SAGE was founded in 1965 by Sara Miller McCune to support the dissemination of usable knowledge by publishing innovative and high-quality research and teaching content. Today, we publish over 900 journals, including those of more than 400 learned societies, more than 800 new books per year, and a growing range of library products including archives, data, case studies, reports, and video. SAGE remains majority-owned by our founder, and after Sara's lifetime will become owned by a charitable trust that secures our continued independence.

Los Angeles | London | New Delhi | Singapore | Washington DC | Melbourne

ADVANCE PRAISE

The book provides an excellent and comprehensive review of the economic landscape of India since 2014. It describes the symptoms of the economic malaise in detail, with evidence instead of rhetoric, and then provides an incisive analysis of the factors that contributed to it. This includes general systemic factors such as over-centralization of policymaking, arbitrary changes in the statistical system, specific policies, such as demonetization, GST reform and protectionism, as well as dealing with the pandemic. From symptoms to diagnostics to prescription, the book takes a clinical look at the state of the economy and the way forward.

Maitreesh Ghatak,
Professor of Economics, London School of Economics

India is at an inflexion point. From 1991 to 2015, India was seen as an emerging economy and a rising power. The economic slowdown since 2016, made worse by the COVID-19 pandemic, recent political and social trends and an increasingly adverse external environment, has brought into question this narrative. Prasanna Mohanty's detailed analysis of recent economic developments and policies reinforces these concerns about India's economic prospects. This book deserves a wide readership.

Sanjaya Baru,
Political Commentator, Policy Analyst and Writer

Prasanna Mohanty's book provides a timely and detailed x-ray into the path taken by the Indian economy in the last decade. It lays out what's gone wrong and what needs to be done by the way of course correction. In this turbulent period, the policy prescriptions underlined in this book offer a well-researched alternative view to getting the Indian economy back on a high growth trajectory.

Rajdeep Sardesai,
Political Analyst, Journalist and Author

Prasanna Mohanty tracks the Indian economic and political policy changes between 2014 and mid-2021, as well as the effects of those on the socio-economic structure of the country in this excellently researched book. He backs his arguments and assertions with data at each and every step. This is an excellent book for any reader interested in the Indian economy.

Prosenjit Datta,
former Editor, Business Today *and* Businessworld

This is a well-argued book with lots of supporting data. It dispassionately analyses the current crisis and traces its roots in economic and political developments in the last three decades. It points to the shortcomings of the official data and presents an alternative picture. It takes into account the exogenous factors and highlights institutional failures and points to their long-term impact. All in all, an eminently readable tome.

Arun Kumar,
Malcolm Adiseshiah Chair Professor,
Institute of Social Sciences and Retd Professor of Economics, JNU

Prasanna Mohanty's book is grounded in a series of 70 exceptionally researched articles he wrote for *Business Today.In* on how to fire up the Indian economy after the prolonged downturn got accentuated by the unexpected intensity of Covid I & II. His eye for detail and the unique ability to deliver sound economic arguments via data are capabilities that make this book very special. In the annals of economic history, I hope that this book will be remembered for its plentiful solutions to the problems plaguing the economy.

Rajeev Dubey,
Editor in Chief, Fortune India;
former Editor of Business Today

With over a decade of experience covering the Indian economy, Prasanna brings out different processes and facets of reforms in India, especially in the last decade, in this book and argues strongly, without rhetoric, why some of those reforms have not worked well…what led to severe slowdown in recent times. While Prasanna's conclusions appear to be implausible in some places, there is no doubt that they are clearly based on data and empirics. In a way, Prasanna's book tries to provide an alternative explanation to the ongoing reforms push, which, some say, is imposed without much evidence, while others argue that it is through conviction.

Professor N. R. Bhanumurthy,
first Vice Chancellor of Bengaluru Dr B. R. Ambedkar School of Economics University (BASE University), a state university of Karnataka

This is a data-backed economic analysis of the Modi government's performance. Data reveal the truth and conceal little. Prasanna Mohanty has carefully collated data from trustworthy sources and laid the record bare. It's rich with data, and everything you want to know about what happened in India is here. It should be on the bookshelf of every policy analyst. The Modi record is bared, and its claims are dared.

Mohan Guruswamy,
Economist and Policy Analyst

AN UNKEPT PROMISE

AN UNKEPT PROMISE

What Derailed *the* Indian Economy

PRASANNA MOHANTY

Los Angeles | London | New Delhi
Singapore | Washington DC | Melbourne

Copyright © Prasanna Mohanty, 2022

All rights reserved. No part of this book may be reproduced or utilized in any form or by any means, electronic or mechanical, including photocopying, recording or by any information storage or retrieval system, without permission in writing from the publisher.

First published in 2022 by

SAGE Publications India Pvt Ltd
B1/I-1 Mohan Cooperative Industrial Area
Mathura Road, New Delhi 110 044, India
www.sagepub.in

SAGE Publications Inc
2455 Teller Road
Thousand Oaks, California 91320, USA

SAGE Publications Ltd
1 Oliver's Yard, 55 City Road
London EC1Y 1SP, United Kingdom

SAGE Publications Asia-Pacific Pte Ltd
18 Cross Street #10-10/11/12
China Square Central
Singapore 048423

Published by Vivek Mehra for SAGE Publications India Pvt Ltd. Typeset in Adobe Caslon 10/13pt by Fidus Design Pvt Ltd, Chandigarh.

Library of Congress Control Number: 2021044826

ISBN: 978-93-5479-186-4 (PB)

SAGE Team: Namarita Kathait, Satvinder Kaur, Madhurima Thapa and Anupama Krishnan

In the memory of Sahir Ludhianvi for his ever-haunting *nazm* 'Jinhe naaz hai Hind par wo kahan hai...'

Thank you for choosing a SAGE product!
If you have any comment, observation or feedback,
I would like to personally hear from you.

Please write to me at **contactceo@sagepub.in**

Vivek Mehra, Managing Director and CEO, SAGE India.

Bulk Sales

SAGE India offers special discounts
for purchase of books in bulk.
We also make available special imprints
and excerpts from our books on demand.

For orders and enquiries, write to us at

Marketing Department
SAGE Publications India Pvt Ltd
B1/I-1, Mohan Cooperative Industrial Area
Mathura Road, Post Bag 7
New Delhi 110044, India

E-mail us at **marketing@sagepub.in**

Subscribe to our mailing list
Write to **marketing@sagepub.in**

This book is also available as an e-book.

CONTENTS

Foreword by Pronab Sen	ix
Acknowledgements	xi
Introduction	1
Chapter I: Institutional Vacuum	23
Chapter II: Masking the Reality	47
Chapter III: Demonetization: First Direct Shock to Economy and People	70
Chapter IV: GST and Other Taxes: Second Shock and Setbacks	91
Chapter V: The Pandemic Catastrophe	115
Chapter VI: AatmaNirbhar Bharat: Turning the Clock Back	149
Chapter VII: New Farm Laws: Opening Farming to Corporate Sector	171
Chapter VIII: New Labour Codes: Weakening Workers, Empowering Employers	189
Chapter IX: Banking 'Reforms': Risks to Finance	209
Chapter X: Privatization: Public Assets, Private Profits	228

Chapter XI: Neoliberal Economics Masquerade	248
Chapter XII: Reimagining Indian Economy	269
Chapter XIII: State of Economy and Future Growth	288
About the Author	307

FOREWORD

Narratives, and not hard facts and figures, have always been the mainstay of democratic politics the world over. So it was in India as well; until 2014, Mr Narendra Modi's election campaign in the run-up to the 2014 General Elections brought about a tectonic shift in Indian political discourse. Data and numbers formed the centrepiece of his speeches, as he spun out the promise that the 'Gujarat model' held for the nation as a whole. It was mesmerizing. Data suddenly became the stuff of politics.

Mr Modi continued in the same vein after becoming the prime minister of India. Every major policy decision was couched in quantitative terms—the status of the issue, what had been done or had not been done in the last 60 years, what would be achieved in the next specified number of years and so on. The narrative was spun around these numbers.

As the policies were implemented, the narratives started to come unstuck. The very data that were used showed that the promises that were held out or the rationale that was given were being belied. The Opposition and the media, understandably and gleefully, latched on to the emerging data to attack the government's position. Prime Minister Modi then unveiled his second major innovation in political discourse, which one could call the 'adaptive' narrative. Since the data could not be changed, the narrative did. The original objective and targets were quietly buried, and new ones took their place. If this was not entirely possible, the responsibility was neatly passed on to others: states, institutions and, sometimes, people themselves. It was done subtly and convincingly. Prime Minister Modi's oratory is so compelling that the people at large bought into the new narratives without serious questioning.

The success of the adaptive narrative technique is only partly due to consummate oratory. It depends mainly on public memory being extremely short. It is not as if this fluidity was not noticed or commented upon. The media did highlight them, and the author of this book is one of the journalists who did so repeatedly. However, the media too has a relatively short attention span. The diversions would be commented upon and then promptly forgotten.

Although at first glance this book is about the performance of the Indian economy during the Modi years, at a different level, it is really a chronicle, an aide memoire if you will, of the manner in which the adaptive narrative technique has been used during this period. This is particularly true of the chapters on demonetization, GST, labour laws, farm laws and the pandemic, but some of the other chapters also hint at this feature.

Adroit use of narratives is unexceptionable in competitive politics, and indeed to be admired when done by a highly skilled practitioner, but there was a darker side to the catapulting of data into mainstream political discourse. Inconvenient data had to be suppressed or made non-comparable with the past; failing which they had to be discredited. This then is the second subtext of this book, and its presence is discernible in many of the chapters. Much of this may not be known to the public at large, but it bears to be repeated.

This is a book on economics by a non-economist, but a person who has been following and writing on the Indian economy for many years. It makes the book eminently accessible to a wide readership since it is shorn of jargon (except the unavoidable minimum) and abstruse theoretical constructs. One may agree with it or not, but hopefully it will make you think.

Dr Pronab Sen

Former Chairman of the National Statistical Commission

ACKNOWLEDGEMENTS

This book couldn't have been possible without Rajeev Dubey, Editor of *Business Today*. He gave me the platform and encouragement to explore and write on various facets of India's economy in the past few years. These writings later developed into this book. I am deeply indebted to him.

During the past many years of my engagement with India's economy, I have had the privilege of learning from some of the best minds in the field in India. They explained the intricacies, provided insights and made economics easy to understand. I am particularly grateful to economists Pronab Sen, Arun Kumar, N. R. Bhanumurthy, Surajit Mazumdar, Satyaki Roy, Vikas Rawal, Sukhpal Singh, R. S. Ghuman, Sukhwinder Singh, R. Nagaraj, Sunil Dharan and Anoop Satpathy. Economist Pulin Nayak read the draft, encouraged me and gave the hope that this book could work.

Special thanks also to P. C. Mohanan, who would always be ready to explain statistical matters, and P. D. T. Achary, who would explain constitutional matters.

However, if there are any flaws in the book, those are mine, not theirs.

I would also like to thank SAGE, particularly editors Manisha Mathews and Namarita Kathait for putting the chapters into place and their production team which gave the book its final shape.

Finally, I thank my family and friends who supported and encouraged me to go through the process and complete the project in the past few months. They include wife Mousumi, daughter Siddhi and friends Parsa Venkateshwar Rao Jr, Asish Sharma and Trithesh Nandan.

INTRODUCTION

One of the biggest ironies of our time is that India is celebrating completion of 75 years of Independence in a year when its 'midnight's tryst with destiny' has visibly soured and it stands demoted from 'electoral democracy' to 'electoral autocracy' and from 'free' to 'partly free' by two global institutions that measure and track evolution of democracies (Freedom House, 2021; V-Dem Institute, 2021).

This is a huge turn in the wrong direction, compared to the ideals imagined and envisioned on the midnight of 14–15 August 1947. This change has facilitated another big wrong turn which is the focus of this book: India's economic growth has derailed and poverty, hunger and inequality stalk people with far greater ferocity than any time in decades. The other irony is that India had recovered well from the fall in its democratic indicators during the Emergency of 1975–1977, but it plunged right back into almost the same depth post-2014 after the change in government.

For a while, it did seem that the dreams of a better future had arrived, with gross domestic product (GDP) growth picking up immediately. In 2015, according to the International Monetary Fund's World Economic Outlook (WEO) report of 2016, India had surpassed China to emerge the fastest growing major economy in the world. That year, the growth rate was 7.3 per cent (the same as India's own estimate of May 2015), surpassing China's growth rate of 6.9 per cent, well above the global average of 3.1 per cent (International Monetary Fund, 2016).

This would change dramatically.

The Pandemic Crisis

In 2020, the COVID-19 hit and the WEO report of April 2021 showed that India had turned into one of the slowest growing economies in the world, with a global rank of 150 out of 194 countries it tracked, as the GDP growth tanked to –7.97 per cent—the same as India's official estimate (it would be *revised to* –7.25% in May 2021, as per which India ranks 142 among 194 countries). China's growth rate was 2.3 per cent and the global average was –3.5 per cent. This is a reversal of 2015. All countries were impacted by the pandemic crisis, but India was hit harder than most and its GDP fell far below the global average, reflecting gross mismanagement of the pandemic (International Monetary Fund, 2021; *Statistics Times*, 2021).

It must be pointed out here that the WEO reports are based on Government of India's data and, hence, do not reflect its own estimations but that of India's. Former Chief Economic Advisor (CEA) Arvind Subramanian, during whose time the new 2011–2012 GDP series was introduced in January 2015, pointed out later that the GDP growth rate was overestimated by 2.5 to 3.7 percentage points per year between 2011–2012 and 2016–2017—a conclusion he had arrived at by comparing the GDP growth rate with 17 high frequency economic indicators. If India's the then CEA didn't believe the 2011–2012 GDP series numbers, there is no question to believe it by any outsider either (Mukherjee, 2019; Subramanian, 2019).

Since then, there have been multiple retrospective revisions in the GDP numbers, masking the real state of the economy even further, prompting former Reserve Bank of India (RBI) Governor Y. V. Reddy to remark that 'in India not only the future is uncertain, even the past is uncertain.' So bad is the state of economy that neither the flawed GDP series nor the retrospective revisions in it could hide the economy's collapse (IANS, 2017).

In this case, one caveat is in order. In spite of the obvious flaws in the 2011–2012 GDP series (detailed in GDP and data vacuum chapter), this book uses the GDP data to present the state of the economy. It strives to provide other evidence, such as national and international studies and surveys, to provide a more realistic picture and support the arguments made.

More than the fall in GDP numbers, it is the accompanying massive loss of lives and livelihoods, causing mass impoverishment, that is a bigger worry. According to the United Nations Conference on Trade and Development (UNCTAD), which used both official (Government of India) data and estimates generated by the United Nations Global Policy Model, Indians lost real income the most among all major economies in the world in 2020–2021 (–27%, compared to the global average of –12.3%) vis-à-vis the average of pre-pandemic income trend since 2017 (UNCTAD, 2021a, 2021b).

The report explained why Indians lost income the most. It stated:

> India's growth performance in 2020 fell below our mid-2020 expectations. Actual fiscal stimulus fell short of initial announcements that suggested a large increase of public spending for pandemic relief. The relief measures adopted were not only much smaller in scale, but also centred on easing supply-side constraints and providing liquidity support rather than aggregate demand support. Moreover, restrictions to people's movement not only severely affected incomes and consumption, they also proved largely unsuccessful in containing the spread of the virus...

In the global context, it explained why the pandemic led to a drastic fall in growth numbers. Among other things, it put the blame on 'a misguided return to austerity after a deep and destructive recession' and 'outdated economic dogmas' followed by developing countries 'with limited fiscal space'. These remarks point to neoliberal (radical right) economic thinking, which is the focus of an entire chapter.

Another global estimate provided the number of Indians likely to have slipped into poverty.

In March 2021, the US Pew Research Center estimated that **75 million Indians** were likely to have impoverished in 2020–2021, accounting for 60 per cent of the global increase in poverty (131 million), post-pandemic of 2020. In contrast, China would see only 1 million of their people impoverished. The break-up showed that out of 75 million, 35 million would be from the low-income group, 32 million would be from the middle-income group and the rest 7 million would be from the upper middle and high-income groups. It defined poor as those surviving at $2 or less per day; low income at $2.1–$10; middle income at $10.2–$20; upper middle at $20.1–$50 and high income at more than $50—all expressed in 2011 purchasing power parities at 2011 prices (Kochhar, 2021).

The headline of this report, 'In the Pandemic, India's Middle Class Shrinks and Poverty Spreads while China Sees Smaller Changes', made another telling point: the Indian middle class that seems beholden to Prime Minister Narendra Modi—clapping hands, banging thalis in balconies on multiple occasions to his call but not outraged at massive loss of lives and livelihoods because of the wrong economics and politics—shrunk by 32 million. It remained unmoved when millions walked past their balconies in distress migration that no other country in the world witnessed, not when thousands perished during the second wave because of lack of hospital beds, oxygen and medicines or when 'liberalized' vaccination policy (for 18–44 age group which the Supreme Court called 'arbitrary and irrational') turned it into a for-profit trade endangering Indians and the world as vaccine shortage hit the global COVAX plan. India went around the world begging for oxygen, medicines, vaccines and every other essential item, resembling more like a Third-World country and a failed state, as one commentator put it, from an aspiring economic superpower a few years ago (Aiyar, 2021b; Chowdhury, 2021b; Supreme Court of India, 2021).

But India's problem didn't start with the pandemic.

The economy was already on a prolonged slowdown due to massive loss of jobs and businesses that the twin shocks of demonetization and GST delivered. The overestimation and retrospective revisions in the GDP couldn't hide the fall.

Before the Pandemic Hit

The GDP growth (2011–2012 series at constant prices) fell from a high of 8.3 per cent in fiscal year (FY) 2017 to just 4 per cent in FY2020 (ending on 31 March 2020), which is less than half. The pandemic lockdown started on the midnight of 24–25 March 2020—a week before the FY ended—and, therefore, couldn't have influenced the FY2020 growth numbers.

The stark reality is captured in the figure below.

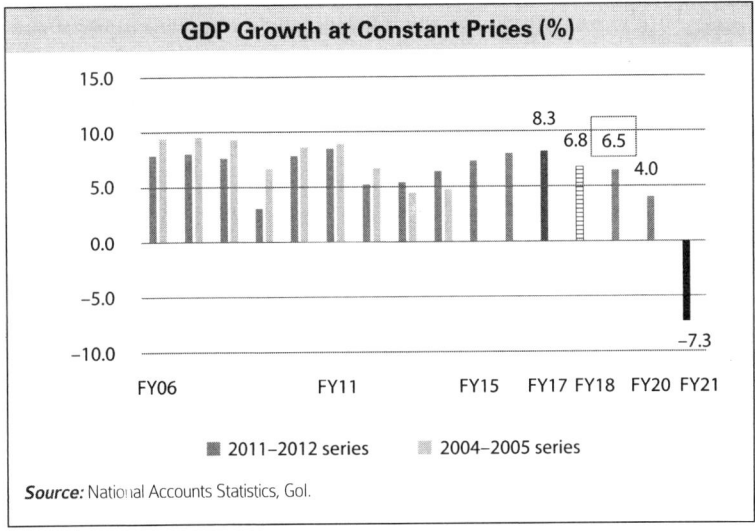

Source: National Accounts Statistics, GoI.

The graph maps growth prior to the change in government in 2014 (using both 2004–2005 and 2011–2012 GDP series) to show that the economy was already slowing down and, after a brief uptick following the adoption of 2011–2012 GDP series (introduced in January 2015), the growth went down again.

The graph also reveals how the demonetization year (FY2017) that wiped out millions of jobs and businesses overnight and devastated informal economy as 86.9 per cent of cash in circulation was banned overnight in a primarily cash-dependent economy clocked the highest growth rate at 8.3 per cent during the entire Modi years. This is not only counterintuitive, but it also reflects the unreliability of the GDP number. The next FY (FY2018) that saw the cumulative impacts of the demonetization and GST grew at a relatively high rate of 6.8 per cent. But then it came crashing down to 4 per cent in FY2020. Given the unreliability of

Introduction 5

the GDP numbers, how much the economy had sunk then or in FY2021 would not be known.

Why India's growth fell to 4 per cent before the pandemic hit is the key to understand its current abyss, especially since its economic fundamentals were never in doubt and it withstood the Great Recession of 2007–2009 rather well (better than other major economies barring China) but here in 2021 India was among the worst performing economies in the world.

The economic misadventures that India had been involved in since 2014 costed it dearly. The first two major direct shocks were the demonetization and GST, and the magnitude of their impact is not known because the Indian government never assessed or collected relevant information (as it did in the case of the pandemic losses of income). Much like the demonetization, the GST led to the closure of more businesses (micro, small and medium enterprises [MSMEs] and trade) and thereby the loss of jobs, particularly in the informal sector, as its very design (input tax credit [ITC]) caused a shift of businesses from informal to formal economy.

By May 2019, for the first time, the Finance Ministry acknowledged, what was known to the rest, that only one engine of the economy, that of public investment, was working and the other three (private investment, domestic consumption and external consumption) had all sputtered out, making the slowdown a structural one, not a cyclical one as the government repeated ad nauseum (Department of Economic Affairs, Ministry of Finance, 2019).

The private investment and external consumption (net exports) engines had sputtered out much earlier. What the Finance Ministry report highlighted was that the main engine of growth, private consumption (contributing 56%–57% of the GDP), was falling, thereby indicating a demand recession in the economy. A demand recession leads to a decline in production and capacity utilization of goods and services, which in turn dries up investment as also revenue, disabling the government to spend and regenerate demand.

When the pandemic hit, a fundamentally weakened economy just collapsed.

What did the economy gain from demonetization? The government made four tall claims: (a) tax-to-GDP ratio drastically improved,

(b) India became 'lesser cash-based economy', (c) it helped reduce black money and (d) tax compliance increased. It concluded that the demonetization, therefore, had been 'greatly beneficial towards national progress'. When official statistics were checked, these claims turned out to be wrong: tax-to-GDP ratio plunged, cash-in-circulation rose dramatically, tax compliance fell and going by the government's logic that more cash translated into more black money, black money increased (Mohanty, 2020; PIB, 2020).

The government made multiple claims about the GST too: one nation, one tax, higher tax efficiency and higher economic growth (2%–2.5%). By mid-2021, various omissions and commissions, like outright refusal to pay states GST compensation that its own law mandates, it is facing existential crisis and the very 'cooperative federalism' it embodies is very much threatened (Aiyar, 2021a).

In the meanwhile, something else was going on without attracting attention. Officially, the AatmaNirbhar Bharat programme was launched in May 2020, which, among other things, imposed import restrictions to promote and protect domestic industries through slogans like 'vocal for local', but it had actually begun in 2014. The then CEA Subramanian wrote a paper showing that India had raised tariff of 60 per cent for 3,200 product categories out of 5,300 products traded with the most favoured nations (MFNs) starting with 2014 (up to 2020). His estimates showed that this led to an *average tariff increase from 13 per cent in 2014 to 17.9 per cent in 2020. In monetary terms, this impacted about $300 billion or about 70 per cent of total MFN imports* (Chatterjee & Subramanian, 2020).

The import substitution policy (import barriers or increase in import tariff) had been a big failure in the past with the growth rate below 4 per cent (derided as 'Hindu' rate of growth). Indians faced high scarcity for essentials such as phones and scooters, and saddled with inferior domestic products that were expensive. Not just Subramanian, even the loudest cheerleader of the government, Arvind Panagariya, former NITI Aayog vice chairman, now back to teaching at the Columbia University, objected to it.

There is a yet another good reason to be wary of import substitution that the AatmaNirbhar Bharat embodies. The trade liberalization of 1991 has significantly altered India's businesses structurally. A 2020 study by Delhi-based government think tank, Institute for Studies in Industrial Development, showed that post-liberalization imports of raw materials and intermediary goods were significantly contributing to exports. Called 'import intensity' (or import components of exported goods), their share had risen sharply from 10.5 per cent in 1993–1994 to 32.5 per cent in 2013–2014 for 'the whole economy'. The maximum rise was in manufacturing from 12.9 per cent to 51 per cent.

What it means is that restricting imports would limit exports, which is not such a good idea as any economists would vouchsafe. Subramanian argued that India's domestic market was not big enough to give a push that a global market could to boost high growth.

Did any external factor play a role in India's pre-pandemic slowdown?

Exogenous Factors

There is no evidence of exogenous factors in pre-pandemic slowdown. For example, the foreign direct investment (FDI) inflows (in US$) witnessed a quantum jump from $36,046 million in FY2014 to ₹45,148 in FY2015 and consistently scaled new highs to reach $74,390 million in FY2020. The trade deficit did go up in FY2018–FY2019 with exports slowing down (in value) which could be because of hike in MFN tariff (from 13% to 17.9% on 3,200 out of 5,300 items between 2014 and 2020). Without a detailed study, it is difficult to say that there were other reasons than the import barriers effecting exports (Chatterjee & Subramanian, 2020; DIPP, 2020).

Natural calamities such as drought and flood damaging agricultural production don't seem to have played a role during FY2015–FY2020. Barring FY2015, there has been no calamitous drought. The average annual growth in agriculture and allied activities was 3.5 per cent (gross value added [GVA] at constant prices) during FY2015–FY2020, same as for the previous six fiscals of FY2009–FY2014. There was only one year of negative agriculture growth during the first period (in FY2015), while there were two in the second (FY2009 and FY2010).

It would be safe to rule out any role of exogenous factors in slowing down India's economy before the pandemic hit. Once the pandemic hit, India compounded its impact through mishandling of both health and economic crises. The government centralized all powers by invoking the National Disaster Management Act (NDMA) of 2005, imposed overnight nationwide lockdown, which was untimely (cases were too few), without planning and preparation, followed by an untimely unlocking amid sharply rising infections and then watched helplessly as millions lost lives and livelihoods and a massive distress migration took place. The second wave caught India unprepared, the government abetted it with superspreader events like the Kumbh and unusually prolonged state elections and then messed up a time-tested universal free vaccination programme to pose a big threat to Indians and the rest of the world (Chowdhury, 2021b).

Absence of Credible Economic Statistics

The impact of all these economic misadventures on the economy and people is not fully known because the government didn't collect relevant information at any stage (as detailed in subsequent chapters), manipulated GDP numbers and suppressed critical information and data.

The first official report to show that the economy is falling apart is the Periodic Labour Force Survey (PLFS) of 2017–2018, which showed massive job loss and a 45-year high unemployment rate. The Azim Premji University studied the unit-level data to state that India lost 9 million jobs between 2011–2012 and 2017–2018 'for the first time in India's history'. India did have a jobless growth in pre-2014 years when jobs were lost in manufacturing, but the overall job creation remained positive, as the Planning Commission of India's (PCI) data on employment generations released in 2014 had shown (Mehrotra & Parida, 2019; MoSPI, 2019; Planning Commission, 2014).

The PLFS of 2018–2019 showed a marginal improvement in the unemployment rate, a gain from the PLFS of 2017–2018, but even that gain (assuming it is correct) would have been wiped out due to the pandemic crisis (MoSPI, 2020).

The last household consumption survey of 2017–2018 was junked after its content was leaked showing that the real expenditure (a proxy for income) had fallen for the first time in 40 years from ₹1,501 per month in 2011–2012 to ₹1,446 per month in 2017–2018, clearly showing that poverty was growing (Jha, 2020).

The NITI Aayog's Sustainable Development Goals (SDGs) report of 2019–2020 showed that poverty, hunger and income inequality increased in 22–25 states/UTs, out of the 28 it mapped, since 2018–2019. The follow-up report for 2020 showed dramatic reversal of fortune with only 2–14 states/UTs showing increase in these indicators, but given the all-round devastation the pandemic caused, leading to the loss of millions of lives and livelihoods and the GDP growth plunging to an all-time low of –7.3% (from 4% in the previous fiscal), this report is highly questionable (NITI Aayog, 2019, 2020).

More so, the National Family Health Survey (NFHS-5) of 2019–2020 had already shown deteriorating nutritional status with children's health (below 5 years) worsening in most states post-NFHS-4 of 2015–2016. Analysis of the report showed rise in child stunting, child wastage and child underweight in 18 of 22 states/UTs mapped. The Global Hunger Index 2020, which presented the pre-pandemic status, ranked India 94 among 107 countries, far below neighbouring Sri Lanka, Bangladesh and Pakistan, and warned, 'In India, like in many other countries, the pandemic is aggravating an already serious hunger situation' (GHI, 2020; Roy, 2020).

All these indicate significant weakening of the economic fundamentals in post-2014 phase and growing impoverishment of the people.

New 'Reforms' That Threaten Future Prospects

The worse is not over yet. The government has unleashed a series of economic 'reforms' the impact of which would be felt in years to come, but it can be said that those would further weaken the economy and impoverish people by prioritizing private business interest over people's well-being. These include new farm laws, new labour codes, banking 'reforms' and privatization of public sector banks (PSB) and other units (public sector undertakings [PSUs]).

Contrary to the government's claims, new farm laws don't promote farmers' interest. Rather these measures are aimed at corporatizing farming by opening a parallel and unregulated market outside state governments-run Agricultural Produce Market Committee (APMC) mandis, notwithstanding the miseries such a move brought to Bihar's farmers after the state dismantled APMC mandis and procurements in 2006 (a small amount of procurement continues nevertheless). The new laws also pose a risk to minimum support price (MSP) and official procurement as per official communications and recommendation of the Commission for Agricultural Costs and Prices (CACP) in its March 2020 report (detailed in the chapter on farm laws), depriving farmers of assured income for their produce, howsoever limited that coverage may be.

During the negotiations with protesting farmers, the government has steadfastly refused to provide a legal guarantee for MSP at such parallel private trade (outside the APMC mandis). Given the impoverished state of Indian farmers (22.5% farm households living below the poverty line as the NITI Aayog report of 2017 showed; 86 per cent of farmers, who are small and marginal, own less than 2 hectares of land and there is high dependence on agriculture for employment in the country [more than 40% of total employment]), corporatization of farming poses a great threat to a large population depending on agriculture.

The new farm laws promote private business in farming and trade by pitting farmers directly against them in price negotiations and contract farming by eliminating the role of states and even courts in governing and resolving disputes in these matters. The US example has shown how it spelt doom for their small farmers. These are detailed in a separate chapter.

Similarly, the new labour codes weaken workers' rights and interests. These codes dilute protections against arbitrary hire-and-fire by expanding the thresholds for applicability of such protections; these code further dilute health and safety protections again by expanding the threshold of protections; and add and expand contractual work by creating a new category called fixed-term employment (FTE) after withdrawing protections against converting permanent employment to short-term contract available in earlier stature; working hours have been increased from 8 hours a day to 12 hours a day and a complete ban has been imposed on strikes—all hard-won rights now stand wiped out (detailed in a separate chapter).

The only benefits for workers the new codes promise are expansions in the coverage of minimum wages and social security (SS). But these are mere promises, sans concrete plans and funds, sans universalization of coverage, sans right to equal-pay-for-equal-work and sans a raise in minimum wages, which remain ₹176 a day as against its internal committee's recommendation of ₹375 a day. Given the fact that 94 per cent of India's workforce is informal, what all this means is that workers' precarity would rise sharply. Past few years have seen disturbing trends: a sharp rise in informal workforce, a loss of salaried/regular jobs, a fall in labour force participation rate and workers' population ratio, indicating a lack of jobs and a reverse migration of workers to low productive agriculture (APU, 2021; Bhardwaj, 2021).

Laws that weaken financial and SS of a vast majority—be it in agriculture or factories and other establishments—wouldn't raise productivity or propel higher economic growth.

Privatization of public assets, including profitable ones, and de-nationalization of banks poses further threats to the financial stability, makes the economy prone to economic crisis and impoverishes people by allowing profit maximization of private businesses to run the economy, determine growth and development.

Privatization of public assets reduces the government's capacity to provide employment and protections to the underprivileged (job reservations can't be expected from private sector). The proposed de-nationalization of banks and allowing corporations to run banks are particularly fraught with risks to financial stability and equitable credit flow. Even developed economies have made course corrections after the Great Depression of 2007–2009 by increasing public share in banking. India nationalized banks in the late 1960s and the 1970s to overcome credit constraints for SMEs, new ventures and rural economy. The lessons have been forgotten.

While private businesses are critical to growth of any economy, official statistics show that India's private corporate sector is heavily indebted and a big loan defaulter, which has caused the current banking crisis in the first place. These are routinely written-off as non-performing assets (NPAs) of banks, which zoomed post-2014, from ₹63,502 crore during FY2005–FY2015 to ₹8.85 lakh crore during FY2015–FY2020, according to the RBI database. Private businesses also need regular bailouts, tax incentives, tax holidays and tax cuts, thereby incentivizing more tax evasion. How wise would it then be to hand over hundreds of PSUs to those corporations?

The pandemic has shown that India's corporate sector (listed companies) is overwhelmingly driven by the principle of maximization of profits. The financial details of more than 4,000 listed companies for Q2 of FY2021 showed highest ever profits in history, which was surpassed in Q3 of FY2021. The Centre for Monitoring Indian Economy's (CMIE) analysis showed that this was achieved, among other things, by reducing jobs and wages at a time of unprecedented job and income crisis. The prime minister's promotion of private 'wealth creators' on the premise that the wealth created thus (through privatization and pro-business policies) would then be redistributed among the rest is entirely misplaced and misleading (Mohanty, 2021).

Experience shows that when the private sector is allowed a greater role in healthcare and education, in post-liberalized era, the costs of both skyrocketed, raising inequalities and deprivations, and taking those beyond the reach of ordinary people. Their role during the pandemic (reluctance to provide services and fleecing of patients) and the gross inadequacies of public healthcare infrastructure have exposed the folly of relying on private business to provide public or social goods. Let this be reminded again that India is home to most of the poor in the world and its inequality and socio-economic deprivations are worse than other major economies.

None of the argument, however, is meant to keep the private sector out or undermine its role. It has a significant role to play but a carte blanche to it means that the Indian government is abdicating its own responsibilities to run the economy and determine India's growth and development priorities according to the needs of the vast majority of people, not a tiny minority. It is constitutionally obliged and owes it to the citizens of this country to work for their interest, not that of private businesses.

Institutional Failures

The seeds of economic distress were sown right at the beginning in 2014 when the PCI was dismantled and a think tank NITI Aayog replaced it. Rather than providing economic logic and evidence to support new ideas or validate existing decisions, it turned into a big cheerleader of all of the government's policies.

From a planned growth model, India turned into a non-planned, top-down and self-serving growth model that has damaged the economy and people. Democratic decision-making, parliamentary debates and scrutiny of laws, public debate and opinion have been given a go-by. Democracy itself has been seriously undermined. Laws are passed as money bills (Aadhaar law and electoral bond) to bypass the Rajya Sabha. Electoral bond has been brought to hide the identity of political doners and bypass scrutiny of the Election Commission and the Companies Act and facilitate the inflow of unaccounted money from private businesses to undermine elections and governance. Democratically elected assemblies and governments in Jammu and Kashmir (J&K) and Delhi have been reduced to vassal states. A discriminatory citizenship law has been brought to target Muslims. Mobs of various kinds have been empowered to attack religious minorities and anyone questioning the government or airing dissent and disagreements.

All these developments have been accompanied with failures of other constitutional and democratic checks and balances. The Supreme Court has shown a remarkable reluctance to uphold fundamental rights, question the government and decide the constitutionality of several critical laws causing widespread distress (abrogation of Article 370, citizenship law, farm laws, Electoral Bond, etc.). Mainstream media, particularly

TV channels with wide reach, have changed the rules of the game by not questioning those in power, rather they have turned compliant and defenders of the government, thereby doing a great disservice to the people (Chishti, 2021; Chowdhury, 2021a).

Democracy and secular politics matter to economic growth. Several multi-country studies tracking decades of development have shown that democracy significantly raises economic growth and secularization precedes high growth, not the other way round. A big part of the blame for worsening democratic and secular order must rest with the citizens, who are empowered by the Constitution of India, for not questioning and seeking accountability from their elected government.

If all of this sounds depressing, it indeed is the case, and the evidence is all around us. But unlike 'fait accompli' attached to the government's narratives supporting its policy decisions, there are sound economic logics and evidence for many other paths to economic growth and elimination of poverty, hunger and inequality.

Most of these solutions are known and have worked in India and abroad. Some are in plain sight but are not adopted. Given the unprecedented spread of poverty, hunger and income inequality in post-2014, by far the best immediate solution is to provide direct income support, which is doable and only needs political will. Not just a dignified life, a healthy, educated and secure population can drive a healthy democracy and a healthy economy.

Another key is to end years of pronounced biases against certain sectors such as agriculture and services. Industry remains everyone's favourite (economists and politicians alike) for obvious reason—money power drives politics and policies. But industry has spectacularly failed India—unlike Western democracies and many Asian giants that have grown by industrialization. Since 1950–1951, agriculture has provided the maximum employment and generated the maximum income. Industry's contribution in both is poor and stagnant. That the services sector has driven India's growth is known, yet how many departments and ministries or policies have been framed for its promotion? None. It continues to remain an appendage of industry and the focus of all policies—new farm and labour laws, privatization and AatmaNirbhar Bharat—is industry.

Once right policies and politics are followed, everything else will fall back into place. India rebuilt itself after a debilitating spell of colonization that wiped out its wealth and de-industrialized it. India rebuilt again in the 1980s and the 1990s by reforming its economy. India has the talent and competence to revive its fortune again, provided the right people are placed in the right positions.

Structure of the Book

All that ails Indian economy and its people now surely didn't just origin in 2014, but this book focuses on how all the key economic policies adopted since 2014 have *reversed most of the gains* India had achieved in earlier decades. As the prime minister for 10 years (which were the best years of growth), Manmohan Singh, tried to rectify many of the distortions that the liberalization of 1991 brought in by him and the then Prime Minister Narasimha Rao. He introduced a series of laws and programmes, including the Forest Rights Act of 2006, Right to Fair Compensation and Transparency in Land Acquisition, Rehabilitation and Resettlement Act of 2013, Mahatma Gandhi National Rural Employment Guarantee Act (MGNREGA) of 2005, National Food Security Act (NFSA) of 2013, to ensure 'inclusive' growth.

Restoring growth and development calls for a detailed diagnosis of what went wrong after 2014. The underlying assumption is that proper **diagnosis** of the flaws, whether inherent or due to poor governance, is essential to find the right remedies. The first six chapters of the book are devoted to analysing the key policy decisions focusing on the ones the impact of which are already known, followed by four chapters on 'reforms' which are yet to fully play out.

Chapter I looks at the gradual weakening of institutional mechanisms for decision-making without which top-down and self-serving policies wouldn't have been possible. Chapter II looks at how India's once highly regarded GDP and statistical system have lost their credibility and ability to reflect the ground realities. Chapter III is devoted to the demonetization of 2016, the first big economic shock that led to massive job and business losses overnight. Chapter IV deals with the second big economic shock: a poorly designed and implemented GST, now facing uncertain future. Chapter V looks at the impact of the third and by far the biggest economic shock: the pandemic outbreak compounded by multiple failures of the government. Chapter VI focuses on another economic misadventure—the AatmaNirbhar Bharat Abhiyan—embodying import substitution that sans economic logic and evidence, and threatens to take India back to 'Hindu' rate of growth.

The other four chapters are on four big bang 'reforms' in progress. Chapter VII looks at the new farm laws that have sparked country-wide farmers' agitation and new labour codes that undermine workers' rights and protections are discussed in Chapter VIII. Chapter IX deals with banking 'reforms' which include privatization of PSBs, a new bad bank for stressed asset resolution and allowing large industries to run their banks. Privatization of other public assets is the subject of Chapter X.

Chapter XI provides neoliberal (radical right) economic concepts and principles underlying government policies to explain why those have hurt rather than help the masses and the economy while enhancing the fortunes of top 1 per cent or top 0.1 per cent of the population. Chapter XII provides alternative economic policies and programmes that could be a better bet for India, correcting many creeping distortions and boosting future growth and development prospects. These solutions are thrown up from the diagnosis of the economy and the state of people. It seeks to impress that much more than just economic policies need to change. Economist and Nobel laureate Stiglitz has repeatedly said that neoliberal economics is a 'political doctrine' meant to serve certain interests, 'never supported by economic theory' and it has been undermining state and democracy for more than 40 years (Thoma, 2008).

Stiglitz explained how neoliberal economics work in money-driven political systems such as the USA and India. He wrote that money power (of private business) translates into political power, ultimately evolving into an economy and democracy of the 1 per cent, for the 1 per cent and by the 1 per cent. The collusion between political power and money power leads to government failures as the powers that enable state to improve societal well-being can be used by some groups or individuals to advance their self-interests at the cost of others. Thus, he wrote that the real problem is 'not the economics but the politics'. India's opaque electoral bond, which facilitates the flow of unaccounted corporate money into politics, is a stark symptom of this cosy nexus (Mohanty, 2019; Stiglitz, 2019).

Thus, economic policies won't change unless the politics promoting them is changed, but politics is beyond the scope of this book, and this is the book's *biggest limitation*. The book, however, strives to emphasize that policies should be evidence-based, made after due deliberations, within the constitutional framework of checks and balances, and there should be no place for presumptive solutions (good intentions but bad policies) or self-serving and top-down ones India is witnessing far more frequently since 2014.

Chapter XIII revisits the state of economy after the pandemic hit and provides a broad indication of India's future growth prospects within the obvious limitations and foolhardiness of such an exercise.

A final word.

The book sans rhetoric. No assertion is made without putting evidence upfront, for which it relies on official statistics, national and international studies, surveys, ground reports and other supportive information. It also strives to focus more on what went wrong and why, so that corrective measures can be taken. Cricketing legend Michael Holding, who recently wrote a book on racism, *Why We Kneel, How We Rise*, provides a good perspective for this approach. Talking about why some parts of his book are a hard read, he said in an interview, 'It had to be hard because unless you recognize why you are sick, you can't cure yourself' (*The Indian Express*, 2021).

References

Aiyar, Y. (2021a, 9 May). The second wave and the Indian state. *Hindustan Times*. https://www.hindustantimes.com/opinion/the-second-wave-and-the-indian-state-101620579557130.html

Aiyar, Y. (2021b, 2 June). GST: End of the road for cooperative federalism? *Bloomberg | Quint*. https://www.bloombergquint.com/gst/gst-end-of-the-road-for-cooperative-federalism

APU. (2021, 5 May). State of working India 2021. Azim Premji University. https://cse.azimpremjiuniversity.edu.in/state-of-working-india/swi-2021/

Bhardwaj, A. (2021, 6 May). CEDA-CMIE bulletin: Manufacturing employment halves in 5 years. CEDA, Ashoka University and CMIE. https://ceda.ashoka.edu.in/ceda-cmie-bulletin-manufacturing-employment-halves-in-5-years/

Chatterjee, S., & Subramanian, A. (2020, October). India's inward (re)turn: Is it warranted? Will it work? (Policy Paper No. 1). Ashoka University. https://www.ashoka.edu.in/static/doc_uploads/file_1603091486.pdf

Chishti, S. (2021, 26 June). India needs closure on these five big cases pending before the SC. *The Quint.* https://www.thequint.com/voices/opinion/five-cases-pending-before-the-supreme-court-pendency-caa-electoral-bonds-money-bill-jammu-kashmir?s=03#

Chowdhury, D. (2021a, 3 May). It isn't just Modi. India's compliant media must also take responsibility for the COVID-19 crisis. *Time.* https://time.com/6033152/india-media-covid-19/

Chowdhury, D. (2021b, 28 May). Modi never bought enough COVID-19 vaccines for India. Now the whole world is paying. *Time.* https://time.com/6052370/modi-didnt-buy-enough-covid-19-vaccine/

Department of Economic Affairs, Ministry of Finance. (2019, March). Monthly economic report. https://dea.gov.in/sites/default/files/MER-March%202019.pdf

Department for Promotion of Industry and Internal Trade, GOI. (2020). Fact Sheet on Foreign Direct Investment (FDI) from April 2000 to December 2020. https://dpiit.gov.in/sites/default/files/FDI%20Factsheet%20December%2020.pdf

Freedom House. (2021). Freedom in the world: Democracy under siege. https://freedomhouse.org/sites/default/files/2021-02/FIW2021_World_02252021_FINAL-web-upload.pdf

GHI. (2020, October). Global hunger index. https://www.globalhungerindex.org/pdf/en/2020.pdf

IANS. (2017, 28 June). Difference of opinion between RBI, govt is not bad: Y. V. Reddy. *Business Standard.* https://www.business-standard.com/article/news-ians/difference-of-opinion-between-rbi-govt-is-not-bad-y-v-reddy-117062800341_1.html

International Monetary Fund. (2016, January). Subdued demand, diminished prospects. World Economic Outlook. https://www.imf.org/en/Publications/WEO/Issues/2016/12/31/Subdued-Demand-Diminished-Prospects

International Monetary Fund. (2021, April). Managing divergent recoveries. https://www.imf.org/en/Publications/WEO/Issues/2021/03/23/world-economic-outlook-april-2021

Jha, S. (2020, 18 February). NSO's consumer spend report showing first fall in 40 yrs won't be released. *Business Standard.* https://www.business-standard.com/article/economy-policy/national-statistical-commission-won-t-release-nso-s-consumer-spend-report-120021800045_1.html

Kochhar, R. (2021, 18 March). In the pandemic, India's middle class shrinks and poverty spreads while China sees smaller changes. Pew Research Center. https://www.pewresearch.org/fact-tank/2021/03/18/in-the-pandemic-indias-middle-class-shrinks-and-poverty-spreads-while-china-sees-smaller-changes/

Mehrotra, S., & Parida, J. K. (2019, October). India's employment crisis: Rising education levels and falling non-agricultural job growth. https://cse.azimpremjiuniversity.edu.in/wp-content/uploads/2020/10/Mehrotra_Parida_India_s_Employment_Crisis_October_2019.pdf

Mohanty, P. (2019, 15 March). India: General elections 2019: Who is funding the electioneering of our political parties? Part I and II. *DailyO, India Today* Group. https://www.dailyo.in/politics/lok-sabha-elections-2019-party-funding-electoral-bonds-national-parties/story/1/29910.html and https://www.dailyo.in/politics/lok-sabha-elections-2019-party-funding-fcra-national-parties-general-elections-2019-political-funding-black-money/story/1/29913.html

Mohanty, P. (2020, 26 November). Rebooting economy 48: Do tax numbers show a healthier economy? *Business Today.* https://www.businesstoday.in/opinion/columns/indian-economy-do-tax-numbers-show-a-healthier-economy-economic-growth/story/423073.html

Mohanty, P. (2021, 21 February). Rebooting economy 69: What do workers gain from growth and profits? *Business Today.* https://www.businesstoday.in/opinion/columns/rebooting-economy-69-what-do-workers-gain-from-growth-and-profits/story/431857.html

MoSPI. (2019). Annual report: Periodic labour force survey, 2017–2018. http://mospi.nic.in/sites/default/files/publication_reports/Annual%20Report%2C%20PLFS%202017-18_31052019.pdf?download=1

MoSPI. (2020). Annual report: Periodic labour force survey, 2018–2019. http://mospi.nic.in/sites/default/files/publication_reports/Annual_Report_PLFS_2018_19_HL.pdf

Mukherjee, A. (2019, 14 June). Modi's suspect GDP numbers have done real damage. *Bloomberg | Quint.* https://www.bloombergquint.com/opinion/modi-s-suspect-gdp-data-have-damaged-india-s-economy

NITI Aayog. (2019, 30 December). SDG India—Index and dashboard 2019–20. https://niti.gov.in/sdg-india-index-dashboard-2019-20#:~:text=The%20

SDG%20India%20Index%202019,qualitative%20assessment%20on%20SDG%2017

NITI Aayog. (2020). SDG India—Index and dashboard 2020–21. https://niti.gov.in/writereaddata/files/SDG_3.0_Final_04.03.2021_Web_Spreads.pdf

PIB. (2020, 8 November). Demonetisation helped to reduce black money, increase tax compliance and given a boost to transparency: PM. https://pib.gov.in/PressReleseDetail.aspx?PRID=1671214

Planning Commission. (2014). Employment across various sectors (in millions), employment elasticity, CAGR & share of employment and GVA: 1999–2000, 2004–05, 2009–10. https://niti.gov.in/planningcommission.gov.in/docs/data/datatable/data_2312/DatabookDec2014%20116.pdf

Roy, T. (2020, 14 December). Child nutrition levels in India worsened over last five years, finds NHFS survey. *The Wire*. https://science.thewire.in/health/child-nutrition-levels-in-india-worsened-over-last-five-years-finds-nhfs-survey/#:~:text=According%20to%20a%20World%20Bank,14%25%2C%20the%20report%20said

Statistics Times. (2021, 29 May). List of countries by projected GDP growth. https://statisticstimes.com/economy/countries-by-projected-gdp-growth.php

Stiglitz, J. (2019). *People, power and profits: Progressive capitalism for an age of discontent.* W. W. Norton.

Subramanian, A. (2019, 29 June). India's GDP mis-estimation: Likelihood, magnitudes, mechanisms, and implications (CID Faculty Working Paper No. 354). Harvard University. https://www.hks.harvard.edu/centers/cid/publications/faculty-working-papers/india-gdp-overestimate

Supreme Court of India. (2021, 31 May). Distribution of essential supplies and services during pandemic. https://main.sci.gov.in/supremecourt/2021/11001/11001_2021_35_301_28040_Judgement_31-May-2021.pdf

The Indian Express. (2021, 28 June). Michael Holding: 'All people of colour who hit out at racism, their careers ended in no time'. https://indianexpress.com/article/sports/cricket/michael-holding-west-indies-cricket-racism-t20-7378608/

Thoma, M. (2008, 7 July). Stiglitz: The end of neo-liberalism? https://economistsview.typepad.com/economistsview/2008/07/stiglitz-the-en.html

UNCTAD. (2021a, 18 March). Global economy gets COVID-19 shot from US stimulus, but pre-existing conditions worsen. https://unctad.org/news/global-economy-gets-covid-19-shot-us-stimulus-pre-existing-conditions-worsen

UNCTAD. (2021b). Out of the frying pan...into the fire? https://unctad.org/system/files/official-document/gdsinf2021d1_en.pdf

V-Dem Institute. (2021). Autocratization turns viral, democracy report 2021. https://www.v-dem.net/files/25/DR%202021.pdf

I INSTITUTIONAL VACUUM

Right after taking charge of the government on 26 May 2014, the prime minister unfurled a series of 'reforms' that would end up severely weakening the economic fundamentals and inflicted immense and eminently avoidable pain and misery on a vast majority of population. All the democratic decision-making processes, and checks and balances fell by the wayside as the government rode roughshod and did what it fancied. Transparency and accountability of government faded from public discourse.

As a result of these 'reforms', beginning with the dismantling of the Planning Commission of India (PCI) in 2014, demonetization of 2016, Goods and Services Tax (GST) of 2017, the AatmaNirbhar Bharat of 2020 and new farm and labour laws of 2020, India's growth plunged to −7.3 per cent in FY2021, turning it into one of the slowest growing economies in the world (ranking 142 of 194 countries), from the fastest growing major economies in 2015. Millions of people lost their lives and livelihoods in these years due to a series of economic misadventures and gross mismanagement of the pandemic (IMF, 2021; MoSPI, 2021; *Statistics Times*, 2021).

None of it could have happened if India's democratic and constitutional mechanisms of decision-making, and checks and balances were working as they did for most part in post-Independence India, save for the Emergency of 1975–1977. This chapter highlights some of these developments.

NITI Aayog Replaces Planning Commission

The first top-down and ill-thought decision of the new government was to declare a sudden decision to dismantle the PCI which Prime Minister Modi announced in his first Independence Day address on 15 August 2014. The PCI, set up in 1950 through an executive order, had prepared 12 five-year plans until 2014 and played a stellar role first in rebuilding and transforming India devastated by the 200-year colonial rule. Second, it laid the foundation of a modern social and economic growth and development model, industrialized India that had been systematically de-industrialized by the colonial masters and also led the reform-era transition of the 1980s and the 1990s.

The PCI's beginning and end marked the highest growth phases in post-Independence India. The contrast between the two phases, however, is sharp. At the beginning, the much-maligned Nehruvian socialist era witnessed a quantum jump in economic growth—the GDP growth jumped 5 times from annual average of 0.8 per cent between 1930–3031 and 1946–1947 to 4.1 per cent between 1950–1951 and 1946–1947—accompanied with a dramatic fall in income inequality that India never saw again. The post-liberalized era brought not only high growth but also high-income inequality (more about which is in the AatmaNirbhar Bharat chapter; Mohanty, 2021).

The PCI has had many flaws and not many shed tears for its demise at the time. It reminded the new government of the Soviet-era planning, control and communism but not China, which too followed the same model while adopting capitalism in late 1970s for high growth. In 2017, a government paper shed light on PCI's dismantling. It stated, 'an internal evaluation in Government revealed that Planning Commission was witnessing policy fatigue necessitating structural changes in central planning process' (Srinivas, 2017).

The NITI Aayog, which replaced the PCI in 2015, produced two documents that mimicked earlier five-year plans: 'Three-year Action Agenda 2017–18 to 2019-20' and 'Strategy for New India @ 75'. The first one recycled the UPA-II (United Progressive Alliance-II) era policies, except reviving two failed and abandoned ones, public–private partnership (PPP) and import substitution of the 1960s and the 1970s.

The second didn't recognize job crisis, the devastations caused by demonetization and GST or the economic slowdown, though the quarterly GDP growth had fallen from 9.7 per cent in Q2 of FY2017 to 5.6 per cent in Q3 of FY2019. This document recycled the UPA era schemes that had by now been relaunched with changed names: Make in India, Skill India, Digital India, Swachh Bharat, Ayushman Bharat, etc. The Aayog also announced Seven-Year Strategy and Fifteen-Year Vision documents, but those never materialized (*Hindustan Times*, 2014; Mohanty, 2020a).

Apparently, the prime minister was not very happy with the results and in 2019 asked central ministries to make five-year plans with well-defined targets and milestones (PTI, 2019a).

'NITI' in the NITI Aayog stands for 'National Institution for Transforming India' and its goals are lofty. Envisioned as a think tank, it was to provide central and state governments with 'relevant strategic and technical advice' across the spectrum of policymaking, disseminate best practices and infuse new policy ideas and specific issue-based support. It ended up as the principal cheerleader of the government (PIB, 2015).

Cheerleading Government

The demonetization paralysed the economy as millions of jobs and businesses were lost overnight. What role the Aayog played in it is not known, but it extended unconditional, strong and steady support even in the face of mounting evidence that it hurt, rather than help, the people and the economy. The then Vice Chairpersons Arvind Panagariya, and his successor, Rajiv Kumar have said that it would have a positive impact in the long run (Mishra, 2018; PTI, 2016).

The same happened with the GST. Its deeply flawed design and implementation caused further loss of jobs and businesses, particularly damaging informal economy. Panagariya listed GST as one of the 'two truly mega reforms' (the other being corporate tax cut of 2019) in 2020; Kumar had already endorsed it, though then CEA Arvind Subramanian described it as an economic shock, along with demonetization. There is no evidence of the Aayog playing any role in its roll-out (Panagariya, 2020; Subramanian, 2018; Thapar, 2017).

It supported the untimely and unplanned lockdown with policy papers and SWOT analyses and predicted that the COVID-19 cases would end on 16 May 2020 by releasing the graph reproduced below (NITI Aayog, 2020a, 2020b; Rawat, 2020).

The following is the extract of NITI Aayog's 24 April presentation on zero virus count on 16 May.

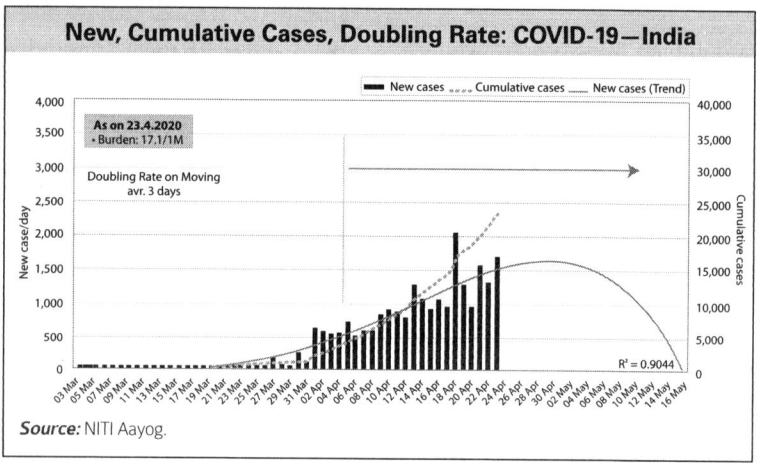

Source: NITI Aayog.

On the appointed day (16 May), India has 90,648 total cases, 4,864 daily cases and 2,871 deaths. A few days later (23 May), the Aayog denied having made this claim and apologized for 'misconception'. By now, it had already claimed that the lockdown had averted 14–29 lakh cases and saved 37,000–78,000 lives based on a model designed for non-COVID-19 diseases (PIB, 2020; PTI, 2020a).

It has nothing to say about the impact of the pandemic on the people and economy yet.

The Aayog has lent uncritical support to three new farm laws, new labour codes and privatization of public banks and other assets. V. K. Saraswat, a member, wrote in support of mere announcement of these 'reforms' without even waiting for these to be spelt out. Kumar too spoke in favour of these 'reforms'. Panagariya wrote that India was facing 'acute problem of credit deprivation' and that there was a need to privatize banks to address it when India was in a 'liquidity trap' to support privatization of banks. The same day (5 February 2021), the Reserve Bank of India's (RBI) monetary policy statement had declared that India's 'systemic liquidity remained in large surplus' (Mohanty, 2021; Panagariya, 2021; PTI, 2020b; RBI, 2021; Saraswat & Ghosh, 2020).

Unlike the PCI, the Aayog doesn't collect or provide data on economic and social developments of states. By not collecting data on the impact of demonetization, GST and the pandemic on the loss of jobs and businesses, it has created an intellectual vacuum as the apex think tank of the government. On the other hand, it acts more like a propaganda wing of the government. A glaring example is that of the GDP back series. It has no locus standi or domain expertise in statistics and yet it stalled the release of back series data of the new GDP of 2011–2012 base (adopted in January 2015) twice for showing higher growth rates during the previous UPA years (2004–2014). When the Aayog released the back series, the growth rates of the UPA years had been lowered. Estimating GDP and its back series are the tasks of the Central Statistics Office (CSO; detailed in the chapter on GDP and data vacuum; Iyer, 2018; Mohanty, 2019).

Weakening of Democratic Checks and Balances

The intellectual vacuum created in post-PCI could have been filled by other institutional mechanisms, like the Parliament, ministries, various advisory and autonomous bodies of the government, independent academic institutions and experts. But if none stood up to be counted, it is because they were undermined and ignored by the political leadership. For example, the role of CEA and Economic Advisory Council to the Prime Minister (EAC-PM) in critical decisions such as demonetization, GST and lockdown is not known; none of them raised red flags when they should have (Mohanty, 2020b).

None of these raised their voices publicly against 'liberalized' vaccination policy that was discriminatory, a veritable profit-making trade in part and endangered well-being of the people and economy. No protest was heard when this policy was modified at the instance of the Supreme Court and yet reserved 25 per cent of vaccines for private hospitals at a substantially higher rates for the 18–44 age group, as against free vaccination for the rest (more of it in the pandemic catastrophe chapter; Ramakumar, 2021a, 2021b).

India's democracy has come under a serious cloud since 2014. Sweden's V-Dem Institute, which measures democracies in the world since 2017, downgraded India from 'electoral democracy' to 'electoral autocracy' in its 2021 report, observing that 'Narendra Modi led the Bharatiya Janata Party (BJP) victory in India's 2014 elections' marked a 'vertical' decline in democracy, 'making it one of the most dramatic shifts among all countries in the world over the past 10 years, alongside autocratizing countries like *Brazil, Hungary,* and *Turkey*' (V-Dem Institute, 2021).

Its graph, reproduced below, mapped this decline through key democratic indicators such as deliberative democracy index, egalitarian democracy index, electoral democracy index, liberal democracy index and participatory democracy index.

The V-Dem Institute has been warning the world about India's democratic decline since 2018, when it said that India was 'at risk' not only because its 'level of democracy has declined significantly

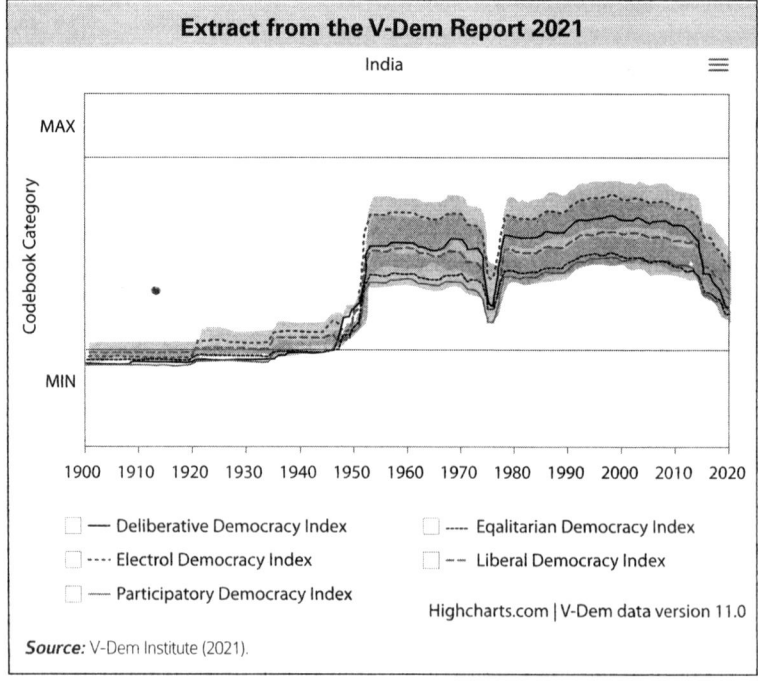

28 AN UNKEPT PROMISE

over the last decade, particularly concerning freedom of speech and alternative source of information, civil society, the rule of law and some electoral prospects' but also that 'autocratization is now manifesting', along with some others such as Brazil, Russia, Turkey and the USA. Its 2020 report stated that the ruling BJP was 'the typical ruling party in autocracies in terms of illiberalism' (V-Dem Institute, 2018, 2020).

The USA's Freedom House also downgraded India in 2021 into 'party free' in political rights and civil liberties, just one rank above 'not free'. It did so by pointing at deterioration in political rights and civil liberties and a spate of communal attacks against Muslims 'since Narendra Modi became prime minister in 2014'. It stated: 'Under Modi, India appears to have abandoned its potential to serve as a global democratic leader, elevating narrow Hindu nationalist interests at the expense of its founding values of inclusion and equal rights for all' (Freedom House, 2021).

Democracy matters for economic growth, apart from people's general well-being.

A multi-institutional and multi-country study led by Massachusetts Institute of Technology (MIT) economist Daron Acemoglu in 2019 concluded that 'democratizations increase GDP per capita by about 20 percent in the long run'. The study examined 184 countries from 1960 to 2010 (50 years) to see the impact of the unprecedented spread of democracy around the world during which 122 democratizations of countries and 71 cases in which countries moved from democracy to a non-democratic type of government (Acemoglu et al., 2019).

The following graph shows the impact of democratization on economic growth.

India would do well to realize that damaging democracy will damage both the economy and the people.

Communal and divisive politics hurts economic growth too.

A multidisciplinary study of 109 countries spanning over 100 years by researchers from the Universities of Bristol (UK) and Tennessee (USA), published in 2018, found that *economic growth comes after* secular polity,

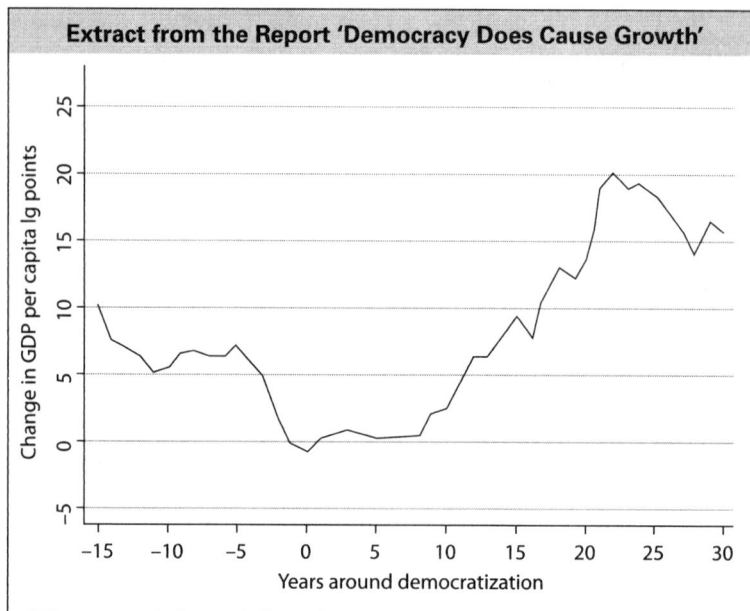

GDP per capita before and after a democratization. This figure plots GDP per capita in log points around a democratic transition relative to countries remaining non-democratic in the same year. We normalize log GDP per capita to 0 in the year preceding the democratization. Time (in years) relative to the year of democratization runs on the horizontal axis.

Source: Acemoglu et al. (2019).

not the other way round. The following graph reproduced from this study shows how growth in the secularization graph is *leading* the development graph (GDP) in these countries (Ruck et al., 2018).

Yet public assaults on Muslims and *Islamophobia* continue to dominate India's politics. From a series of *mob lynching* in the name of cow protection and communal riots, the pandemic witnessed Muslims being blamed for the spread of the pandemic. The Tablighi Jamaat was the target during the first wave until three high courts came to their rescue and during the second wave it were the 16 Muslim members of the Covid War Room of the Bruhat Bengaluru Mahanagara Palike, which ended with a BJP leader's associates being arrested in the bed scam (Asif, 2021; Halarnkar, 2021; Mohanty, 2020c; Peerigo, 2020; *The Wire*, 2021).

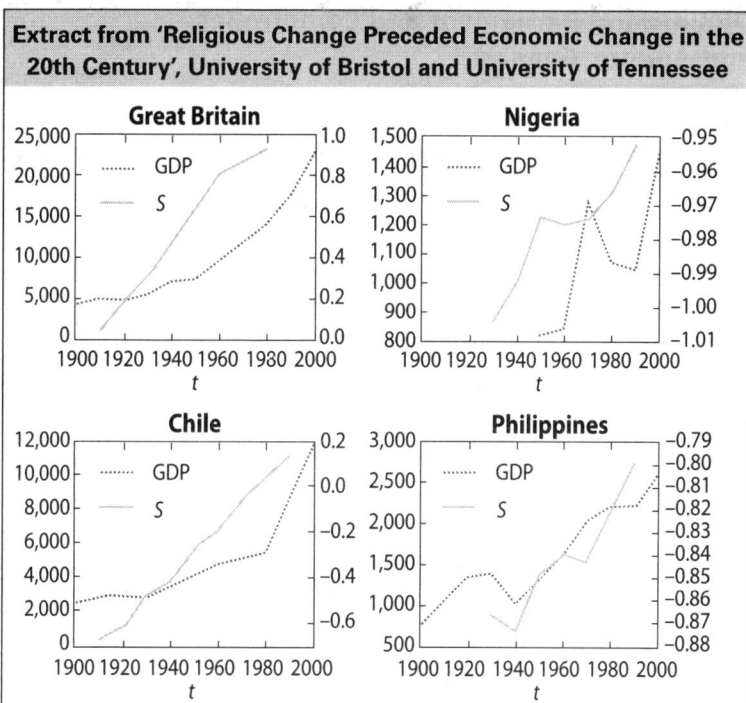

Time series of secularization versus GDP per capita, from four illustrative countries, over the 20th century. Each red line represents the mean secularization score, S_t, of the birth cohort in decade, t, for that country. Each blue line represents the mean GDP per capita (normalized to 1990 US$) during decade t in that country.

Source: Ruck et al. (2018).

Yet the political establishment hasn't gone for a course correction. Instead, reliance on fake news, propaganda, misleading claims and hyperboles continues. For instance, on 14 June 2021, the prime minister told G7 leaders that India was their 'natural ally' in defending democracy, freedom of thought and liberty from 'authoritarianism', among other threats (Mihindukulasuriya, 2020; PTI, 2021a).

That India's democracy is under a cloud is not just because of the V-Dem Institute's downgrading. The evidence is all around. Let us look at a few instances.

Diminishing Parliament and Comptroller and Auditor General

Prime Minister Modi bowed on its steps and called the Parliament as the 'temple of democracy' while stepping in for the first time in 2014 (PTI, 2014).

But over the years, the role of the Parliament in law making and holding the government accountable has significantly diminished. On the contrary, it has been used to undermine the very democracy it is supposed to uphold.

A glaring example is passage of the Jammu and Kashmir (J&K) Reorganisation Act of 2019 and a resolution together which revoked the state's special status under Article 370 and downgraded it to two union territories (UTs). These go-aheads by the Parliament allowed the centre to shut down the state and its people with a complete ban on the Internet and mobile services for a long time and put thousands of people, including prominent political leaders, in jail without charge to prevent democratic protests (Human Rights Watch, 2019; PTI, 2019b).

Another was the amendment to the Government of National Capital Territory of Delhi Act in March 2021. Amid the raging second wave of the pandemic, the amendment which declared Delhi's Lieutenant Governor (LG), a nominee of the centre and an unelected individual, as Delhi's 'government' was passed by the Parliament. This reduced the real government, Delhi's elected legislature and Council of Ministers to adjuncts of the LG. Former secretary general of the Lok Sabha P. D. T. Achary wrote that this amendment turned the Constitution on its head since the LG is neither a member of the Legislative Assembly nor is he/she accountable to it. Declaring a central government's nominee as 'government' is travesty of both democracy and the Parliament (Achary, 2021; Ministry of Law and Justice, 2021).

Both J&K and Delhi have now turned vassal states of the centre, with its nominee ruling there, instead of elected assemblies and Council of Ministers.

Curtailed Sessions

After the new government came to power in 2014, the Parliament has seen steady erosion of its role in law making. Its committees, like department-related standing committees, select and joint committees, which scrutinize key legislations before being debated and passed in both houses, have been kept out of key legislations like the J&K Reorganisation Act of 2019, which abrogated the state's special status (Article 370) and its bifurcation; discriminatory Citizenship Amendment Act (CAA) of 2019 (on the basis of religion); amendment to the Unlawful Activities (Prevention) Act (UAPA) of 2019 designating individuals as 'terrorists', as against groups earlier and the three new farm laws were passed bypassing such committees (Sahu, 2020).

Data-driven portal IndiaSpend's analysis showed that during Modi's first term (2014–2019), only 25 per cent of bills were referred to parliamentary committees, compared to 71 per cent under the UPA-II (2004–2009) and 60 per cent under the UPA-I (2009–2014) and that only about 10 per cent of bills introduced during the second term between May 2019 and September 2020 had been referred to committees. It revealed many other disturbing trends: no committee met during the national lockdown, even virtual meetings were not allowed; meetings and duration of meetings were far less than earlier; several standing committees took partisan approach to prevent discussion on key issues likely to embarrass the government and dissent notes were not allowed (Ali, 2020).

Several legislations have been passed as money bill to bypass the Rajya Sabha in which the government lacks a majority. Article 110 of the Constitution states that a bill is considered a money bill 'only' when it contains provisions related to taxation, borrowing of money, expenditure from or receipt to the Consolidated Fund of India, etc. It can be introduced in and passed by the Lok Sabha. Although the Rajya Sabha can debate and recommend amendments, it can't pass or force its views (Indian Kanoon, n.d.; PRS, 2015).

Several key legislations of doubtful claims of being money bill have been passed. These include the Aadhaar law, which mandates the use of Aadhaar identity card for banking and other essential services, thereby compromising privacy (held as fundamental right by the apex court) and electoral bond, which turns electoral funding opaque and beyond the scrutiny of the Election Commission and disclosure norms of the Companies Act of 2013. Although the Supreme Court upheld the Aadhaar law as money bill, the dissenting judgement of

Justice D. Y. Chandrachud described bypassing of the Rajya Sabha 'a fraud on the Constitution' (Khaitan, 2020; Supreme Court of India, 2018).

Unlike the US Congress, the Parliament has had no role to play in managing the pandemic. It didn't formulate stimulus or relief packages. In fact, its sessions were curtailed in 2020 and 2021 due to the pandemic. French political scientist Christophe Jaffrelot wrote that under the new government, the Lok Sabha and the Rajya Sabha had ceased to be key places for debate and wondered: 'How do you make democracy work without a representative body?' (Jaffrelot & Jumle, 2020; Mohanty, 2020d).

A big reason for the diminishing role of the Parliament is also the weak political opposition. The less said the better. The opposition has been so ineffective, dispirited and invisible that the UK's *Financial Times* wrote in 2020 that 'the annihilation of India's political opposition is almost complete' (*Financial Times*, 2020).

In the meanwhile, India's top auditor, the Comptroller and Auditor General of India (CAG), which plays a critical role in bringing accountability to government's financial management and played a key role in exposing several high-profile cases of financial improprieties in the Bofors deal, allocation of captive coal blocks, 2G spectrum auction and Commonwealth Games in recent decades, has remained subdued. Its role in the biggest corruption scandals to hit post-2014 was the Rafale deal (2016) which was effectively buried by the CAG producing a 'redacted' report, withholding critical information on 'commercial details' like pricing of the fighter jets that would have revealed financial misconduct (CAG, 2019; Philippin, 2021; Ram, 2019; Sridhar, 2019).

A right to information (RTI) query revealed in 2021 that in the past five years of the Modi government, the total number of CAG reports relating to central government ministries and departments had fallen by 75 per cent—from 55 in 2015 to just 14 in 2020 (Vikram, 2021).

Ambiguity of Supreme Court and Media

The Supreme Court of India, as the final interpreter of the Constitution and upholder of the constitutional rights of citizens, is key to India's constitutional democracy and its checks and balances. Its functioning too has come under, particularly since four of the most senior judges (next to the Chief Justice of India [CJI]) called an unprecedented press conference in January 2018 to warn that unless the apex court 'is preserved and it maintains its equanimity', India's 'democracy will not survive'. They raised several concerns about the functioning of the court from selective assignment of cases to the CJI not listening to them (BBC, 2018).

Several key legislations challenged for their constitutional validity remain undecided. These include (a) the CAA of 2019, which introduced religion-based citizenship for outsiders but excluded Muslims, spreading panic and protests across the country; (b) the opaque electoral bond of 2017; (c) the new farm laws of 2020 that usurp states' power and threatens farmers' interests, sparking a prolonged protest and (d) the J&K Reorganisation Act of 2019 (ANI, 2021; Bhardwaj, 2021; PTI, 2021b).

The court has been accepting the government's affidavits in a 'sealed cover', thereby denying a fair trial and natural justice. It began in 2016 with the court asking the RBI to identify big corporate defaulters owning more than ₹500 crore to banks and spread to the cases involving electoral bond, Rafale deal, National Register of Citizens in Assam and others (Manju, 2016; *The Print*, 2019).

The court has been found wanting in protecting fundamental rights of people and being selective in approach. An RTI query revealed in February 2021 that 58 habeas corpus petitions were pending, the oldest one being from 2005. When a TV anchor known for proximity to the government applied for bail in 2020, the court was prompt and granted the relief but not to others with the CJI saying that he wanted to discourage the use of Article 32—a constitutional right to citizens to move the apex court for protection of fundamental rights (Bar and Bench, 2021; IANS, 2020; Rajagopal, 2020).

The court's independence of the apex court has been questioned also because former CJI Justice Ranjan Gogoi got nominated to the Rajya Sabha less than six months after retirement in 2019 and, more recently, Justice Arun Mishra was appointed chairman of the National Human Rights Commission a year after describing Modi as a 'versatile genius' as a serving judge. In 2014, former CJI Justice P. Sathasivam was appointed Governor of Kerala less than six months after his retirement (Nair, 2020; *The Indian Express*, 2014, 2021).

In 2020, former Chief Justice of Delhi High Court Justice A. P. Shah lamented that the only institution capable of stopping the death of democracy was aiding it (Shah, 2020).

There have been some good judgements, like the 2018 one declaring right to privacy as a fundamental right; declaring the 'liberalized' vaccine policy for 18–44 age group as 'arbitrary and irrational', leading to its partial rollback and dismissal of sedition case against journalist Vinod Dua, upholding a journalist's right to criticize government, even brutally (Rajagopal, 2021; Supreme Court of India, 2021).

But the true success lies in surge of such instances than dearth.

Another key institution of democratic checks and balances is media—the watchdog of democracy. The mainstream media, particularly a large number of television channels with a wider reach and a segment of print media, have turned the rule of the game upside down by stopping to hold the government accountable.

Recently, the *Time* magazine held India's 'compliant' and 'servile media' partly responsible for it. It described how many English and Hindi news channels and regional news outlets are 'unabashedly pro-Modi' and 'routinely exaggerated the government's successes and either glossed over its failures or spun ways to pin them on Modi's discontents: the opposition, liberals, Muslims, activists, leftists, protesters, NGOs, and other assorted "anti-nationals"'. It did note some change in regional papers which highlighted under-reporting of deaths but stated that was because the scale of damages had become too difficult to hide (Chowdhury, 2021).

A compromised media compromises economic growth too.

A multinational study covering more than 150 countries, published by UNESCO in 2008, examined the co-relation between free press and different dimensions of development (including GDP, health and education), poverty, governance and conflict/violence. It concluded that there indeed existed a 'good co-relation' and a 'positive influence'. Barring some exceptions, it stated that countries that did not have press freedom suffered from governance problems and rested its case by observing: 'A free press constitutes an instrument of development as such, in the same way as education or investment' (UNESCO, 2008).

Amartya Sen had once famously observed that there had never been a famine in a democratic society or even in India since Independence because famine was not even possible when the press was free as it would expose any shortage in time to force corrective measures (Hamilton, 2020).

Silence of Citizens

There is yet another big threat to India's growth story: silence of its citizens.

Voters elect and decide their governments, thereby holding governments accountable. Indians, particularly the educated and empowered middle class, have stopped questioning the government or expressing outrage at its policies, seemingly inured to the immense and avoidable pain that fellow citizens have been going through since the 2016 demonetization.

Former Finance Minister P. Chidambaram captured the essence in his article 'The Tragedy of the Missing Middle'. He wrote:

> It is disappointing to see the middle class indifferent to the over-100 days of protests of the farmers at Singhu and Tikri. Except when the horror on Nirbhaya was perpetrated, the middle class distanced itself from the police excesses in JNU and AMU, the anti-CAA protests at Shaheen Bagh and elsewhere and, shamefully, the plight of the millions of migrant workers who trekked hundreds of kilometres to their homes following the sudden lockdown on March 25, 2020.... Police firings and encounters do not seem to stir their conscience. Arbitrary arrests of social activists, writers and poets or harassment of Opposition political leaders do not seem to shake them out of their complacency.... (Chidambaram, 2021)

Noam Chomsky once said, 'As long as the general population is passive, apathetic, diverted to consumerism or hatred of the vulnerable, then the powerful can do as they please, and those who survive will be left to contemplate the outcome' (Chomsky, 2021).

In the meanwhile, dissent has turned into being 'anti-national' and seditious.

The centre has ruthlessly been cracking down on all voices of dissent and protests by using harsh sedition (IPC 124A) and anti-terror law UAPA of 1967. Scores of academics, human rights activists, lawyers, students and journalists have been incarcerated and many are languishing in jail without bail. There has been a remarkable surge in sedition and anti-terror cases. A study showed that 96 per cent of sedition cases filed against Indians for criticizing politicians and governments over the last decade were registered after 2014 (Article14, 2021).

As for the anti-terror case, the government told the Rajya Sabha that 5,922 people were arrested under the UAPA between 2016 and 2019 of which only 132 were convicted (*The Hindu*, 2021).

The U.S. Department of State expressed serious concerns about democratic and human rights violations in its 2020 Human Rights Report, which included 'unlawful and arbitrary killings, including extrajudicial killings perpetrated by police'; 'arbitrary arrest and detention by government authorities'; 'restrictions on freedom of expression and the press'; 'use of criminal libel laws to prosecute social media speech, censorship, and site blocking'; 'overly restrictive rules on nongovernmental organizations'; 'restrictions on political participation', etc. (U.S. Department of State, 2021).

To sum up, India's politics needs to change, not just for people's wellbeing in terms of democratic rights but also for their financial health through democratic checks and balances on arbitrary economic policies.

Takeaways

⇨ Dismantling of the PCI created a policy and planning vacuum that the NITI Aayog has failed to fill.
⇨ The Parliament, political opposition, the CAG, judiciary and media have failed to provide robust checks and balances necessary for sound policymaking.
⇨ India's democracy and its secular politics have weakened, which bodes ill for future growth prospects.
⇨ Citizens have turned indifferent to the pain of fellow citizens and have stopped questioning the government they voted for.
⇨ The institutional failure that India is witnessing is structural and, hence, is unlikely to change until political changes happen.

References

Acemoglu, D., Naidu, S., Restrepo, P., & Robinson, J. A. (2019, 14 January). Democracy does cause growth. *Journal of Political Economy*. https://economics.mit.edu/files/16686

Achary, P. D. T. (2021, 20 March). Centre's Delhi amendment bill is at odds with Supreme Court's ruling and the Constitution. *The Wire*. https://thewire.in/law/delhi-amendment-bill-centre-lieutenant-governor-supreme-court

Ali, S. (2020, 14 September). Parliamentary panels' role, functioning at all-time low, data show. *IndiaSpend*. https://www.indiaspend.com/parliamentary-panels-role-functioning-at-all-time-low-data-show/

ANI. (2021, 10 March). SC tags petitions challenging constitutional validity of farm laws. *The New Indian Express*. https://www.newindianexpress.com/nation/2021/mar/10/sc-tags-petitions-challenging-constitutional-validity-of-farm-laws-2274812.html

Article14. (2021, 23 May). Our New Database Reveals Rise in Sedition Cases in the Modi Era. https://www.article-14.com/post/our-new-database-reveals-rise-in-sedition-cases-in-the-modi-era

Asif, M. M. (2021, April). Virulence of Hindutva. In V. Chaturvedi (Ed.), *Perspectives on Asia* (pp. 154–165). Asia Shorts and *Journal of Asian Studies*. https://www.asianstudies.org/wp-content/uploads/Chapter-11-Asif.pdf

Bar and Bench. (2021, 22 February). 58 habeas corpus petitions pending before Supreme Court, oldest is from 2005: RTI response. https://www.barandbench.com/news/litigation/58-habeas-corpus-petitions-pending-before-supreme-court-oldest-2005-rti

BBC. (2018, 12 January). India Supreme Court judges: Democracy is in danger. https://www.bbc.com/news/world-asia-india-42660391

Bhardwaj, D. (2021, 29 March). Electoral bonds: After SC order activists, oppn point out loopholes. *Hindustan Times*. https://www.hindustantimes.com/india-news/electoral-bonds-after-sc-order-activists-oppn-point-out-loopholes-101616974039304.html

CAG. (2019). *Performance audit report of the Comptroller and Auditor General of India on capital acquisition in Indian Air Force* (Report No. 3). https://www.humanrightsinitiative.org/download/C&AG-AirForce-CapitalAcq-PerfAudit-Report3-2019.pdf

Chidambaram, P. (2021, 14 March). The tragedy of the missing middle. *The Indian Express*. https://indianexpress.com/article/opinion/columns/middle-class-politics-farmers-protest-p-chidambaram-7227195/

Chomsky, N. (2021, 31 March). Chomsky Noam, tweet of March 31, 2021. https://twitter.com/noamchomskyT/status/13769995545040

Chowdhury, D. R. (2021, 3 May). It isn't just Modi. India's compliant media must also take responsibility for the COVID-19 crisis. *Time*. https://time.com/6033152/india-media-covid-19/?s=03

Financial Times. (2020, 6 August). The annihilation of India's political opposition is almost complete. https://www.ft.com/content/bf8b2503-a9cf-4506-b947-e476f7656f0c

Freedom House. (2021). Freedom in the world: Democracy under siege. https://freedomhouse.org/sites/default/files/2021-02/FIW2021_World_02252021_FINAL-web-upload.pdf

Halarnkar, S. (2021, 27 March). Turning India over to the mob, video by video. *Scroll*. https://scroll.in/article/990688/turning-india-over-to-the-mob-video-by-video

Hamilton, L. (2020, 31 October). Amartya Sen said no democracy, with a free press, has ever had major famines. *The Print*. https://theprint.in/pageturner/excerpt/amartya-sen-said-no-democracy-with-free-press-has-had-major-famines/534152/

Hindustan Times. (2014, 15 August). PM Narendra Modi scraps Planning Commission. https://www.hindustantimes.com/india/pm-narendra-modi-scraps-planning-commission/story-EJdGN4v0ETFV1SJZEeFy1J.html

Human Rights Watch. (2019, 16 September). India: Free Kashmiris arbitrarily detained. https://www.hrw.org/news/2019/09/16/india-free-kashmiris-arbitrarily-detained

IANS. (2020, 16 November). SC is trying to discourage use of Article 32 after surge in petitions: CJI. *Business Standard.* https://www.business-standard.com/article/current-affairs/sc-is-trying-to-discourage-use-of-article-32-after-surge-in-petitions-cji-120111600809_1.html

Indian Kanoon. (n.d.). Article 110 in the Constitution of India. https://indiankanoon.org/doc/72095/

Iyer, P. V. (2018, 7 December). Three years ago, key statistics panel revised UPA growth up, Niti Aayog rejected it. *The Indian Express.* https://indianexpress.com/article/india/key-statistics-panel-revised-upa-growth-up-niti-aayog-rejected-it-5482457/

Jaffrelot, C., & Jumle, V. (2020, 15 October). Under Modi government, Lok Sabha and Rajya Sabha have ceased to be key places for debate. *The Indian Express.* https://indianexpress.com/article/opinion/columns/narendra-modi-government-parliament-lok-sabha-rajya-sabha-6725428/

Khaitan, T. (2020, 7 August). Killing a constitution with a thousand cuts: Executive aggrandizement and party-state fusion in India. *Law & Ethics of Human Rights, 14*(1), 49–95. https://www.degruyter.com/document/doi/10.1515/lehr-2020-2009/html

Manju, A. B. (2016, 17 February). Supreme Court asks RBI to submit list of large loan defaulters. *DNA.* https://www.dnaindia.com/business/report-supreme-court-asks-rbi-to-submit-list-of-large-loan-defaulters-2178604

Mihindukulasuriya, R. (2020, 31 January). Nearly 18,000 Twitter accounts spread 'fake news' for BJP, 147 do it for Congress: Study. *The Print.* https://theprint.in/politics/nearly-18000-twitter-accounts-spread-fake-news-for-bjp-147-do-it-for-congress-study/356876/

Ministry of Law and Justice. (2021, 28 March). The Government of National Capital Territory of Delhi (Amendment) Act, 2021. *The Gazette of India.* https://www.livelaw.in/pdf_upload/gnctd-amendemnt-bill-391206.pdf

Mishra, R. (2018, 10 January). I strongly support demonetisation. *Business Line.* https://www.thehindubusinessline.com/opinion/i-strongly-support-demonetisation/article9842384.ece

Mohanty, P. (2019, 13 November). GDP base year row: What's the problem with re-basing India's growth calculations. *Business Today.* https://www.businesstoday.in/current/economy-politics/gdp-base-year-row-whats-the-problem-with-rebasing-indias-growth-calculations-indian-economy-gross-domestic-product/story/390180.html

Mohanty, P. (2020a, 1 June). Coronavirus lockdown XVIII: Why India urgently needs SOPs for decision-making. *Business Today*. https://www.businesstoday.in/current/economy-politics/coronavirus-lockdown-india-urgently-needs-sop-for-decision-making-migrant-workers-economy-fiscal-deficit/story/405243.html

Mohanty, P. (2020b, 11 September). Rebooting Economy XXVI: Derailment of economy is not 'act of God', it is 'art of misdirection'. *Business Today*. https://www.businesstoday.in/opinion/columns/india-derailment-of-indian-economy-is-not-an-act-of-god-it-is-art-of-misdirection-job-loss-unemployment-gdp/story/415820.html

Mohanty, P. (2020c, 11 November). Rebooting economy 44: India's journey from one of the fastest growing economies in 2015 to slowest in 2020. *Business Today*. https://www.businesstoday.in/opinion/columns/rebooting-economy-44-indias-journey-from-one-of-the-fastest-growing-economies-in-2015-to-slowest-in-2020/story/421644.html

Mohanty, P. (2020d, 17 November). Rebooting economy 46: Who is designing India's growth path? *Business Today*. https://www.businesstoday.in/opinion/columns/indian-economy-who-is-designing-indias-growth-path-atma-nirbhar-bharat-demonetisation-economic-lockdown/story/422135.html

Mohanty, P. (2021, 10 February). Rebooting economy 66: Is India facing credit deprivation to warrant corporation banks? *Business Today*. https://www.businesstoday.in/opinion/columns/rebooting-economy66-is-india-facing-credit-deprivation-to-warrant-corporation-banks/story/430868.html

MoSPI. (2021, 31 May). Provisional estimates of annual national income 2019–2020 and quarterly estimates of gross domestic product for the fourth quarter (Q4) of 2019–2020. https://mospi.gov.in/documents/213904/416359//PRESS%20NOTE%20PE%20and%20Q4%20estimates%20of%20GDP1600850161778.pdf/661ea24e-9ac7-1444-94f2-be87f79d773e

Nair, S. K. (2020, 19 March). As former CJI Ranjan Gogoi takes oath as Rajya Sabha member, opposition walks out. *The Hindu*. https://www.thehindu.com/news/national/former-cji-ranjan-gogoi-takes-oath-as-rajya-sabha-member/article3`6321.ece

NITI Aayog. (2020a, 30 April). Why lockdown is the best strategy for India to fight COVID-19? https://niti.gov.in/why-lockdown-best-strategy-india-fight-covid-19

NITI Aayog. (2020b, 11 May). Covid-19 in India: A swot analysis. https://niti.gov.in/covid-19-india-swot-analysis

Panagariya, A. (2020, 14 October). Six years of reforms: Modi has established his reformist credentials alongside PMs like Rao and Vajpayee. *The Times of India.* https://timesofindia.indiatimes.com/blogs/toi-edit-page/six-years-of-reforms-modi-has-established-his-reformist-credentials-alongside-pms-like-rao-and-vajpayee/

Panagariya, A. (2021, 5 February). Corporates for banking: To address India's credit scarcity problem, allow corporate houses to set up banks. *The Times of India.* https://timesofindia.indiatimes.com/blogs/toi-edit-page/corporates-for-banking-to-address-indias-credit-scarcity-problem-allow-corporate-houses-to-set-up-banks/

Peerigo, B. (2020, 22 October). It was already dangerous to be Muslim in India. Then came the Coronavirus. *Time.* https://time.com/5815264/coronavirus-india-islamophobia-coronajihad/?s=03

Philippin, Y. (2021, 4 April). Sale of French Rafale jet fighters to India: How a state scandal was buried. *Mediapart.* https://www.mediapart.fr/en/journal/international/040421/sale-french-rafale-jet-fighters-india-how-state-scandal-was-buried?utm_source=facebook&utm_medium=social&utm_campaign=Sharing&xtor=CS3-66

PIB. (2015, 1 January). Government constitutes National Institution for Transforming India (NITI) Aayog. https://pib.gov.in/newsite/PrintRelease.aspx?relid=114268

PIB. (2020, 22 May). 14 lakh–29 lakh cases averted, 37,000–78,000 lives saved due to timely decision of lockdown, we are on the right track: Government. https://pib.gov.in/PressReleseDetail.aspx?PRID=1626137

PRS. (2015, 22 December). Money bills vs. other bills. PRS Legislative Research. https://www.prsindia.org/theprsblog/money-bills-vs-other-bills

PTI. (2014, 20 May). Modi describes Parliament as 'temple of democracy'. *Business Standard.* https://www.business-standard.com/article/politics/modi-describes-parliament-as-temple-of-democracy-114052000994_1.html

PTI. (2016, 30 November). Demonetisation to benefit economy in long run: Panagariya. *Business Line* (updated on 15 January 2018). https://www.thehindubusinessline.com/economy/demonetisation-to-benefit-economy-in-long-run-panagariya/article9401841.ece

PTI. (2019a, 11 June). PM Modi asks top officials to come out with five-year plan for each ministry, impactful decisions. *Business Today.* https://www.businesstoday.in/current/economy-politics/pm-modi-asks-top-officials-to-come-out-with-five-year-plan-for-each-ministry-impactful-decisions/story/355171.html

PTI. (2019b, 6 August). Par nod for revoking spl status for J-K, splitting state into 2 UTs; PM says momentous. *Business Standard.* https://www.

business-standard.com/article/pti-stories/par-nod-for-revoking-spl-status-for-j-k-splitting-state-into-2-uts-pm-says-momentous-119080601604_1.html

PTI. (2020a, 23 May). Never said COVID-19 cases will be zero by May 16: NITI Aayog member. NDTV. https://www.ndtv.com/india-news/niti-aayog-member-vk-paul-never-said-covid-19-cases-will-be-zero-by-may-16-2233705

PTI. (2020b, 30 October). India to pursue self-reliance, encourage domestic entrepreneurs, says Rajiv Kumar. *The Hindu*. https://www.thehindu.com/business/Economy/india-to-pursue-self-reliance-encourage-domestic-entrepreneurs-says-rajiv-kumar/article32982327.ece

PTI. (2021a, 14 June). India natural ally of G7 in defending democracy, freedom of thought: PM. *Business Standard*. https://www.business-standard.com/article/current-affairs/india-natural-ally-of-g7-in-defending-democracy-freedom-of-thought-pm-121061300903_1.html

PTI. (2021b, 15 June). SC to hear plea challenging centre's notification on citizenship to non-Muslim refugees in 2 weeks. *The Wire*. https://thewire.in/law/iuml-caa-citizenship-non-muslim-refugees-mha-supreme-court

Rajagopal, K. (2020, 11 November). Supreme Court grants interim bail to Arnab Goswami, two others in 2018 abetment to suicide case. *The Hindu*. https://www.thehindu.com/news/national/supreme-court-grants-bail-to-arnab-goswami-two-others-in-2018-abetment-to-suicide-case/article33073472.ece

Rajagopal, K. (2021, 3 June). Journalists entitled to protection against sedition, says Supreme Court. *The Hindu*. https://www.thehindu.com/news/national/supreme-court-quashes-sedition-case-against-journalist-vinod-dua/article34713763.ece

Ram, N. (2019). Investigative reports by N. Ram on the Rafale deal. *The Hindu*. https://www.thehindu.com/news/national/investigative-reports-by-n-ram-on-the-rafale-deal/article26447043.ece

Ramakumar, R. (2021a, 26 April). Whose intellectual property is Bharat Biotech's publicly funded Covaxin? India deserves an answer. *Scroll*. https://scroll.in/article/993257/why-its-vital-for-indians-to-know-who-owns-intellectual-property-rights-to-bharat-biotechs-covaxin

Ramakumar, R. (2021b, 8 June). Modi forced to change tack but new vaccine policy still promotes inequity and inefficiency. *The Wire*. https://thewire.in/government/modi-forced-to-change-tack-but-new-vaccine-policy-still-promotes-inequity-and-inefficiency

Rawat, M. (2020, 17 May). In April, govt predicted zero new Covid-19 case by May 16. What went wrong? *India Today*. https://www.indiatoday.in/news-analysis/story/health-ministry-covid19-pandemic-case-prediction-graph-1678917-2020-05-17

RBI. (2021, 5 February). Monetary policy statement, 2020–21, resolution of the Monetary Policy Committee (MPC) February 3–5, 2021. https://rbidocs.rbi.org.in/rdocs/PressRelease/PDFs/PR105055BEF93017054F9BAF12623CBCCE60DB.PDF

Ruck, D. J., Bentley, A. R., & Lawson, D. J. (2018). Religious change preceded economic change in the 20th century. American Association for the Advancement of Science. https://advances.sciencemag.org/content/advances/4/7/eaar8680.full.pdf

Sahu, S. N. (2020, 21 September). The way farm bills passed in Rajya Sabha shows decline in culture of legislative scrutiny. *The Wire*. https://thewire.in/politics/farm-bills-rajya-sabha-legislative-scrutiny

Saraswat, V. K., & Ghosh, A. (2020, 4 June). Modi's Atmanirbhar package paves way for Make in India 2.0 in post-Covid world. *The Print*. https://theprint.in/opinion/modis-atmanirbhar-package-paves-way-for-make-in-india-2-0-in-post-covid-world/434929/

Shah, A. P. (2020, 18 September). The only institution capable of stopping the death of democracy is aiding it. *The Wire*. https://thewire.in/law/supreme-court-rights-uapa-bjp-nda-master-of-roster

Sridhar, V. (2019, 15 March). CAG report: A whitewash job. *Frontline*. https://frontline.thehindu.com/the-nation/article26373546.ece

Srinivas, V. (2017, 16 August). Planning Commission to NITI Aayog: Making strategies for transforming India. PIB. https://pibindia.wordpress.com/2017/08/16/planning-commission-to-niti-aayog-making-strategies-for-transforming-india/

Statistics Times. (2021, 29 May). List of countries by projected GDP growth. https://statisticstimes.com/economy/countries-by-projected-gdp-growth.php

Subramanian, A. (2018, 29 November). 'Demonetisation was a massive, draconian, monetary shock', says Arvind Subramanian in his new book. *Mint*. https://www.livemint.com/Industry/PL1a49BBpiMN2r2VRhvOrN/demonetisation-arvind-subramanian-book-of-counsel-modi-jaitl.html

Supreme Court of India. (2018, 26 September). Justice K. S. Puttaswamy (Retd.) versus Union of India and others. https://main.sci.gov.in/supremecourt/2012/35071/35071_2012_Judgement_26-Sep-2018.pdf

Supreme Court of India. (2021, 31 May). Supreme Court judgement in suo motu case regarding 'distribution of essential supplies and services during pandemic'. https://main.sci.gov.in/supremecourt/2021/11001/11001_2021_35_301_28040_Judgement_31-May-2021.pdf

Thapar, K. (2017, 7 November). Interview: Rajiv Kumar, NITI Aayog Chief, defends demonetisation. *The Wire*. https://thewire.in/economy/rajiv-kumar-niti-aayog-chief-defends-demonetisation

The Hindu. (2021, 10 February). Parliamentary proceedings | 2.2% of cases registered under the UAPA from 2016–2019 ended in court conviction. https://www.thehindu.com/news/national/22-of-cases-registered-under-the-uapa-from-2016-2019-ended-in-court-conviction/article33804099.ece

The Indian Express. (2014, 4 September). Ex-CJI Sathasivam is governor, jurists say it may lead to more 'political intervention'. https://indianexpress.com/article/india/india-others/ex-cji-sathasivam-appointed-kerala-governor/

The Indian Express. (2021, 3 June). Nine months after he retired from SC, Justice Arun Mishra is NHRC chief. https://indianexpress.com/article/india/justice-arun-mishra-nhrc-chairman-7340811/

The Print. (2019, 15 April). Sealed-cover doctrine: SC ensuring secrecy or excluding Indians from public debate? https://theprint.in/talk-point/sealed-cover-doctrine-sc-ensuring-secrecy-or-excluding-indians-from-public-debate/221754/

The Wire. (2021, 26 May). Bengaluru: BJP MLA's aide arrested in bed booking scam case. https://thewire.in/government/bengaluru-bjp-mlas-aide-arrested-in-bed-booking-scam-case

U.S. Department of State. (2021, 30 March). India 2020 human rights report. https://www.state.gov/wp-content/uploads/2021/03/INDIA-2020-HUMAN-RIGHTS-REPORT-1.pdf

UNESCO. (2008). Press freedom and development: An analysis of correlations between freedom of the press and the different dimensions of development, poverty, governance and peace. https://unesdoc.unesco.org/ark:/48223/pf0000161825_eng

V-Dem Institute. (2018). Democracy for all?: V-Dem annual democracy report 2018. https://www.v-dem.net/media/filer_public/68/51/685150f0-47e1-4d03-97bc-45609c3f158d/v-dem_annual_dem_report_2018.pdf

V-Dem Institute. (2020, 26 October). New global data on political parties: V-Party. https://www.v-dem.net/media/filer_public/b6/55/b6553f85-5c5d-45ec-be63-a48a2abe3f62/briefing_paper_9.pdf

V-Dem Institute. (2021). Autocratization turns viral, democracy report 2021. https://www.v-dem.net/files/25/DR%202021.pdf

Vikram, K. (2021, 7 March). CAGed? Top audit body's reports on Centre's money management down by 75 per cent. *The New Indian Express*. https://www.newindianexpress.com/thesundaystandard/2021/mar/07/caged-top-audit-bodys-reports-on-centres-money-management-down-by-75-per-cent-2273200.html

IMF. (2021, April). Managing divergent recoveries (World Economic Outlook). https://www.imf.org/en/Publications/WEO/Issues/2021/03/23/world-economic-outlook-april-2021

II MASKING THE REALITY

The dismantling of the PCI robbed India of a platform for open debate, framing of policies and plans for the entire country and created an intellectual vacuum that the NITI Aayog failed to provide. This was followed by another significant misadventure—introduction of a structurally flawed GDP series in January 2015 to artificially raise the growth rate. The new GDP series also marked the beginning of wholesome data manipulations to mask harsh economic realities.

The new GDP series with 2011–2012 as base was introduced on 30 January 2015. It was significantly influenced by a secret, untried and untested database called MCA-21 of the Ministry of Corporate Affairs (MCA). The MCA-21 provided estimates for industry and services output but is a self-populated (by companies themselves) and, hence, unreliable and unverified. Four years later, in 2019, its flaws were partly revealed by the National Sample Survey Office (NSSO). By now, the new GDP series had raised India's growth rate, thereby surpassing that of China to emerge as the fastest growing major economies in the world overnight. The International Monetary Fund's (IMF) WEO report of January 2016 showed that India's GDP grew at 7.3%, outpacing China's 6.9%, in 2015 (International Monetary Fund, 2016).

Overestimating GDP Numbers

The new 2011–2012 GDP series significantly increased the growth rates of FY2013 and FY2014 from 4.5 per cent and 4.7 per cent under the 2004–2005 series to 5.1 per cent and 6.9 per cent, respectively. Since multilateral agencies such as the World Bank (WB), the IMF and various UN bodies use 'official data' provided by respective governments, India got a fresh coat of paint while the underlying economic fundamentals had not changed. This would unravel a few years later (MoSPI, 2015).

The new series showed a structural change in the economy. The share of agriculture and industry went up, while that of services went down. In FY2012, the agriculture's share (of GVA at current prices) went up marginally from 17.9 per cent to 18.4 per cent but that of industry's leaped up from 19 per cent to 23.7 per cent—close to the target of 25 per cent which Make in India had set in 2014 without a sweat. Its major component, manufacturing, went up from 12.9 per cent to 17.3 per cent—another significant leap. The services' share went down from 63.2 per cent to 58 per cent (MoSPI, 2015).

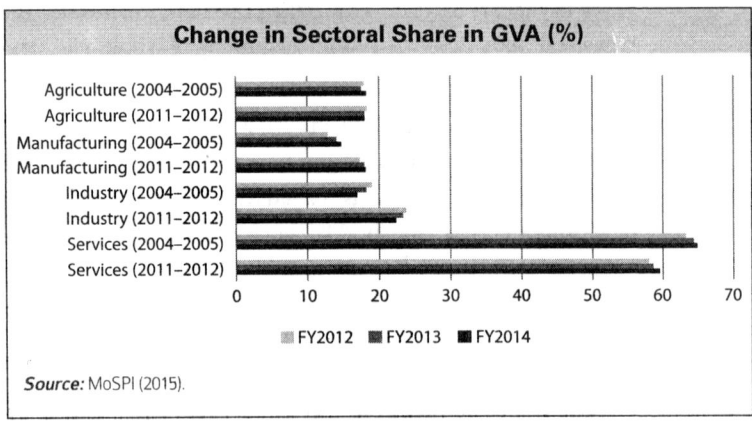

These changes happened due to two major changes in estimating the GDP numbers: (a) the use of MCA-21 data for the first time, which provide balance sheets of registered companies in mining, manufacturing and services, and (b) shifting of some of the sub-components of 'trade, hotels, transport and communication' from services to industry (Bhanumurthy, 2018b).

NSSO and Former CEA Expose GDP Numbers

Four years later in April 2019, the MCA-21 database was exposed for its flaws by the NSSO, a government body. Its report, 'Technical Report on Services Sector Enterprises in India 2016–17', stated that when the MCA-21 data for the services sector companies (not manufacturing ones) were verified, 45 per cent of the units turned out to be defective: 'About **45%** of MCA units were found to be out-of-survey/casualty…' (NSSO, 2019).

What it meant was that 45 per cent of the services sector units in the MCA-21 (a) don't exist, (b) don't operate or (c) are engaged in unrelated activities, thus providing a misleading picture. The NSSO also pointed out that such error in other databases used earlier in the economic census (EC) and business registers of states had an error margin of **18 per cent**, far lower than 45 per cent.

A couple of months later, in June 2019, another revelation was made.

The then CEA Arvind Subramanian, who had by now resigned from his post and joined the Harvard University, wrote a paper saying that the new GDP series overestimated growth 'from 2.5 percentage points per year (without electricity) to 3.7 percentage points per year (with electricity)' during the period of 2011–2012 and 2016–2017. According to his paper, the growth during this period should have been 4.5 per cent, rather than close to 7 per cent that the new GDP series claimed (Subramanian, 2019a).

He used 17 key indicators from 2001–2002 to 2017–2018, correlated with GDP growth and produced independently of the CSO—the government body tasked with preparing the GDP estimates. These indicators included electricity consumption, two-wheeler sales, commercial vehicle sales, tractor sales, airline passenger traffic, foreign tourist arrivals, railway freight traffic, index of industrial production (IIP), etc. Then, he compared India with 71 high- and middle-income countries by estimating a relationship between a set of indicators and GDP growth for the pre- and post-2011 periods.

He pointed out 'two major policy implications' of this overestimation in the GDP: (a) growth must be restored as a key policy issue as accurate growth estimate is 'critical for internal policymaking' and accomplish other objectives and (b) quality and integrity of data need to be improved to 'restore the reputational damage suffered to data generation in India across the board' from GDP to employment to government accounts.

About the methodology and data used for the 2011–2012 GDP series, he commented:

> A variety of evidence suggests that the *methodology changes* introduced for the post-2011 GDP estimates led to an *over-estimation of GDP growth*. Given the *nature of the data, and the impossibility for researchers to reproduce* the detailed methodology underlying the GDP estimates, the results in the paper are by no means the final word. (Subramanian, 2019a)

Predictably, Subramanian was challenged and was told that his analysis was based on indicators and associated assumptions. None questioned the use of defective MCA-21 data set, though two months later, in June 2019, it was merged into the National Statistics Office (NSO). In response, Subramanian made another explosive revelation.

He wrote, in his July 2019 paper 'Validating India's GDP Growth Estimates':

> Since the underlying (GDP) data *are not available publicly*, nobody outside the CSO can 'estimate GDP'. Outsiders can only check to see whether the GDP estimates are plausible, broadly satisfying some macro-consistency checks. That is what my GDP paper attempted to do: not to estimate but to cross-check and validate the CSO figures. (Subramanian, 2019b)

P. C. Mohanan, a career statistician and former acting chairman (Sep 2018–Jan 2019) of the National Statistical Commission (NSC)—the apex body for standard setting, quality control, regulation of statistical data collected by multiple ministries and departments, including the NSSO—revealed that never in the past did India use a data set like the MCA-21 which was not in the public domain, implying that no untested, secret data set had been used for GDP estimates until 2015 and that all data sets used have always been in the public domain (Mohanty, 2019c).

The Case of GDP Back Series (November 2018)

The credibility of GDP number was further eroded when the back series data, which should have been released in January 2015, was held back for more than three years. When it was released in November 2018, it had already lost credibility.

The release of back series data preceded an unsavoury episode.

Minutes before it, the NITI Aayog and the Ministry of Statistics and Programme Implementation (MoSPI) had deferred the back series estimates of an NSC subcommittee, headed by Professor N. R. Bhanumurthy of the National Institute of Public Finance and Policy (NIPFP). This subcommittee's report had been in July 2018. What the Aayog and MoSPI found unacceptable series were two double-digit growth rates in the UPA era—10.2 per cent in FY2008 and 10.8 per cent in FY2011. They said that they needed more information and clarifications to approve it (Bhanumurthy, 2018a; Waghmare, 2018).

The involvement of the Aayog is questionable as it neither has locus standi nor domain expertise in this area. The MoSPI is the administrative ministry for the CSO, which is responsible for preparing the GDP and its back series and, hence, it has the mandate to accept or reject the CSO's estimates. Why did then the NSC constituted a subcommittee to prepare the back series instead of the CSO doing it? The NSC is the apex body for standard setting and technical clearance for all statistics outside the administrative control of the MoSPI.

The mystery would be revealed a few days later on 7 December 2018.

On that day, an investigative report stated that the Aayog had dismissed the CSO's back series estimates three years ago in 2015. The reason was same: higher growth rates during the UPA years under the GDP series of 2011–2012. The CSO had finalized the back series from 2004–2005 to 2011–2012, as is the usual practice. Before it was to be released, a meeting took place in which the then Aayog's Vice Chairman Arvind Panagariya rejected it. The report quoted the then NSC Chairman Pronab Sen saying: 'Niti Aayog took just one look at the growth rates which were going higher after 2004–05 and said, "We can't allow it"'. There was a question on the robustness of relationships, for example, between MCA and RBI data (Iyer, 2018).

The NSC subcommittee's back series estimates need attention for raising the methodology and data sets used for the preparation of the 2011–2012 GDP series.

Its back series went back to 1993–1994, instead of the usual 1951–1952, highlighting the problems with new methodology and the use of MCA-21 data set which prevented this. First, it said that the MCA-21 data set was available from 2007–2008 but not comparable and 'unusable due to issues of taxonomy units or unit reporting problems'. This data set was stabilized only after 2011–2012. Second, because of this, it had to depend on private, non-official database of the CMIE for determining manufacturing and services output. Besides, it had to rely on the CMIE for determining construction output too. This had never been the case in the past (Bhanumurthy, 2018a).

The following extract (box) from its report would make it all clear.

Extract from NSC Subcommittee Report on Back Series Calculation

V.1 Back Series Compilation Based on Revised Methodology

V.1.1 The new series of National Accounts Statistics(NAS) with base year 2011–12 have been revised and released on 29th January, 2015. Whenever a new series of NAS is introduced with an updated base period, it is an accepted practicle to link the old series to the new series to provide a comparable set of national accounts statistics for users.

V.1.2 The appraoch followed in this method is the same as was followed for compilation of the new series to the extent similar data sets were available. Thus, estimates of GVA have been compiled separately for different institutional sectors. Public corporations and general government sector were backcasted by splicing. Private Corporate sector was back casted using CMIE data due to non availability of reliable MCA data sets. The unincorporated sector were backcasted by indicators used in the new series.

V.1.3 To elaborate, MCA21 data have been used to estimate the corporate segments of the economy in the new series. While the MCA data is available from 2006-07 under an e-govermance initative of thr GOI but not on comparable basis. For the past years although data was available but was unusable due to issue of taxonomy units or unit reporting problems. The data set stabilised only after 2010-11 onwards. Thus in order to backcast the series from 2004–05 till 2010–11, CMIEs PROWESS database was used.

V.1.4 In the case of manufacturing sector, for the private corportae sector, ASI growth rates of this sector have been used whichwere available for the period.

V.1.5 in the case of construction sector, for estimating the value of output of construction materials, value of outputs was estimated from dataset of CMIE for related companies.

The back series that was released in November 2018 (ahead of general elections of May 2019), had been prepared by the CSO. The Aayog held a press conference to release it. The back series had cut down two double-digit growth rates of FY2008 and FY2011 to single digits 7.7 per cent and 8.5 per cent, respectively. This was proudly displayed also as reproduced below (MoSPI, 2018).

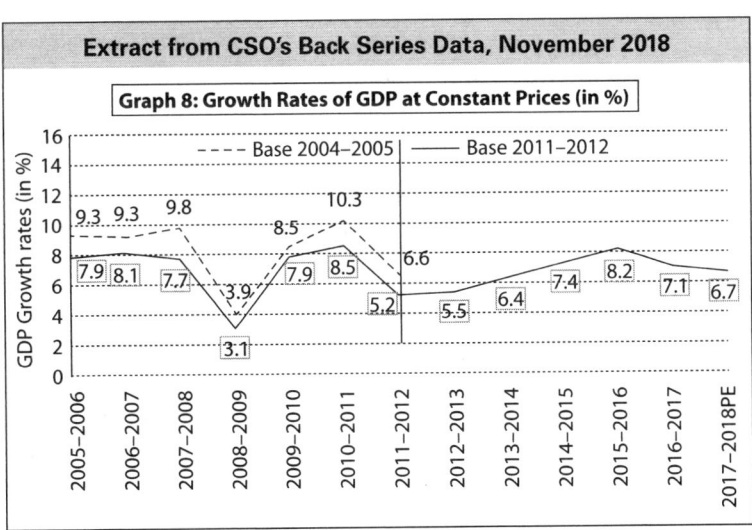

This back series went only up to 2004–2005, not 1950–1951, thus leaving a critical gap and reducing its ability to provide a long-term comparative

Masking the Reality

data to analyse growth rates in previous decades. For this very reason, it would have to be junked sooner than later.

There are other problems with the 2011–2012 GDP series.

Why Retrospective Revisions in GDP?

That the 2011–2012 GDP is a vanity project for the government is not in doubt. This idea has been reinforced because of multiple retrospective revisions, provoking former RBI Governor Y. V. Reddy to comment: 'In India not only the future is uncertain, even the past is uncertain. So, they keep revising the data' (IANS, 2017).

The revisions started soon after the back series data were released. In January 2019, the GDP growth for FY2017, the demonetization fiscal, was raised from 6.6 per cent to 8.2 per cent and then, in January 2021, it was further raised to *8.3 per cent*. Another round of revisions raised the growth for FY2019 from 5.9 per cent to 6.1 per cent and then 6.5 per cent (RE1, 2021) but reduced that for FY2020 from *5 per cent to 4.2 per cent and then 4 per cent* (RE1, 2021).

How such revisions help the government?

One, as the FY2017 growth of 8.3 per cent shows, it falsifies the adverse impact of demonetization that the country witnessed. Two, a lower growth rate of FY2020 heightens the base effect to take the FY2021 growth rate higher than the reality. In May 2021 (private equity [PE]), this is exactly what happened and one more revision took the FY2021's growth from −8 per cent to −7.3 per cent.

One important caveat is in order here.

GDP measures the monetary value of final goods and services produced (output) in an economy in a specific time (one FY) and which are bought by the final user. It is not a measure of many other things associated with economic growth, like, it is not a measure of well-being of the masses, their happiness, wealth and income equity or damage to environment (air, water and soil pollution and illness and death they cause imposing cost on the economy) that growth in output brings. There is a large body of literature on these aspects and the very economist who formulated GDP first (then called gross national product), Nobel laureate Simon Kuznets (1971), also said so and worked to address them. An alternate to GDP remains a work-in-progress. Hence, the GDP numbers discussed earlier should be taken in right perspective and other indicators of people's well-being and economic health shouldn't be ignored (Mohanty, 2020e, 2020f; Philipsen, 2015).

Data Suppression or Quality Check Issues?

Fiddling with vital economic statistics is routine. When a leaked report of the NSSO's PLFS of 2017–2018 appeared in February 2019, stating that India's unemployment rate had touched a 45-year-high at 6.1 per cent, it was immediately dismissed by raising data quality issues. After the government secured a second term in May 2019, this report was released. By that time, P. C. Mohanan, the then acting chairman of the NSC, and an independent member J. V. Meenakshi (one of the three members NSC is supposed to have), had resigned in protest against gross neglect of the NSC (Jha, 2019a; Mohanty, 2019a).

The Azim Premji University would later analyse the unit-level data of the PLFS 2017–2018 to say that *9 million jobs* had been lost 'for the first time in India's history', between 2011–2012 and 2017–2018 (Mehrotra & Parida, 2019).

In November 2019, another NSSO report, Household Consumer Expenditure Survey of 2017–2018, got leaked and hit the headlines saying that 'real' household consumption expenditure (MPCE) had fallen for the first time in 40 years from ₹1,501 in 2011–2012 to ₹1,446 in 2017–2018. This report was never released on 'data quality issue' and objections from an expert committee—the running theme for the government for all inconvenient data. Later, some parts of this report regarding health and education expenditures were released separately but not the full report (ANI, 2019; Jha, 2019a).

Later, it was revealed that the said expert committee had made no such recommendations. On the contrary, it corroborated the findings, along with those of the PLFS of 2017–2018, and found that the fall in consumption expenditure matched with the fall in rural wages between

2011–2012 and 2017–2018 that the PLFS report of 2017–2018 had thrown up (Jha, 2019c, 2020).

That poverty is creeping on would be later confirmed by none other than the Aayog. In December 2019, it released 'SDG India—Index & Dashboard 2019–20', which, unbeknown to it, carried damning data (NITI Aayog, 2019).

A comparison of poverty, hunger and income inequality scores of 28 states and UTs that it had mapped in 2019 with the baseline index it had prepared in 2018 showed that poverty went up in 22 states, hunger in 24 states and income inequality in 25 states/UTs (Mohanty, 2020a).

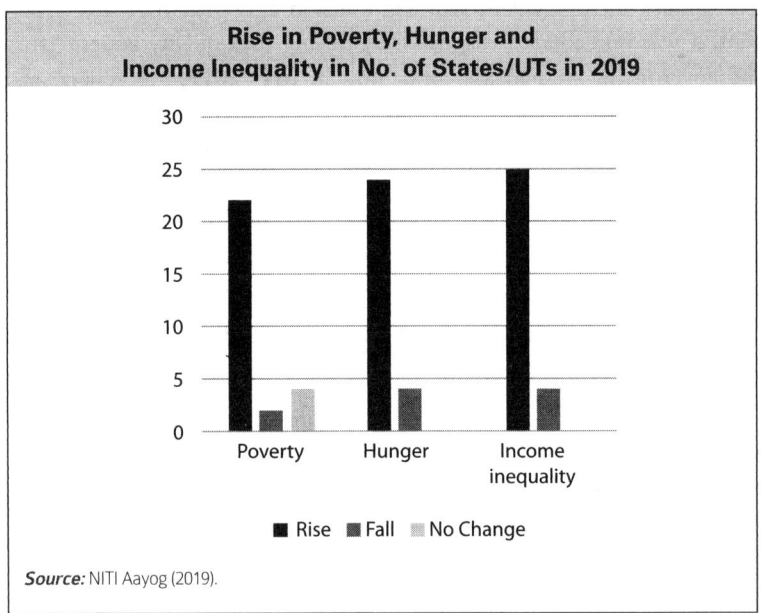

Source: NITI Aayog (2019).

India's brazen fiddling with data so provoked experts that *108 eminent economists and social scientists* from across the globe, including Nobel laureate Abhijit Banerjee, issued a public statement expressing their concerns over 'political interference' and asked the prime minister to restore 'institutional independence', 'integrity' and 'credibility' of the statistical organizations (*The Print*, 2019).

It provoked a bizarre response. While the government ignored the economists and sociologists, a group of 131 chartered accountants, who have little knowledge or expertise in this area, issued a public statement dismissing the economists and social scientists as 'politically motivated and baseless', and vouched for the integrity of India's statistical system and high growth (Mathew, 2019).

India's statistical system has had an enviable reputation globally. Even developed economies admired the modern Indian statistical system developed by legendary P. C. Mahalanobis, who founded the Indian Statistical Institute, shaped and served in the PCI and pioneered methodologies for large-scale surveys in the early decades of independent India. As late as 2005, two economists, Angus Deaton and Valerie Kozel, wrote 'most countries can only envy India's statistical capacity' (Deaton & Kozel, 2005).

That is no more the case.

When the Aayog released India's SDG Index for 2020 in June 2021 (NITI Aayog, 2021), it showed that the growing poverty, hunger and income inequality of 2019 had dramatically disappeared. Among the 28 states/UTs it mapped, poverty fell in 25, hunger in 23 and income inequality in 13. It didn't explain how this miracle happened, except lavishing praises on its and government's various initiatives. It didn't reckon, the year 2020 saw the pandemic crisis, an overnight lockdown that saw the economy collapse—the GDP growth fell to −7.3 per cent in FY2021 from 4 per cent in FY2020—with millions losing jobs and businesses. By 31 March 2021, the pandemic had caused *12.2 million infection cases and 162,927 deaths*—entailing far higher health expenditure and further impoverishment (Our World in Data, n.d.).

The US Pew Research Center estimated that *75 million* Indians would have slipped into poverty (60% of all in the world), 35 million of them into extreme poverty (below $2 dollar of living expense per day) due to the pandemic in 2020 (Kochhar, 2021).

In fact, the pandemic saw the suppression of critical epidemiological data that could have helped in containing the damages by understanding of the spread of the virus better, preparing and managing the healthcare, which collapsed.

A group of over *200 scientists and medical researchers* issued repeated statements and expressed their anguish at the government's refusal to release critical data relating to the patterns and severity of the infections for more than a year for their analysis. India wasn't doing enough analysis of its own in any case. They wrote to the prime minister cautioning that 'India's inability to adequately manage the spread of the infection had resulted largely from its epidemiological data being either not systematically collected or denied to the scientific community.' They also complained that India's AatmaNirbhar Bharat policy had made the import of scientific equipment and reagents 'extremely tedious and time-consuming' and that it had reduced their ability to sequence coronavirus genomes for surveillance (Mudur, 2021).

The situation remains unchanged.

The government asked scientists to remove infection-prevalence data of epidemic hotspots in 10 cities that the national serosurveys conducted by the Indian Council of Medical Research (ICMR) had thrown up. Such information would have helped understanding the evolution of the virus—early detection of far more infectious mutant 'delta' that caused havoc in India and abroad during the second wave—and why the virus spreads faster in some cities than others and why infection prevalence was much the same in districts generating few or zero cases and relatively with many cases. All these hampered analysis and meaningful interventions by scientists. Worse, India didn't release daily or total infection cases, presenting insignificant and even irrelevant data such as 'positivity', 'recovery' and 'active' cases, after deleting the previous day's data. Only such data were released that gave a false sense of well-being (Mudur, 2020; Narayanan, 2021).

The devastating second wave would see India scouring the world for oxygen, medicines and vaccines, resembling a Third-World country and a failed state. The gross under-reporting of cases and deaths would hit national and international media, and courts would reprimand leading to upward revisions in deaths in some cases. A Patna high court directive would see a 73 per cent rise in deaths in Bihar by recounting the deaths over a few weeks (Aiyar, 2021; Gamio & Glanz, 2021; Kumar, 2021).

Fiscal Mismanagement and Fiscal Responsibility and Budget Management at Risk

Data suppression and fudging has marred fiscal numbers also, making mockery of the Fiscal Responsibility and Budget Management (FRBM)

Act of 2003. This law seeks to keep budgetary profligacy in check by limiting fiscal deficit and debt-to-GDP ratio: 3.3 per cent and 60 per cent of the GDP, respectively. But this has been rendered useless through two methods: (a) exaggerating growth projections in revenue collections that lower revenue and fiscal deficits and (b) off-budget borrowings for budgetary spending that hides actual fiscal deficit.

For example, the FY2021 budget projected a 10 per cent GDP growth, translating into corresponding high growth in revenue, when the first advance estimates (AEs) had already projected the previous year's growth (FY2020) at 5 per cent, which eventually fell to 4 per cent. By doubling the projected growth for FY2021, the budget's fiscal calculations were bound to go away, which it did, though the pandemic crisis hit hard and FY2021 growth fell to –7.3 per cent. At the time, the pandemic had already struck China and the situation demanded circumspection. But then this had become a routine (Mohanty, 2020d, 2020g; MoSPI, 2020).

Similarly, off-budget borrowings happened earlier also but became far more pronounced to beat the FRBM compliance. Public sector entities were asked routinely to borrow 'huge' amounts from the market to run their affairs, which didn't get reflected in the budget and hence had no impact on the debt-to-GDP ratio. The Food Corporation of India (FCI) and National Bank for Agriculture and Rural Development, for example, kept borrowing from the market. The CAG has repeatedly flagged this and the lack of transparent disclosures of expenditures (Mohanty, 2020b).

The government has used 'strategic disinvestment' the tabs for which were picked up by PSUs such as Oil and Natural Gas Corporation (ONGC), Power Finance Corp (PFC), National Thermal Power Corporation (NTPC) and others, often involving heavy borrowing from the market which doesn't get reflected in the budget. The ONGC, once a cash-rich 'navaratna', is now dried out with its 'cash and bank balances' falling to ₹968.2 crore in FY2020, from ₹10,798.9 crore in FY2016—a fall of 91 per cent—and is also saddled with a huge 'net debt' of ₹11,704 crore in FY2020, according to its annual report of 2019–2020 (Mohanty, 2020c; ONGC, 2020).

The extent of hidden, off-budget borrowing became evident in the budget for FY2022 when it showed an expenditure of ₹1.3 lakh crore on fertilizer subsidy against the budgeted ₹71,309 crore (1.9 times more) and ₹4.2 lakh crore on food subsidy, against the budgeted ₹1.2 lakh crore (3.5 times more; Mohanty, 2021b).

Data Vacuum

The Parliament session of September 2020 will go down in history for the government admitting that it had no data on critical matters. In response to a series of questions, it said that it had no data on the following: (a) job loss of migrant workers due to the lockdown, (b) death of health workers and sanitation workers fighting the pandemic, though India honoured them by petal showers from the sky (helicopters flew all around the country for that) and by banging utensils, blowing conch shells and lighting candles in balconies, (c) death of migrant workers who walked home during the lockdown, (d) death of policemen on pandemic duty, (e) number of informal workers, who were hit the hardest due to the lockdown, (f) number of suicides by students during the lockdown, etc. (Mohanty, 2020h; Yahoo, 2020).

The budget for FY2022 was a classic example as it was framed without such critical information and more: how many slipped into poverty and how many suffered healthcare and education deprivations even in the face of growing evidence (Mohanty, 2021a).

The other aspect is ignoring inconvenient data.

Overlooking Crucial Data

Not just the Aayog's report on poverty, hunger and income inequality, the Global Hunger Index 2020 ranked India at 94 (of 107 it mapped), far below neighbouring Sri Lanka, Bangladesh and Pakistan, indicating worsening condition of Indians. It gave a timely warning too: 'In India, like in many other countries, the pandemic is aggravating an already serious hunger situation' (GHI, 2020).

In December 2020, the government's own National Health Survey (NHS-5) of 2019–2020 showed an alarming situation of nutrition. The nutritional level among children worsened since the last survey (NHS-4) of 2015–2016. An analysis of its data stated that 18 of the 22 states and UTs saw a rise in child stunting, wastage and underweight (children under the age of 5) during the period. It also marked a reversal of the earlier trend of improvement in child nutrition. Some of the states (Kerala, Gujarat, Maharashtra, Goa and Himachal Pradesh) which had lowered their rates of stunting in the previous decade reported a rise; 16 states and UTs (of the 22 surveyed) recorded a rise in children severely wasted and underweight in comparison to the previous round (Roy, 2020).

Meanwhile, the National Crime Records Bureau stopped releasing suicide data for 2017 and 2018 to deny information on farmer suicides—which was among the multiple issues raised by farmers' agitations seeking a higher MSP—razing all over the country. When those reports were finally released in 2019, the reports showed a decline in farmer suicides (now divided into categories of cultivator and farm labour), but the annual rate was still higher than 10,000.

Something else came to notice. Suicides by unemployed, self-employed and daily wagers were rising sharply because of economic distress and economy slowdown, which surpassed suicides among farmers. The number of suicides by daily wagers crossed 30,000 in 2019 and that of unemployed and self-employed was approximately 15,000.

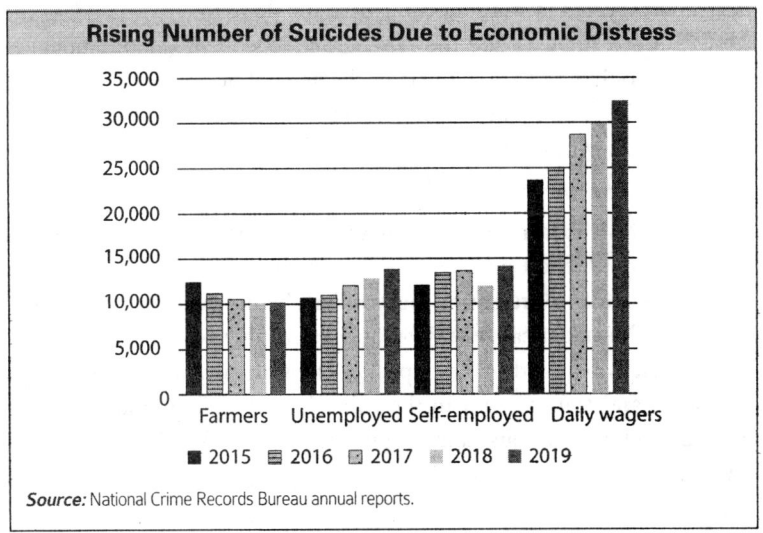

The budgets for FY2021 and FY2022 didn't take note of it. The cumulative impact of data suppression, non-collection or not taking cognizance of critical data is that there is little hope of these being addressed, progressively worsening the real financial health of people and the economy.

Endangered Glory of India's Statistical System

India's statistical system has also come under severe strain after 2014. In the midst of the 2019 general elections, the government restructured the entire statistical system quietly (MoSPI, 2019a).

With this order, NSO and its constituents—NSSO and CSO—became 'integral parts of the main ministry'; NSSO and CSO merged into NSO and secretary to the ministry (MoSPI) became the new head of NSO and, as such, also the Chief Statistician of India (CSI). This restructuring turned MoSPI secretary into Chief Statistical Officer—a reversal of existing arrangement—making a bureaucrat as CSI.

A little explanation is needed to understand how this compromises the statistical system.

The CSI is the functional head of the statistical system and the NSC is the apex body for standard setting, quality control, regulation of statistical data collected by multiple ministries and departments, including the MoSPI. Both the CSI and the NSC are independent (autonomous) in their functioning and are not part of the general bureaucracy. They were brought in 2006 to ensure autonomy and transparency to the statistical system in line with the recommendation of the Rangarajan Commission report of 2001 (Rangarajan, 2001).

What the restructuring meant was that the NSSO ceased to exist as an autonomous body and became a part of the general bureaucracy. In the absence of oversight by independent bodies such as the CSI and the NSC, the statistical system became vulnerable to political interference. What is required is the opposite. The statistical system needs full autonomy and transparency in the collection, compilation and dissemination of statistical data, and it must also be insulated from political interference (Mohanty, 2019b).

The NSSO has played a significant role in collecting a variety of socio-economic data through National Sample Surveys (NSS), starting with 1950. It was known as National Statistical Survey Organisation then, renamed as NSSO in 1974 after reorganizing NSS activities (under one office rather than two earlier), and it played a very critical role in policymaking. Its merger has caused apprehensions about the credibility of such exercises now.

When this restructuring happened, it was disclosed that the NSC (set up in 2005) would become a statutory body to give it more teeth. That would have been a move in the right direction. But in 2019, a draft National Statistical Commission Bill proposed it 'to be a body corporate' for which 'the decision of the Central Government, whether a question is of policy or not shall be final'. It proposed to include the CEA and RBI's deputy governor as ex officio members. All these sparked fears of it being a government's handmaiden and toothless. Pronab Sen, the first NSC chairman, reacted to it by saying:

> It is worse than the current model because at least in the current model, the NSC Chairman is a Minister-of-State, and in the government, these things matter. When you have a body outside the government, he would essentially be treated as a PSU chairman and that would make a difference to how bureaucrats treat him. (Bhattacharya, 2020; MoSPI, 2019b)

While the draft remained a draft, the NSC was reconstituted in its old form (Suneja, 2019).

Takeaways

⇨ The 2011–2012 GDP series is neither credible nor capable of reflecting ground realities.

⇨ Critical socio-economic data must not be suppressed, overlooked or remain uncollected. These are essential for evidence-based decision-making and strategic investments for future. Data are considered public good and, hence, the sooner India corrects itself, the quicker will it benefit its people and economy.

⇨ Prudence demands that statistical system shouldn't be turned into a vanity project for the government of the day.

References

Aiyar, Y. (2021, 9 May). The second wave and the Indian state. *Hindustan Times*. https://www.hindustantimes.com/opinion/the-second-wave-and-the-indian-state-101620579557130.html

ANI. (2019, 15 November). Consumer expenditure survey not to be released due to 'data quality issues', Congress targets government. *Business Standard*. https://www.business-standard.com/article/news-ani/consumer-expenditure-survey-not-to-be-released-due-to-data-quality-issues-congress-targets-government-119111501821_1.html

Bhanumurthy, N. R. (2018a, 15 July). Report of the Committee on Real Sector Statistics. MoSPI. http://mospi.nic.in/sites/default/files/committee_reports/Report_of_the_committee_on_real_sector_statistics_2182018.pdf

Bhanumurthy, N. R. (2018b, 31 August). Misreading the GDP report. *The Indian Express*. https://indianexpress.com/article/opinion/columns/indian-economy-gdp-in-upa-nda-government-narendra-modi-bjp-congress-5333346/

Bhattacharya, P. (2020, 4 February). The battle to save India's statistical system. *Mint*. https://www.livemint.com/news/india/the-battle-to-save-indias-statistical-system-11580746495555.html

Deaton, A., & Kozel, V. (2005). Data and dogma: The great Indian poverty debate. https://www.princeton.edu/~deaton/downloads/deaton_kozel_great_indian_poverty_debate_wbro_2005.pdf

Gamio, L., & Glanz, J. (2021, 25 May). Just how big could India's true covid toll be? *The New York Times.* https://www.nytimes.com/interactive/2021/05/25/world/asia/india-covid-death-estimates.html?referringSource=articleShare

GHI. (2020, October). Global hunger index. https://www.globalhungerindex.org/pdf/en/2020.pdf

IANS. (2017, 28 June). Difference of opinion between RBI, govt is not bad: Y. V. Reddy. *Business Standard.* https://www.business-standard.com/article/news-ians/difference-of-opinion-between-rbi-govt-is-not-bad-y-v-reddy-117062800341_1.html

International Monetary Fund. (2016, January). *World Economic Outlook.* https://www.imf.org/external/pubs/ft/weo/2016/update/01/#:~:text=The%20Updated%20Forecast,and%203.6%20percent%20in%202017.&text=Growth%20in%20advanced%20economies%20is,and%20hold%20steady%20in%202017

Iyer, P. V. (2018, 7 December). Three years ago, key statistics panel revised UPA growth up, Niti Aayog rejected it. *The Indian Express.* https://indianexpress.com/article/india/key-statistics-panel-revised-upa-growth-up-niti-aayog-rejected-it-5482457/

Jha, S. (2019a, 6 February). Unemployment rate at four-decade high of 6.1% in 2017–18: NSSO survey. *Business Standard.* https://www.business-standard.com/article/economy-policy/unemployment-rate-at-five-decade-high-of-6-1-in-2017-18-nsso-survey-119013100053_1.html

Jha, S. (2019b, 15 November). Consumer spend sees first fall in 4 decades on weak rural demand: NSO data. *Business Standard.* https://www.business-standard.com/article/economy-policy/consumer-spend-sees-first-fall-in-4-decades-on-weak-rural-demand-nso-data-119111401975_1.html#:~:text=The%20survey%20%E2%80%94%20Key%20Indicators%3A%20Household,Rs%201%2C501%20in%202011%2D12.&text=In%20cities%2C%20it%20rose%20by,report%20reviewed%20by%20Business%20Standard

Jha, (2019c, 21 November). 'Consumer spend survey: Panel didn't flag quality issues, ask for scrapping. *Business Standard.* https://www.business-standard.com/article/economy-policy/consumer-spend-survey-panel-didn-t-flag-quality-issues-ask-for-scrapping-119112001535_1.html

Jha, S. (2020, 18 February). NSO's consumer spend report showing first fall in 40 yrs won't be released. *Business Standard.* https://www.business-standard.com/article/economy-policy/national-statistical-commission-won-t-release-nso-s-consumer-spend-report-120021800045_1.html

Kochhar, R. (2021, 18 March). In the pandemic, India's middle class shrinks and poverty spreads while China sees smaller changes. Pew Research Center.

https://www.pewresearch.org/fact-tank/2021/03/18/in-the-pandemic-indias-middle-class-shrinks-and-poverty-spreads-while-china-sees-smaller-changes/

Kumar, R. (2021, 10 June). Bihar Covid death toll increases by 73% after HC-ordered review. *Hindustan Times.* https://www.hindustantimes.com/india-news/bihar-covid-death-toll-increases-by-73-after-hc-ordered-review-101623264310365.html

Mathew, J. C. (2019, 19 March). 131 CAs vouch for India's growth statistics, term call by 108 economists to save statistical system politically motivated. *Business Today.* https://www.businesstoday.in/top-story/131-cas-vouch-for-india-growth-statistics-terms-call-by-108-economists-to-save-statistical-system-politically-motivated/story/328979.html

Mehrotra, S., & Parida, J. K. (2019, October). *India's employment crisis: Rising education levels and falling non-agricultural job growth* (CSE Working Paper No. 2019-04). Azim Premji University. https://cse.azimpremjiuniversity.edu.in/wp-content/uploads/2019/10/Mehrotra_Parida_India_Employment_Crisis.pdf

Mohanty, P. (2019a, 28 March). Data fudging: Dressing up GDP and budget numbers does no good to economy. *Business Today.* https://www.businesstoday.in/current/economy-politics/data-fudging-dressing-up-gdp-and-budget-numbers-does-no-good-to-economy/story/331960.html

Mohanty, P. (2019b, 2 June). Agenda for new government: Independence of statistical organisations. *India Today.* https://www.indiatoday.in/india/story/agenda-for-next-government-restoring-credibility-of-data-1540524-2019-06-02

Mohanty, P. (2019c, 23 November). GDP base year row: What's the problem with re-basing India's growth calculations. *Business Today.* https://www.businesstoday.in/current/economy-politics/gdp-base-year-row-whats-the-problem-with-rebasing-indias-growth-calculations-indian-economy-gross-domestic-product/story/390180.html

Mohanty, P. (2020a, 8 January). Budget 2020: Niti Aayog shocker; poverty, hunger and income inequality up in 22 to 25 states and UTs. *Business Today.* https://www.businesstoday.in/union-budget-2020/news/budget-2020-niti-aayog-shocker-poverty-hunger-income-inequality-up-in-22-to-25-states-uts-poor-indians/story/393404.html

Mohanty, P. (2020b, 24 January). Budget 2020: Off-budget financing—A riddle wrapped in enigma. *Business Today.* https://www.businesstoday.in/union-budget-2020/news/budget-2020-off-budget-financing-central-government-extent-not-known-cag-modi-govt/story/394588.html

Mohanty, P. (2020c, 25 January). Budget 2020: Strategic disinvestment, a questionable source of off-budget financing. *Business Today.* https://

www.businesstoday.in/union-budget-2020/news/budget-2020-strategic-disinvestment-as-source-of-off-budget-financing/story/394626.html

Mohanty, P. (2020d, 15 March). Rebooting economy XXVII: Fiscal mismanagement threatens India's economic recovery. *Business Today.* https://www.businesstoday.in/opinion/columns/indian-economy-fiscal-management-threatens-indias-economic-recovery-covid19-crisis/story/416024.html

Mohanty, P. (2020e, 2 June). Unravelling GDP growth I: More growth is producing more inequality and misery. *Business Today.* https://www.businesstoday.in/current/economy-politics/gdp-growth-indian-economy-economic-growth-income-inequality-poor-wealthy-coronavirus-lockdown-covid-19/story/408375.html

Mohanty, P. (2020f, 30 June). Unravelling GDP growth II: Why GDP measures output, not people's well-being. *Business Today.* https://www.businesstoday.in/current/economy-politics/unravelling-gdp-growth-indian-economy-measures-output-not-peoples-well-being-economic-growth/story/408517.html

Mohanty, P. (2020g, 3 September). Rebooting economy XXIV: 7 critical GST flaws govt needs to address at the earliest. *Business Today.* https://www.businesstoday.in/opinion/columns/gst-structural-and-operational-flaws-govt-needs-to-address-at-the-earliest-indian-economy/story/415001.html

Mohanty, P. (2020h, 17 November). Rebooting economy 46: Who is designing India's growth path? *Business Today.* https://www.businesstoday.in/opinion/columns/indian-economy-who-is-designing-indias-growth-path-atma-nirbhar-bharat-demonetisation-economic-lockdown/story/422135.html

Mohanty, P. (2021a, 30 January). Rebooting Economy 63: Budgeting FY22 with critical information gaps. *Business Today.* https://www.businesstoday.in/union-budget-2021/columns/indian-economy-budgeting-fy22-with-critical-information-gaps/story/429601.html

Mohanty, P. (2021b, 6 February). Rebooting economy 64: Budget numbers don't add up to 10% or more growth in FY22. *Business Today.* https://www.businesstoday.in/union-budget-2021/columns/indian-economy-budget-numbers-dont-add-up-to-10-or-more-growth-in-fy22/story/430462.html

MoSPI. (2015, 30 January). New series estimates of national income, consumption expenditure, saving and capital formation (base year 2011–12). http://mospi.nic.in/sites/default/files/press_release/nad_press_release_30jan15.pdf

MoSPI. (2018, 28 November). National accounts statistics: Back-series 2004-05 TO 2011-12. PIB. https://pib.gov.in/newsite/PrintRelease.aspx?relid=186002

MoSPI. (2019a, 23 May). Order of restructuring MoSPI. http://mospi.nic.in/sites/default/files/iss-orders/Order_Restructuring%20of%20MoSPI%2023052019.pdf?download=1

MoSPI. (2019b, 19 December). Draft National Statistical Commission Bill 2019. http://mospi.nic.in/sites/default/files/nscbill/nscbilld.pdf

MoSPI. (2020, 7 January). Press note on first advance estimates of national income, 2019-20. http://mospi.nic.in/sites/default/files/press_release/Presss%20note%20for%20FAE%202019-20.pdf

Mudur, G. S. (2020, 20 September). How Covid numbers were hushed up. *The Telegraph.* https://www.telegraphindia.com/india/how-covid-numbers-were-hushed-up/cid/1792482

Mudur, G. S. (2021, 30 April). Covid: India's research community asks Modi for data on patterns and severity of infections. *The Telegraph.* https://www.telegraphindia.com/amp/india/covid-india-research-community-asks-modi-to-release-data-on-patterns-and-severity-of-infections/cid/1814074?__twitter_impression=true

Narayanan, N. (2021, 1 February). False remedies: The Modi government's woeful record of suppressing information on COVID-19. *Caravan.* https://caravanmagazine.in/health/modi-government-suppressing-information-covid-19

NITI Aayog. (2019, 30 December). SDG 2019: SDG India—Index & dashboard 2019-20. https://niti.gov.in/sdg-india-index-dashboard-2019-20

NITI Aayog. (2021, June). SDG 2020: SDG India—Index & dashboard 2020-21. https://niti.gov.in/writereaddata/files/SDG_3.0_Final_04.03.2021_Web_Spreads.pdf

NSSO. (2019). Technical report on services sector enterprises in India 2016–17. http://mospi.nic.in/sites/default/files/publication_reports/Final%20TR%2074th%20Round_compressed.pdf

ONGC. (2020). Annual report, 2019–20: Making a strategic move. https://www.ongcindia.com/wps/wcm/connect/31cce834-fb8f-49c1-a2c4-38df2f712f7c/ONGC_AR_2019-20.pdf?MOD=AJPERES&CONVERT_TO=url&CACHEID=ROOTWORKSPACE-31cce834-fb8f-49c1-a2c4-38df2f712f7c-noD1QT5

Our World in Data. (n.d.). Coronavirus pandemic (COVID-19)—The data. https://ourworldindata.org/coronavirus-data?country=~IND

Philipsen, D. (2015). *The little big number: How GDP came to rule the world and what to do about it.* Princeton University Press. https://academic.oup.com/ahr/article-abstract/121/2/536/2581903?redirectedFrom=PDF

Rangarajan, C. (2001). Background of the National Statistical Commission (NSC). MoSPI. http://mospi.nic.in/background-national-statistical-commission-nsc#:~:text=A%20Commission%20set%20up%20by,Official%20Statistics%20in%20the%20country

Roy, T. (2020, 14 December). Child nutrition levels in India worsened over last five years, finds NHFS survey. *The Wire.* https://science.thewire.in/health/child-nutrition-levels-in-india-worsened-over-last-five-years-finds-nhfs-survey/#:~:text=According%20to%20a%20World%20Bank,14%25%2C%20the%20report%20said

Subramanian, A. (2019a, 29 June). *India's GDP mis-estimation: Likelihood, magnitudes, mechanisms, and implications* (Working Paper No. 354). Harvard University. https://www.hks.harvard.edu/centers/cid/publications/faculty-working-papers/india-gdp-overestimate

Subramanian, A. (2019b, July). Validating India's GDP growth estimates (CID Faculty Working Paper No. 357). Harvard University. https://growthlab.cid.harvard.edu/files/growthlab/files/2019-07-cid-wp-357-india-gdp.pdf

Suneja, K. (2019, 27 May). National Statistical Commission to get more teeth in 100 days. *The Economic Times.* https://economictimes.indiatimes.com/news/economy/policy/national-statistical-commission-to-get-more-teeth-in-100-days/articleshow/69527914.cms?from=mdr

The Print. (2019, 14 March). Economic statistics in a shambles; need to raise a voice: An appeal from 108 economists & social scientists across the world. https://cdn-live.theprint.in/wp-content/uploads/2019/03/1552578453615_Press-Release-14-3-2019-Economic-Statistics-in-Shambles.pdf

Waghmare, A. (2018, 13 November). Govt heeds economists' advice, defers releasing GDP back series data. *Business Standard.* https://www.business-standard.com/article/economy-policy/govt-heeds-economists-advice-defers-releasing-gdp-back-series-data-118111201753_1.html

Yahoo. (2020, 23 September). Lynchings, migrant deaths, student suicides: 20 things Union govt doesn't have data on. https://in.news.yahoo.com/lynchings-migrant-deaths-student-suicides-131246018.html?guccounter=1&guce_referrer=aHR0cHM6Ly93d3cuZmFjZWJvb2suY29tLw&guce_referrer_sig=AQAAAHWIETGvP4B2WibCk0d1SRX4V5I5GGIweTFIZi0QT_Pe_4t3i9gblOCE0wjKbGpvS3jJ5d5qcDhnNSQhvmIIQyOuIIr18kxXhVGJRon5SfvWPVrtpa2WODip-Oh8cfrlX22GS-w6alvxxzNhXtMgewuc-v0zbkZ-VS-WpHZl3zzF

III DEMONETIZATION

First Direct Shock to Economy and People

The demonetization marked Prime Minister Narendra Modi's nightly 'aakashvani' style of decision-making.

At 8 PM on 8 November 2016, he appeared on television to tell the people that from midnight (four hours away), he was banning all high currency notes of ₹500 and ₹1,000. It was the first 'shock and awe' operation, which sucked out 86.9 per cent of the cash or ₹15.4 lakh crore of ₹17.9 lakh crore of currency in circulation (CIC), at one stroke, paralyzing all economic activities. India being a cash-dependent economy, a large part of which is informal (contributing 50% to the GDP), there was simply no money to be paid for work, particularly to a huge population of casual and daily wagers (RBI, 2017).

India queued up outside banks almost daily for months as cash was rationed, starting with ₹2,000 a day. While the limit was slowly raised, there was another problem. None of the new currencies fitted the 2.2 lakh ATMs, leading to recalibration and further delays. More than 100 people died in these queues in the first month (PTI, 2016a; Worstall, 2016).

Nobel laureate Amartya Sen called it 'despotic' and 'disaster':

> It (demonetization) undermines notes; it undermines bank accounts; it undermines the entire economy of trust. That is the sense in which it is despotic.... In the last 20 years, the country has been growing very fast. But it is all based on acceptance of each other's word. By taking despotic action and saying we had promised but won't fulfill our promise, you hit at the root of this.
> (PTI, 2016b)

Arun Shourie, former minister in the Atal Bihari Vajpayee government and senior journalist, said: 'This is a government by "ilhaam" (revelation). The Prime Minister has the "ilhaam" one night that demonetization should be done and he does it. In any case it was a bold step. I have to remind you suicide too is a bold step.' He dismissed demonetization as 'the largest *money laundering* scheme', a charge which many others repeated (*The Wire*, 2017).

That it had gone horribly wrong was obvious right from the next morning, but the prime minister appealed people to give him 50 days to prove that his objectives and intentions were right (to eliminate black money, terror funding and fake currencies), failing which he would be ready to face punishment at any 'chowk' that people may fix (Gatty & Johnson, 2016).

The prime minister termed demonetization as a 'mahayagna of honesty' to kill black money resulting from 70 years of corruption, and that it was hurting those more who had ill-gotten money than ordinary honest citizens. He equated the situation as similar to a family's tolerance of the lingering odour of wall paint while decorating the house for a marriage and that, though there is some discomfort in everything, the 'intention behind it must be well-meaning'. Yet fun was made of Indians' sufferings in Japan, relishing how people had planned marriages but there was simply no cash in hand. However, newspapers were awash with news of lavish marriages in the family of Central Minister Nitin Gadkari and Bellary's mining baron Reddys (who have been in and out of the BJP) in November and December 2016 involving more than 50,000 guests and a large number of chartered flights were used—negating Modi's claims of inconveniencing the rich in any way (*Financial Express*, 2016; IANS, 2016; *The Hindu*, 2016; Yadav, 2016).

Imaginary Benefits

The government remained quiet for the next four years and then made tall claims about its successes. On 8 November 2020, Modi and his Finance Minister Nirmala Sitharaman made several bizarre claims through a series of tweets. Had they checked official statistics, they wouldn't have, but fact or truth never comes in the way of propaganda.

They made four basic claims: (a) 'tax/GDP ratio drastically improved', (b) 'made India a lesser cash-based economy', (c) 'helped reduce black money, increase tax compliance', gave a 'boost to transparency' and concluded that the demonetization (d) has been 'greatly beneficial towards national progress' (Mohanty, 2020d; PIB, 2020).

Official statistics said the opposite.

Tax-to-GDP Plunge, India Turned More Cash-based

The latest data show that gross tax (central) as a percentage of GDP took a big hit post-demonetization and GST (FY2017, FY2018).

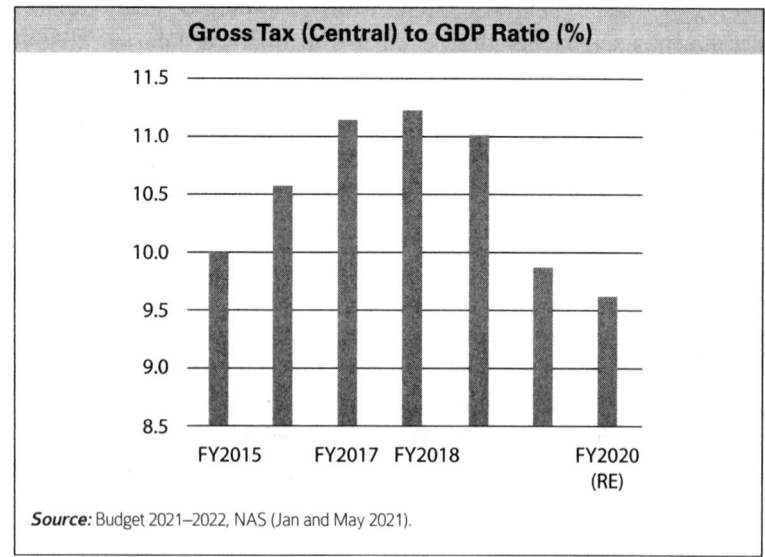

Source: Budget 2021–2022, NAS (Jan and May 2021).

It never touched the UPA-era high of FY2008 (12.1%). In June 2020, this had officially been announced by the Central Board of Direct Taxes five months before that Modi and Sitharaman misled India (Seth, 2020).

The second big claim was that India turned less-cash economy. Nothing could be farther from the truth. The RBI's weekly CIC data from 4 November 2016—four days before the demonetization—to 6 November 2020 (two days before the prime minister's claim) showed that CIC had sharply risen. On 4 November 2016, the CIC was ₹17.98 lakh crore, which climbed up to ₹27.3 lakh crore on 6 November 2020—a rise by 51.7 per cent. In FY2021, currency-to-GDP ratio jumped to a high of 14.7 per cent of GDP (12% in FY2020), growing at 17.2 per cent (14% in FY2020; RBI, 2021).

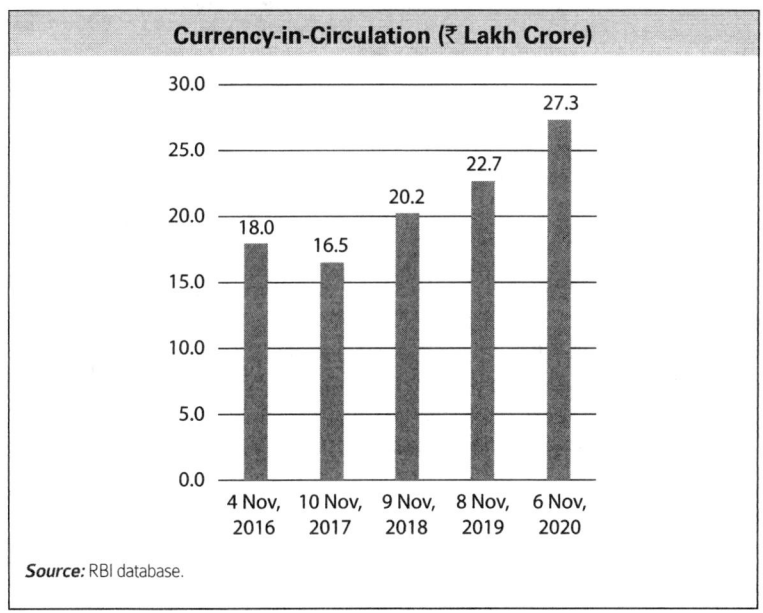

Source: RBI database.

The goal of making India a cashless economy was put forward as an afterthought, after the government realized that its three stated objectives—eliminate black money, terror funding and fake counterfeit currencies—were flawed. The most obvious beneficiary of it was a new payment bank that used the prime minister's face on its front-page ads and turned unicorn in double quick time.

Going by the government's own logic, more CIC meant more black money in the economy, not less. RBI's occasional paper of 2020, 'Modelling and Forecasting Currency Demand in India: A Heterodox Approach' stated that post-demonetization years (FY2018, FY2019 and FY2020) witnessed 'extraordinary jump' in CIC that it had seen only thrice in the previous 50 years. According to a table in the paper, reproduced below, previous cash surges occurred when nominal GDP growth was high at 14.7–16.6 per cent. But the post-demonetization surge (FY2018–FY2020) occurred when nominal GDP was far lower at 9.8 per cent (RBI, 2020).

Extract from RBI's Occasional Paper, July 2020

High Phases of CIC Growth during 1997–2020

Phase	CIC Growth		Average Nominal GDP Growth	Inflation	Interest Rate (%)
	Average	Range		(CPI-IW)	Deposit Rates
1987–1988 to 1989–1990	17.3	14.2–20.4	15.7	8.2	9.5
1993–1994 to 1995–1996	19.8	17.1–22.6	16.6	9.2	11.0
2005–2006 to 2008–2009	17.0	16.5–17.4	14.7	6.6	7.7
2017–2018 to 2019–2020	22.7	14.2.37.0	9.3	5.3	6.7

Source: DBIE, RBI; author's calculations.

The government's claim that the demonetization pushed digital payments was also misleading. Digital payment was going up steadily until the demonetization but fell afterwards. The following graph uses RBI data from its annual reports (from FY2010 to FY2021) and includes all digital modes of payments systems/methods: real-time gross settlement, credit transfers, debit transfers, card payments and prepaid payment instruments.

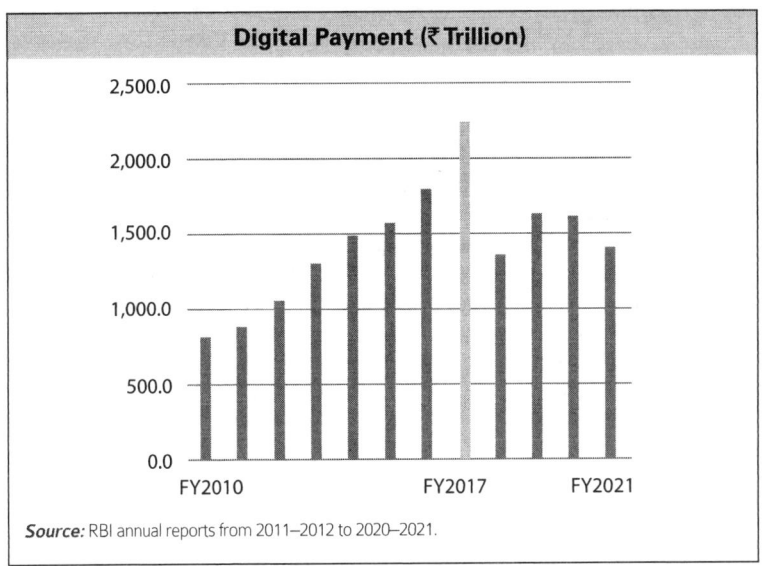

Source: RBI annual reports from 2011–2012 to 2020–2021.

Tax Compliance

It was also claimed in the 8 November 2020 statement that tax compliance had improved since (a) 'self-assessment tax of more than ₹13,000 crore was paid by targeted non-filers', (b) 3.04 lakh persons who deposited cash of ₹10 lakh or more but had not filed IT return were 'identified' and (c) 2.9 lakh such identified non-filers responded and paid self-assessment tax of ₹6,531 crore.

None of this requires demonetization. These are routine exercises of the Income Tax Department (ITD). The ITD is identifying millions of non-filers and 'dropped filers' (who stop filing returns) through the non-filers monitoring system (NMS) for more than a decade. The NMS tracks annual information returns, Centralised Information Branch data and tax deducted at source/tax collected at source statements for this. The third Tax Administration Reforms Commission (TARC) of 2014 said that the NMS identified *2.2 million* non-filers with potential tax liabilities in 2014—up from *0.2 million* in 2013—reproduced below (Mohanty, 2020a; TARC, 2014).

The real issue here is what happens after such identification. The fall in the tax-to-GDP ratio shows that the follow-up action is poor.

> **Extract from Third TARC Report of 2014**
>
> **Non-filers monitoring system**
>
> The non-filers monitoring system was conceptualised to prioritise action on non-filers with potential tax liabilities. Data analysis was carried out in January 2013 to identify non-filers about whom information was available in AIR, CIB data and TDS/TCS return. Algorithms were applied in January 2014 and 22.09 lakh non-filers with potential tax liabilities were identified. Instructions has been issued to the field authorities to take appropriate action against non-filers for Assessment Years (AY) 2008–09 to 2010–11 (in cases where a TDS deductor had made payments of ₹5 lakh and above after deducting tax at source, but recipients of income or deductees did not file their income tax returns). Data analysis identified 34.28 lakh non-filers with potential tax liabilities (2.19 lakh case in 2013 and 22.09 lakh case in 2014).[216]

The efficiency of self-assessment tax is also questionable. Former Finance Minister Arun Jaitley had said as much. In his 2018 budget speech, talking about the presumptive income scheme that allows taxpayers to choose a predetermined tax slab and pay tax accordingly without maintaining tax records, he said: 'Under this scheme, 41% more returns were filed during this year which shows that many more persons are joining the tax net under simplified scheme. However, the *turnover shown is still not encouraging*' (Mohanty, 2020c).

This is because entrepreneurs and traders take advantage of the scheme to switch to lower tax slabs.

Further, on 19 September 2020, Minister of State for Finance Anurag Thakur confirmed in writing to the Lok Sabha, in reply to a question, that only *about 1 per cent of Indians actually pay tax*. He said: 'Yes, approximately, for Financial Year 2018–19 till Feb 2020, 5.78 Crore Returns of Income were filed by individual taxpayers out of which *1.46 Crore individual taxpayers filed Returns declaring income above ₹5 Lakh.*' As per the Finance Act of 2019, taxpayers with annual incomes of up to ₹5 lakh are not required to pay income tax from assessment year (AY) 2020–2021 (Lok Sabha Secretariat, 2020).

No such data are available in public domain to throw more light on it. Tax data are not only not updated on a timely basis, but they also reveal more trivial than critical information to be of any use (Income Tax Department, n.d.).

The Indian government may take pride in demonetization, but the world actually warned against it. Gita Gopinath, IMF's chief economist, issued a global warning in 2018, saying that no macroeconomist would recommend demonetization to any developing or advanced country. Later, in 2018, she later published a paper (co-authored with economists from the Harvard University and the RBI, among others) showing that India's GDP shrunk by 2 percentage points in that quarter (Q4 of FY2017) due to cash shortage (Chodorow-Reich et al., 2018; Venkatesh, 2018).

Former CEA Arvind Subramanian wrote in November 2018:

> Demonetisation was a massive, draconian, monetary shock: in one fell swoop 86% of the currency in circulation was withdrawn. Real GDP growth was clearly affected by demonetisation. Growth had been slowing even before, but after demonetisation the slide accelerated. In the six quarters before demonetisation growth *averaged 8% and in the seven quarters after, it averaged about 6.8%* (with a four-quarter window, the relevant numbers are 8.1% before and 6.2% after). (Subramanian, 2018)

The demonetization was actually a misnomer. High-value currencies are demonetized primarily for two purposes: to be replaced with currencies of higher value if high inflation reduces their real value, or to eliminate the high presence of counterfeit currencies. Neither was the case for India then. Besides, ₹500 and ₹1,000 notes were replaced with ₹2,000 notes.

There is an interesting episode associated with it. Nobel laureate (2017) economist Richard Thaler tweeted, supporting the demonetization immediately, at 8.41 PM on 8 November 2016 (Modi's announcement came at 8 PM): 'his is a policy I have long supported. First step toward cashless and good start on reducing corruption.' Eleven minutes later, he tweeted again, at 9 PM, when he was told that ₹500 and ₹1,000 notes were being replaced with ₹2,000 notes: 'Really? Damn' (Pandathil, 2017).

Embarrassed, Rashtriya Swayamsevak Sangh (RSS) ideologue S. Gurumurthy, now a member of the RBI board, said that the ₹2,000 notes would be 'phased out' gradually, which is what has happened, though inflation has been well under control for years (Kanwal, 2016).

Harvard versus Hard Work

There was another interesting twist. The first and second AEs (AE1 and AE2) showed that the demonetization has had no impact on the economy, but the growth for FY2017 would be 7.1 per cent, which was higher than expected and more than China's 6.8 per cent for October–December quarter of 2016, enabling India to retain its tag of world's fastest growing major economy. Modi immediately launched an attack on Harvard economists Amartya Sen and Larry Summers in March 2017, saying that 'a poor man's (referring to himself) who through his hard work is trying to improve the economy' stood vindicated over 'people at Harvard' (Guha, 2017; PTI, 2017).

It is a different matter that GDP growth for FY2017 climbed up to 8.2 per cent in January 2018 and 8.3 per cent in January 2021, making the demonetization year the fastest growing FY after Modi came to power and remains so till now.

The phrase *Harvard versus hard work* first emerged in 2014, when Modi targeted former finance minister and a Harvard alumni P. Chidambaram for ridiculing his knowledge of economics. At a rally in Tamil Nadu, Modi said:

> He (Chidambaram) said Modi's knowledge of economics can be written behind a postage stamp.... He thinks nobody else is more intelligent than him. Only if you paste the postal stamp will the letter be delivered. I have proved myself through delivery (in Gujarat)...you (Chidambaram) are educated from a big university. I am from a poor background from a small village. The finance minister is from Harvard. I am from hardwork. Do we need Harvard or hard work for the development of the country? (PTI, 2014)

Whose Idea Was It?

Who proposed demonetization? Who drafted and vetted it? What economic logic was provided? What were the precise goals? Who all were consulted? No answer is available as a tight veil of secrecy has been maintained until now. The Cabinet meeting was called minutes before the announcement and the prime minister was quoted as telling his ministers: 'I have done all the research and, if it fails, then I am to blame.' No further detail is known (Reuters, 2016).

Later, it was revealed that former RBI Governor Raghuram Rajan had opposed it verbally and in written communication from the RBI. The approval came after his term ended and Urjit Patel replaced him months ahead of the 'aakashvani'. The minutes of the RBI's board meeting revealed (through RTI) that concerns were raised over the justifications offered by the government, particularly about the impact on black money and counterfeit notes (*The Wire*, 2019).

Two names figured prominently in media about the possible mastermind: RSS ideologue S. Gurumurthy and Pune-based RSS activist Anil Bokil. Gurumurthy's name figures because of his explicit support to demonetization ahead of the announcement. He wrote in a daily on 22 June 2016:

> With the credit off-take falling in a rising economy, the RBI ought to be clearly seeing where the vitamin of money comes from to finance the higher growth. The new finance is sourced in an unprecedented rise in cash holdings which have risen to ₹15 lakh crore in 2015–16 with the share of high denomination notes in the total currency in circulation rising from 33 per cent to 85 per cent in 2015–16... (Gurumurthy, 2016; Thakurta, 2018)

But the face that hit media more was Anil Bokil, founder of a Pune-based think tank Arthakranti Pratishthan set up in 2014. He claimed that he had been advocating demonetization for several years and that he had met Modi several times to present his idea. He also gave details of his meetings, the last one in 2016 and demonetization was one of four ideas he gave (Busvine & Jain, 2016; Ghadyalpatil, 2016; Guha, 2017).

A few months after the demonetization, the prime minister's party, Bharatiya Janata Party (BJP), registered its biggest ever election win in Uttar Pradesh (February–March 2017) during which speculations were rife that the real motive was to starve the Opposition of cash, particularly among journalists covering the elections. Credible or not, the number of candidates contesting this election fell by 30 per cent (Rawat, 2017).

There was a third candidate.

State Bank of India Flags Unaccounted Money and Predicts Windfall Gain

Much before anyone had heard the word *demonetization*, the largest PSB, State Bank of India (SBI), red-flagged 'puzzling' rise in cash (in its newsletter *EcoWatch* of March 2016, now called EcoWrap) 8 months before the demonetization. It hinted that 'demonetization' could happen in the near future.

The paper stated that there was a 25 per cent spurt during April–January of FY2016, against the corresponding previous year, which was puzzling and needs to be investigated because (a) *inflation was declining*, (b) *nominal growth had collapsed* and (c) the IIP growth was negative for the previous two months, indicating that higher cash in hand had not led to

---

Extract from State Bank's *EcoWatch*, March 2016

If we were to draw a link between such production surge and usage of cash, it may be possible that demonetization may have already started to happen prior to the Government withdrawing high value notes from circulation (as per unconfirmed available reports, higher currency denomination notes may be discontinued in the near future so as to tackle the menace of unaccounted money). If this is true and the Government gives a window to people to declare unaccounted money in the budget over the next 6 months, this demonetization trend may actually increase manifold.

To sum up, such a currency increase defies logic and has many diverse explanations and needs analysis. One way out of this issue would be popularizing the digital and electronic channels. The total number of POS Machines and ATMs in the country is around 12,70,208 and 1,92,208 respectively. This is highly inadequate for a population of 1.3 trillion people.

Source: SBI (2016).

a rise in demand for goods. It also stated that the government had started withholding high value notes and that 'as per unconfirmed available reports, higher currency notes may be discontinued in the near future as to tackle the menace of unaccounted money.' The following extract is from that newsletter now not available on the SBI's website (SBI, 2016).

The idea of 'windfall gain' from the demonetization first surfaced a week after the demonetization. On 14 November 2016, SBI's CEA Soumya Kanti Ghosh wrote in a business daily ('Demonetisation and Note Burning'): 'Based on such estimates (three plausible scenarios), roughly around ₹4.5 *lakh crore* of money could disappear from the system.' On 23 November 2016, he wrote again in the same daily (titled 'Grappling with Demonetisation Windfall'), bringing down the windfall gain down to ₹2.4–4.8 *lakh crore* which 'will not be converted and remain outside the banking system' (Ghosh, 2016a, 2016b; Mohanty, 2020b).

That never happened and 99.3 per cent banned notes came back to the system—the RBI confirmed it two years later. That failure of the windfall gain, however, led to a wild goose chase.

The ITD was set out to search the missing windfall gain, but nothing was found. This loss would then set the centre after the RBI and seek money from its reserves. A committee under former RBI Governor Bimal Jalan would later facilitate it. The RBI transferred ₹1.76 *lakh crore* in August 2019. What happened to this money is an interesting story narrated in the next chapter (*Business Today*, 2019; Worstall, 2017).

The surprising element was that the government actually believed in a windfall gain of ₹3–4 lakh crore, assuming that currency notes to this extent wouldn't come back and that the RBI would pass it on to the government as its liabilities would have been reduced by this amount.

Was It Meant to Serve Private Business?

In December 2016, more than a month after the demonetization, Tony Joseph, former editor of *Businessworld* and author of bestselling book *Early Indians*, wrote what the headline said: 'The real reasons for demonetisation might be hiding in plain sight.' He said that demonetization was pre-planned and not a botched operation in implementation, as many believed, and that it aimed at promoting private companies in digital payment (Joseph, 2016).

This article deserves to be quoted at some length.

To substantiate that it wasn't a botched operation, but that the immense pain inflicted on people for months (cash rationing, delay in availability of cash, etc.) was a pre-planned exercise, he quoted three key players: the prime minister, the then finance minister and the then RBI governor. He quoted the prime minister saying, among other things, 'I always said the government's measure will *bring a degree of inconvenience* but this short-term pain will pave way for long-term gains.' The then Finance Minister Arun Jaitley said, among other things, 'RBI has been *releasing currency as per schedule*. The aim of demonetisation has been to move towards digital transactions.' The then RBI Governor Urjit Patel said, 'The decision has not been taken in haste but *after detailed deliberations....* The central bank and government were conscious of certain immediate difficulties for the public and all efforts were made to mitigate them.'

Joseph argued that cash rationing and delayed replenishment were not because of 'poor execution' or 'monumental mismanagement' as former Prime Minister Manmohan Singh had described it, rather it was a pre-planned operation to force people into digital payment. He drew attention to two immediate developments to argue his case: (a) within hours of the announcement, Paytm released front-page newspaper ads with the prime minister's face to promote digital payment and (b) a few weeks later, newborn payment banks of Reliance Industries and Airtel announced plans to create merchant networks for digital payments.

He pointed out that the move to promote digital payment started more than a year earlier when 11 new payment banks were given licences. A series of quick moves were made thereafter to promote digital payments. He further argued that the real motive was not to check corruption since the two major corruption scandals of the time, the Aircel-Maxis and AgustaWestland deals, didn't involve cash transactions but bank transfers to companies in India and abroad.

Wait. There is more evidence that the demonetization had been planned for a long period of time.

In 2017, former RBI Governor Raghuram Rajan disclosed in his book *I Do What I Do*, after the end of his term, that he was approached by the government for his views on demonetization in February 2016 and he rejected it 'orally'. He explained: 'Although there might be long-term benefits, I felt the likely short-term economic costs would outweigh them, and felt there were *potentially better alternatives* to achieve the main goals. I made these views known in no uncertain terms.' In his view, black money hoarders find ways to divide their hoard into many smaller pieces, and a fair amount of cash is typically in gold and that he would prefer focusing more on the incentives that lead to the generation of black money (Rajan, 2017).

Later, he wrote, the RBI was asked to prepare a note on it, which it did. The note outlined the potential costs and benefits, as well as the preparation and time that would be needed in case the government decided to go ahead and warned about the consequences if the preparation was inadequate. Rajan also explained that people would find out ways to *infuse (unaccounted) money back into the system without paying tax* and that a fair amount of unaccounted cash was typically in the form of gold, which is even harder to catch. The government was immune to all of this.

In December 2016, a reputed business paper revealed that in February–March 2016, Madhya Pradesh and Haryana had approached the NIPFP to evaluate Anil Bokil's proposals (mentioned earlier). The NIPFP submitted its report (working paper) a week after the demonetization, which stated:

> The demonetisation undertaken by the government *is a large shock to the economy....* While it has been argued that the cash that would be extinguished would be 'black money' and hence, should be rightfully extinguished to set right the perverse incentive structure in the economy, *this argument is based on impressions rather than on facts.* While the facts are not available to anybody, it would be foolhardy to argue that this is the only possibility.... (NIPFP, 2016)

Weeks after demonetization, it emerged that the BJP had gone on a land-buying spree all over India before the demonetization was announced, with a BJP MLA from Bihar disclosing that the money for it had come from the headquarters (*Catch News*, 2017; *The Indian Express*, 2016).

Nevertheless, demonetization was a ham-handed affair requiring 74 notifications from the government and the RBI in the first 50 days (Joshi, 2021).

Damage Demonetization Caused

This would never be known because official reports were wishy-washy and private assessments were patchy. None looked at the immense pain it inflicted on the ordinary people and the informal economy. It was the beginning of India's fall from a democratic to an autocratic country where people no longer mattered.

For example, the RBI's report of 10 March 2017, titled 'Macroeconomic Impact of Demonetisation—A Preliminary Assessment', stated:

> The analysis in this paper suggests that demonetisation has impacted various sectors of the economy in varying degrees; however, in the affected sectors, the adverse impact was **transient** and felt mainly in November and December 2016. The impact moderated significantly in January 2017 and dissipated by and large by mid-February, reflecting the fast pace of remonetisation. (Emphasis added; RBI, 2017)

The Economic Survey of 2016–2017, released in January 2017, stated: 'Demonetisation has had short-term costs but holds the potential for long term benefits.' About short-term costs, it stated that the 'magnitudes of short-term costs remain uncertain', but it listed several long-term benefits, including 'reduced corruption, greater digitalization of the economy, increased flows of financial savings, and greater formalization of the economy, all of which could eventually lead to higher GDP growth, better tax compliance and greater tax revenues'.

In September 2018, the 'Task Force for Drafting the New Income Tax Law' report showed that the corporate investment had fallen by 58.9 per cent from ₹10.3 lakh crore in FY2016 (AY 2016–2017) to ₹4.3 lakh crore in FY2017 (AY 2017–2018; *The Hindu*, 2019).

In 2018, the Agriculture Ministry submitted a report to the Parliamentary Standing Committee on Finance saying that millions of farmers had been affected (no cash meant no trading in agriculture produce), but this was withdrawn and replaced with another one that declared 'no adverse impact' of demonetization. The Ministry also issued a show-cause notice to two directors and a joint secretary for the first report (Nair, 2018).

As the GDP numbers show, the economy went on a tailspin post-demonetization, making mockery of such assertions in government reports. Later, Rajan said that the demonetization killed 10–12 million jobs (Mumbai Congress, 2019).

'Grand Cultural Revolution'?

Apart from the economic and political aspect, something else attracted attention at the time which pointed to India's rapid fall as a democratic country.

Venkaiah Naidu, then Union Minister for Urban Development, Information and Broadcasting, who would become the speaker of the Lok Sabha and then the vice-president of India, wrote in a national daily about the 'new cultural revolution' a few days into the demonetization, when millions of Indians were queueing up outside banks. He described demonetization as a part of *'grand cultural revolution* that the PM is working on' aimed at *behaviour change* for building a 'new India' (Naidu, 2016).

Given that this came amid all-round panic, loss of jobs and businesses, cash rationing and a display of fortitude by the people, Naidu's exposition probably meant *subservience* of people to the *commands of the strong leader*. Indians would keep paying a heavy price for such medieval subservience for years to come.

Takeaways

⇨ Demonetization marked the beginning of a top-down, arbitrary and self-serving decision-making through 'aakashvani' that would endure.

⇨ No democratic institution stood up to protest it, emboldening the autocratic streak of the new government.

⇨ Demonetization caused massive overnight loss of livelihood, hit informal economy hard but the damages were never properly or fully assessed, displaying a rare apathy of an elected government to people's pain and harm to the economy.

⇨ This also accelerated economy growth which was slowing down but artificially propped up by the new GDP series of 2011–2012, which overestimated growth numbers.

References

Business Today. (2019, 26 August). RBI board approves transfer of ₹1.76 lakh crore to centre. https://www.businesstoday.in/current/economy-politics/breaking-rbi-board-approves-transfer-of-rs-1-7-lakh-crore-to-centre-jalan-committee/story/375481.html

Busvine, D., & Jain, R. (2016, 10 December). Who knew about Modi's secret demonetisation plan? *Mint.* https://www.livemint.com/Politics/PZJjaYIbSXITq8gIrZePnL/How-closely-guarded-was-Narendra-Modis-demonetisation-plan.html

Catch News. (2017, 10 February). Before Modi banned ₹500, ₹1000 notes BJP was busy investing in real estate. http://www.catchnews.com/india-news/bjp-bought-land-worth-crores-just-before-note-ban-1480019920.html

Chodorow-Reich, G., Gopinath, G., Mishra, P., & Narayanan, A. (2018). Cash and the economy: Evidence from India's Demonetization. https://scholar.harvard.edu/files/crgmn_demonetization.pdf

Financial Express. (2016, 4 December). 50 chartered planes for Nitin Gadkari's daughter's wedding says report; minister refutes claim. https://www.financialexpress.com/india-news/50-chartered-planes-for-nitin-gadkaris-daughters-wedding-says-report-minister-refutes-claim/463714/

Gatty, H. R., & Johnson, T. A. (2016, 14 November). PM Modi on demonetisation: Bear pain for 50 days, then punish me. *The Indian Express.* https://indianexpress.com/article/india/india-news-india/demonetisation-of-rs-500-rs-1000-notes-pm-modi-bear-pain-for-50-days-then-punish-me-4373933/

Ghadyalpatil, A. (2016, 22 November). Meet Anil Bokil, the man who gave Narendra Modi the idea of demonetisation. *Mint.* https://www.livemint.com/Politics/Ik4IpJUvejB3bIDm0VWKgN/Meet-Anil-Bokil-the-man-who-gave-Narendra-Modi-the-idea-of.html

Ghosh, S. K. (2016a, 14 November). Demonetisation and note burning. *Business Standard.* https://www.business-standard.com/article/opinion/soumya-kanti-ghosh-demonetisation-and-note-burning-116111401590_1.html

Ghosh, S. K. (2016b, 23 November). Grappling with demonetisation windfall. *Business Standard.* https://www.business-standard.com/article/opinion/grappling-with-demonetisation-windfall-116112301447_1.html

Guha, K. (2017, 5 March). It takes hard work to get through Harvard—And it's dangerous for Modi to imply otherwise. *Scroll.in.* https://scroll.in/article/830952/it-takes-hard-work-to-get-through-harvard-and-its-dangerous-for-modi-to-imply-otherwise

Gurumurthy, S. (2016, 22 June). Rajan: The exit that was inevitable. *The New Indian Express.* https://www.newindianexpress.com/opinions/columns/s-gurumurthy/2016/jun/22/Rajan-The-exit-that-was-inevitable-883797.html

IANS. (2016, 16 November). Mining baron Reddy splurges on daughter's lavish wedding. *Business Standard.* https://www.business-standard.com/article/news-ians/mining-baron-reddy-splurges-on-daughter-s-lavish-wedding-116111600997_1.html

Income Tax Department. (n.d.). CBDT releases direct taxes data. https://www.incometaxindia.gov.in/Pages/Direct-Taxes-Data.aspx

Joseph, T. (2016, 19 December). The real reasons for demonetisation might be hiding in plain sight. *The Indian Express.* https://indianexpress.com/article/blogs/demonetisation-implementation-cash-crunch-digital-payments-cashless-transactions-4435312/

Joshi, R. (2021, 1 January). The hollowing out of democracy. *Deccan Herald.* https://www.deccanherald.com/amp/opinion/comment/the-hollowing-out-of-democracy-934065.html?__twitter_impression=true

Kanwal, R. (2016, 12 December). New ₹2,000 notes to be phased out within 5 years, says RSS ideologue Gurumurthy. *India Today.* https://www.indiatoday.in/india/story/2000-notes-new-currency-phased-out-rss-demonetisation-note-ban-357084-2016-12-12

Lok Sabha Secretariat. (2020, 19 September). Unstarred question no. 1231. http://loksabhaph.nic.in/Questions/QResult15.aspx?qref=17514&lsno=17

Mohanty, P. (2020a, 24 February). Taxing the untaxed III: Is govt oblivious to leakages in direct tax collection? *Business Today*. https://www.businesstoday.in/current/economy-politics/taxing-the-untaxed-is-govt-oblivious-to-leakages-in-direct-tax-collection-corporate-non-corporate-taxes/story/396799.html

Mohanty, P. (2020b, 11 September). Rebooting economy XXV: How a series of economic misadventures derailed India's growth story. *Business Today*. https://www.businesstoday.in/opinion/columns/indian-economy-how-a-series-of-economic-misadventures-derailed-indias-growth-story-gdp/story/415727.html

Mohanty, P. (2020c, 17 October). Rebooting economy XXVII: Fiscal mismanagement threatens India's economic recovery. *Business Today*. https://www.businesstoday.in/opinion/columns/indian-economy-fiscal-management-threatens-indias-economic-recovery-covid19-crisis/story/416024.html

Mohanty, P. (2020d, 26 November). Rebooting economy 48: Do tax numbers show a healthier economy? *Business Today*. https://www.businesstoday.in/opinion/columns/indian-economy-do-tax-numbers-show-a-healthier-economy-economic-growth/story/423073.html

Mumbai Congress. (2019, 10 February). Demonetisation killed the informal sector, 10–12 million jobs were lost: Former RBI Governor Raghuram Rajan. https://twitter.com/incmumbai/status/1094514256257503234; https://newscentral24x7.com/demonetisation-effects-rbi-modi-informal-sector-10-12-million-jobs-lost-raghuram-rajan/amp/?__twitter_impression=true

Naidu, M. V. (2016, 29 November). The new cultural revolution. *The Indian Express*. https://indianexpress.com/article/opinion/columns/demonetisation-effect-rbi-economy-gdp-4400464/

Nair, S. K. (2018, 27 November). Ministry withdraws note ban report. *The Hindu*. https://www.thehindu.com/news/national/ministry-withdraws-note-ban-report/article25608445.ece?homepage=true

NIPFP. (2016, 14 November). *Demonetisation: Impact on the economy* (NIPFP Working Paper No. 182). https://www.nipfp.org.in/media/medialibrary/2016/11/WP_2016_182.pdf

Pandathil, R. (2017, 10 October). Richard Thaler did not endorse Narendra Modi's demonetisation; his tweet on ₹2,000 is still relevant. *Firstpost*. https://www.firstpost.com/business/richard-thaler-did-not-endorse-narendra-modis-demonetisation-his-tweet-on-rs-2000-is-still-relevant-4127071.html

PIB. (2020, 8 November). Demonetisation helped to reduce black money, increase tax compliance and given a boost to transparency: PM. https://pib.gov.in/PressReleseDetail.aspx?PRID=1671214

PTI. (2014, 8 February). Modi tears into Chidambaram, says hard work not Harvard pays. *News18*. https://www.news18.com/news/politics/modi-tears-into-chidambaram-says-hard-work-not-harvard-pays-667181.html

PTI. (2016a, 23 November). 40 per cent ATMs recalibrated to dispense new currency. *Business Today*. https://www.businesstoday.in/current/economy-politics/40-per-cent-atms-recalibrated-to-dispense-new-currency/story/240936.html

PTI. (2016b, 30 November). Demonetisation a despotic action, says Amartya Sen. *The Wire*. https://thewire.in/economy/demonetisation-a-despotic-action-says-amartya-sen

PTI. (2017, 1 March). Hard work more powerful than Harvard: PM Narendra Modi. *The Economic Times*. https://economictimes.indiatimes.com/news/politics-and-nation/hard-work-more-powerful-than-harvard-pm-narendra-modi/articleshow/57410764.cms?utm_source=contentofinterest&utm_medium=text&utm_campaign=cppst

Rajan, R. (2017). *I do what I do*. Harper Business.

Rawat, V. S. (2017, 6 March). Demonetisation effect: Fewer candidates fought 2017 UP poll. *Business Standard*. https://www.business-standard.com/elections/uttar-pradesh-assembly-elections-2017/demonetisation-effect-fewer-candidates-fought-2017-up-poll-117030600517_1.html

RBI. (2017, 10 March). Macroeconomic impact of demonetisation—A preliminary assessment. https://rbidocs.rbi.org.in/rdocs/Publications/PDFs/MID10031760E85BDAFEFD497193995BB1B6DBE602.PDF

RBI. (2020). Modelling and forecasting currency demand in India: A heterodox approach. https://rbidocs.rbi.org.in/rdocs/Publications/PDFs/0OCCASIONALPAPERSVOL41NO1202028B707351EED4867BD95CFA38D4B2280.PDF

RBI. (2021). Annual report 2020–21. https://rbidocs.rbi.org.in/rdocs/AnnualReport/PDFs/0RBIAR202021_F49F9833694E84C16AAD01BE48F53F6A2.PDF

Reuters. (2016, 9 December). Demonetisation: If it fails, then I am to blame, PM Modi told cabinet. *The Indian Express*. https://indianexpress.com/article/india/who-knew-modis-black-money-move-kept-a-closely-guarded-secret/

SBI. (2016, March). *State Bank EcoWatch* (Issue no. 25). https://www.dropbox.com/s/7yzugi4oirueuu0/SBI%20EcoWatch-March2016.pdf?dl=0

Seth, D. (2020, 24 June). India's tax-GDP ratio plunges to 9.88% in FY20, lowest in 10 years. *Business Standard*. https://www.business-standard.com/article/economy-policy/india-s-tax-to-gdp-ratio-plunges-to-a-decade-low-of-9-88-in-fy20-120060801629_1.html

Subramanian, A. (2018, 28 November). 'Demonetisation was a massive, draconian, monetary shock', says Arvind Subramanian in his new book. *Mint*. https://www.livemint.com/Industry/PL1a49BBpiMN2r2VRhvOrN/demonetisation-arvind-subramanian-book-of-counsel-modi-jaitl.html

TARC. (2014, November). Tax administration reforms in India: Spirit, purpose and empowerment (Third report of TARC). https://www.dea.gov.in/sites/default/files/TARC3rdReport.pdf

Thakurta, P. G. (2018, 8 August). The importance and unimportance of S. Gurumurthy. *The Wire*. https://thewire.in/economy/gurumurthy-demonetisation-modi-swamy

The Hindu. (2016, 14 November). Demonetisation has equalised the rich and the poor, claims Modi. https://www.thehindu.com/news/national/Demonetisation-has-equalised-the-rich-and-the-poor-claims-Modi/article16447877.ece

The Hindu. (2019, 21 August). Report of the task force for drafting the new income tax law. https://www.thehindu.com/news/resources/report-of-the-task-force-for-drafting-the-new-income-tax-law/article29214463.ece

The Indian Express. (2016, 25 November). BJP leaders bought many parcels of land before demonetisation, claims report. https://indianexpress.com/article/india/india-news-india/bjp-leaders-bought-many-parcels-of-land-before-demonetisation-claims-report-4394500/

The Wire. (2017, 4 October). Arun Shourie compares demonetisation to suicide, calls it 'largest money-laundering scheme'. https://thewire.in/economy/arun-shourie-demonetisation-modi-gst

The Wire. (2019, 11 March). Minutes of RBI's pre-note ban board meeting raise questions over decision-making process. https://thewire.in/economy/rbis-board-meeting-on-demonetisation-raises-more-questions-over-decision-making-process

Venkatesh, M. (2018, 2 October). Would not suggest demonetisation to any country: New IMF chief economist Gita Gopinath. *The Print*. https://theprint.in/economy/would-not-suggest-demonetisation-to-any-country-new-imf-chief-economist-gita-gopinath/128447/

Worstall, T. (2016, 8 December). India's demonetisation kills 100 people apparently—This is not an important number. *Forbes*. https://www.forbes.com/sites/timworstall/2016/12/08/indias-demonetisation-kills-100-people-apparently-this-is-not-an-important-number/?sh=22460867237a

Worstall, T. (2017, 17 January). India's demonetisation—3-4 lakh crore untaxed cash deposited, IT department to investigate. *Forbes*. https://www.forbes.com/sites/timworstall/2017/01/10/indias-demonetisation-3-4-lakh-crore-untaxed-cash-deposited-it-department-to-investigate/?sh=4bfccd805ac6

Yadav, P. (2020, 8 November). Twitter link to Modi's video of November 12, 2016. https://twitter.com/priyapyadav18/status/1325334898694004741

IV GST AND OTHER TAXES

Second Shock and Setbacks

Before the economy could recover from the 'massive, draconian, monetary shock' of demonetization, as the then CEA Arvind Subramanian later described it, the Indian government brought a major tax reform by way of GST which delivered a second shock to the economy. Business activities were disrupted for months, small and medium industries shut down and more jobs were lost. The devastations it caused would not be fully known because the Indian government made no attempt to assess, just as it didn't in the case of demonetization.

The GST was introduced with a midnight session of the Parliament on 30 June–1 July 2017, like the one when India gained Independence in 1947. It was described as 'a second freedom fight'. Prime Minister Narendra Modi said that it was a 'good and simple tax' which would end tax terrorism and inspector raj, fight black money and corruption, epitomize cooperative federalism and, just as Sardar Patel had united all principalities post-Independence, the GST would unite India into one market (*The Times of India*, 2017).

It was a sensible and significant tax reform which backfired. Let's understand this with the help of hindsight.

GST Has Structural Flaws

The GST subsumed eight central and nine state indirect taxes, including service tax, VAT, excise, entry tax, etc., and yet it is different from those in design. It is levied on value additions at all stages of production of goods and services, from manufacturing to final consumption, and is a destination-based tax, unlike the others which were origin-based (place of production), thus altering the revenue generation of producer states and consumption states. Apart from equally sharing the revenue, states are compensated for loss of taxes and rights.

However, its structural flaws have become apparent over the years.

The *first* is leaving out three high-value goods: petroleum and petroleum products, alcohol for human consumption and electricity. Both the centre and the states collect a large amount of tax on these. Keeping those out of the GST, states retained some control over revenue. The *second* is a large number of tax slabs: 0 per cent, 0.25 per cent, 3 per cent, 5 per cent, 12 per cent, 18 per cent, 28 per cent, composite tax of 1 per cent (for below ₹1.5 crore turnover) and a cess over and above 28 per cent on sin and luxury goods. Cess collections go to the central kitty and is meant for compensating states for their revenue loss.

Zero-tax slab (of the nine) counts because 149 items are listed under it and need to be factored in while determining tax liability of a firm. The multiplicity of slabs goes against the global experience that Subramanian had, in his 2015 report on GST, warned against by stating: 'Ideally, the GST should aspire to a single rate, which would then also be the standard rate. Since 2000, about *90 per cent of countries* that have adopted a VAT have chosen to have a single rate.' His report recommended three tax rates: 12 per cent (centre plus states) covering most items with two standard rates varying between 17 per cent and 18 per cent (CBIC, 2015).

The rates are discriminatory too. For example, luxury items of rough diamond, precious and semi-precious stones attract 0.25 per cent GST and polished diamonds, gold, platinum and silver ornaments attract 3 per cent. But humble tendu leaves used for bidi making by the rural poor, 'katha', a wood extract used in 'paan' and biscuits given to poor children in Anganwadi centres attract 18 per cent GST (CBIC, 2017).

In simple words, the GST rate is high on items consumed by the poor and low on those consumed by the rich/wealthy. Although economists argue that high tax on luxury items distorts market and choices (discretionary spending), as against essential items (people tend to avoid paying high tax on discretionary items, goes the logic), this tax regime goes against the cardinal principle of the ability to pay. The argument for a lower rate on luxury items may make sound business sense but not economic sense as it burdens the poor more.

The *third* flaw is its complex implementation mechanisms which impose very high cost of compliance. For example, a pan-Indian firm (a cycle/motorcycle maker or a potato chips/cold drink maker) needs to file *988 GST returns* every single year. That is because it has to file two monthly returns, GSTR-1 (outward supply of goods and services) and GSTR-3B (summarized details with input tax claims) every month (24 in a year) and two annual returns of GSTR-9 and GSTR-9C (GST audit) to both central and state governments. With 28 states and 9 UTs after J&K's downgrading, it needs to file 962 returns to states/UTs (24×37 + 2×37) and another 26 to central government (24 GSTR-1 and GSTR-3B in a year, one GSTR-9 and one GSTR-9C).

The actual documentation is far more daunting and costly. Ask GST experts and they will tell you that a firm needs to track all its warehouses and office establishments in every state every month to file the returns. All this requires enormous paperwork, manpower deployment and establishment costs on more than 10 million companies registered for the GST. Plus, a team of officials to police the system. More than three years after the GST was introduced, the centre is still struggling with the return formats and IT system (Mondal, 2020).

A WB study of 2018 stated that India's GST was more complex (with high and multiple tax rates) than the comparable systems in *115 countries*, adding to the cost of compliance and *incentivized tax evasion* (World Bank, 2018).

The *fourth* flaw is input tax credit (ITC). At every stage of production, a firm needs to pay tax and since the final tax is on output, it is allowed to reclaim all taxes paid on inputs (raw materials and intermediate goods). This is an unnecessary exercise and has had a debilitating impact on small and medium businesses. Economist Arun Kumar explains this why. He says that small firms with annual turnovers of less than ₹40 lakh (earlier ₹20 lakh) are exempted from the GST and need not be registered, which means that bigger firms buying from them can't claim ITC. Thus, bigger firms don't source their inputs from small and unorganized businesses, thereby damaging the latter's business.

The downside of ITC became stark when the centre was asked to waive GST on Covid-related essentials (oxygen, medicines and equipment) during the devastating second wave in 2021, and India was seeking global aid. Finance Minister Nirmala Sitharaman ruled out carte blanche exemption, saying: 'If full exemption from GST were given, the domestic producers of these items would be unable to offset taxes paid on their inputs and input services and would pass these on to the end consumers by increasing their price' (*Bloomberg | Quint*, 2021).

Operational Flaws Became Evident

The implementation too has been defective. As a result, more than three years after its rollout, GST is not fully operational. The GST Network (GSTN), the IT backbone of the GST, is not ready yet. Technical glitches and several rounds of training to officials in 2018 and 2019 didn't help. The private players engaged to run the system proved inefficient and were replaced in 2019 with a government entity (Ministry of Finance, 2019a; Mohanty, 2020d).

The inoperative GSTN meant no automatic matching of vouchers and, thus, refund of ITC claims is without verification. This has led to a flourishing business in fake input claims. The government told the Rajya Sabha that fake claims of ₹11,518.6 crore were detected during July 2017–May 2019. The CAG flagged this and other anomalies. Its March 2021 report stated:

> During the current audit, we noticed that owing to the continuing *extensions in the roll out* of simplified return forms, and *delay in decision making*, the originally envisaged system-verified flow of ITC through 'invoice matching' is yet to be implemented and a non-intrusive e-tax system still remains unimplemented. The GST return system is still a *work in progress* despite more than three years of GST roll out.
> (CAG, 2019, 2021; Ministry of Finance, 2019b)

A key return not yet rolled out is GSTR-9C, providing for GST tax audit details. Its rollout is extended every year, the last one advancing it to April 2021. As a result, the GST liabilities, validity of refund claims, etc., of firm go unaudited.

It is not difficult to imagine that the GST could have been made simpler and effective. Economist Arun Kumar, who has written extensively on the subject including a book, argues that the main culprit is ITC provision which should be removed. Since the final burden is on consumers, the GST should be 'last-point' tax, like the sales tax earlier, eliminating the enormous burden of filing and tracking who paid what to whom to claim the tax credit at every stage of production, without reducing tax collection. He argues that this would help the unorganized sector (enterprises outside the purview of GST) also as without ITC they would be back in business. The gain to the unorganized sector would far outweigh the loss to the organized sector that this change may bring. He says that since 5 per cent of firms pay 95 per cent of taxes, as former Finance Minister Arun Jaitley used to claim, it wouldn't matter much if some firms don't pay GST. Focusing on simplifying the system and making it more efficient would pay better dividend.

A Good Example of Cooperative Federalism

State governments gave up their right to tax (loss of revenue) on a large number of goods and services, other than petrol and petroleum products, alcohol for human consumption and electricity. They are compensated for the loss of right and revenue through a cess with a guarantee of 14 per cent growth every year for the next five years (it ends in 2022).

But as the GST collections didn't match the expectations problems erupted. Budget documents show a 31.4 per cent growth in its collection in FY2019—a year after it was introduced—but the next FY saw the growth slipping to 3 per cent and then shrinking to –13.9 per cent in FY2021 (RE). At the GST Council meeting of September 2019 (FY2020) at Goa, the centre told states its difficulty in paying the compensation. Ironically, the same day (20 September), the government declared the corporate tax cut of ₹1.45 lakh crore. A few weeks earlier, the RBI had announced the transferring of ₹1.76 lakh crore of surplus to the government (*Business Today*, 2019; Magazine, 2021; PIB, 2019).

The inability to pay the GST compensation snowballed into a major crisis in September 2020 (FY2021) when the centre outrightly refused to pay, blamed lack of fiscal resources on the pandemic, famously describing it as an 'Act of God', and asked states to borrow from either the RBI or from the open market to meet the shortfall. What remained unstated was that the GST had failed to deliver, and the centre's mismanagement of the economy was adversely impacting it.

As the following figure shows, the centre's estimates of GST have also been always off the mark even before the pandemic hit the economy, reflecting both unrealistic assessments and projections.

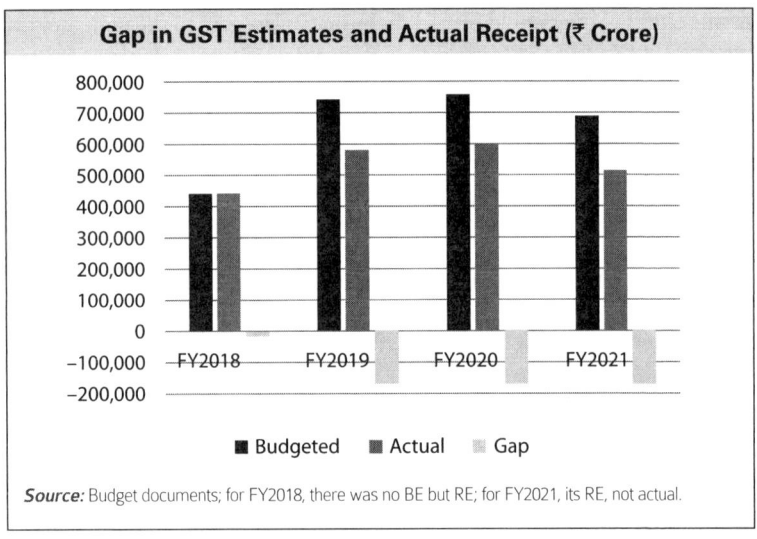

The centre's suggestion to states to borrow the shortfall threatened to break 'cooperative federalism'. It violated its own law, the Goods and Services Tax (Compensation to States) Act of 2017, which provides a statutory guarantee for the compensation as well as an annual increase of 14 per cent in the compensation. Later, the centre decided to borrow the shortfall from the RBI and 'lend' it to states, not transfer, as it should have been the case. In FY2021, it 'lent' ₹1.1 lakh crore and in FY2022 it

96 AN UNKEPT PROMISE

proposes to lend ₹1.58 lakh crore (*Business Today*, 2021; Ministry of Law and Justice, 2017; PTI, 2020).

It is in this context that the Subramanian Committee's caution over difficulties in adopting GST in a federal structure becomes relevant. The report stated that many other large federal systems such as the EU, Canada, Brazil, Indonesia, China and Australia faced serious challenges. Some were overly centralized, depriving the sub-federal levels of fiscal autonomy (Australia, Germany, and Austria); where there was a dual structure (as India was to adopt), they were either administered independently creating multiple tax bases and rates (Brazil, Russia and Argentina). None of them had managed to overcome these disadvantages and India needed to find its own answers. The USA had desisted from adopting such a tax system altogether. The warnings were ignored (CBIC, 2015).

There are other reasons for a setback to cooperative federalism. As against a promise of 42 per cent devolution of taxes from the divisible pool, the actual was 33–35 per cent during the 14th Finance Commission period. As against states' demand to remove GST on Covid-related essentials, a host of items such as medical oxygen, ventilators, ventilator masks, cannula and helmet, testing kits, inflammatory diagnostic kits, hand sanitizer, gas/electricity/other furnaces for cremation, ambulances, etc., continue to attract 5 per cent tax (brought down from 12%–28% as a temporary relief in June 2021; Aiyar, 2021; PIB, 2021; *The Hindu*, 2021).

Tall Claims and Real Impact

The prime minister claimed all credits for the GST by telling the Parliament in February 2020 that it was his brainchild and he was its architecture. It wouldn't be unfair, therefore, to put the blame for everything that has gone wrong with it on him. As chief minister of Gujarat, he had strongly opposed GST for years by branding it as 'retrograde in nature and completely against the tenets of fiscal federalism', among others (*Deccan Chronicle*, 2017; Mohan, 2020).

While pushing for GST, several tall claims were made. In 2009, chairman of the 13th Finance Commission, Vijay Kelkar, wrote:

> Preliminary results indicate that the growth in GDP can be between *2–2.5%* with the implementation of a well-designed GST. The increase in exports can be between *10–14%*. It is indeed a staggering impact and demands an energetic action to usher in a well-designed GST at an early date. (Kelkar, 2009)

Kelkar's report, 'Report of the Task Force on Goods & Services Tax' of the same year, referred to a study by the National Council of Applied Economic Research (NCAER) to repeat its conclusion which stated that GST could boost growth by *0.9–1.7 per cent*, much lower than what Kelkar claimed in his article. The NCAER finding was based on two assumptions: full employment and that 50 per cent of indirect taxes remain embedded and 'stick' to production and distribution (NCAER, 2009; Thirteenth Finance Commission, 2009).

Former Finance Ministers Pranab Mukherjee and Arun Jaitley too had made similar claims (Jha, 2015; PTI, 2010).

Economist Arun Kumar explained in his 2019 book *Ground Scorching Tax* how the claims that GST would boost growth by lowering prices, facilitate ease of doing business, reduce distortions and increase efficiency, etc., which had been provided to justify it, were found to be incorrect. Even the organized sector floundered, but a bigger pain was inflicted on the unorganized sector which lost business to the organized sector because of ITC. The flawed design and implementation of the GST adversely impacted business climate, reducing investment. He argued that the GST would have an adverse impact because 'most of the advantages (of the GST) would accrue to the organized sector which would expand at the expense of the unorganized sector and this would lead to a fall in growth rate of the economy and to greater inequality' (Kumar, 2019).

The actual impact of the GST on economic growth is not known, though enough ground reports and odd official reports show that it damaged the economy. In 2018, the Tamil Nadu government tabled a report on MSMEs in the assembly which stated two remarkable developments post-GST: (a) 50,000 units were shut in one year in 2017–2018 and (b) a dramatic rise in the registration of MSMEs came to a halt. Not all of it was due to the GST for sure, but this was one of the four factors that were listed for these developments, the others being demonetization, flood and cyclone (*The Hindu*, 2018).

The All India Manufacturers' Organisation representing MSMEs reported in 2018 that traders and MSMEs had lost around 3.5 million jobs in the past few years, primarily due to the GST and demonetization (Narasimhan & Babu, 2018).

The other big claim about the GST was the elimination of black money. The argument was that as inputs and outputs would get into a paper trail monitored separately by the centre and states, it would bring down transactions conducted in black markets. Instead, it led to a flourishing market in fake GST ITC claims. Kumar argues that black money economy is run by 'the triad' consisting of the ruling elite of the country (corrupt businessmen, corrupt politicians and corrupt executive), which derives enormous benefit out of it and hence only lip service is paid about its elimination (Kumar, 2019).

It isn't just the GST which has caused problems. India's entire tax structure is regressive and the new tax policies post-2014 have made it more so.

India's Regressive Tax Structure

One of the first things the new government did post-2014 was to abolish wealth tax from FY2016 even as French economist Thomas Piketty was telling the world that inequality had risen sharply and that the rich needed to be taxed. Then, in September 2019, corporate tax was cut to the tune of ₹1.45 lakh crore amid a prolonged economic slowdown and fiscal resource crunch.

On the other hand, the poor have been burdened with high tax as petrol and diesel get costlier even as price of the crude falls. The impact of it all can be seen in the following graphs.

The first graph shows corporate tax and income tax collections. For the first time in more than a decade, corporate tax collections fell below income tax in FY2021, indicating a higher tax burden on non-corporate entities. Ironically, corporations pay tax *on their profits*, while income tax is paid by non-corporate entities such as partnership firms, individuals and Hindu Undivided Family (HUF) *on their incomes*.

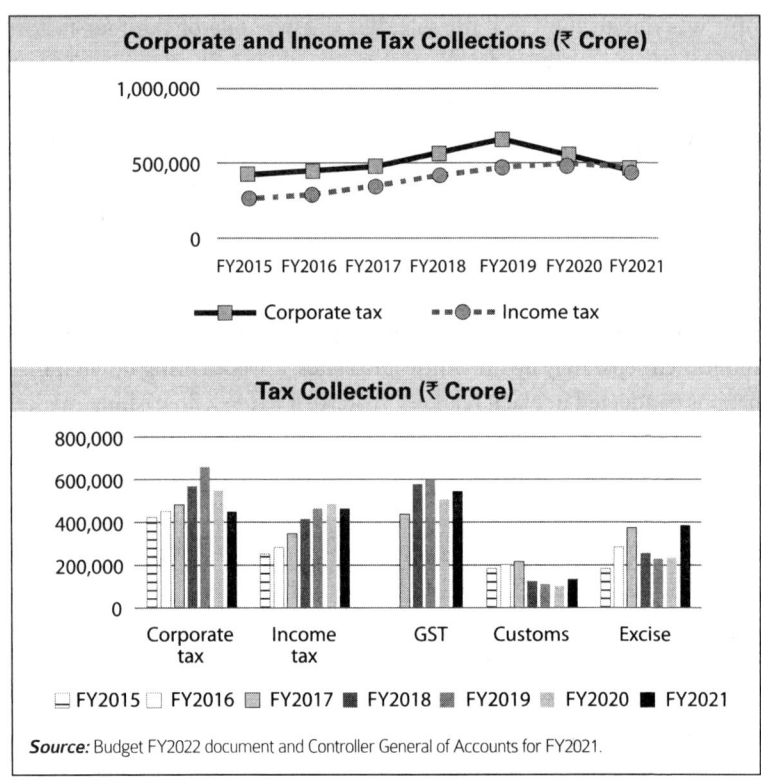

Source: Budget FY2022 document and Controller General of Accounts for FY2021.

The second graph shows rising excise duty collections because of rising excise on petrol and diesel. The crude prices crashed in 2014 as the new government took over but the retail price of petrol and diesel kept going up, reaching ₹100 per litre in 2021. The average annual Brent price of crude peaked at $111.6/barrel in 2012 and began sliding rapidly reaching the lowest point of $43.67 in 2016 and then went up to $71.34 in 2018 but fell to $41.96 in 2020 and $61.82 in 2021 (as on 7 May 2021; Sönnichsen, 2021).

The average annual growth in excise duty between FY2015 and FY2021 has been a robust 14.6 per cent, while that of corporate tax has been 3 per cent (using budget FY2022 data updated for FY2021 with the Controller General of Account's latest data released in June 2021). Average annual growth in gross tax revenue is 7.9 per cent during the period.

The high growth in excise is a burden on the poor, rather than the rich, because it is well known that the poor are the major consumers. A consumption mapping study by the centre showed that 61.42 per cent of petrol was being consumed by two-wheelers and 2.34 per cent by three-wheelers, while cars consumed 34.35 per cent; in case of diesel, commercial vehicles carrying goods and buses consumed 37.8 per cent and tractors 13 per cent, while cars and utility vehicles for private use consumed only 13.15 per cent (PPAC, 2014).

There are many more anomalies with India's tax system.

Higher Burden on Indirect Tax

India's tax regime continues to be regressive with indirect taxes contributing more. Indirect tax doesn't distinguish between rich and poor (capacity to pay); direct tax is on the income levels and thus based on ability-to-pay principle. Longer term mapping of direct and indirect tax as percentage of GDP shows that after narrowing down of the gap in 2010, it started widening.

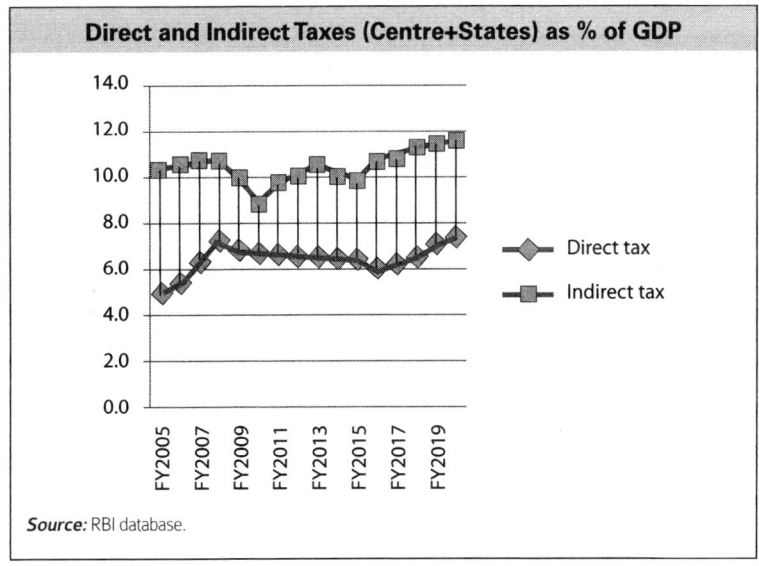

This is in sharp contrast to developed economies where the share of direct tax is more. The Organisation for Economic Co-operation and Development (OECD) average share of direct tax in 2018 was 67.3 per cent of the total tax collection. For the corresponding year FY2019 for India, the share of direct tax was 38.3 per cent, just the opposite (OECD, 2020).

Even direct tax is regressively designed as the burden is more on (a) smaller taxpayers, rather than larger corporations and (b) more on individuals than corporations.

Bigger Corporations Pay Less Tax

The budget documents have been showing how the 'effective tax rate' (the ratio of total taxes [including surcharge and education cess but excluding dividend distribution tax] to the total profits before taxes (PBT) expressed in percentage) is higher for smaller companies, demonstrating how tax incentives and deductions benefit larger companies more than smaller companies.

Here is a comparative state of effective tax rates and ratio of total income to PBT.

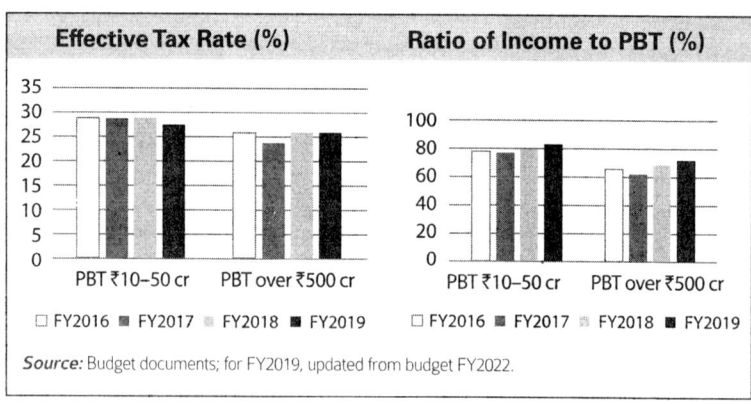

The first graph shows corporations making bigger profits (more than ₹500 crore) are paying less effective tax rate than those making smaller profits of ₹10–50 crore. The second graph reflects the impact of tax incentives. It is higher for corporations making bigger profits, taking the ratio of total income to PBT lower than those making smaller profits.

The budget documents have stopped updating these data after FY2019.

A sensible government would have attempted tax reforms to reverse the trend. Instead, there is an attempt to hide tax incentives and revenue foregone.

Revenue Foregone for Corporations

Another measure of higher tax concessions to corporations vis-à-vis non-corporate and individuals is revenue foregone. For the past few years, the government is hiding this by masking it by the following means:

- The term 'revenue foregone' has been replaced with 'revenue impact of tax incentives' to give a positive spin.
- It stopped showing central excise revenue foregone from FY2018, saying that it was merged with the GST even when petroleum and petroleum products are out of GST's ambit and earns a huge sum from central excise. Revenue foregone in GST is not provided, thus hiding a part of revenue foregone.
- It divided indirect tax concessions into 'conditional' and 'unconditional' ones and then said the 'unconditional' ones should not be counted as revenue foregone since it is meant for all and because of certain policy imperatives.
- It stopped adding 'conditional' indirect tax foregone in the total.

It is precisely because of this that the revenue foregone has dropped from more than ₹5 lakh crore in FY2014 and FY2015 to less than ₹1 lakh crore in later years.

Further, the FY2021 budget used a new trick to suppress revenue foregone for corporations by basing its estimates on FY2019, though it would have had all details by then. This was done to avoid showing the corporate tax cut of ₹1.45 lakh crore declared in September 2019 (FY2020) and should be counted as revenue foregone for FY2020.

This trick was repeated in the FY2022 budget too. Its calculations were based on revenue foregone of FY2019, which meant the corporate tax cut of ₹1.45 lakh crore is yet to be part of the official record of revenue foregone.

The graph below shows the impact of adding the corporate tax cut, 'unconditional' revenue foregone (as used to be the case for budget documents until FY2016) for custom duty but not for excise in the absence of data.

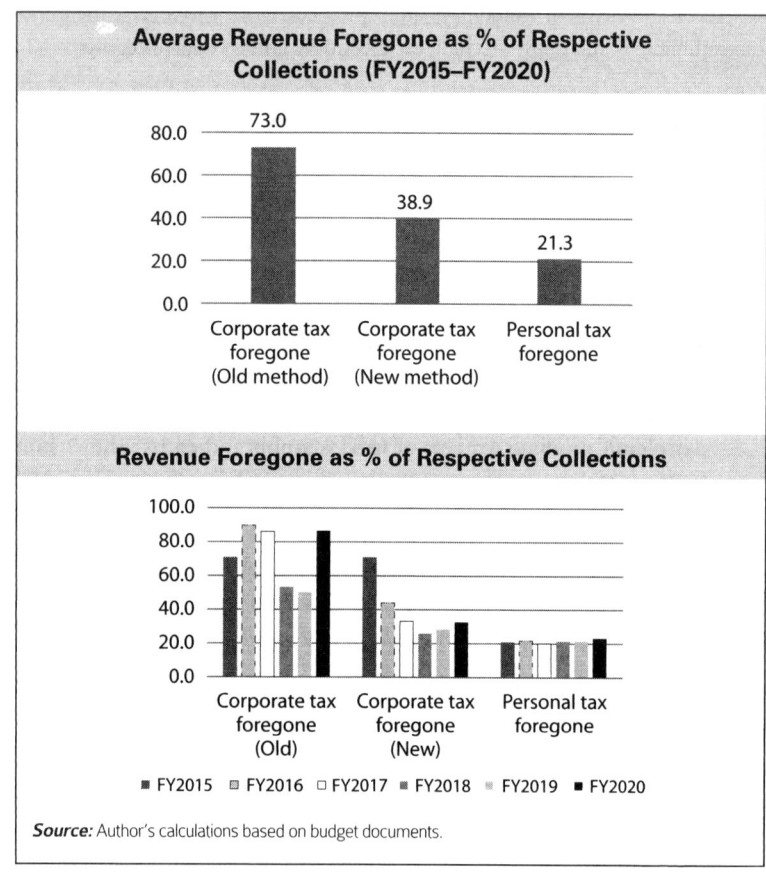

Source: Author's calculations based on budget documents.

The first graph shows the percentage of revenue foregone to total respective tax collections during FY2015–FY2020. Corporations win hands down with their share of revenue foregone at 73 per cent under the old method (before FY2016) and 38.9 per cent under the new method that uses several tricks to hide the actual state. Yet it is far more than 21.3 per cent than the rest.

The second graph shows year-wise trend under the new method. The skewed nature of taxation (tilted in favour of potentially bigger taxpayers) is evident: personal tax foregone is visibly far lower than corporate tax collection.

Another noticeable feature is the fall in corporate tax foregone, particularly drastically in FY2018. One reason could be the fall in imports due to high tariff, leading to less custom duty paid and foregone for corporations.

Former CEA Subramanian and Chatterjee of Pennsylvania State University pointed out in their 2020 study that import tariff had been significantly hiked after 2014, *particularly in 2018* when it was raised for 2,500 product categories. They wrote:

> Between 1991 and 2014, average MFN tariffs *declined from 125 percent to 13 percent. Since 2014, there have been about 3,200 tariff increases* at the HS-6 digit level (on most-favored-nation imports), a strikingly large increase. As a result, the *average tariff has increased from 13 percent to nearly 18 percent*. The largest increases occurred in *2018 when there were nearly 2,500 tariff increases* amounting to nearly 4 percentage points. We estimate that the tariff increases affected import categories that amount to about *$300 billion or about 70 percent of total imports*. (Chatterjee & Subramanian, 2020)

These increase amount to 60 per cent of total import items (3,200 out of 5,300 product categories). Did that actually impact imports? Yes, official data show the growth in imports came crashing down from a high of 17.4 per cent in FY2018 to –0.8 per cent in FY2020 (further detailed in the chapter on AatmaNirbhar Bharat).

Tax Havens, Double Taxation Avoidance Treaty, General Anti-Avoidance Rule and Tax Evasion Are in Whose Favour?

India's other tax laws are also heavily tilted in favour of corporations, as its record in curbing use of tax havens and shell companies for checking tax evasion is very poor.

Both FDI inflows and outflows have been primarily through tax havens, a trend that continues post-2014. The following graph maps the inflows and outflows through well-known tax havens such as Singapore, Mauritius, Netherlands, USA, UK, Cayman Islands and Cyprus common to both. As is evident, the share of tax havens is about 80 per cent or more.

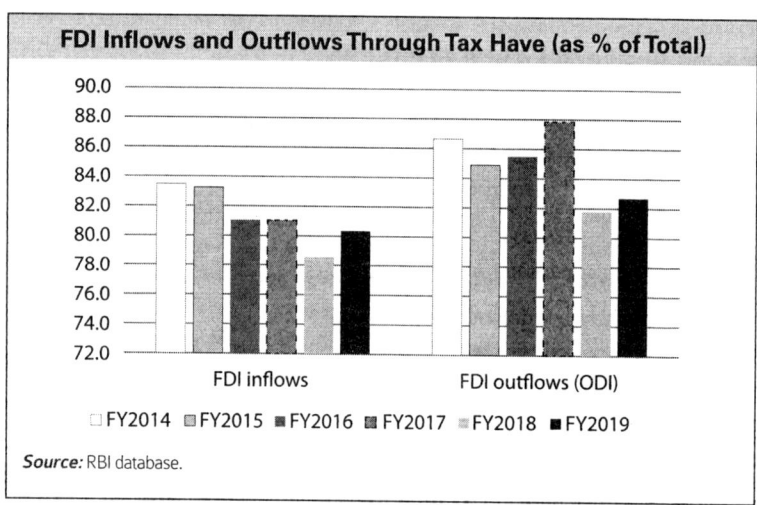

Tax havens' involvement of the possibilities of round-tripping and 'phantom' FDI in which shell companies play a very useful role. These are well known and officially acknowledged phenomena, but little attention is paid unless a big financial scam hits the headlines. Global studies show that at least 37.5 per cent of FDIs flowing through tax havens are 'phantom' FDIs or FDIs meant for tax evasion, rather than real investment. These FDIs pass through empty corporate shells that have no real business activities and primarily exist to evade tax (Mohanty, 2019b, 2020b, 2020f).

Unmindful of the pitfalls, the new government liberalized the FDI regime, emphasized more on quantitative inflows, rather than achieving the original policy objectives of technology transfers, marketing expertise, promotion of exports and creation of jobs, etc. (Mohanty, 2019a).

More so since big multinational companies are known for tax evasion by profit-shifting and other mechanisms.

In December 2019, UK-based transparency campaign group Fair Tax accused the big six US tech firms—Amazon, Facebook, Google, Netflix, Apple and Microsoft—of avoiding paying $100 billion in tax (or ₹730,000 crore at exchange rate of ₹73) in a decade between 2010 and 2019. The gap between the headline tax rates and actual tax paid—better understood as effective tax rate—was even higher during the period—$155.3 billion (₹1,133,690 crore at exchange rate of ₹73; Fair Tax, 2019).

Leading global financial newspaper *Financial Times* carried out its investigation by examining 25 years of financial statements of the world's 10 biggest public companies by market capitalization in nine sectors. It found multinationals paying lower tax than a decade earlier and the *gap* between reporting of what they *expect to pay in tax, and the actual payments* had grown because some US companies were *parking cash or booking profits overseas* (Toplensky, 2018).

These studies were limited in coverage but provide windows to global practices. The OECD-G20 initiative, 'Action Plan on Base Erosion and Profit Shifting' (BEPS), to check tax avoidance estimated that globally *$240 billion were being lost every year* (or ₹17.4 lakh crore a year at exchange rate of ₹73) due to tax avoidance (OECD, 2013).

Corporations use various ways to evade tax.

The Fair Tax's investigation revealed that multinationals *shift their revenue and profits to tax havens* abroad, such as Bermuda, Ireland, Luxembourg and the Netherlands. While Bermuda is a no-tax jurisdiction, others are low-tax jurisdictions. They exploit various loopholes in taxation systems, colourful named 'Double Irish', 'Single Malt' and 'Dutch Sandwich'—one more combination of it.

The Silicon Six's operations outside the USA accounted for 52 per cent of their booked revenue and *64 per cent of their booked profits*. But the tax liability from these operations was just *8.4 per cent* of the identified foreign profits—a mere third of their consolidated tax charge of 25.3 per cent. Studies have shown that these companies make different disclosures to their shareholders and tax authorities (Mohanty, 2020a).

Tax havens expert Gabriel Zucman of the UC Berkeley presented his latest findings in a graph to show how US corporations are increasing profit-shifting to avoid tax up from about 30 per cent in the 1980s to more than 50 per cent in 2018. The graph is reproduced below (Mohanty, 2020e).

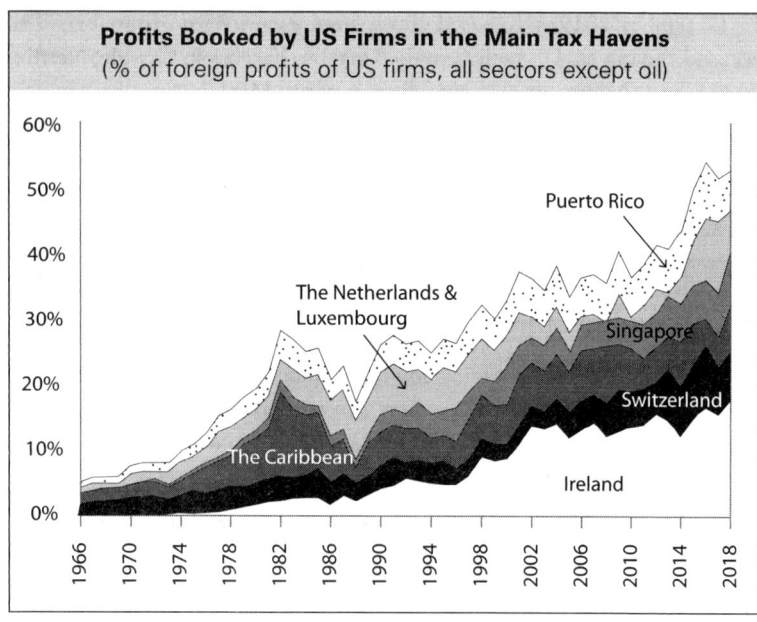

The Silicon Six and other multinationals operate in India and the tax havens they operate through also figure prominently in India's FDI inflows and outflows, as shown in the earlier graph.

There is no contemporary study on profit-shifting in India. NBER's 2020 report, 'The Missing Profits of Nations', provided an estimate on the basis of 2015 data of *tax loss due to profit-shifting* by domestic and foreign corporations operating in India. It showed that, compared to the effective corporate tax of 21 per cent in the USA, it was 10 per cent in India, and corporate tax loss due to profit-shifting was 8 per cent in India, against 14 per cent in the USA (Tørsløv et al., 2018).

India is among 135 countries who are collaborating to end tax through a 15-point BEPS action plan of OECD-G20 mentioned earlier, which is in various stages of implementation in different countries. One of these is ending double taxation avoidance treaties (DTATs) with tax havens or zero/low tax jurisdictions.

India has signed DTAT with close to 90 countries, some of which are known tax havens such as Singapore, Mauritius, Cyprus and others.

It has renegotiated such treaties with Mauritius and Singapore in 2017 but, as an analysis by the Tax Justice Network showed, these are partial and do not plug all loopholes. These are also self-defeating as multinational and domestic companies would simply shift their operations to other tax havens such as the Netherlands, Virginia Islands or any other to avoid tax (Fowler, 2019; Mohanty, 2020e).

Extended Deadline of Anti-tax Avoidance General Anti-Avoidance Rule

Way back in 2012, concerns about tax evasion led to the General Anti-Avoidance Rules (GAAR) of 2012 in the Income Tax Act of 1961, but that has not been implemented yet. Immediately, the Shome Committee was set up to examine its implementation (apparently due to resistance from industry) which concurred with the objective and stated, 'On considerations of economic efficiency, fiscal justice and revenue productivity, a taxpayer should not be allowed to use legal structures or transactions exclusively to avoid tax' (Shome Committee, 2012).

The GAAR of 2012 was introduced followed by the hugely controversial tax dispute over telecom major Vodafone buying Hutchison Essar's India operations in a tax haven, the Cayman Islands, in 2007. The GAAR provides that certain transactions would be 'impermissible avoidance arrangement' if (a) the main purpose is to obtain tax benefit and (b) it has one of the following characteristics: (i) it creates rights and obligations that are not normally created between parties dealing at arm's length, (ii) it results in the misuse or abuse of the provisions of the tax law, (iii) it lacks commercial substance and (iv) it is carried out by means or in a manner which is normally not employed for an authentic (bona fide) purpose (DSM, 2012).

But then the Shome Committee recommended that the implementation of the GAAR should be deferred until FY2017 for administrative reasons (lack of preparations, training and clarity on some concepts). Since then, the deadline is being extended. Last heard, it was deferred till 31 March 2021. In the meanwhile, several advanced economies have enacted the GAAR, prominent among them are the USA, the UK, France, Germany, the Netherlands, Canada, New Zealand, China, Poland and Australia (CTC, 2020; Mohanty, 2020a, 2020c).

Takeaways

⇨ GST failed to produce the result it was expected to.

⇨ GST is yet to be fully rolled out more than three years after its rollout.

⇨ India's tax system is regressive and imposes higher burden on poor and relatively smaller taxpayers rather than following cardinal principles of ability to pay and equity.

⇨ India has been lax in checking tax evasion and avoidance by corporations.

References

Aiyar, Y. (2021, 2 June). GST: End of the road for cooperative federalism? *Bloomberg | Quint.* https://www.bloombergquint.com/gst/gst-end-of-the-road-for-cooperative-federalism

Bloomberg | Quint. (2021, 9 May). Nirmala Sitharaman defends GST on Covid drugs, equipment. https://www.bloombergquint.com/business/nirmala-sitharaman-defends-gst-on-covid-drugs-equipment

Business Today. (2019, 26 August). RBI Board approves transfer of ₹1.76 lakh crore to centre. https://www.businesstoday.in/current/economy-politics/breaking-rbi-board-approves-transfer-of-rs-1-7-lakh-crore-to-centre-jalan-committee/story/375481.html

Business Today. (2021, 29 May). GST Council meet: Centre to borrow ₹1.58 lakh cr to compensate states, says FM. *Business Today.* https://www.businesstoday.in/current/economy-politics/gst-council-meet-centre-to-borrow-rs-158-lakh-cr-to-compensate-states-says-fm/story/440280.html

CAG. (2019). *Report of the Comptroller and Auditor General of India for the year ended March 2018* (Report no. 11). Department of Revenue. https://cag.gov.in/uploads/download_audit_report/2019/Report_No_11_of_2019_Compliance_Audit_of_Union_Government_Department_of_Revenue_Indirect_Taxes_Goods_and_Services_Tax.pdf

CAG. (2021). *Report of the Comptroller and Auditor General of India for the year ended March 2019 and March 2020* (Report no. 1). Department of

Revenue. https://cag.gov.in/uploads/download_audit_report/2021/Union_INDT_GST-CA__1_2021-0605ada1e04e151.14994928.pdf

CBIC. (2015, 4 December). Report on the revenue neutral rate and structure of rates for the Goods and Services Tax (GST). https://www.cbic.gov.in/resources//htdocs-cbec/gst/cea-rpt-rnr-new.pdf;jsessionid=71DC3546AF252574B0FAA31CF317C85B

CBIC. (2017). Rate of GST on goods. https://cbic-gst.gov.in/pdf/goods-rates-booklet-03July2017.pdf

Chatterjee, S., & Subramanian, A. (2020, October). *India's inward (re)turn: Is it warranted? Will it work?* (Policy Paper No. 1). Ashoka University. https://www.ashoka.edu.in/static/doc_uploads/file_1603091486.pdf

CTC. (2020, 24 April). Circular no. 10/2020. https://twitter.com/CTCConnect/status/1254784901171122177

Deccan Chronicle. (2017, 1 July). PM Modi opposed UPA's GST in 2013. https://www.deccanchronicle.com/nation/politics/010717/pm-modi-opposed-upas-gst-in-2013.html

DSM. (2012, 28 June). Draft guidelines regarding implementation of General Anti Avoidance Rules (GAAR) in terms of section 101 of the Income Tax Act, 1961. https://www.incometaxindia.gov.in/Communications/Circular/910110000000000734.htm

Fair Tax. (2019, December). The silicon six and their $100 billion global tax gap. https://fairtaxmark.net/wp-content/uploads/2019/12/Silicon-Six-Report-5-12-19.pdf

Fowler, N. (2019). India and the renegotiation of its double tax agreement with Mauritius: An update. Tax Justice Network. https://www.taxjustice.net/2019/04/04/india-and-the-renegotiation-of-its-double-taxation-avoidance-agreement-with-mauritius-an-update/

Jha, L. K. (2015, 17 April). FM Arun Jaitley says GST to increase GDP by 1–2 per cent. *Business Today.* https://www.businesstoday.in/current/economy-politics/gst-to-increase-gdp-by-1-2-per-cent-fm-arun-jaitley/story/218230.html

Kelkar, V. (2009, 1 December). A well-designed GST can boost GDP growth by 2%. *Business Today.* https://www.businesstoday.in/moneytoday/expert-view/a-welldesigned-gst-can-boost-gdp-growth-by-2percent/story/8474.html

Kumar, A. (2019). *Ground scorching tax.* Penguin.

Magazine, A. (2021, 28 August). Govt blames Covid, but payment stalled year ago. *The Indian Express.* https://indianexpress.com/article/business/economy/covid-19-gst-coronavirus-centre-state-6572818/

Ministry of Finance. (2019a, 9 July). *Removal of private sector entities from GSTN* (Rajya Sabha Unstarred Question No. 1800). https://pqars.nic.in/annex/249/Au1800.pdf

Ministry of Finance. (2019b, 9 July). *Missing GST taxpayers* (Rajya Sabha Unstarred Question No. 1785). https://pqars.nic.in/annex/249/Au1785.pdf

Ministry of Law and Justice. (2017). The Goods and Services Tax (Compensation to States) Act, 2017. https://www.cbic.gov.in/resources//htdocs-cbec/gst/gst-compensation-to-states-act.pdf;jsessionid=B884971A12CC30FF39EF97D86BAC6D7D

Mohan, A. (2020, 7 February). Current architecture of GST is my brainchild, says PM Narendra Modi. *Business Standard*. https://www.business-standard.com/article/politics/current-architecture-of-gst-is-my-brainchild-says-pm-narendra-modi-120020700065_1.html

Mohanty, P. (2019a, 5 September). Decoding slowdown: FDI inflows trend shows all's not well; growth drops to single digits. *Business Today*. https://www.businesstoday.in/current/economy-politics/foreign-direct-investment-fdi-falls-further-decoding-slowdown-more-capital-outflows-indian-economy/story/377419.html

Mohanty, P. (2019b, 7 October). Reality check: RBI's casual approach to round-tripping menace. *Business Today*. https://www.businesstoday.in/current/economy-politics/rbi-round-tripping-central-bank-casual-approach-reality-check-fdi-investments-shell-companies/story/383371.html

Mohanty, P. (2020a, 13 March). Taxing the untaxed V: What paralyses India from enforcing anti-tax avoidance law. *Business Today*. https://www.businesstoday.in/current/economy-politics/taxing-the-untaxed-v-india-anti-tax-avoidance-law-gaar-corporate-tax-multinationals-finance-ministry/story/398176.html

Mohanty, P. (2020b, 27 March). Taxing the untaxed IX: Is India blissfully ignorant to the menace of shell companies? *Business Today*. https://www.businesstoday.in/current/economy-politics/taxing-the-untaxed-india-shell-companies-threat-global-economy-indian-economy-black-money/story/399411.html

Mohanty, P. (2020c, 6 May). Coronavirus lockdown XII: Why the wealthy should be taxed more. *Business Today*. https://www.businesstoday.in/current/economy-politics/coronavirus-lockdown-indias-wealthy-tax-government-npas-bad-loans-super-rich-black-money/story/402967.html

Mohanty, P. (2020d, 3 September). Rebooting economy XXIV: 7 critical GST flaws govt needs to address at the earliest. *Business Today*. https://www.businesstoday.in/opinion/columns/gst-structural-and-operational-flaws-govt-needs-to-address-at-the-earliest-indian-economy/story/415001.html

Mohanty, P. (2020e, 14 September). Rebooting economy XXVII: Fiscal mismanagement threatens India's economic recovery. *Business Today*. https://www.businesstoday.in/opinion/columns/indian-economy-fiscal-management-threatens-indias-economic-recovery-covid19-crisis/story/416024.html

Mohanty, P. (2020f, 4 December). Taxing the untaxed VI: What are tax havens and why they matter to India. *Business Today*. https://www.businesstoday.in/current/economy-politics/taxing-the-untaxed-income-tax-havens-india-black-money-fdi-inflows-outflows-money-laundering/story/398614.html

Mondal, D. (2020, 31 July). Two years of hard work comes to naught as govt junks new GST return format. *Business Today*. https://www.businesstoday.in/current/economy-politics/two-years-of-hard-work-comes-to-naught-as-govt-junks-new-gst-return-format/story/411663.html

Narasimhan, T. E., & Babu, G. (2018, 15 December). Traders, MSMEs saw 3.5 mn job losses due to note ban, GST, other factors. *Business Standard*. https://www.business-standard.com/article/economy-policy/traders-msme-sector-lost-3-5-mn-jobs-in-4-5-yrs-over-note-ban-gst-survey-118121500645_1.html

NCAER. (2009, December). *Moving to Goods and Services Tax in India: Impact on India's growth and international trade* (Working Paper No. 103). https://www.ncaer.org/publication_details.php?pID=30

OECD. (2013). Action plan on base erosion and profit shifting. https://www.oecd.org/ctp/BEPSActionPlan.pdf

OECD. (2020). Revenue statistics 2020: Tax revenue trends in the OECD. http://www.oecd.org/tax/tax-policy/revenue-statistics-highlights-brochure.pdf

PIB. (2019, 20 September). Corporate tax rates slashed to 22% for domestic companies and 15% for new domestic manufacturing companies and other fiscal reliefs. https://pib.gov.in/Pressreleaseshare.aspx?PRID=1585641

PIB. (2021, 12 June). Change in GST rates on goods being used in Covid-19 relief and management. https://pib.gov.in/PressReleasePage.aspx?PRID=1726525

PPAC. (2013). All India study on sectoral demand of diesel & petrol. https://www.ppac.gov.in/WriteReadData/Reports/201411110329450069740AllIndiaStudyonSectoralDemandofDiesel.pdf

PTI. (2010, 22 July). GST to make India a $2 trillion economy: Pranab Mukherjee. *The Economic Times*. https://economictimes.indiatimes.com/news/economy/finance/gst-to-make-india-a-2-trillion-economy-pranab-mukherjee/articleshow/6201907.cms?from=mdr

PTI. (2020, 5 December). All states accept centre's borrowing plan for GST shortfall. *Bloomberg | Quint*. https://www.bloombergquint.com/gst/jharkhand-opts-in-all-states-accept-centres-borrowing-plan-for-gst-shortfall

Shome Committee. (2012). Final report on General Anti Avoidance Rules (GAAR) in Income-tax Act, 1961. https://www.finmin.nic.in/sites/default/files/report_gaar_itact1961.pdf

Sönnichsen, N. (2021, 7 June). Brent crude oil price annually 1976–2021. Statista. https://www.statista.com/statistics/262860/uk-brent-crude-oil-price-changes-since-1976/

The Hindu. (2018, 8 June). What revival? Close to 50,000 MSMEs Shut Up Shop in Tamil Nadu in Past Year. https://www.thehindu.com/news/national/tamil-nadu/what-revival-close-to-50000-units-shut-shop-in-past-year/article24107824.ece

The Hindu. (2021, 1 June). Congress CMs protest against exclusion from GoM on GST waiver for COVID-19 products. https://www.thehindu.com/news/national/cong-ministers-omission-from-gom-on-gst-exemption-to-covid-19-relief-material-deliberate/article34698358.ece

The Times of India. (2017, 1 July). GST: Freedom at midnight from tax terrorism, says PM Modi. http://timesofindia.indiatimes.com/articleshow/59394375.cms?utm_source=contentofinterest&utm_medium=text&utm_campaign=cppst

Thirteenth Finance Commission. (2009, 15 December). Report of the Task Force on Goods & Services Tax. https://fincomindia.nic.in/writereaddata/html_en_files/oldcommission_html/fincom13/discussion/report291209.pdf

Toplensky, R. (2018, 11 March). Multinationals pay lower taxes than a decade ago. *The Financial Times*. https://www.ft.com/content/2b356956-17fc-11e8-9376-4a6390addb44

Tørsløv, T. R., Ludvig, S. W., & Zucman, G. (2018). *The missing profits of nations* (NBER Working Paper No. 24701). NBER. https://www.nber.org/system/files/working_papers/w24701/w24701.pdf

World Bank. (2018, 1 January). Implementation of India's Goods and Services Tax: Design and International Comparison. https://documents.worldbank.org/en/publication/documents-reports/documentdetail/918831542619297197/implementation-of-india-s-goods-and-services-tax-design-and-international-comparison

V THE PANDEMIC CATASTROPHE

India was on a prolonged slowdown when the pandemic hit in early 2020 and India locked down from the midnight of 24–25 March 2020. The GDP growth had sequentially fallen from 8.3 per cent in FY2017 to 4 per cent in FY2020, which ended 6 days after the lockdown began.

The two big engines of the economy had already failed: consumption demand and private investment. The third engine, net exports, has been swinging wildly in the past few years due to import substitution policy since 2014, which has impacted both imports and exports (detailed in AatmaNirbhar Bharat chapter) and hence unreliable. That left the only engine working and capable of driving growth: government expenditure and investment, which didn't rise to the occasion. The GDP growth in FY2022 fell to –7.3 per cent and India's rank fell to 142 in comparative growth table (International Monetary Fund, 2021; Statistics Times, 2021).

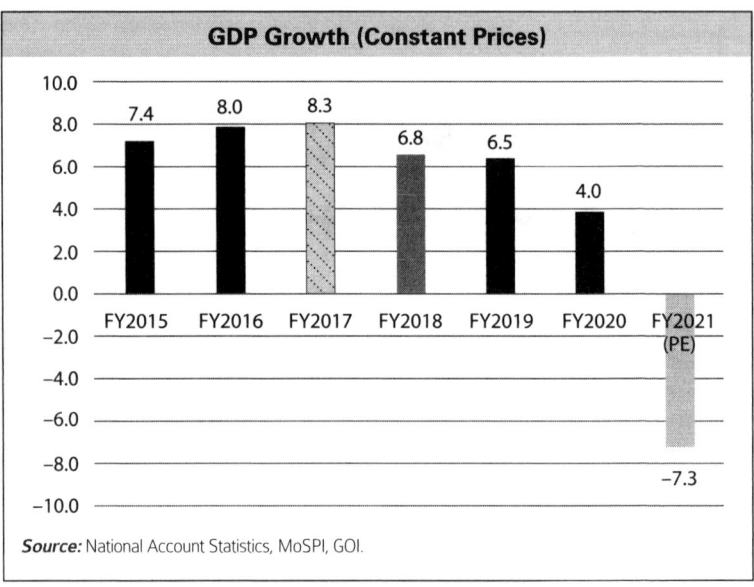

Source: National Account Statistics, MoSPI, GOI.

State of Economy before the Pandemic Hit

The Monthly Economic Report of the Finance Ministry on May 2019 was the first to ring an alarm bell over the pre-pandemic economic slowdown after paying the usual homilies. It read:

> The Indian economy is the fastest growing major economy and is projected to grow faster in the coming years. However, India's economy appears to have *slowed down* slightly in 2018–19. The proximate factors responsible for this slowdown include declining growth of private consumption, tepid increase in fixed investment, and muted exports.... (Ministry of Finance, 2019)

To understand what it meant, the growth rates of GDP components (expenditure)—private consumption (PFCE), government expenditure (GFCE), investment (GFCF), exports and imports (exports minus imports are considered for GDP calculations)—need to be looked at. The graph above maps their growth since FY2015 (MoSPI, 2021).

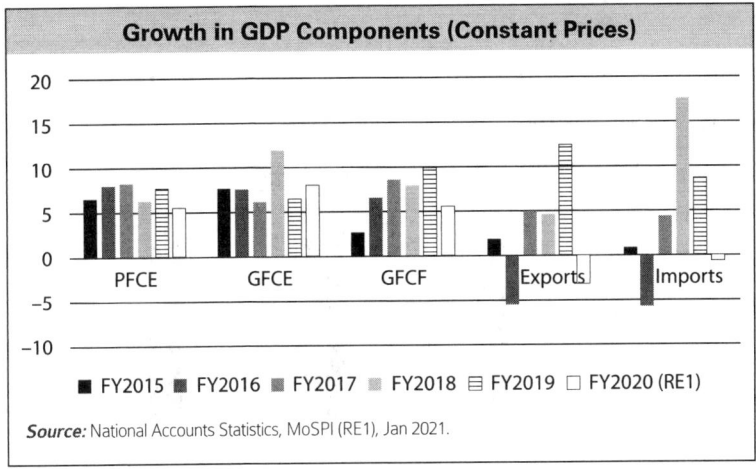

Source: National Accounts Statistics, MoSPI (RE1), Jan 2021.

According to the figure above, as the pandemic hit India:

1. Growth in private consumption—the main engine of growth contributing to 56–57 per cent to the GDP—was falling from a high of 8.1 per cent in FY2017 to 5.5 per cent in FY2020.
2. Growth in government expenditure (GFCE)—contributing about 10 per cent to the GDP—was falling from a high of 11.9 per cent in FY2018 to 7.9 per cent in FY2020.
3. Growth in investment (GFCF)—contributing about 32 per cent to the GDP—was falling from a high of 9.9 per cent in FY2019 to 5.4 per cent in FY2020.
4. Growth in exports and imports were wildly fluctuating and turned negative in FY2020.

The sectoral growth showed that while growth in agriculture and services were positive in FY2020, industry and its largest component, manufacturing, had taken a big hit, shrinking well below the zero mark in FY2020. The services sector was slowing down, though it still grew by more than 6 per cent in FY2020.

The slowing down of private consumption (PFCE) seen in the earlier graph had impacted industrial production as measured by capacity utilization (CU) and IIP. CU fell below 70 per cent for the first time in a decade in all four quarters of FY2020. Last

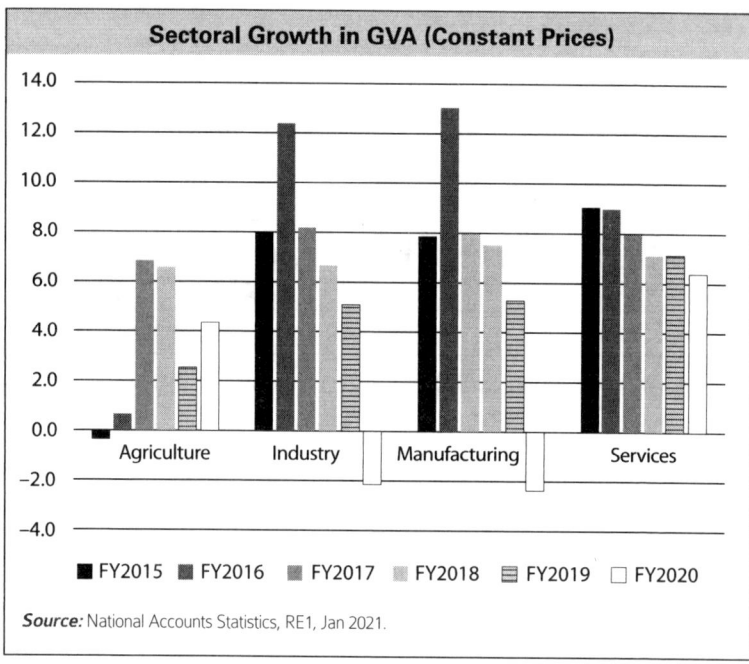

time, it had touched 80 per cent in Q4 of FY2011. Growth in manufacturing IIP (annual) turned negative for the first time in FY2020 since the new GDP series of 2011–2012 started to –1.4 per cent.

The following graph, taken from the RBI's 2020 report, maps this fall on a quarterly basis. CU is on the left-hand-side axis and growth in manufacturing is on the right-hand-side axis (RBI, 2020a).

Lower production of goods and services also meant lower demand for capital investment by industry. While the growth in bank credit to the non-food sector fell from 8.6 per cent in FY2015 to 6.7 per cent in FY2020, it was only 0.7 per cent and 0.6 per cent, respectively, for industry and, its component, large industry. Counter-intuitively, growth in credit to industry in FY2017 was negative when the GDP grew at 8.3 per cent—maximum in the 2011–2012 series. That was the year of demonetization too.

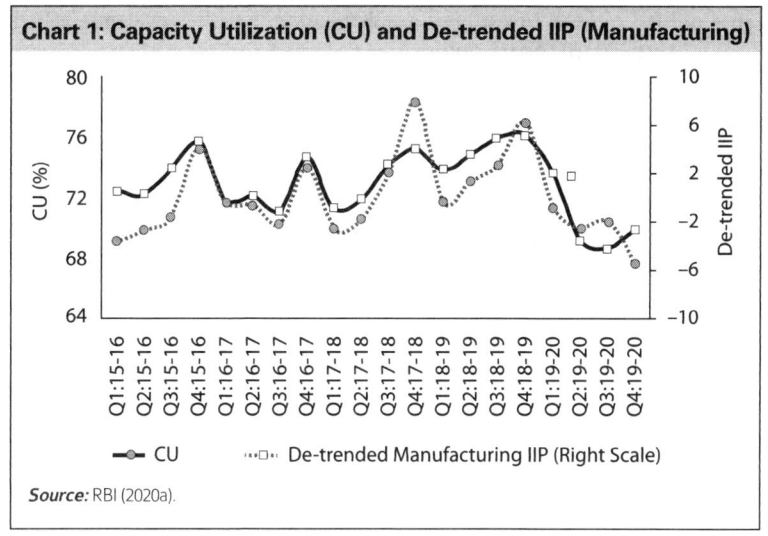

Source: RBI (2020a).

When industry's need for fresh investment is absent, it makes little difference to the supply of cheap credit, except for boosting stock markets. That is why the massive corporate tax cut in September 2019 (₹1.45 lakh crore) when revenues were drying up and growth had slowed down neither made

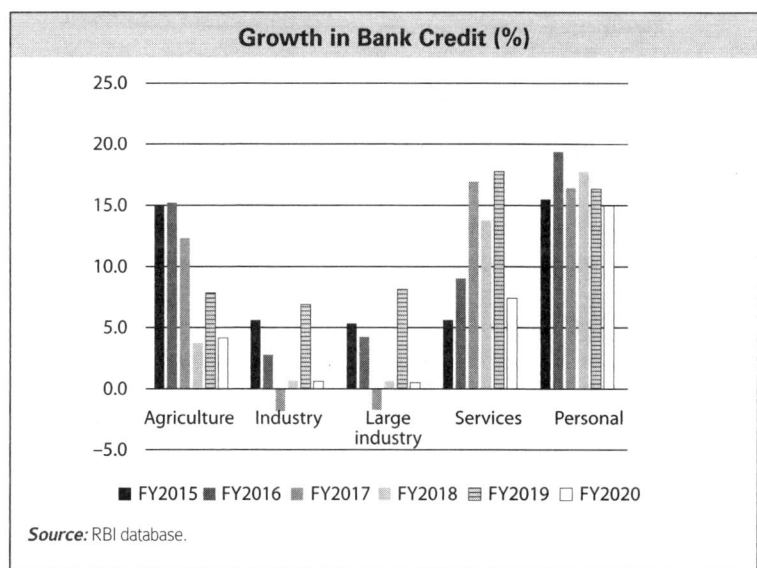

Source: RBI database.

The Pandemic Catastrophe | 119

sense nor led to fresh investment or job creation that the government had promised. The RBI's 2019–2020 annual report later revealed that the tax cut was used for 'debt servicing, build-up of cash balances and other current assets rather than restarting the capex cycle' (RBI, 2020b).

Decline in Household Income

The growth slowdown and massive job and business losses due to demonetization and GST impoverished Indians, which was reflected in a declining trend in household savings from FY2015 level. If compared with FY2012 level, the fall is even more stark. Household savings are the biggest source of investment for the economy, contributing to more than 60 per cent of gross domestic savings. Gross household savings fell to 19.6 per cent in FY2020 from a high of 23.6 per cent in FY2012 (MoSPI, 2021).

A remarkable feature of this fall is the decline in physical assets (including gold and silver ornaments), while net financial savings (savings minus borrowings) remained virtually flat. The decline in physical assets (house, land, farm implements, gold and silver ornaments, etc.), particularly from

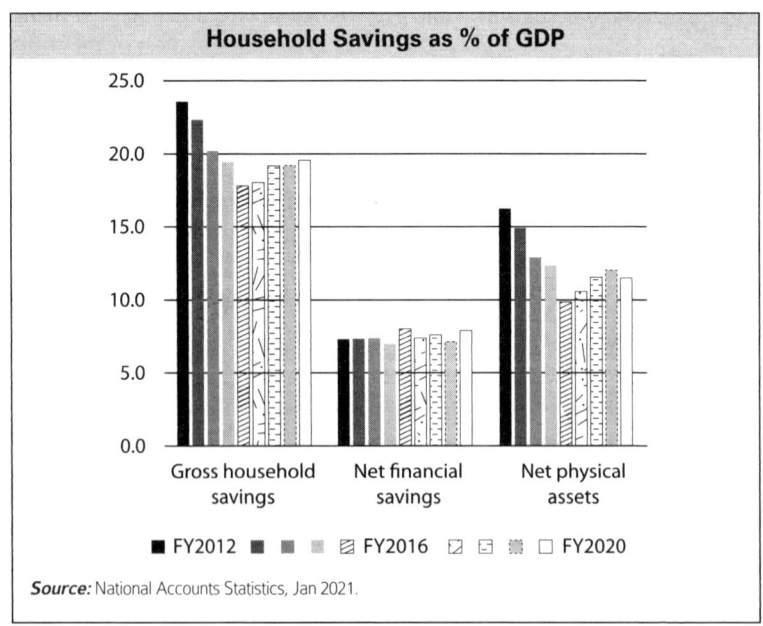

FY2012 and FY2015 levels, could mean liquidation of physical assets to meet existential needs such as food, health, education and marriage. The maximum dip in gross household savings and physical assets was in FY2016—the year of demonetization.

In India, household consumption expenditure survey is used as a proxy for household incomes and financial health. The last one was in 2011–2012. The 2017–2018 survey results were withheld for showing a fall for the first time in 40 years from monthly per capita consumer expenditure (MPCE) of ₹1,501 in 2011–2012 to ₹1,446 in 2017–2018. No fresh survey has been carried even in the face of demonetization and GST, which would have reduced it further (Jha, 2019).

The per capita GDP is not a suitable measure for financial health of households as it reflects the combined income of households, governments and corporations. Further, household incomes include non-corporations, such as partnership firms, trusts and HUF. Yet growth in per capita disposable income (per capita GNDI) fell to 6.8 per cent in FY2020 from a high of 12.2 per cent in FY2013 (MoSPI, 2021).

The previous few years witnessed a sharp decline in rural and corporate wages also, which is another evidence of growing impoverishment of people. An SBI research paper showed that both urban and rural wage growths had slowed down, further reducing consumption demand. Urban wages (nominal) fell from high double digit (peaked at 20.5% in FY2011) down to single digit in FY2019 due to financial crisis (growing NPAs first in banks and then non-banking financial companies [NBFCs] in 2018 with the collapse of Infrastructure Leasing & Financial Services [IL&FS]). Rural wage (nominal) growth also declined from high double digits (peaked at 27.7% in FY2014) to less than 5 per cent during FY2017–FY2019 (reproduced below; Dey, 2019).

The previous chapters have elaborated many economic and political misadventures that created intellectual and information vacuum, weakened democratic checks and balances and removed scope for public debates, consultations and dissent. All of these opened the space for non-planned, top-down and self-serving policymaking that inflicted immense and avoidable pain on the people and devastated informal economy, which contributes about 50 per cent to the GDP. Fiscal mismanagement, ineptitude and incompetence in managing the economy have also contributed

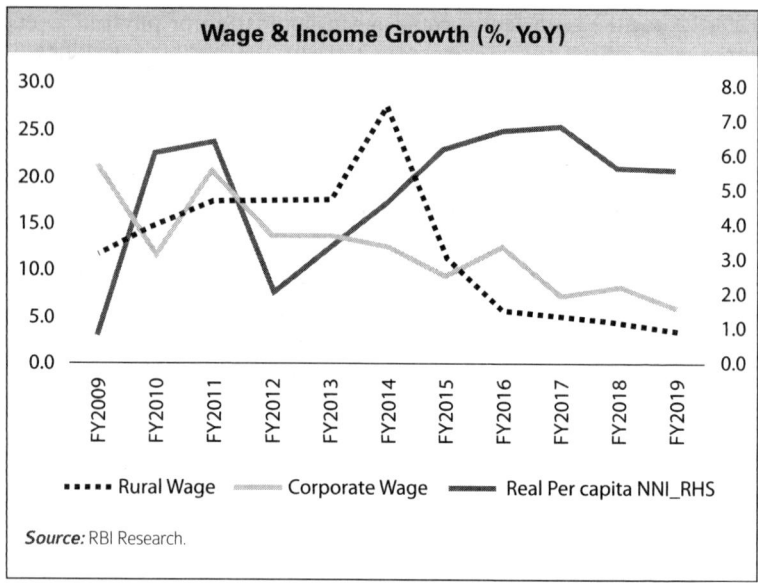

Source: RBI Research.

to the slowing down of growth rate to 4 per cent in FY2020 and the consequent poverty of the people (Mohanty, 2020b; NSC, 2012).

Then the pandemic struck.

First Wave of the Pandemic

On 24 March 2020, the prime minister announced a pandemic lockdown during a national address at 8 PM. He said that the entire country would completely shut down all social and economic activities and impose a strict curfew on all but for emergency services at four hours' notice. There was no prior consultation even with central ministries as an RTI response will reveal later (PIB, 2020c; Purohit & Parmar, 2021).

It was one of the most stringent in the world, as a comparative study by Oxford University showed. The sudden announcement created panic, trapping people everywhere, in bus stands, railway stations and airports. People rushed to the markets and banks to stock up daily provisions and cash. The government revoked the NDMA of 2005 to enforce a 24×7 curfew (*India Today*, 2020).

This was unnecessary for many reasons.

By 23 March, most states/UTs had imposed localized lockdowns. The centre's statement of the day was: '30 States/UTs have imposed complete lockdown in the entire States/UTs covering 548 districts'; '3 States/UTs have imposed lockdown in certain areas of their territories (58 districts) and 1 UT has imposed closure of some activities in their areas.' Only Sikkim and Mizoram (12 districts) had not done so. There was no palpable panic, and the restrictions were localized (PIB, 2020b).

Untimely Locking and Unlocking

The lockdown was untimely too. On 25 March, India's total Covid-19 cases were 657 with total 12 deaths.

When the unlocking began on 1 June, it was the time to lock down. The total cases stood at 1.98 lakh, daily cases 7,761 and total deaths 5,608 on 1 June. The following graph maps how the lockdown and unlocking panned out.

The pandemic was mismanaged. Although the centre invoked the NDMA and micromanaged every activity, poor management was evident. On 26 March, a day after the lockdown, Cabinet Secretary Rajiv

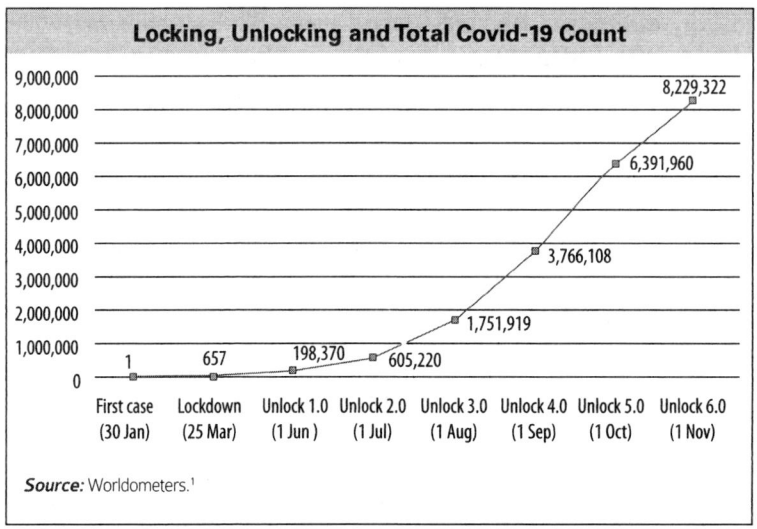

Source: Worldometers.[1]

---

[1] https://www.worldometers.info/coronavirus/#countries

Gauba wrote to chief secretaries of states/UTs telling them about a gap between 'more than 15 lakh incoming international passengers', who had come in during 18 January–23 March, and those being monitored. These were the potential carriers of the virus. Since the letter also claimed that the centre was monitoring all international airports, it showed its own mishandling (Gauba, 2020).

Distress Migration

India witnessed a mass distress migration that no other country witnessed. In its affidavit to the Supreme Court on 31 March, it said, '5–6 lakh persons' had walked hundreds of miles to their homes in rural India by then, within 7 days of the lockdown and expressed fear that the virus would spread to rural areas which had 'remained untouched so far'. Then it said that *one-third of the 'barefoot' migrants* could be carrying the virus. By August, 54 per cent of total cases were reported from rural areas. Yet there was little attempt to provide shelter, food, testing or quarantine facilities to the migrants. The task was left to states/UTs. Millions of migrant workers had been trapped in urban areas and walked home with family and luggage in sheer desperation, having lost jobs and shelters (factory owners and landlords evicted them; Bindra & Sharma, 2020; Pandey, 2020; SBI, 2020b; Supreme Court of India, 2020).

When Delhi provided buses to ferry them, FIRs were filed against 44 DTC drivers for violating the curfew. Special trains would start only in May, until then the migrants were beaten and humiliated by police across the country. In all, 11.4 million workers went back to their rural homes and about 971 perished on the way due to exhaustion and accidents, with 96 dying in trains (ANI, 2020; Ministry of Labour and Employment, 2021; Paliath, 2021).

Ironically, the Indian Railways, which ferried 6.29 million workers and their families (of 11.4 million who went back) charged full ticket prices and made a profit of ₹*428 crore*, as it revealed in response to an RTI query. The Railways is fully public owned and entirely run and managed with public money. A national crisis was not the time for profit-making, especially after it declared to donate ₹151 crore to the PM CARES Fund—a supposedly public charitable trust headed by

Prime Minister Narendra Modi but is run as a private body not open to public scrutiny or subject to the RTI Act of 2005 (Jain, 2021; Ministry of Railways, 2020).

Migrant workers received neither cash assistance nor rations. More than a year later, there is still no database, no policy and no ration for these migrant workers. On 11 June 2021, the apex court ordered states/UTs to provide free ration to migrants, irrespective of whether they have ration cards or not, and also questioned the centre's claim of providing them free ration when the one-nation-one-ration-card scheme had not been implemented fully (Paliath, 2021; PTI, 2021d).

The OECD countries protected 50 million jobs during their lockdowns by using their existing 'job retention (JR) schemes', which also 'buttressed aggregate demand by supporting the incomes of workers'. The USA spent millions on unemployment allowance; one report stated that by mid-February 2021, 18 million workers were getting such benefits. It didn't track job loss, paid no unemployment allowances and its new labour codes passed during the pandemic don't even mention it (Liu, 2021; Mohanty, 2020e; OECD, 2020).

Healthcare Collapsed

As expected, the pandemic exposed India's poor healthcare infrastructure. When the daily cases hit close to 100,000 in September 2020, all states, particularly metro cities of Delhi and Mumbai, found hospital beds and healthcare workers grossly inadequate and the healthcare was *on the brink of collapse*. India already had a *shortage of 600,000 doctors and 2 million nurses*. Private healthcare, which dominates the healthcare sector, was forced into pandemic care by using the *NDMA of 2005*, as most of them had closed shop (Mohanty, 2020a; Wallen, 2020).

The AatmaNirbhar Bharat relief packages of more than ₹20 lakh crore earmarked ₹15,000 crore for ramping up healthcare, but the fine print stated that only *₹7,774 crore* were allocated for FY2020, and the rest for the next four years. The total packages of ₹23.66 lakh crore only had a fiscal outgo of 1.6 per cent of the GDP, the SBI's estimates showed, the rest were liquidity infusion by way of cheap credit, credit guarantee schemes, etc. (PIB, 2020d; SBI, 2020b).

In November 2020, the Parliamentary Standing Committee on Health exposed multiple failures of India's pandemic care, warning against a second wave and asked the centre to prepare for it. All of this would be ignored. Some of the key points the panel made were as follows:

1. Inadequate healthcare spending with no focused budget for Covid.
2. Inadequate primary and secondary healthcare infrastructure and staffing in many areas.
3. Need higher investment 'in public health' and decentralization of healthcare.
4. Disruption of medical services for non-Covid patients during lockdown paralyzed the delivery of essential healthcare services, leading to hundreds of non-Covid deaths, such as pregnant women and children.
5. Out-of-pocket expenditure 'may have further driven many families to below poverty line'.
6. Arriving at a sustainable pricing model to treat Covid patients could have averted many deaths.
7. 'Private hospitals charging exorbitant medical fees' which were beyond the reach of many people.
8. 'A second wave of COVID has been witnessed in European countries and the Committee, therefore, feels that India must also be prepared'; there should be no superspreading festive events; healthcare infrastructure should be strengthened and 'adequate production of oxygen' should be ensured (Parliament of India, 2020).

Yet not one additional hospital was set up by the centre during the pandemic, though 'bhoomi puja' was held for a grand temple in Ayodhya (August 2020), two Boeing aircrafts were brought for VVIPs at ₹8,400 crore (October 2020), the Central Vista redevelopment was sanctioned (₹20,000 crore) and the Motera stadium in Gujarat was rebuilt (opened in February 2021; Mohanty, 2020d; PTI, 2020b).

Private Healthcare

Private healthcare, *providing/controlling 78 per cent and 74 per cent* of inpatient care in urban and rural areas, respectively, failed to rise up to the occasion. In spite of invoking the NDMA, the CEO of the National Health Authority had to 'appeal' for help. Several states issued multiple warnings to provide non-Covid care, as most of them had closed shop (Bhushan, 2020; Mohanty, 2020b; Kumar & Singh, 2016).

The centre showed a marked favour towards private healthcare. While RT-PCR tests for Covid were free in government hospitals, private hospitals were allowed to charge ₹4,500—far more than ₹600 at which the test kit was being supplied by the centre (HC, 2020).

Meanwhile, private healthcare continued to fleece patients as the centre didn't cap vital items like N95 masks, personal protective equipment, face shields, goggles and charges for hospital beds and intensive cares. For Delhi's private hospitals, the centre fixed very high rates and then, on court intervention, cut down hospitalization charges by one-third. The new rates were beyond the reach of ordinary households, ranging from ₹8,000 to ₹18,000 per day for a hospital bed, when the average household monthly income (MPCE) of Indians is less than ₹1,500, as the 2017–2018 NSSO survey of household consumption expenditure had shown (Bhuyan, 2020; Ministry of Home Affairs, 2020).

In the midst of the pandemic, the centre, through the NITI Aayog and budget for FY2021, pressed for the PPP model with a viability gap funding (VGF) of 40 per cent for building new private medical colleges, not hospitals. Both asked states to hand over government district hospitals to these colleges for running, besides providing unencumbered land and other incentives for these private medical colleges (Ministry of Finance, 2020; Sharma, 2020a).

Non-scientific Remedies

In the meanwhile, the centre turned backwards and actively promoted untested and unscientific traditional systems of cure such as Ayurveda, homeopathy, Unani and Siddha for the Covid treatment. The Ministry of Ayush asked people to sip water boiled with *tulsi* (*Ocimum sanctum*) and take 'Arsenicum album 30' (a homeopathic drug) as a cure. One minister asked people to sunbathe and another promoted 'Bhabhiji' papad as a cure. 'Gaumutra party' was organized in Delhi to promote cow urine as the cure (The Week, 2020; PIB, 2020a, PTI, 2020a; Shukla, 2020).

Prime Minister Modi talked in favour of *Ayurveda* at the World Economic Forum (WEF) conclave in January 2021. V. K. Paul, NITI Aayog member at the forefront of India's fight against the pandemic, told people to consult Ayurveda practitioners and consume *chyawanprash* and *kadha* (a brew of herbs and spices). Just before the devastating second wave hit, Health Minister Vardhan and his cabinet colleague Nitin Gadkari launched yoga guru Ramdev's herbal concoction *Coronil* in February 2021, presenting it as 'the first evidence-based medicine for corona' approved by the WHO, which promptly denied it (*Hindustan Times*, 2021; Menon, 2021; PM India, 2021).

Devastating Second Wave

In spite of advance warning of a second wave from the parliamentary panel in November 2020 and repeated warning from the scientists of Indian SARS-CoV-2 Genomics Consortium in early March 2021, which also alerted about the 'Delta' variant taking hold, India was grossly unprepared when it hit and peaked in April–May 2021 (Ghoshal & Das, 2021).

India emerged as the epicentre of the global pandemic as it drove up the global numbers dramatically with daily cases reaching 400,000 and daily deaths reaching 4,000 in May 2021 as against less than 100,000 daily cases and only 2,000 daily deaths during the first wave of the pandemic. The WHO described the Indian situation 'beyond heartbreaking' (Reuters, 2021; Slater, 2021).

In fact, devastations were waiting to happen.

State after state had shut down temporary special Covid-care centres that had been set up in January and February 2021, thereby reducing capacity, some of these, such as Delhi, Uttar Pradesh, Karnataka, Maharashtra, were hit harder. India organized two big superspreader events: the Kumbh at Haridwar and prolonged 8-phase elections in West Bengal and other states in March–April 2021. About *9.1 million people* took to mass bathing and, as feared, cases spread to Gujarat, Madhya Pradesh, Odisha and other states (Rawat, 2021). Uttarakhand saw *1800 per cent spike*. It *spread the variants* prevalent in one region to another region (Pandey, 2021, 10 May; *The Indian Express*, 2021b; *The Quint*, 2021).

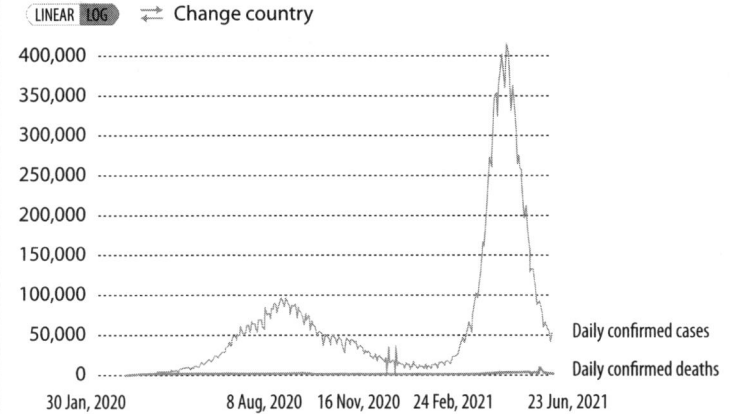

The same happened with the state elections. The states that held elections saw a *huge spike* in virus cases and deaths; the panchayat elections in Uttar Pradesh reportedly claimed more than *1,600 teachers* on poll duty (Menon and Goodman, 2021; *India Today*, 2021).

In the midst of a raging second wave, the Prime Minister held a series of election rallies and boasted about a massive public gathering. That is not surprising because he had already claimed success against the virus by telling the WEF in January 2021 that India '*saved humanity from a big disaster* by containing corona effectively'. Health Minister Harsh Vardhan declared in March that India was 'in the *end game* of the COVID-19 pandemic'; he also dismissed the second wave saying "I don't think it is some classical second wave or something" (NDTV, 2021; PM India, 2021; PTI, 2021a; Salyal, 2021).

While India had locked down at the total cases of 657 in 2020, the prime minister ruled out a national lockdown and asked states to create

The Pandemic Catastrophe

'micro-containment zones' on 20 April 2021—the day India reported 295,158 daily cases and 2,023 daily deaths[2] (ANI, 2021).

As people died inside and outside of hospitals due to a lack of oxygen, equipment, medicines and hospital beds, people desperately took to social media to send SOS messages. There was no central helpline to assist them. While domestic media remained circumspect, international media reported that the system had *collapsed*, people had been 'abandoned' to their fate during the gravest crisis in the past 100 years and the Indian state, confronted with the catastrophe, literally 'melted away' (*The Economist*, 2021a; *The Guardian*, 2021a, 2021b).

Such was the state that an Indian Army commander sought Bollywood actor Sonu Sood's help to set up a 200-bed Covid care hospital at the Jaisalmer military station. The Youth Congress, and its hitherto unknown leader B. V. Srinivas, emerged as the saviour to which foreign ambassies ran for help (Chhina, 2021a, 2021c; *Scroll.in*, 2021a).

Waking up belatedly, India sent an SOS for oxygen, medicines, equipment and vaccines. *Over 40 countries*, including the USA, the UK, China and Russia, rushed immediate supplies. Hundreds of tonnes of emergency relief supplies reached India, but were held up for days at the Delhi airport because the government was unsure about the GST rates to be applied even as hospitals and people made desperate SOS calls and many died without help. The pile was freed only after public outcry and court intervention (Mohan, 2021; Roche, 2021; Saikia & Sharma, 2021).

Rural areas were left to fend for themselves without tests, doctors, hospital beds and medicines. Multiple high courts and the apex court had to intervene and issue daily directives to the centre and states for ensuring better healthcare. For days, India was haunted by unclaimed bodies floating in the Ganga, thousands buried in its sand banks in Uttar Pradesh, Bihar and other rivers in Madhya Pradesh (Dubey, 2021; Mishra, 2021; *Scroll.in*, 2021b).

Vaccines: From Self-sufficient to Importer

The vaccine remains the only effective antidote to the virus that can save from the pandemic, but India failed here too.

---

[2] https://ourworldindata.org/coronavirus-data?country=~IND

First, it *delayed* in the ordering of vaccines. Developed countries such as the USA, the UK, Australia, Japan and Germany placed their vaccine orders (for Pfizer-BioNTech, Moderna, Novavax, Janssen, AstraZeneca, etc.) from May 2020 onwards. India waited till *January 2021* to order domestically developed Covaxin and AstraZeneca. *Orders were placed only for 16.5 million doses*, which was grossly inadequate for a country of 1.34 billion people, while countries with smaller populations had placed 150–800 million doses. Japan, which had a lower caseload, ordered 220 million (Mudur, 2021).

Second, India didn't spend any money on vaccine development—as it told the Supreme Court in an affidavit—unlike Western countries, which poured in billions of dollars. The Serum Institute of India (SII) producing Covishield was committed to supply 50 per cent of the vaccines to poor countries. Nevertheless, India controlled the export of Covishield (directing how many doses should be sent and when) and turned exports into a photo op (Prabhala & Menghaney, 2021a; Supreme Court of India, 2021a).

Third, the prime minister undermined vaccination by telling chief ministers amid the second wave on 8 April 2021 that 'we had won the war without vaccines' in response to their complaints of vaccine shortages. Earlier, in March 2021, Vardhan had told the Lok Sabha that all adults need not be vaccinated and there would be no universal vaccination (Ghosh, 2021; Sharma, 2021; *The Indian Express*, 2021a).

Fourth, India exported more vaccine abroad in its 'Vaccine Maitri' programme than it used for its own people, as it claimed in the UN. Then it stopped the export of vaccines altogether, thereby wrecking the global *COVAX plan*, under which the SII had received license to manufacture AstraZeneca's Covishield and supply vaccines to 92 poor countries, including India, thereby covering 50 per cent of the world population (4 billion). By stopping export and attempting to doing so, it created a risk of prolonging the pandemic for the world. Its neighbours Bangladesh, Nepal and Sri Lanka faced severe vaccine shortages because of this (Chowdhury, 2021; Prabhala & Menghaney, 2021; PTI, 2021b).

Then it sought vaccines from abroad, which is ironic as India is the largest vaccine maker in the world, manufactures more than *60 per cent of all vaccines sold* across the globe. But the public infrastructure was kept idle and two private manufacturers, SII producing Covishield and Bharat Biotech (BB) producing Covaxin, were granted monopolies, ignoring their limited capacities. India turned from a *mass exporter of vaccines to net importer* causing further global concern because it was part of the global plan to vaccinate 91 poor countries (Chowdhury, 2021; Roy et al., 2020).

India didn't evoke *compulsory licensing* to ramp up vaccine production, even though the Covaxin was based on the SARS-CoV-2 strain isolated in the National Institute of Virology in Pune, which functions under the ICMR, which transferred this strain to BB for the vaccine. India opposed evoking compulsory licensing, telling the Supreme Court about 'serious, severe and unintended adverse consequences' but lobbied hard *patent waiver* at the WTO not over all vaccines but also other Covid medicines (Ramakumar, 2021; Sidhartha, 2021; Supreme Court of India, 2021a).

An investigative report stated that India's seven public vaccine manufacturing institutes, which ensured vaccine security for decades, were 'sitting idle'. Yet, when Russian vaccine Sputnik V was approved, it was given to the private firm SII by the centre, despite SII's apparent failure to meet its commitment to supply vaccines to 91 poor countries (PTI, 2021c; Varshney, 2021).

India's vaccine shortage and reliance on foreign supply could have been avoided if the country had enacted mandatory licencing and allowed public sector firms to operate.

Truth be told, India's pandemic vaccine programme was misdirected from the get-go.

Covaxin was cleared under suspicious circumstances in a 'clinical trial mode', without its efficacy known, in January 2021, when a host of approved vaccines, including Covishield manufactured by India's SII, was available. The WHO didn't approve it in the absence of adequate data until the end of June 2021 (Parashar, 2021a; Ravikumar, 2021).

India started producing Sputnik V which hadn't received the WHO's approval. Further, accused of not spending to ramp up production, India promptly announced paying ₹1,500 crore for 300 million doses to an

Indian private vaccine manufacturer, Biological E, which was *undergoing third phase of trial* for efficacy (*Mint*, 2021; *The Indian Express*, 2021d).

Then, there was the 'liberalized' vaccine policy.

'Liberalized' Vaccine Policy

In another disastrous decision, the centre unilaterally reversed India's time-tested universal vaccination programme by announcing a 'Liberalised and Accelerated Phase 3 Strategy of Covid-19 Vaccination' on 19 April 2021 for *18–44 age group*.

Under this policy, two private vaccine manufacturers, SII and BB, were 'empowered' to supply *50 per cent* of their vaccines to states and in the open market 'at a pre-declared price'. The reason? The policy statement read:

> This would 'augment vaccine production as well as availability, incentivising vaccine manufacturers to rapidly ramp up their production as well as attract new vaccine manufacturers, domestic and international. It would also make pricing, procurement, eligibility and administration of vaccines open and flexible, allowing all stakeholders the flexibility to customise to local needs and dynamics'. (PIB, 2021a)

This meant the following: (a) the responsibility of vaccinating 18–44 age group was passed on to state governments and private hospitals, and (b) private companies were now allowed to fix differential pricing. The SII promptly priced Covishield at ₹400 per dose for states (later reduced to ₹300) and at ₹600 per dose for private hospitals; the BB priced Covaxin at ₹600 and ₹1,200, respectively, for states and private hospitals. The centre was buying both at *₹150 per dose* (ENS Economic Bureau, 2021; Raghavan, 2021).

Later, it was revealed that the 'liberalization' policy was against the advice of the National Technical Advisory Group on Immunisation (NTAGI) and the decision was taken without considering the availability of vaccines or ramping up capacity. It was also revealed by the private manufacturers that the differential pricing had the prior approval from the highest authority, with whom they had 'shared details on the cost of production and markup' (*The Economic Times*, 2021a; Singh, 2021; *The Economic Times*, 2021b).

The Supreme Court called the 'liberalized' policy 'arbitrary and irrational', prima facie violating Article 14 (right to equality before law) and Article 21 (right to life), and questioned the government on the logic of 'paid vaccination' when ₹35,000 crore had been allocated in the budget. It also questioned the precondition of registering to the CoWIN app, reminding the centre of the digital divide and deprivations of rural population (Roy, 2021a, 2021b; Supreme Court of India, 2021b).

A week later, the 'liberalized' policy was partially rolled back. The centre decided to buy the states' share of 25 per cent vaccines, taking the central procurement to 75 per cent. The rest 25 per cent was left for private trade between private manufacturers and private hospitals (*The Hindu*, 2021).

The centre then fixed a private trade rate between private hospitals and private manufacturers: Covishield at ₹780, Covaxin at ₹1,100 and Sputnik V (being produced by SII) at ₹1,145 per dose, including 5 per cent GST and ₹150 service charges (PIB, 2021b).

Then the centre increased the gap between two doses of Covishield from 6–8 weeks to 12–16 weeks on 13 May amid rising cases and vaccine shortage, saying that this was recommended by the scientific group NTAGI based on real-life evidence of the UK. Several members of the NTAGI later disclosed that they didn't back doubling the gap, rather they proposed increasing the gap to 8–12 weeks as advised by the WHO (Das & Ghoshal, 2021c).

Under-reporting

The official data on the devastation caused by the second wave in number of cases and deaths are grossly under-reported. *The Economist*'s estimates showed that the actual deaths were *six times* higher during the second wave. Its estimates of May 2021 showed that when India was reporting about 4,000 deaths a day, there were 6,000–31,000 excess deaths per day. *The New York Times* estimate showed that by 24 May, India more likely had 539 million Covid-19 cases, against the official number of 26.9 million, and 1.6 million deaths against the official number of 307,231. Dr Bhramar Mukherjee of the Institute for Health Metrics and Evaluation, University of Washington, estimated India's under-reporting of cases by a factor of 20 and that of deaths by a factor of 4 or 5 (Gamio & Glanz, 2021; Mukherjee, 2021; *The Economist*, 2021b, 2021c).

The government dismissed these reports as 'misinformed', 'baseless' and 'false', but ground reports proved otherwise. Two intrepid reporters checked out crematoriums in six cities—Patna, Kanpur, Jamnagar, Morbi, Rajkot and Porbandar—across three states of Gujarat, Uttar Pradesh and Bihar to claim that the actual death count was 3 to 30 times more than the official data (Purohit & Aafaq, 2021).

Later in June, Bihar carried out a survey at the Patna High Court's directive, and the total death toll jumped from 5,424 to 9,375 on 8 June (73% rise). Jharkhand's survey revealed a 43 per cent increase in deaths in April–May 2021 from what had been registered in April–May 2019. In Telangana, the scrutiny of death certificates found 'excess deaths' registered with the municipality of Hyderabad during April–May 2021, which was more than *10 times* the officially recorded 3,275 Covid deaths for the corresponding period in the entire state (Kumar, 2021; Ramani, 2021).

Under-reporting of deaths is not unusual. The latest Census report on medical certification of cause of death, released in June 2021, states that only 20.7 per cent registered deaths were medically certified for cause in 2019. This is a fall by 0.4 percentage point from 2018 (21.1%). There have been complaints of hospitals not certifying Covid deaths as per the WHO guidelines, forcing the Supreme Court to ask for proper guidelines to certify Covid deaths (Office of the Registrar General of India, 2021; Vaidyanathan, 2021).

A major cause of under-reporting by India is also because of its low Covid testing. Worldometers' data show that by the end of June 2021, India's Covid tests per million was abysmally low at less than 0.29 million, while the average of the top 10 countries with highest cases was 1 million or *3.5 times more*.

Global Comparison

Globally, the USA tops the list in total number of Covid cases at 34.5 million, India is second at 30.1 million, as on 25 June 2021. In terms of death count, India is third (393,338) after the USA (618,685) and Brazil (509,282). If per million cases and deaths are considered, India's counts are on the lower side, meaning it has done better.

The following graph provides a comparative picture of per million total cases and deaths for the top 5 countries in terms of total number of cases.

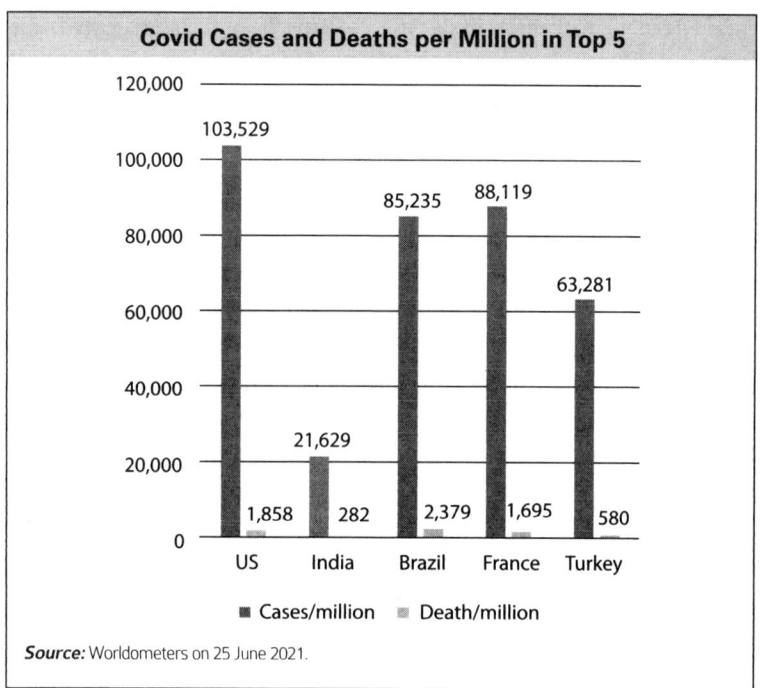

However, this is also the case with African and Asian countries. The Worldometer, which provides data for 49 Asian (including India) and 58 African countries, shows that the average of total cases per million for these 107 countries is 20,417 and total deaths per million is (on average) 227.15, which are less than India's. Why these numbers are less for African and Asian countries is a matter of scientific study.

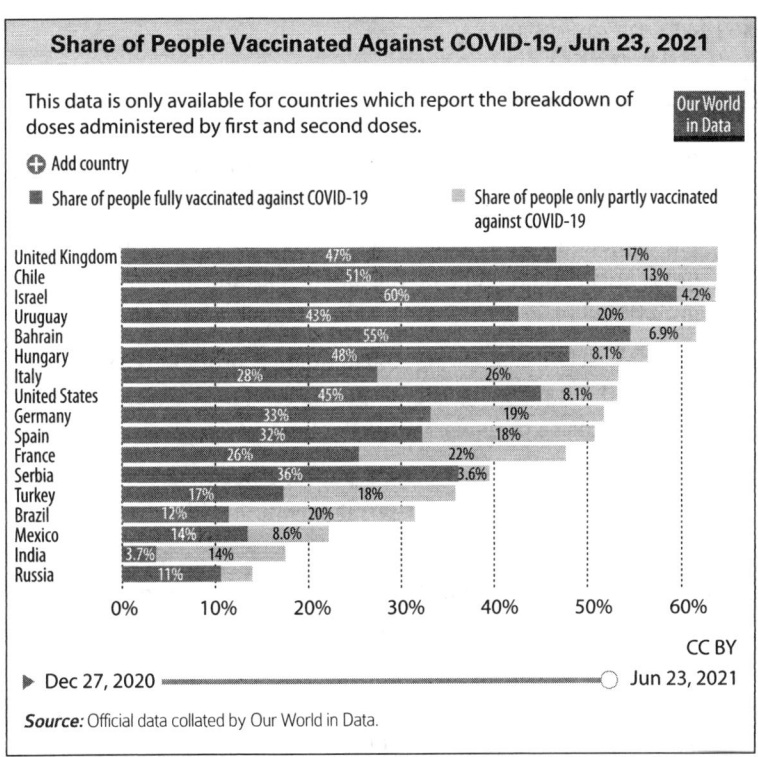

India's botched vaccination drive has ensured that once the vaccine maker of the world now lags by far behind when it comes to vaccinating its population. A comparative analysis shows that India had managed to vaccinate only 3.7 per cent of its population fully and 14 per cent partially (single dose) as on 25 June 2021. Global leaders such as the UK had fully vaccinated 47 per cent of its population, Israel 51 per cent, the USA 45 per cent, France 26 per cent, Turkey 17 per cent and Brazil 12 per cent in comparison.

Since vaccine is the best bet against Covid-19 and the threat of a third wave with 'Delta Plus' has been already recognized as a variant and three other variants are emerging as a new concern, India must vaccinate its entire population at the earliest. Else, India risks a prolonged pandemic (Akbar, 2021).

Takeaways

- Before the pandemic hit, India's growth had been sinking with FY2020 growth down at 4 per cent from 8.3 per cent in FY2017.
- The pandemic hit all countries, but India was hit harder due to gross mismanagement of the pandemic and the economy. Its growth fell to −7.3 per cent—one of the slowest in the world.
- Ignoring science, abjuring consultations, promoting pseudoscience and not planning and preparing for the situation cost India dearly in terms of unwarranted deaths and sickness.
- The pandemic exposed India's pathetic healthcare system and the policy of promoting for-profit private healthcare at the cost of public healthcare.
- Its botched vaccination drive has endangered lives of Indians and that of 91 poor countries depending on India for Covishield supply.
- India has fully vaccinated a small fraction of its population. It needs to ramp up vaccination without delay.

References

Akbar, S. (2021, 28 June). Watch out for four emerging variants of coronavirus, warn health experts. *The Times of India*. https://timesofindia.indiatimes.com/india/experts-watch-out-for-four-emerging-variants/articleshow/83907102.cms

ANI. (2020, 1 April). FIR against DTC drivers. https://www.dropbox.com/s/3351402aj2lrtac/FIR%20against%20DTC%20drivers.jpg?dl=0

ANI. (2021, 20 April). PM Modi urges states to consider lockdowns as last option, focus on micro-containment zones. https://www.aninews.in/news/national/general-news/pm-modi-urges-states-to-consider-lockdowns-as-last-option-focus-on-micro-containment-zones20210420221102/

Bhushan, I. (2020, 16 April). Private sector must be a wholehearted partner of government in fight against COVID-19. *The Indian Express*. https://indianexpress.com/article/opinion/columns/india-coronavirus-lockdown-covid-19-economy-6364409/

Bhuyan, A. (2020, 4 June). From treatment to medical gear, patients paying more in COVID times. *IndiaSpend.* https://www.indiaspend.com/from-treatment-to-medical-gear-patients-paying-more-in-covid-times/

Bindra, J., & Sharma, N. C. (2020, 1 April). Coronavirus: Govt tells SC one-third of migrant workers could be infected. *Mint.* https://www.livemint.com/news/india/covid-19-govt-tells-sc-one-third-of-migrant-workers-could-be-infected-11585643185390.html

Chhina, M. A. S. (2021, 22 May). Army brass frowns as CO writes to Sonu Sood for help with Covid facility equipment. *The Indian Express.* https://indianexpress.com/article/india/army-brass-frowns-as-commanding-officer-writes-to-sonu-sood-for-covid-facility-equipment-7324876/

Chowdhury, D. R. (2021, 28 May). Modi never bought enough COVID-19 vaccines for India. Now the whole world is paying. *Time.* https://time.com/6052370/modi-didnt-buy-enough-covid-19-vaccine/

Das, K. N., & Ghoshal, D. (2021, 15 June). Exclusive Indian scientists: We didn't back doubling of vaccine dosing gap. Reuters. https://www.reuters.com/world/india/exclusive-indian-scientists-we-didnt-back-doubling-vaccine-dosing-gap-2021-06-15/

Dey, M. (2019, 14 August). SBI Ecowrap—Root cause of the current demand slowdown (Issue 32). SCRIBD. https://www.scribd.com/document/424933186/SBI-Ecowrap-Root-Cause-of-the-Current-Demand-Slowdown-002

Dubey, M. D. (2021, 14 June). With no tests and no treatment, people in rural India are dying of COVID-like symptoms. *Gaon Connection.* https://en.gaonconnection.com/covid19-rural-india-villages-coronavirus-tests-antigen-rtpcr/

ENS Economic Bureau. (2021, 25 April). Covaxin rates: ₹600 for states; ₹1,200 for hospitals. *The Indian Express.* https://indianexpress.com/article/india/covaxin-rates-rs-600-for-states-rs-1200-for-hospitals-7287845/

Gamio, L., & Glanz, J. (2021, 25 May). Just how big could India's true Covid toll be? *The New York Times.* https://www.nytimes.com/interactive/2021/05/25/world/asia/india-covid-death-estimates.html?referringSource=articleShare

Gauba, R. (2020, 26 March). D.O. No. 272/2/1/2020-Cab. III. https://www.dropbox.com/s/4t6wargs8r8z7yr/MHA%2015%20lakh%20entered%20India.pdf?dl=0

Ghosh, A. (2021, 8 April). We defeated Covid once without a vaccine, important to test, track, treat: PM Modi tells CMs. *The Print.* https://theprint.in/health/we-defeated-covid-once-without-a-vaccine-important-to-test-track-treat-pm-modi-tells-cms/636702/

Ghoshal, D., & Das, K. (2021, 3 May). Exclusive scientists say India government ignored warnings amid coronavirus surge. Reuters. https://www.reuters.

com/world/asia-pacific/exclusive-scientists-say-india-government-ignored-warnings-amid-coronavirus-2021-05-01/

Hindustan Times. (2021, 13 April). VK Paul recommends chyawanprash, Ayurveda; experts criticise remarks. https://www.hindustantimes.com/india-news/paul-recommends-chyawanprash-ayurveda-experts-criticise-remarks-101618340743478-amp.html?__twitter_impression=true

India Today. (2020, 10 April). India implements strictest lockdown in the world, lags in testing: Expert. https://www.indiatoday.in/india/story/india-implements-strictest-lockdown-in-the-world-lags-in-testing-expert-1665604-2020-04-10

India Today. (2021, 22 May). UP Teachers' Union claims 1,600 died in poll duty in contrast to Yogi govt's claims of 3 deaths. https://www.indiatoday.in/coronavirus-outbreak/video/up-teachers-union-claims-1-600-died-in-poll-duty-in-contrast-to-yogi-govt-s-claims-of-3-deaths-watch-1805679-2021-05-22

International Monetary Fund. (2021, April). *Managing divergent recoveries.* https://www.imf.org/en/Publications/WEO/Issues/2021/03/23/world-economic-outlook-april-2021

Jain, A. (2021, 25 February). Why Does PM CARES not qualify as a 'public authority' under the RTI Act? *The Wire.* https://thewire.in/law/pm-cares-fund-trust-deed-supreme-court

Jha, S. (2019, 15 November). Consumer spend sees first fall in 4 decades on weak rural demand: NSO data. *Business Standard.* https://www.business-standard.com/article/economy-policy/consumer-spend-sees-first-fall-in-4-decades-on-weak-rural-demand-nso-data-119111401975_1.html#:~:text=The%20survey%20%E2%80%94%20Key%20Indicators%3A%20Household,Rs%201%2C501%20in%202011%2D12.&text=In%20cities%2C%20it%20rose%20by,report%20reviewed%20by%20Business%20Standard

Kumar, R. (2021, 10 June). Bihar Covid death toll increases by 73% after HC-ordered review. *Hindustan Times.* https://www.hindustantimes.com/india-news/bihar-covid-death-toll-increases-by-73-after-hc-ordered-review-101623264310365.html

Kumar, V., & Singh, P. (2016). Access to healthcare among the Empowered Action Group (EAG) states of India: Current status and impeding factors. *National Medical Journal, 29*(5), 267–273. https://pubmed.ncbi.nlm.nih.gov/28098080/#affiliation-1

Liu, J. (2021, 10 March). Biden signs $1.9 trillion stimulus package—Here's what it includes for unemployment. *CNBC.* https://www.cnbc.com/2021/03/10/unemployment-benefit-updates-in-the-american-rescue-plan-stimulus.html

Menon, S. (2021, 2 March). Coronavirus: The misleading claims about an Indian remedy. *BBC.* https://www.bbc.com/news/56172784

Menon, S., & Goodman, J. (2021, 29 April). India Covid crisis: Did election rallies help spread virus? *BBC.* https://www.bbc.com/news/56858980

Ministry of Finance. (2019, 1 May). Monthly economic report, March 2019. https://dea.gov.in/sites/default/files/MER-March%202019.pdf

Ministry of Finance. (2020, 1 February). Budget 2020–2021: Speech of Nirmala Sitharaman. https://www.indiabudget.gov.in/doc/bspeech/bs202021.pdf

Ministry of Home Affairs. (2020, 17 May). Order no. 40-3/2020-DM-I(A). https://www.mha.gov.in/sites/default/files/MHAOrderextension_1752020_0.pdf

Ministry of Labour and Employment. (2021, 8 February). Lok Sabha unstarred question no. 1056. http://164.100.24.220/loksabhaquestions/annex/175/AU1056.pdf

Ministry of Railways. (2020, 20 July). Information sought by Shri Ajay Bose, under the RTI Act, 2005. https://www.dropbox.com/s/whgtqx37i8cxixo/Ajay%20Bose%20railway%20profit.pdf?dl=0

Mint. (2021, 24 June). WHO uncovers problems at Sputnik V Covid-19 vaccine at Russia's Ufa plant. https://www.livemint.com/news/world/who-uncovers-problems-at-sputnik-v-covid-19-vaccine-plant-at-ufa-in-russia-11624478980637.html

Mohan, G. (2021, 4 May). A long wait: Indian diaspora sends Covid aid, but it gets stuck in the process. *India Today.* https://www.indiatoday.in/coronavirus-outbreak/story/a-long-wait-indian-diaspora-sends-covid-aid-but-it-gets-stuck-in-the-process-1798879-2021-05-04

Mohanty, P. (2020a, 29 April). Coronavirus lockdown XI: Why India's health policy needs a course correction. *Business Today.* https://www.businesstoday.in/current/economy-politics/coronavirus-lockdown-covid-19-india-health-policy-healthcare-private-hospitals/story/402405.html

Mohanty, P. (2020b, 18 May). Coronavirus lockdown XV: Not just stimulus 2.0, getting fiscal mathematics right is critical too. *Business Today.* https://www.businesstoday.in/current/economy-politics/coronavirus-lovkdown-economic-stimulus-package-fiscal-deficit-covid-19-pandemic/story/404137.html

Mohanty, P. (2020c, 27 July). Rebooting economy X: COVID-19 puts question mark on private sector's efficiency in healthcare. *Business Today.* https://www.businesstoday.in/opinion/columns/indian-economy-covid19-private-sector-healthcare-public-hospitals-coronavirus/story/411219.html

Mohanty, P. (2020d, 11 November). Rebooting economy 44: India's journey from one of the fastest growing economies in 2015 to slowest in 2020. *Business Today.* https://www.businesstoday.in/opinion/columns/rebooting-economy-44-indias-journey-from-one-of-the-fastest-growing-economies-in-2015-to-slowest-in-2020/story/421644.html

Mohanty, P. (2020e, 4 December). Rebooting economy 50: Economic reforms for whom and for what? *Business Today*. https://www.businesstoday.in/opinion/columns/indian-economy-economic-reforms-for-whom-and-for-what-demonetisation-gst-farm-laws/story/423976.html

MoSPI. (2021, 29 January). Press note on first revised estimates of national income, consumption expenditure, saving and capital formation for 2019–20. http://mospi.nic.in/sites/default/files/press_release/PressNote_FRE%20 2019-20%20-%20Website.pdf

Mudur, G. S. (2021, 19 April). How India landed in Covid vaccine mess. *The Telegraph*. https://www.telegraphindia.com/india/how-we-landed-in-covid-vaccine-mess/cid/1812969

Mukherjee, B. (2021, 29 May). The latest data from @BhramarBiostat, @themojostory. https://twitter.com/BDUTT/status/1398504561300541443

NDTV. (2021, 17 April). 'Have never ever seen such huge crowds at a rally': PM Modi in Asansol. https://twitter.com/ndtv/status/1383419909128933377

NSC. (2012). Report of the Committee on Unorganised Sector Statistics. https://www.lmis.gov.in/sites/default/files/NSC-report-unorg-sector-statistics.pdf

OECD. (2020, 12 October). Job retention schemes during the COVID-19 lockdown and beyond. http://www.oecd.org/coronavirus/policy-responses/job-retention-schemes-during-the-covid-19-lockdown-and-beyond-0853ba1d/

Office of the Registrar General of India. (2021, June). Report on medical certification of cause of death 2019. https://censusindia.gov.in/2011-Documents/mccd_Report1/MCCD_Report_2019.pdf

Paliath, S. (2021, 24 March). A year after exodus, no reliable data or policy on migrant workers. *IndiaSpend*. https://www.indiaspend.com/governance/migrant-workers-no-reliable-data-or-policy-737499

Pandey, G. (2020, 22 April). Coronavirus in India: Desperate migrant workers trapped in lockdown. *BBC*. https://www.bbc.com/news/world-asia-india-52360757

Pandey, G. (2021, 10 May). India Covid: Kumbh mela pilgrims turn into super-spreaders. *BBC*. https://www.bbc.com/news/world-asia-india-57005563

Parashar, S. (2021, 23 May). Government steps in to expedite WHO approval for Covaxin. *The Times of India*. https://timesofindia.indiatimes.com/india/government-steps-in-to-expedite-who-approval-for-covaxin/articleshow/82869339.cms

Parliament of India. (2020, 21 November). The outbreak of pandemic COVID-19 and its management. https://rajyasabha.nic.in/rsnew/Committee_site/Committee_File/ReportFile/14/142/123_2020_11_15.pdf

PIB. (2020a, 29 January). Advisory for Corona virus. https://pib.gov.in/PressReleasePage.aspx?PRID=1600895

PIB. (2020b, 23 March). Important announcement: 30 states/UTs announce complete lockdown in the entire state/UT covering 548 districts. https://twitter.com/PIB_India/status/1242133894427787267

PIB. (2020c, 24 March). PM calls for complete lockdown of entire nation for 21 days. https://pib.gov.in/newsite/PrintRelease.aspx?relid=200658

PIB. (2020d, 9 April). Government of India sanctions ₹15000 crores for India COVID-19 emergency response and health system preparedness package. https://pib.gov.in/PressReleaseframePage.aspx?PRID=1612534

PIB. (2021a, 19 April). Government of India announces a liberalised and accelerated Phase 3 strategy of Covid-19 vaccination from 1st May. https://www.pib.gov.in/PressReleasePage.aspx?PRID=1712710

PIB. (2021b, 9 June). PIB's bulletin on Covid-19. https://www.pib.gov.in/PressReleasePage.aspx?PRID=1725676

PM India. (2021, 28 January). PM's address at the World Economic Forum's Davos dialogue. https://www.pmindia.gov.in/en/news_updates/pms-address-at-the-world-economic-forums-davos-dialogue/

Prabhala, A., & Menghaney, L. (2021, 2 April). The world's poorest countries are at India's mercy for vaccines. It's unsustainable. *The Guardian.* https://www.theguardian.com/commentisfree/2021/apr/02/india-in-charge-of-developing-world-covid-vaccine-supply-unsustainable

PTI. (2020a, 19 March). Coronavirus: MoS Health Ashwini Kumar Choubey says sunlight kills virus. *India Today.* https://www.indiatoday.in/india/story/coronavirus-ashwini-kumar-choubey-sunlight-1657436-2020-03-19

PTI. (2020b, 1 October). First of two VVIP planes costing ₹8,400 cr arrives in India; custom-made B777 will fly PM, president and VP. *Firstpost.* https://www.firstpost.com/india/first-of-two-vvip-planes-costing-rs-8400-cr-arrives-in-india-custom-made-b777-will-fly-pm-president-and-vp-8871161.html

PTI. (2021a, 7 March). Harsh Vardhan says India is in the endgame of Covid-19 pandemic. *Hindustan Times.* https://www.hindustantimes.com/india-news/harsh-vardhan-says-india-is-in-the-endgame-of-covid-19-pandemic-101615128329364.html

PTI. (2021b, 27 March). Supplied more COVID-19 vaccines globally than immunising own people: India tells UN. *Business Today.* https://www.businesstoday.in/current/economy-politics/supplied-more-covid-19-vaccines-globally-than-immunising-own-people-india-tells-un/story/435058.html

PTI. (2021c, 4 June). Serum Institute gets DCGI nod to manufacture Sputnik V COVID-19 vaccine in India. *The Hindu*. https://www.thehindu.com/news/national/serum-institute-gets-dcgi-nod-to-manufacture-sputnik-v-covid-19-vaccine-in-india/article34729671.ece

PTI. (2021d, 12 June). SC asks states, UTs to implement 'one nation, one ration card' scheme. *Business Standard*. https://www.business-standard.com/article/current-affairs/sc-asks-states-uts-to-implement-one-nation-one-ration-card-scheme-121061200046_1.html

Purohit, J., & Parmar, A. (2021, 22 March). Who did Modi government consult before the corona lockdown? A BBC investigation. *BBC*. https://www.bbc.com/hindi/india-56478320

Purohit, K., & Aafaq, Z. (2021, 30 April). BJP states hiding Covid-19 deaths are endangering India's health response. *Article 14*. https://www.article-14.com/post/bjp-states-hiding-covid-19-deaths-are-endangering-india-s-health-response?s=03

Raghavan, P. (2021, 25 April). Serum Institute's ₹600/dose for Covishield in private hospitals is its highest rate the world over. *The Indian Express*. https://indianexpress.com/article/india/serum-institute-covishield-price-india-world-7286635/

Ramakumar, R. (2021, 26 April). Whose intellectual property is Bharat Biotech's publicly funded Covaxin? India deserves an answer. *Scroll.in*. https://scroll.in/article/993257/why-its-vital-for-indians-to-know-who-owns-intellectual-property-rights-to-bharat-biotechs-covaxin

Ramani, S. (2021, 13 June). Excess deaths in Hyderabad are 10 times the official COVID-19 toll for Telangana. *The Hindu*. https://www.thehindu.com/news/cities/Hyderabad/excess-deaths-in-hyderabad-are-10-times-the-official-covid-19-toll-for-telangana/article34807214.ece

Ravikumar, S. (2021, 6 January). Criticism mounts over India's 'abrupt' approval of COVAXIN. *Reuters*. https://www.reuters.com/article/health-coronavirus-india-vaccine-idINKBN29B0YH

Rawat, S. (2021, 30 April). 9.1 million thronged Mahakumbh despite Covid-19 surge: Govt data. *Hindustan Times*. https://www.hindustantimes.com/cities/dehradun-news/91-million-thronged-mahakumbh-despite-covid-19-surge-govt-data-101619729096750.html

RBI. (2020a, 3 April). OBICUS survey on the manufacturing sector—Q4: 2019–20. https://rbidocs.rbi.org.in/rdocs/Publications/PDFs/OBICUSR494AD20ADC479440DDAE9F97BDA3E4826F.PDF

RBI. (2020b, 21 August). Annual report 2019–20. https://rbidocs.rbi.org.in/rdocs/AnnualReport/PDFs/0RBIAR201920DA64F97C6E7B48848E6DEA06D531BADF.PDF

Reuters. (2021, 26 April). Situation in India 'beyond heartbreaking', WHO chief says. https://www.reuters.com/world/india/situation-india-beyond-heartbreaking-who-chief-says-2021-04-26/

Roche, E. (2021, 29 April). Over 40 countries to assist India in its battle against second Covid wave. *Mint*. https://www.livemint.com/news/india/india-to-get-assistance-from-over-40-nations-to-fight-second-covid-19-wave-11619704474199.html

Roy, A., Rocha, E., & Das, K. N. (2020, 10 December). Not without India: World's pharmacy gears up for vaccine race. Reuters. https://www.reuters.com/article/health-coronavirus-india-vaccine-idUSKBN28K10E

Roy, R. (2021a, 2 May). 'Centre's vaccine policy prima facie detrimental to right to health, centre should consider revisiting it to withstand the scrutiny of articles 14, 21': Supreme Court. *Live Law*. https://www.livelaw.in/amp/top-stories/supreme-court-centres-vaccine-policy-prima-facie-detrimental-to-right-to-health-article-14-21-173474?__twitter_impression=true

Roy, R. (2021b, 31 May). 'People are not getting vaccine slots; getting distress calls': Supreme Court questions Co-WIN registration requirement for vaccination. *Live Law*. https://www.livelaw.in/top-stories/supreme-court-questions-cowin-registration-requirement-for-vaccination-174946

Saikia, A., & Sharma, S. (2021, 3 May). Where are the 300 tonnes of emergency Covid-19 supplies that have landed in Delhi in last five days? *Scroll.in*. https://scroll.in/article/993973/where-are-the-300-tonnes-of-emergency-covid-19-supplies-that-have-landed-in-delhi-in-last-five-days

Salyal, A. S. (2021, 22 March). Covid case surge not a classic 2nd wave, says Harsh Vardhan. *Hindustan Times*. https://www.hindustantimes.com/cities/chandigarh-news/covid-case-surge-not-a-classic-2nd-wave-says-harsh-vardhan-101616355287082.html

SBI. (2020a, 15 May). Package for poor: Uttar Pradesh and West Bengal account for 27% of street vendors. https://bank.sbi/documents/13958/3312806/Ecowrap_20200515.pdf

SBI. (2020b, 17 August). Ecowrap. https://www.sbi.co.in/documents/13958/3312806/170820-SBI+Ecowrap+-+The+Good%3B+The+Bad%3B+The+Ugly.pdf/38684abb-d48c-6f80-45ad-bd1351c51c05?t=1597644350762

SBI. (2020c, 13 October). Conditional fiscal stimulus at a minimal 0.2% of GDP. https://sbi.co.in/documents/13958/3312806/141020-Ecowrap_20201013.pdf/9d3197d0-4738-5b67-5df8-5feaa4d86f7e?t=1602653238250

SBI. (2020d, 12 November). Government announces a slew of measures in Atmanirbhar 3.0. https://www.sbi.co.in/documents/13958/3312806/13112020_Ecowrap_20201112.pdf/8f0d6832-538f-392d-cef9-5ef848adc78c?t=1605254146366

Scroll.in. (2021a, 2 May). Youth Congress gives oxygen to NZ embassy after it asks for help on Twitter, then deletes tweet. https://scroll.in/latest/993852/youth-congress-gives-oxygen-to-nz-embassy-after-it-asks-for-help-on-twitter-then-deletes-tweet

Scroll.in. (2021b, 15 May). Covid: NHRC calls for special law to uphold dignity of dead as bodies found along Ganga river. https://scroll.in/latest/994970/covid-nhrc-calls-for-special-law-to-uphold-dignity-of-dead-as-bodies-found-along-ganga-river

Sharma, H. (2020, 23 May). NITI Aayog to states: Speed up medical colleges on PPP model. *The Indian Express.* https://indianexpress.com/article/india/niti-aayog-to-states-speed-up-medical-colleges-on-ppp-model-6423201/

Sharma, N. (2021, 19 March). Not all adults in India to be vaccinated against Covid-19. *The Economic Times.* https://economictimes.indiatimes.com/industry/healthcare/biotech/healthcare/not-all-adults-in-india-to-be-vaccinated-against-covid-19/articleshow/81587115.cms?utm_source=contentofinterest&utm_medium=text&utm_campaign=cppst

Shukla, A. (2020, 24 July). Union minister launches 'Bhabhiji' papad, says will help drive away Covid-19. *Hindustan Times.* https://www.hindustantimes.com/india-news/union-minister-launches-bhabhiji-papad-says-will-help-drive-away-coronavirus/story-jG9B7sUEQbWRN7ANhkdrYJ.html

Sidhartha. (2021, 8 May). Not just vaccine, India seeks patent waiver for Covid meds too. *The Times of India.* https://timesofindia.indiatimes.com/business/india-business/not-just-vax-india-seeks-patent-waiver-for-covid-meds-too/articleshow/82471616.cms

Singh, S. (2021, 26 April). For those who think the 2 pharma cost announced differential & exorbitant vaccine pricing on their own and without centre in the loop. | 'In a meeting presided over by the prime minister on April 20, vaccine manufacturers had shared details on the cost of production and markup.' https://twitter.com/SushantSin/status/1386554322079477760/photo/1

Slater, J. (2021, 19 April). India's devastating outbreak is driving the global coronavirus surge. *The Washington Post.* https://www.washingtonpost.com/world/interactive/2021/india-covid-cases-surge/?utm_campaign=wp_main&utm_medium=social&utm_source=facebook

Slater, J., & Masih, N. (2021, 8 May). In India's surge, a religious gathering attended by millions helped the virus spread. *The Washington Post.* https://www.washingtonpost.com/world/2021/05/08/india-coronavirus-kumbh-mela/?request-id=46ae8d55-92dd-43de-83e0-c02427c42fc5&pml=1

Statistics Times. (2021, 29 May). List of countries by projected GDP growth. https://statisticstimes.com/economy/countries-by-projected-gdp-growth.php

Supreme Court of India. (2020, 31 March). *Alakh Alok Srivastava v. Union of India.* https://www.livelaw.in/pdf_upload/pdf_upload-371969.pdf

Supreme Court of India. (2021a, 7 May). In distribution of essential supplies and services during pandemic. https://www.livelaw.in/pdf_upload/centres-affidavit-in-suo-moto-covid-case-supreme-court-393164.pdf

Supreme Court of India. (2021b, 31 May). Suo Motu writ petition (civil no. 3 of 2021). https://main.sci.gov.in/supremecourt/2021/11001/11001_2021_35_301_28040_Judgement_31-May-2021.pdf

The Economic Times. (2021a, 21 May). Shots for 18-44-Year Group Was Not Part of the Plan, Says Chief of Body That Detailed Vaccine Rollout. https://economictimes.indiatimes.com/news/politics-and-nation/shots-for-18-44-yr-group-was-a-political-decision/articleshow/82812610.cms?utm_source=contentofinterest&utm_medium=text&utm_campaign=cppst

The Economic Times. (2021b, 26 April). Vaccine pricing plan shared with centre before announcement, say officials. https://economictimes.indiatimes.com/industry/healthcare/biotech/pharmaceuticals/vaccine-pricing-plan-shared-with-centre-before-announcement-says-officials/articleshow/82250409.cms

The Economist. (2021a, 8 May). India's national government looks increasingly hapless; Confronted with catastrophe, the state has melted away. https://www.economist.com/asia/2021/05/08/indias-national-government-looks-increasingly-hapless

The Economist. (2021b, 15 May). Modelling Covid-19's death toll: There have been 7m–13m excess deaths worldwide during the pandemic. https://www.economist.com/briefing/2021/05/15/there-have-been-7m-13m-excess-deaths-worldwide-during-the-pandemic

The Economist. (2021c, 12 June). More evidence emerges of India's true death toll from Covid-19. https://www.economist.com/asia/2021/06/12/more-evidence-emerges-of-indias-true-death-toll-from-covid-19

The Guardian. (2021a, 21 April). 'The system has collapsed': India's descent into Covid hell. https://www.theguardian.com/world/2021/apr/21/system-has-collapsed-india-descent-into-covid-hell

The Guardian. (2021b, 21 April). India's government has abandoned its citizens to face a deadly second wave alone. https://www.theguardian.com/commentisfree/2021/apr/21/indias-government-abandoned-citizens-deadly-second-covid-wave

The Hindu. (2021, 7 June). Government will revert to centralised procurement of vaccines, says Modi. https://www.thehindu.com/news/national/prime-minister-narendra-modi-addresses-the-nation-on-june-7-2021/article34753292.ece

The Indian Express. (2021a, 9 April). Coronavirus India highlights: PM Modi asks CMs to focus on micro-containment. https://indianexpress.com/article/india/india-coronavirus-second-wave-live-updates-lockdown-curfew-rules-cases-deaths-vaccination-7262037/

The Indian Express. (2021b, 26 April). State after state shut down special Covid centres just before 2nd wave. https://indianexpress.com/article/india/state-after-state-shut-down-special-covid-centres-just-before-2nd-wave-7289078/

The Indian Express. (2021c, 5 May). Winning praise for Covid relief work, IYC chief Srinivas says: 'Helping everyone in need, don't want to do politics on this'. https://indianexpress.com/article/cities/bangalore/iyc-chief-srinivas-says-we-are-helping-everyone-want-to-do-politics-7303447/

The Indian Express. (2021d, 4 June). In a first, centre will pay ₹1,500 crore to reserve 30 crore doses of new vaccine. https://indianexpress.com/article/india/centre-signs-deal-with-hyderabad-based-biological-e-for-30-crore-covid-19-vaccine-doses-7342015/

The Quint. (2021, 8 May). After Kumbh, Uttarakhand sees 1800% jump in COVID-19 cases. https://www.thequint.com/coronavirus/spike-covid-cases-uttarakhand-haridwar-maha-kumbh-mela-superspreader

The Week. (2020, 14 March). Hindu Mahasabha holds 'cow urine party' to fight coronavirus, plans more parties. https://www.theweek.in/news/india/2020/03/14/hindu-mahasabha-organises-cow-urine-party-to-fight-coronavirus-plans-more.html

Vaidyanathan, A. (2021, 24 May). 'Is there policy on Covid death certificates?' Supreme Court to centre. NDTV. https://www.ndtv.com/india-news/is-there-policy-on-covid-death-certificates-supreme-court-to-centre-2448356

Varshney, V. (2021, 17 April). COVID-19 vaccines: Waiting for advantage India. *Down To Earth.* https://www.downtoearth.org.in/news/health/covid-19-vaccines-waiting-for-advantage-india-76543

Wallen, J. (2020, 16 September). India's healthcare system on brink of collapse again as it hits five million Covid-19 cases. *The Telegraph.* https://www.telegraph.co.uk/global-health/science-and-disease/indias-healthcare-system-brink-collapse-hits-five-million-covid/

VI AATMANIRBHAR BHARAT

Turning the Clock Back

Defining AatmaNirbhar Bharat

The prime minister unveiled his concept of AatmaNirbhar Bharat as the way (*Eshah Panthah*) to turn India into an economic superpower during the pandemic lockdown in May 2020. Although the phrase resonates with noble ideals, it still lacks clarity. Is it self-reliance or self-sufficiency? Both phrases have been used in the same sentence to explain it: 'The state of the world today teaches us that a (AatmaNirbhar Bharat) "self-reliant India" is the only path. It is said in our scriptures—*Eshah Panthah*. That is—self-sufficient India' (Embassy of India, Moscow, 2020; Mishra, 2020; Mohanty, 2020; Press Information Bureau, 2020).

He listed 'five pillars' to achieve AatmaNirbhar Bharat:

> (i) Economy, which brings in quantum jump and not incremental change; (ii) Infrastructure, which should become the identity of India; (iii) System, based on 21st century technology driven arrangements; (iv) Vibrant Demography, which is our source of energy for as self-reliant India; and (v) Demand, whereby the strength of our demand and supply chain should be utilized to full capacity.

Apparently, his Cabinet colleagues were taken by surprise and had no concept note to fall back on. They issued statements branding all their routine activities as part of the AatmaNirbhar Bharat Abhiyan—from rationing of food grains that started during the Second World War to defence procurement, education, skilling, etc. (Mohanty, 2020).

A 'special economic package' of ₹20 lakh crore to 'boost' AatmaNirbhar Bharat was added, which included not only measures to manage the lockdown-induced hardship but also a wide range of 'reforms' that, as would be revealed later, were of little use in the current health and economic crises: new farm laws, new labour codes, privatization of public assets such as airports, power distribution systems, atomic energy (later national banks would be added to the list), private participation in 'planetary exploration', commercialization of coal and boosting private investment through VGF. Finally came the import substitution policy with a clarion call of 'vocal for local' and 'local for global' (Ministry of Finance, 2020).

The AatmaNirbhar Bharat came for sharp criticism from economists and experts, including the prime minister's loudest cheerleader Arvind Panagariya who had, by now, resigned as vice chairman of the NITI Aayog and returned to teaching at the Colombia University.

Former CEA to the Modi government, Arvind Subramanian, and co-author Shoumitro Chatterjee, from the Pennsylvania State University wrote panning the import substitution policy. They argued:

> India is turning inward. Domestic demand is assuming primacy over export-orientation and trade restrictions are increasing, reversing a 3-decade trend. This shift is *based on three misconceptions, which we dispel*: that India's domestic market size is big, India's growth has been based on domestic not export markets, and export prospects are dim because the world is deglobalizing. (Chatterjee & Subramanian, 2020a, 2020b; Subramanian & Chatterjee, 2020)

They pointed out that India had embarked on import substitution right from 2014, thereby reversing the liberalized policies and wrote:

> Between 1991 and 2014, average MFN tariffs *declined from 125 percent to 13 percent*. Since 2014, there have been about *3,200 tariff increases* at the HS-6 digit level (on most-favored-nation imports), a strikingly large increase. As a result, the *average tariff has increased from 13 percent to nearly 18 percent*. The largest increases occurred in *2018 when there were nearly 2,500 tariff increases* amounting to nearly 4 percentage points. We estimate that the tariff increases affected import categories that amount to about *$300 billion or about 70 percent of total imports*.

The increase in tariff affected 60 per cent import items (3,200 out of 5,300 product categories).

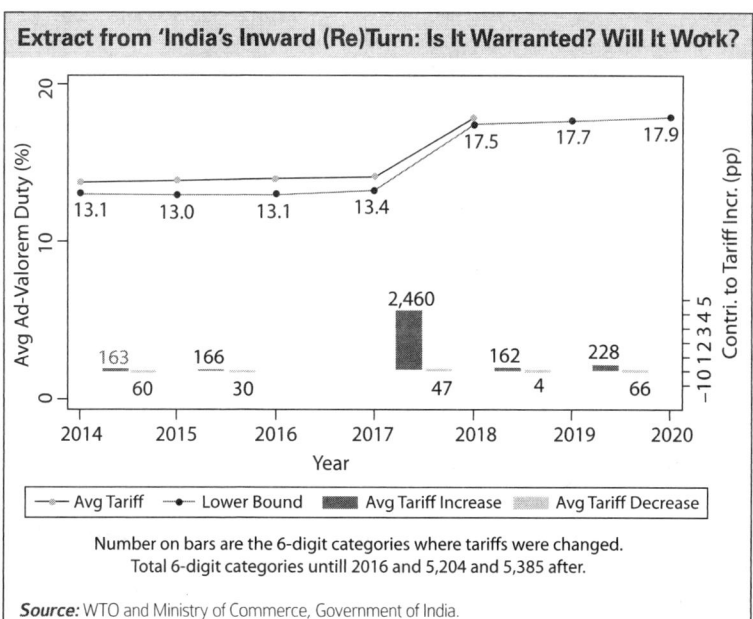

AatmaNirbhar Bharat 151

Quite predictably, this policy caused serious damage to both imports and exports. The following graphs show how both exports and imports plummeted post-FY2018 in absolute numbers and growth rates, particularly after the massive hike in import tariffs in 2018 as Subramanian and his co-author had pointed out. They had argued that it is the global market which is big enough to provide a big boost to India's growth, not the domestic market.

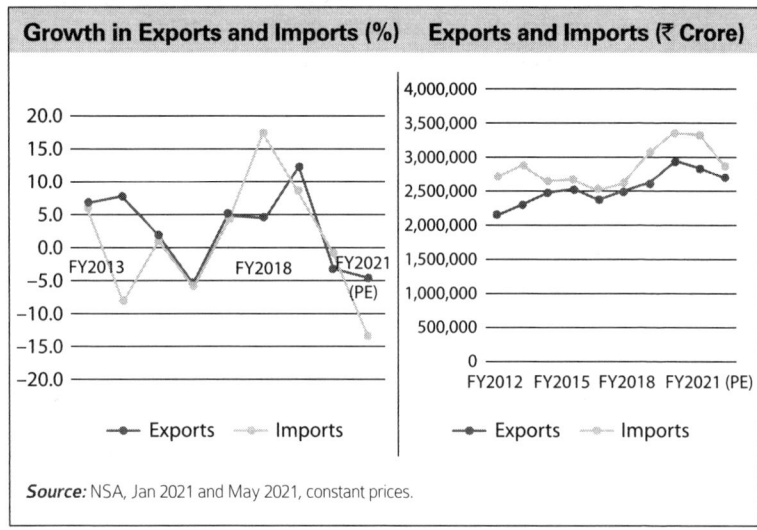

Source: NSA, Jan 2021 and May 2021, constant prices.

It needs further study to decipher why the rapid changes took place before FY2018. However, it is clear that exports and imports are linked more significantly than probably realized, and a fall in imports that the AatmaNirbhar Bharat seeks to achieve actually pulls down exports too, depriving India to benefit from global trade. The following study brought clarity to this.

Less Imports, Less Exports

Delhi-based Institute for Studies in Industrial Development (ISID) published a study 'Import Intensity of India's Manufactured Export—An Industry Level Analysis' in 2020, which examined how India's exports have become increasingly dependent on imports (Paul & Kumar, 2020).

It found that post-liberalization, import of raw materials and intermediary goods had increased and 'contributed to the growing exports of India'. It estimated 'import intensity' or import components of exported goods and found that for the 'whole economy', import intensity had risen from 10.5 per cent in FY1994 to 32.5 per cent in FY2014, and that for manufacturing had increased much more significantly up from 12.9 per cent to 51 per cent. In manufacturing, import substitution had risen most in petroleum products from 5.8 per cent to 91.4 per cent.

Its findings are mapped below.

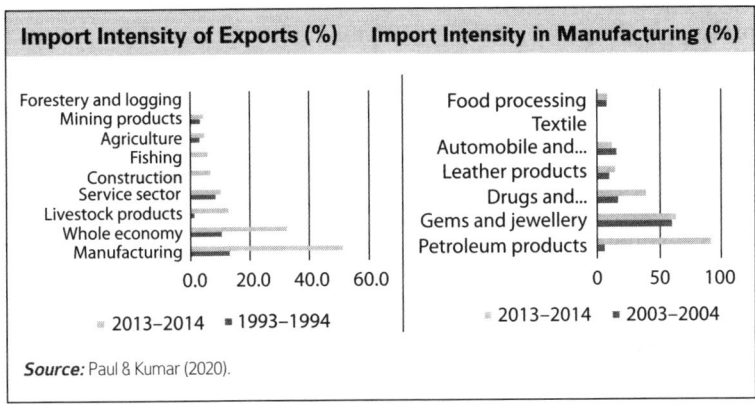

Source: Paul & Kumar (2020).

What the study made clear is that reducing imports would reduce exports and, hence, its capacity to boost India's growth.

A rattled Panagariya dismissed the idea in an interview and warned the government against falling into the trap of local businesses. He said that this move would allow less efficient producers to get into market and won't be competitive or contribute much to export (Panagariya, 2020).

In the 1960s and the 1970s, when the import substitution policy was last tried, India's average growth rate was 3.5 per cent. World over, this was derided as 'Hindu' rate of growth. Post-reform in the 1980s and then the big bang reform of 1991 pushed growth at a much higher rate. Post-trade liberalization of 1991, India's exports had grown riding on the import of raw materials and intermediate products, and are now heavily dependent on these imports.

Architecture of Aatmanirbhar Bharat

The pandemic lockdown called for relief and fiscal stimulus to tide over the period in which all social and business activities (except for emergency services) had been shut down. The AatmaNirbhar Bharat packages, announced in several rounds, did provide for additional ration and a token of cash transfers for cooking gas, etc., but the fiscal spending was very little. The packages were predominantly about liquidity infusion by way of cheap credit, credit guarantee schemes for MSMEs and 'reforms' for the future.

By mid-June, when India had already announced a ₹20 lakh crore package as the prime minister had promised, a national daily provided comparative data on stimulus packages of major economies to show that India's fiscal spending or 'fiscal stimulus (as % of GDP)' was the lowest at 1.2 per cent of GDP. In contrast, Singapore had provisioned 10.4 per cent, the USA 9 per cent, Germany and Canada 6.9 per cent, the UK 5.6 per cent, Brazil 4.5 per cent and China 2.6 per cent of their GDP (Roychoudhury, 2020).

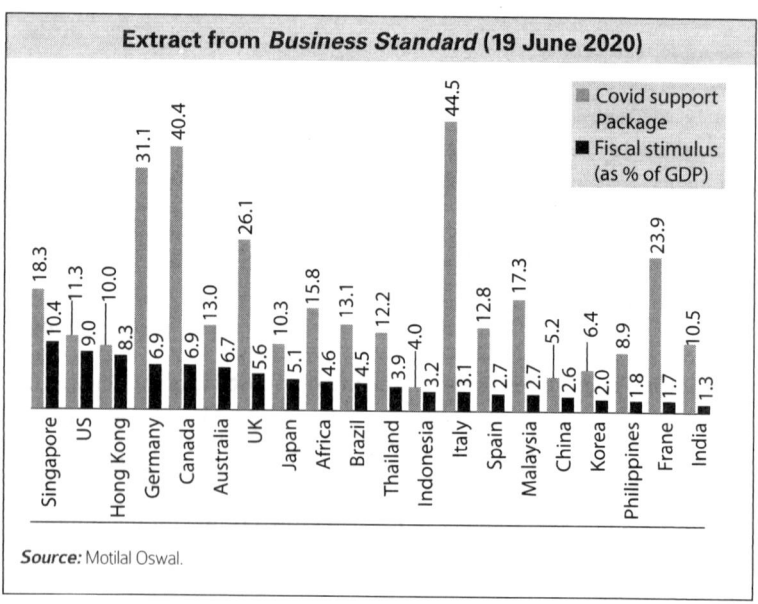

Source: Motilal Oswal.

In all, the AatmaNirbhar Bharat packages amounted to ₹23.66 lakh crore. As estimated by the SBI, the actual fiscal spending was only 1.6 per cent of the GDP (0.5%, 0.8% and 0.21% for the packages 1, 2 and 3, respectively; SBI 2020a, 2020b, 2020c).

The pre-pandemic state of the economy was known. The economy was slowing down for 8 quarters, from 8.2 per cent in Q4 of FY2018 to 3.1 per cent in Q4 of FY2020 (ending on 31 March 2020, a week after the lockdown). By this time, the growth in private consumption (PFCE), the main driver contributing about 56–57 per cent to the GDP, had slowed down from a high of 8.1 per cent in FY2017 to 5.5 per cent in FY2020; the growth in government expenditure (GFCE), contributing about 10 per cent to the GDP, had fallen from a high of 11.9 per cent in FY2018 to 7.9 per cent in FY2020 and the growth in investment (GFCF), contributing about 32 per cent to the GDP, had fallen from a high of 9.9 per cent in FY2019 to 5.4 per cent in FY2020.

A complete lockdown of economic activities meant that except for government expenditure (GFCE), all others were hit hard. Therefore, fiscal spending should have got the priority, but it didn't.

The key to understanding the design of AatmaNirbhar Bharat is the underlying economic thinking, the key points of which are narrated in the following paragraphs.

Fiscal Austerity

Fiscal austerity is an important neoliberal (radical right) economic concept as per which the fiscal deficit should be limited to 3 per cent of GDP and debt-to-GDP ratio should be limited to 60 per cent. The IMF has been imposing on about 100 countries worldwide since 1985. India adopted its norms when it sought its loan in 1991 to tide over the foreign exchange crisis. Later, it became part of the FRBM Act of 2003 (IMF, 2017; Ministry of Finance, 2003).

When the pandemic struck, India's fiscal deficit was double at 6 per cent and debt-to-GDP ratio was touching 70 per cent. India didn't want to further raise either and hence a tight fiscal approach to the pandemic, though a number of economists, including Nobel laureates Amartya Sen and Abhijit Banerjee and former RBI Governor Raghuram Rajan, made fervent and repeated appeals to the government to go for higher fiscal spending without bothering about fiscal deficit and debt but they were ignored. Nobel laureate Joseph Stiglitz specifically warned the USA against fiscal austerity and wrote that 'the true danger is austerity.' He explained the economic logic: lower government spending would constrain GDP growth and cause higher debt-to-GDP ratio, contrary to what fiscal austerity sought to achieve (Sen et al., 2020; Stiglitz, 2020).

In 2016, three top IMF economists admitted that fiscal austerity was self-defeating after studying its impact on economic growth in more than 100 countries over a long period of time. They concluded: '…in practice, the episodes of fiscal consolidation have been followed, on average, by drops rather than by expansion in output' (Ostry et al., 2016).

The Indian government didn't care and, by the time it said that it realized the mistake and promised to spend more, it was December 2020—by when India had already undergone three quarters of recession. When it presented its budget for FY2022 on 1 February 2021, there was very little growth in fiscal spending: mere 1 per cent rise in the budgeted spending over FY2020 (RE; Mohanty, 2021a).

The emphasis on higher fiscal spending is because monetary policy has its limitations when demand is depressed, which can be revived through higher fiscal spending and, as demand picks up, private investment will come in. Else, excess liquidity will remain idle, creating a liquidity trap as India is witnessing.

Liquidity Infusion

Infusing liquidity (supply-side solution) to address recession is yet another neoliberal economic (monetarist) thinking, though multiple global experiences have shown that this doesn't work when demand is depressed and unemployment is high (Krugman, 2009).

As the lockdown progress, the RBI cut repo rate from 4.4 per cent to 4 per cent on 22 May 2020) and cash reserve ratio (CRR) from 4 per cent to 3 per cent on 28 March 2020. Until 31 October 2020, it had infused ₹12.7 lakh crore through its various instruments as part of the AatmaNirbhar Bharat drive (Sharma, 2020).

What happened to its liquidity infusion? Most of it got parked in its own reverse repo account—a safe place where banks earn 3.35 per cent interest—when banks don't want to lend or there are no takers for credit. The following graphs map the trajectory of reverse repo account deposits.

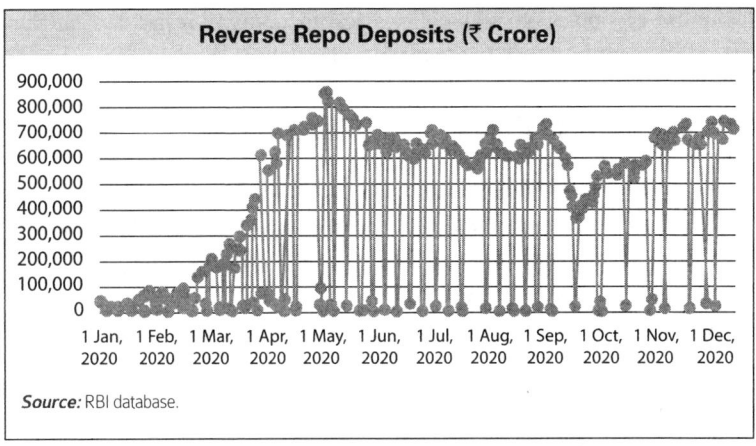

Source: RBI database.

It was a classic 'liquidity trap' waiting to happen. Since such data are available daily, the RBI knew right from day one that cheap credit was a wasteful strategy. Yet it has persisted in doing the same. Its Financial Stability Report of 11 January 2021 explained how easy credit posed 'macrofinancial risks' to the economy as 'unintended consequences' of the monetary and fiscal measures pursued to push economic recovery and, if continued, it would lead to *economic impairment and delay the recovery*. It further stated that its macro-stress tests for 'credit risks' showed that the gross NPA ratio of scheduled commercial banks (SCBs) was likely to increase from 7.5 per cent in September 2020 to 13.5–14.8 per cent by September 2021 (RBI, 2021a).

In February 2021, it declared India to be in a state of 'credit surplus', which is 'engendering easy financial conditions'; warned of impending 'macrofinancial risks' and liquidity trap if the liquidity infusion continued and blamed the government's fiscal and monetary policies for such a situation. Later, it put the blame for low credit offtake on the pre-pandemic slowdown, pandemic loss of business and growing stressed assets in large businesses (RBI, 2021b, 2021c).

In spite of all such fears, if the RBI has maintained the key rates, repo and CRR, it is because of its balancing act. It perceives, correctly, that India's problem is a weak demand, which translates into weak demand for credit, and that tightening credit wouldn't help generating demand. The risk is when the excess liquidity gets into market and creates volatility. That is another reason for economists to seek higher fiscal spending to revive demand, but the government has stuck to the neoliberal supply-side solutions.

Privatization of PSUs

Privatization too is a neoliberal concept pushed by the IMF. Two of the AatmaNirbhar packages, of 16 May and 17 May 2020, focused on privatization and ease of doing business. Privatizations included entry of private players to strategic areas and outright sales of public assets (Ministry of Finance, 2020a; Ministry of Finance, 2020b).

The 16 May package included 'structural reforms' listing private participation in coal and other mining activities, defence production, aviation, space research, particularly in 'planetary exploration', privatization of airports, power distribution and atomic energy sector. The 17 May package talked about enhancing the *ease of doing business*.

Privatization has been pushed in the name of private sector efficiency, for which there is little evidence. In 2015, the UNDP published analysis of all existing global studies on comparative efficiencies of public and private sectors and reached at three conclusions: (a) 'no model of ownership'—public, private or mixed—'is intrinsically more efficient' than the other; (b) literature broadly comparing efficiency 'lacks rigour', more of 'opinion pieces' and sectoral literature (health and education) 'is more rigorous although often inconclusive' and (c) efficiency under all ownership models 'depends on competition, regulation, autonomy and wider issues of institutional development' (Rao, 2015).

Nevertheless, the AatmaNirbhar Bharat devoted considerable energy.

Ease of Doing Business

As for improving the ease of doing business ranking, a WB project, India did remarkably well to jump from a rank of 142 in 2014 to 63 in 2019.

But in August 2020, the WB stopped publishing this index after finding a number of irregularities in data and ranking. It has been under a cloud for some years, which led to the resignation of Paul Romer as chief economist of the WB in 2018 (Chaudhary, 2020).

But there is more to it. An improved ranking should lead to a higher inflow of FDIs. India saw that the growth in FDI inflows dropped dramatically during this period—from 25 per cent in FY2015 to 1 per cent in FY2018 and 2 per cent in FY2019, before rising to 20 per cent in FY2020. Even a 25 per cent growth in FY2015 is too low compared to 40 per cent to 155 per cent from FY2005 to FY2008. Although in absolute numbers (US$) the FDI inflows have been going up, there are doubts about what the FDI inflows is doing as it hasn't helped in boosting the GDP growth. India's growth slowed down to 4 per cent even before the pandemic hit. Besides, most of the FDI inflows (over 80%) is routed through well-known tax havens such as Singapore, Mauritius and the Netherlands (DIPP, 2021; Mohanty, 2018, 2021b).

Foreign Assistance

The AatmaNirbhar Bharat is a misnomer.

Prime Minister Modi has been consistently seeking foreign help in making India self-sufficient in every area. Days after unveiling his AatmaNirbhar Bharat, on 23 July, Modi invited US companies to invest in Indian agriculture inputs and machinery, agriculture supply chain, food processing sector, fisheries and organic produce and healthcare under the very same AatmaNirbhar Bharat Abhiyan (*Business Today*, 2020).

In September 2020, he again invited global investors to make India AatmaNirbhar Bharat while addressing the US-India Strategic Partnership Forum. Hard-selling AatmaNirbhar Bharat, he said: 'It ensures that India's strengths act as a global force multiplier… "AatmaNirbhar Bharat" is about transforming India from being just a passive market to an active manufacturing hub at the heart of global value chains.' In October 2020, he addressed Invest India Conference in Canada where he sold new farm and labour laws to woo Canadian investors to invest in India and make it great: 'These reforms will support our efforts to build an AatmaNirbhar Bharat or self-reliant India. By working towards self-reliance, we seek to contribute to global good and prosperity' (Banakar, 2020; MEA, 2020).

Bombay Plan 1944 and Nehruvian Idea of AatmaNirbhar Bharat

Prime Minister Modi and his colleagues often blame Pandit Nehru for all that ails India now.

The argument goes that India turned socialist, stifled private enterprises, built inefficient public sector units that need to be sold off now and government started running business all because of Pandit Nehru. In short, Pandit Nehru is responsible for everything that doesn't work 56 years after his death (Nehru died in 1964).

What is forgotten is that much before Nehru rolled out his Five-Year plans, built basic industries, which were virtually non-existent and private sector was unwilling to invest in long-term projects for many reasons and run most of the economic activities, it was the doyens of industry who had proposed all this and more to make India self-reliant and improve the living conditions of the people.

That was the Bombay Plan of 1944, authored by such illustrious names as J. R. D. Tata, G. D. Birla, Sir Ardeshir Dalal, Sri Ram, Kasturbhai Lalbhai, A. D. Shroff and John Mathai. They were the first ones to propose a larger and stronger role for government with 'state ownership', 'state control' and 'state management' of production, distribution, consumption, investment, foreign trade and exchange, and wages and working conditions, etc. (Mohanty, 2021c).

They were the ones who proposed 'a planned economic development', 'nationalization' and 'public supervision and control' of industries. Their stated goals were to 'improve the standard of living of the masses', reduce 'disparities of income', 'inequalities' and make India 'self-sufficient'. In all of this, their own role was to be secondary and under the control of government/state.

Their vision document was actually called 'Memorandum Outlining a Plan of Economic Development for India', but it came to be known after the city to which the authors belonged (Thakurdas et al., 1944).

Many economic historians have pointed out the similarities (intellectual debt) between the Bombay Plan of 1944 and the post-Independence India's first *three Five-Year plans as well as the Industrial Policy Resolutions of 1948 and 1956*. Economist V. Ananth Krishna has been quoted as categorically stating that 'the Nehruvian era witnessed the implementation of the Bombay Plan; a substantially interventionist state and an economy with a sizeable public sector' (Sanyal, 2012).

Former Prime Minister Manmohan Singh said at the centenary celebrations of J. R. D. Tata in 2004: 'As a student of economics in 1950s and later as a practitioner in government, I was greatly impressed by the "Bombay Plan" of 1944. *In many ways, it encapsulated what all subsequent plans have tried to achieve…*' (PTI, 2004).

Why did the then doyens of industry envision an overwhelming role for state and not for the private sector?

One big reason is their little faith in private enterprises to deliver.

The document stated that it advocated a larger role for government/state as *unrestricted private enterprises* under the *capitalistic system* of production have *not served the interests of consumers and the community* generally as satisfactorily as they should have, and it recognized 'that the existing economic organization, based on private enterprise and ownership, has *failed to bring about a satisfactory distribution of the national income.*' The experience of the Great Depression of 1929, caused by the unbridled greed of private enterprises, must have had a serious impact on the authors.

The other view is that 'the State belongs to the people and is but a means of securing the fulfilment of the individual's rights'; '*planning is not inconsistent with a democratic organization* of society' and that 'the *distinction between capitalism and socialism has lost much of its significance* from a practical standpoint.'

Contemporary history shows that India's private sector wealth creators are more interested in creating private wealth with public assets and public money. In return, they have created the entire banking stress and have run away with their own wealth and unpaid bank loans (detailed in the chapter on privatization).

India's Golden Age of Growth: Growth with Equity

This author has been arguing that India's golden era of India's growth and development, post-Independence, was the time when Pandit Nehru was the prime minister. Those years witnessed unprecedented and dramatic rise in economic growth and income equality.

The data set that provides the growth numbers of Nehru's post-Independence years as prime minister is the 2004–2005 GDP series (the 2011–2012 GDP series stops at 2004–2005). It shows that the average annual growth in the GDP was 4.1 per cent (constant prices) in 13 years between 1951–1952 and 1963–1964.

The significance of this growth number can be understood by comparing it with that of the preceding and succeeding years.

The pre-Independence era data set that most professional economists and other experts use is provided in economist S. Sivasubramanian's book *The National Income of India in the Twentieth Century*, published in 2000. It says that India's average annual growth (constant prices) was *0.9 per cent, 0.8 per cent and 0.8 per cent* during 1900–1901 to 1946–1947 (47 years), 1900–1901 to 1929–1930 (30 years) and 1930–1931 to 1946–1947 (17 years), respectively, at 1948–1949 prices.

This means that during Nehru's time, the GDP growth achieved a *quantum jump of 4.6 to 5.1 times* from the pre-Independence era (of 0.8–0.9 per cent growth).

Writing about this quantum jump, economist Arvind Virmani, who compared the growth rate of 30 years before Independence (1917–1946) and after Independence (1951–1979), wrote that 'this GDP growth rate was *five times* the average rate of growth of 0.7% per annum during the 30-year period from 1917 to 1946.' India's annual average growth rate was 3.5 per cent (constant prices) during 1951–1979, but during Nehru's years (1951–1964) it was 4.1 per cent, that is, *5.9 times* (Virmani, 2004).

In post-Nehru era, the highest growth was witnessed during the new millennium. The 2011–2012 GDP series shows that the average annual growth in 15 years between FY2006 and FY2020 is 6.7 per cent (constant prices). This is a small jump of *1.6 times over the Nehru-era growth*, notwithstanding more than 30 years of liberalization, which began in the 1980s before the big push of 1991 came.

To achieve the Nehruvian quantum jump, the GDP needs to grow at an annual average of *19–21 per cent over a decade and more. This seems far-fetched given that the FY2020 growth (pre-pandemic)* was just 4 per cent (constant prices), which is less than the average annual growth of the Nehru era.

As for growth with equity, French economists Thomas Piketty and Lucas Chancel presented India's income inequality in their 2017 book *Indian Income Inequality, 1922–2015: From British Raj to Billionaire Raj?* (Chancel & Piketty, 2017).

It provides three graphs (among others) that demonstrate how income quality started rising in Nehru's era and plunged in post-1980 reform era, particularly after the 1991 liberalization.

The following graph shows how the income share of the bottom 50 per cent people rose and fell.

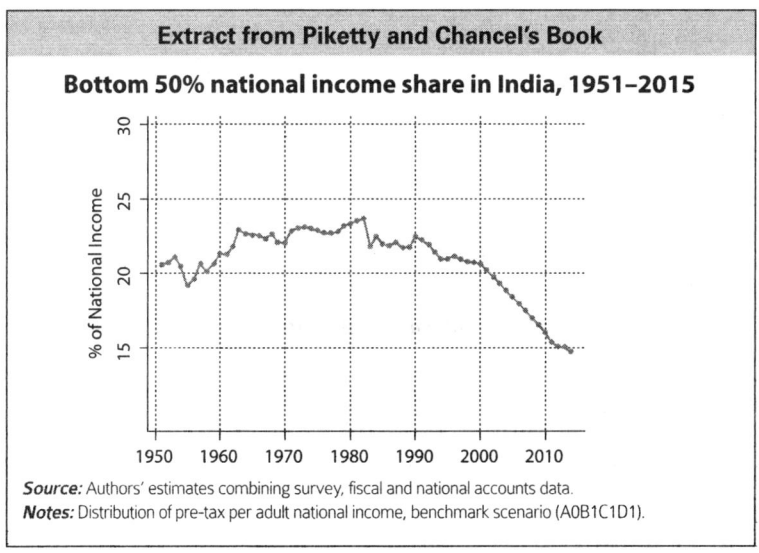

As can be seen, the fall began as the post-1980 reform era and accelerated post-1991 liberalization.

The next one shows how India's 40 per cent middle class (below top 10% and above bottom 50%) has also been short-changed.

Their share (black line) touched its peak of 23.6 per cent in 1982–1983 and then crashed to 14.9 per cent in 2014–2015. Simultaneously that of the top 10 per cent zoomed post-2000, creating a yawning gap that is unlikely to be bridged anytime.

The next one shows how the share of top 1 per cent zoomed.

Extract from Piketty and Chancel's Book. Left: Income of Top 10 Per Cent Was Lower than Middle 40 Per Cent until 2000 and Then Zoomed. Right: Income of Top 1 Per Cent Zoomed Post-1991 Liberalization

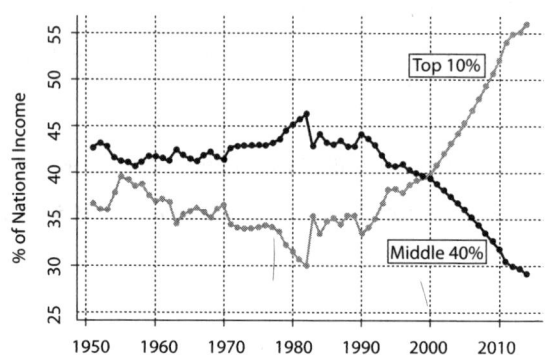

Top 10% vs. Middle 40% national income shares in India, 1951–2015

Source: Authors' estimates combining survey, fiscal and national accounts data.
Notes: Distribution of pre-tax per adult national income, benchmark scenario (A0B1C1D1).

Top 1% national income share in India, 1922–2015

Source: Authors' estimates combining survey, fiscal and national accounts data.
Notes: Distribution of pre-tax per adult national income, benchmark scenario (A0B1C1D1).

Piketty and Chancel explained that this was caused by the free-market neoliberal economics (radical capitalism) adopted by India, starting with the 1980s and then the big push in 1991.

So long as Modi's push for selling off public assets to private wealth creators and handing over running the economy to them continues, the Nehru era's equity is difficult to dream of.

How It Hurts the Poor

The growth with equity model that Nehru gave changed in the liberalized era. Now, the growth went up but so did income inequality when the private sector gained the upper hand in running the economy. The PSUs allowed India 'positive discrimination' through job reservations for the underprivileged Scheduled Castes, Scheduled Tribes and later the Other Backward Classes. With the dismantling of PSUs, such support to the underprivileged will be lost.

The ideological fountain of Modi's BJP, the RSS has been anti-reservation and anti-positive discrimination, notwithstanding periodic refutations. Mohan Bhagwat, the present RSS chief, has repeatedly called for a review of the reservation policy. Manmohan Vaidya, a prominent RSS ideologue, went to the extent of saying that reservation was not required in India as it promoted separatism (ANI, 2017; Sharma & Ghosh, 2019; Shepherd, 2019).

Prime Minister Modi, in fact, brought a 10 per cent reservation for the economically poor upper castes as a counter (one of RSS's arguments for discontinuing reservation is equal opportunity for all as Vaidya said in 2017) just ahead of the 2019 general elections and soon after his party lost state elections in Rajasthan, Madhya Pradesh and Chhattisgarh. Remarkably, this came after quota agitations by Jats in Haryana, Patels in Gujarat and Marathas in Maharashtra, who are all socio-economically powerful and yet have been demanding reservations (Jats and Marathas have already got it and it is before the Supreme Court for violating its earlier judgement of limiting reservations to less than 50%; Varma, 2019).

It is no rocket science that privatization of public assets reduces the state's capacity to redress inequalities.

Takeaways

The AatmaNirbhar Bharat has four key downsides for the economy and the people:

⇨ It eliminates the possibilities of export-led growth and threatens to take India back to 'Hindu' rate of growth.

⇨ It threatens with inferior products at high costs of the pre-reform and pre-liberalization era.

⇨ It threatens to reduce the state capacity to address income inequality.

⇨ It aims to serve private interest, not public.

⇨ It failed to revive the economy even before the second wave hit.

References

ANI. (2017, 20 January). RSS against reservation, says it promotes 'separatism' in India. *Business Standard.* https://www.business-standard.com/article/news-ani/rss-against-reservation-says-it-promotes-separatism-in-india-117012001256_1.html

Banakar, P. (2020, 4 September). India is becoming one of leading attractions for FDI, says PM as he woos global investors. *The New Indian Express.* https://www.newindianexpress.com/nation/2020/sep/04/india-is-becoming-one-of-leading-attractions-for-fdi-says-pm-as-he-woos-global-investors-2192170.html

Business Today. (2020, 23 July). India received foreign investment of $20 billion amid pandemic: PM Modi at India–Idea's summit. https://www.businesstoday.in/current/economy-politics/india-received-foreign-investment-of-20-billion-amid-pandemic-pm-modi-at-india-idea-summit/story/410764.html

Chancel, L., & Piketty, T. (2017, July). *Indian income inequality, 1922–2015: From British raj to billionaire raj?* (Working Paper No. 11). https://wid.world/document/chancelpiketty2017widworld/

Chatterjee, S., & Subramanian, A. (2020a, 15 October). To embrace atmanirbharta is to choose to condemn Indian economy to mediocrity. *The Indian Express.* https://indianexpress.com/article/opinion/columns/india-trade-domestic-market-exports-covid-19-6725538/

Chatterjee, S., & Subramanian, A. (2020b, October). *India's inward (re)turn: Is it warranted? Will it work?* (Policy Paper No. 1). Ashoka University. https://www.ashoka.edu.in/static/doc_uploads/file_1603091486.pdf

Chaudhary, A. (2020, 28 August). World Bank probes irregularities in ease of business report data. *Bloomberg | Quint.* https://www.bloombergquint.com/global-economics/world-bank-probes-irregularities-in-ease-of-business-report-data

DIPP. (2021). Quarterly fact sheet on FDI from April, 2000 to December 2020. https://dipp.gov.in/sites/default/files/FDI%20Factsheet%20December%2020.pdf

Embassy of India, Moscow. (2020, 12 May). Prime Minister Shri Narendra Modi's address to the nation on 12.5.2020. https://indianembassy-moscow.gov.in/press-releases-13-05-20.php

IMF. (2017, March). Fiscal rules at a glance. https://www.imf.org/external/datamapper/fiscalrules/Fiscal%20Rules%20at%20a%20Glance%20-%20Background%20Paper.pdf

Krugman, P. (2009, 6 September). How did economists get it so wrong? *New York Times Magazine.* https://www.nytimes.com/2009/09/06/magazine/06Economic-t.html

MEA. (2020, 8 October). Prime minister's keynote address at the Invest India Conference in Canada. https://mea.gov.in/Speeches-Statements.htm?dtl/33105/Prime_Ministers_Keynote_Address_at_the_Invest_India_Conference_in_Canada

Ministry of Finance. (2003, 26 August). Fiscal Responsibility and Budget Management Act, 2003 (Act No. 39 of 2003). https://www.dea.gov.in/sites/default/files/FRBM%20Act%202003%20and%20FRBM%20Rules%202004.pdf

Ministry of Finance. (2020a, 16 May). Finance minister announces new horizons of growth; structural reforms across eight sectors paving way for Aatma Nirbhar Bharat. https://pib.gov.in/PressReleasePage.aspx?PRID=1624536

Ministry of Finance. (2020b, 17 May). Finance Minister announces government reforms and enablers across seven sectors under Aatma Nirbhar Bharat Abhiyaan. https://pib.gov.in/PressReleasePage.aspx?PRID=1624661

Mishra, U. (2020, 17 August). ExplainSpeaking on economy | Atmanirbhar Bharat: A brief and not-so-affectionate history. *The Indian Express.* https://indianexpress.com/article/explained/explainspeaking-atmanirbhar-bharat-a-brief-and-not-so-affectionate-history-6556627/

Mohanty, P. (2018, 1 November). World Bank ease of doing business ranking: Higher FDI inflows is okay, but why is it not boosting economic growth? *Firstpost.* https://www.firstpost.com/business/world-bank-ease-of-doing-business-ranking-higher-fdi-inflows-is-okay-but-why-is-it-not-boosting-economic-growth-5486281.html

Mohanty, P. (2020, 14 November). Rebooting economy 45: What is AatmaNirbhar Bharat and where will it take India? *Business Today.* https://www.businesstoday.in/opinion/columns/indian-economy-what-is-aatmanirbhar-bharat-and-where-will-it-take-india/story/421952.html

Mohanty, P. (2021a, 6 February). Rebooting economy 64: Budget numbers don't add up to 10% or more growth in FY22. *Business Today.* https://www.businesstoday.in/union-budget-2021/columns/indian-economy-budget-numbers-dont-add-up-to-10-or-more-growth-in-fy22/story/430462.html

Mohanty, P. (2021b, 19 February). Rebooting economy 68: How private wealth creators are serving Indian economy and people. *Business Today.* https://www.businesstoday.in/opinion/columns/rebooting-economy-68-how-private-wealth-creators-are-serving-indian-economy-and-people/story/431736.html

Mohanty, P. (2021c, 27 February). Rebooting economy 70: The Bombay plan and the concept of AatmaNirbhar Bharat. *Business Today.* https://www.businesstoday.in/opinion/columns/rebooting-economy-70-the-bombay-plan-and-the-concept-of-aatmanirbhar-bharat/story/432495.html

Ostry, J. D., Loungani, P., & Furceri, D. (2016, June). Neoliberalism: Oversold? *Finance & Development, 53*(2). https://www.imf.org/external/pubs/ft/fandd/2016/06/ostry.htm

Panagariya, A. (2020, 27 August). India cannot be export powerhouse without being open to imports: Panagariya. *Business Standard.* https://www.business-standard.com/article/economy-policy/india-cannot-be-export-powerhouse-without-being-open-to-imports-panagariya-120082700163_1.html

Paul, M., & Kumar, R. A. (2020, February). *Import intensity of India's manufactured exports—An industry level analysis* (Working Paper No. 220). Institute for Studies in Industrial Development. http://isid.org.in/wp-content/uploads/2020/05/WP220.pdf

Press Information Bureau. (2020, 12 May). English rendering of Prime Minister Shri Narendra Modi's address to the nation on 12.5.2020. https://pib.gov.in/PressReleseDetail.aspx?PRID=1623418

PTI. (2004, 24 August). Manmohan Singh and the 1944 Bombay plan. Rediff. com. https://www.rediff.com/money/2004/aug/24plan.htm

Rao, S. (2015). Is the private sector more efficient? A cautionary tale. UNDP. https://gsdrc.org/document-library/is-the-private-sector-more-efficient-a-cautionary-tale/

RBI. (2021a, 11 January). RBI releases the financial stability report. https://www.rbi.org.in/Scripts/BS_PressReleaseDisplay.aspx?prid=50949

RBI. (2021b, 5 February). Monetary policy statement, 2020–21, resolution of the Monetary Policy Committee (MPC), February 3–5, 2021. https://rbidocs.rbi.org.in/rdocs/PressRelease/PDFs/PR105055BEF93017054F9BAF12623CBCCE60DB.PDF

RBI. (2021c, February). RBI bulletin, *LXXV*, (2). https://rbidocs.rbi.org.in/rdocs/Bulletin/PDFs/BULLETIN022021_FE4E546C0F8F24B5DBE1E40914D1E21A9.PDF

Roychoudhury, A. (2020, 19 June). India's Covid-19 pandemic fiscal cost lowest among major nations: Report. *Business Standard*. https://www.business-standard.com/article/economic-revival/india-s-covid-19-pandemic-fiscal-cost-lowest-among-major-nations-report-120061900105_1.html

Sanyal, A. (2012). The Bombay plan: A forgotten document. https://nzsac.files.wordpress.com/2012/05/bombayplanfornzsac.pdf

SBI. (2020a, 15 May). Package for poor: Uttar Pradesh and West Bengal account for 27% of street vendors. https://bank.sbi/documents/13958/3312806/Ecowrap_20200515.pdf

SBI. (2020b, 13 October). Conditional fiscal stimulus at a minimal 0.2% of GDP. https://sbi.co.in/documents/13958/3312806/141020-Ecowrap_20201013.pdf/9d3197d0-4738-5b67-5df8-5feaa4d86f7e?t=1602653238250

SBI. (2020c, 12 November). Government announces a slew of measures in Atmanirbhar 3.0. https://www.sbi.co.in/documents/13958/3312806/13112020_Ecowrap_20201112.pdf/8f0d6832-538f-392d-cef9-5ef848adc78c?t=1605254146366

Sen, A., Rajan, R., & Banerjee, A. (2020, 17 April). Huge numbers may be pushed into dire poverty or starvation...we need to secure them. *The Indian Express*. https://indianexpress.com/article/opinion/coronavirus-india-lockdown-economy-amartya-sen-raghuram-rajan-abhijit-banerjee-6364521/

Sharma, A., & Ghosh, D. (2019, 19 August). Mohan Bhagwat calls for talks on reservation in 'atmosphere of harmony'. NDTV. https://www.ndtv.com/india-news/mohan-bhagwat-rss-chief-for-dialogue-on-quota-says-need-atmosphere-of-harmony-2087292

Sharma, M. (2020, 12 November). Govt announces Atmanirbhar Bharat 3.0; claims COVID stimulus now worth ₹29.8 lakh crore. *Business Today*. https://www.businesstoday.in/current/corporate/govt-announces-atmanirbhar-bharat-30-covid-stimulus-worth-rs-29-lakh-crore/story/421809.html

Shepherd, K. I. (2019, 21 August). Is abrogation of reservation on the cards? *The Wire*. https://thewire.in/rights/mohan-bhagwat-rss-reservation

Stiglitz, J. (2020, 30 April). Four priorities for pandemic relief efforts. Roosevelt Institute. https://rooseveltinstitute.org/publications/four-priorities-for-pandemic-relief-efforts/

Subramanian, A., & Chatterjee, S. (2020, 14 October). India's export opportunities could be significant even in a post-COVID world. *The Indian Express*. https://indianexpress.com/article/opinion/columns/india-trade-economy-coronavirus-impact-covid-6723899/

Thakurdas, P., Tata, J. R. D., Birla, G. D., Dalal, A., Ram, S., Lalbhai, K., Shroff, A. D., & Matthai, J. (1944). A plan of economic development for India, Parts One and Two. http://www.isec.ac.in/Plan_%20of_%20economic_%20development_%20for_%20India.pdf

Varma, G. (2019, 7 January). Elections 2019: Modi govt woos upper castes with 10% reservation. *Mint*. https://www.livemint.com/Politics/dl06Li5kVrxXMBaDuy0iTL/Narendra-Modi-govt-approves-10-reservation-for-economically.html

Virmani, A. (2004, February). *India's economic growth: From socialist rate of growth to Bharatiya rate of growth* (Working Paper No. 122). Indian Council for Research on International Economic Relations (ICRIER). http://www.icrier.org/pdf/wp122.pdf

VII NEW FARM LAWS

Opening Farming to Corporate Sector

The new farm laws passed during the pandemic lockdown sparked widespread unrest. Ironically, these laws have been brought through the backdoor, behind the backs of Indian farmers. First, these laws were brought through ordinances during the pandemic lockdown of June 2020, then these were pushed through the Parliament, again during the pandemic lockdown in September 2020, with little debate and after dismissing all objections from the Opposition, including the demand for scrutiny by a parliamentary panel. Although it is a state subject, states were not consulted, as an RTI response would reveal to negate the government's claim of prior stakeholders' consultation. Rather, states were disenfranchised. Its long-time key ally, Shiromani Akali Dal, left the government in protest. While farmers sat on dharna at multiple locations outside Delhi, the prime minister didn't meet or listen to their objections, nor did he show any inclination to heed (Jebaraj, 2021; *The Indian Express*, 2020; *The Wire*, 2020).

These laws opened farming to corporate sector, something that the USA did 40 years ago during the Reagan era of neoliberal push. Before examining how these laws work, it is prudent to look at what happened to US farmers.

US Corporations Ate Up Small Farmers

A day after the protesting farmers completed 100 days of their sit-in outside Delhi in March 2021, a national daily carried a chilling account of the American farmers 40 years after the corporate sector entered farming. The writer is a US-based Indian IITian Bedabrata Pain, an ex-NASA scientist and award-winning filmmaker, who had set out on a 10,000 km journey to rural America to document their story. The title of the article was: 'How "Big Ag" Ate Up America's Small Farms' (Pain, 2021).

Some of the key points that Pain listed as 'Big Ag'—gigantic agrobusinesses—took over America's farming are as follows:

1. Farm gate prices collapsed and land value decimated as farmers' land was gobbled up by Big Ag even as the landless started toiling under onerous contract farming.
2. Production cost of wheat went up threefold in 20 years, while the farm gate price is just at the level of 1865 Civil War.
3. Giant corporations used financial clouts to control the market, depress farm gate prices and buy infrastructure for a song to a point where small farms became unsustainable.
4. Big Ag now controls everything from 'farm to fork' and from seeds to grocery shops. Four large firms control 80 per cent of chemical fertilizers, grain trading, dairy production, meat supply and almost 100 per cent of farm machinery.
5. Government money flows to the corporations in the form of write-offs, market facilitation and crop insurance.
6. Over 70 per cent of the $50 billion subsidies go to top 20 per cent farms.
7. Average food prices shot up by more than 200 per cent in 40 years, while earnings of the bottom 90 per cent increased by 25 per cent.
8. Small farmers constitute 90 per cent of all farms but produce 25 per cent of the market value.
9. In February 2020, the median US farm income was a –$1,400.
10. Farmers' share in retail price has declined from 50 per cent in the 1950s to less than 15 per cent today.

11. Of all US poultry farmers, 75 per cent now live below the poverty line.
12. Loan default rates, bankruptcy filings are on the rise, and farmers' suicide rate is 4–5 times higher than the national average.
13. As farm income dwindled, local businesses such as seed suppliers, granaries, repair shops, schools and hospitals started disappearing from rural America.

In the 1980s, President Ronald Reagan introduced laws doing away with price supports, subsidies and slashed loan programmes—all in the name of making US agriculture globally competitive. President Clinton brought the Freedom to Farm Act of 1996 into law which removed the link between income support, payment and farm prices and eliminated several New Deal era (post-1929 Roosevelt era reforms) initiatives; subsidies were sought to be phased out in 7 years—all of this to make US agriculture more market oriented (Pain, 2021).

Will it be any different for India?

New Farm 'Reform' Laws

The three new farm laws at the centre of controversy are as follows: Farmers' Produce Trade and Commerce (Promotion and Facilitation) Act, 2020; the Farmers (Empowerment and Protection) Agreement on Price Assurance and Farm Services Act, 2020, and Essential Commodities (Amendment) Act, 2020. The first law deals with trade and the second with contract farming and both are of utmost concern to farmers. The third relates to stock and price regulation of essential commodities.

The following concerns flow from the first law which

1. Allows *parallel and unregulated private markets* for trading in farm produce outside of the state government-regulated APMC mandis where all government procurement takes place at the MSP. These are also the mandis where farmers engage in the open market trading with private businesses under the supervision of state government.
2. *Disincentivizes APMC mandis* by doing away with mandi taxes that private businesses pay and are used for mandis' maintenance

and farmers' welfare, in these parallel, unregulated private markets. The law is silent on who will set up and run the new markets and provide infrastructure since state governments are kept completely out of its affairs.

3. Doesn't provide for trade at *MSP price or set floor price or any other mechanism* to determine price and ensure that farmers get fair and remunerative price for their produce in these private markets. Farmers will deal directly with private businesses without government supervision or control.
4. Bars legal recourse and courts from resolving disputes arising out of direct deals between farmers and private business. The law states, 'No civil Court shall have jurisdiction to entertain any suit or proceedings in respect of any dispute....'
5. Hands over judicial power for dispute resolution to relatively junior-level executives, such as subdivisional magistrate (SDM) and divisional magistrate (DM; Ministry of Law and Justice 2020c; Mohanty, 2020a).

The second law opens up the entire country for contract farming in which farmers will, again, deal directly with private businesses without state governments' regulation and oversight. State governments' contract laws become infructuous. Farmers are at the mercy of executives for dispute resolution, as courts of law are barred from dispute resolution (Ministry of Law and Justice, 2020a).

The third law is a concern for both farmers and consumers as the amendment to the Essential Commodities Act of 1955 allows higher limits for private businesses to hold stocks of agriculture produce, stocking fears of hoarding, black marketing and price manipulations. This is detrimental to both farmers and consumers. Further, this law removes several key food items from the list of essential commodities which are subject to price control. These include cereals, pulses, potato, onions, edible oilseeds and oils. The impact of this change would be felt by consumers in mid-2021 when food inflation started to rise with prices of pulses and edible oils soaring now that price control is gone (Dash & Gupta, 2021; Ministry of Law and Justice, 2020b).

Unregulated Markets Are Cause of Worry

Many myths have been peddled by the government while pushing through the first law (Ministry of Law and Justice, 2020c). Its introductory paragraph states that the law is meant to provide 'freedom of choice' in the sale and purchase of farmers' produce and 'facilitates remunerative prices through competitive alternative trading channels…outside the physical premises of markets or deemed markets notified under various State agricultural produce market legislations', among other things.

The Shanta Kumar Committee, set up by the Modi government, said in its 2015 report that 'only 6 percent of total farmers in the country' have gained directly from official procurement (at APMC mandis). This means that 94 per cent of farmers sell their produce in open market. There is no bar on those 6 per cent to sell in open market either (Kumar, 2015).

So the new law is not giving 'freedom of choice' to farmers but to private business. Section 6 of the law makes it very clear. It states: 'No market fee or cess or levy, by whatever name called, under any State APMC Act or any other State law, shall be levied' in the private markets. Since this fee, cess or levy is paid by private business (to states, not the central government), it is a freedom of choice and material gain for them to buy without paying tax.

Farmers are worried because Bihar did the same in 2006 by abolishing its APMC law and dismantling MSP-based procurement (though occasionally some amount of procurement takes place in the abandoned APMC mandis) and farmers of Bihar are in deep trouble because of it.

The Bihar Experience

Once Bihar dismantled APMC mandis and procurement, its farmers were completely at the mercy of private businesses. Several studies have shown how they suffered.

In 2013, an interstate ministerial report stated that dismantling of the APMCs in Bihar was *'not in the interest of farmers* and needs orderly marketing'. It stated that the infrastructure of mandis had deteriorated and that Bihar was back to building new mandis. In 2019, a study by the

NCAER stated that private investment in new markets and strengthening existing mandis 'did not take place' and 'farmers are left to the mercy of traders who *unscrupulously fix lower prices*', leading to 'low price realization and instability in prices' (Ministry of Agriculture & Farmers' Welfare, 2013; Pohit et al., 2019).

According to a 2020 study by the University of Pennsylvania, which studied three different agricultural market systems in India—Punjab's regulated market, Bihar's unregulated market and Odisha's partly regulated market for their relative efficacy—Bihar's market infrastructure had 'deteriorated' because private players 'do the minimum' to keep operations running. But, more importantly, it stated that the regulated markets (APMC mandis) of Punjab provided 30–35 per cent more money than partly regulated Odisha and unregulated Bihar markets. Even public procurement in Odisha and Bihar fetched lower than Punjab prices. It also found that while Punjab farmers sold 75–97 per cent of their produce in regulated APMC mandis (for five crops of paddy, wheat, maize, mustard and potato it studied), Odisha farmers sold 20–35 per cent and Bihar farmers 3–9 per cent in their APMC mandis (Chatterjee et al., 2020).

It concluded that 'those who have access to the public procurement machinery *unequivocally benefit both from a higher price and lower uncertainty in their income stream.*'

That Bihar farmers lost out is borne by official records on farmers' income available for 2002–2003 and 2012–2013 (NSSO). The Doubling of Farmers Income (DFI) Committee, headed by Ashok Dalwai (set up in 2016), analysed these data sets to make startling revelations: (a) the income of Punjab farmers benefitting from the APMC–MSP system was *3.3 times* more than Bihar's in 2002–2003 which went up to *4.9 times* in 2012–2013 and (b) Punjab farmers' income (at 2011–2012 prices) grew at 3.2 per cent, while Bihar's shrunk to *–1 per cent* during this period. Since Bihar dismantled the APMC–MSP system in 2006, its farmers should have seen a rise, not a fall, in income during this period (Ministry of Agriculture & Farmers' Welfare, 2017b; Mohanty, 2020c).

No wonder, during the October–November 2020 Bihar elections, farmers were demanding restoration of the APMC system and full-fledged MSP-based procurement for improving their return. News about Bihar farmers' woes is routine. One report says that Bihar farmers send their produce to Punjab for a better price realization; another says that since trading system is rigged in favour of traders (who cheat on weight, moisture level and everything else), very few go to mandis to sell their produce. Yet another report says that farmers of Sitamarhi and Sheohar districts are looking at Nepal to sell their sugarcane since the local sugar mill has closed (Bera, 2021; IANS, 2018; Parth, 2021; Ray 2020, 2021a, 2021b; Singh, 2020, 2021).

None of it means that the APMC–MSP system works perfectly. There are many flaws that need to be fixed. Attempts have been made for decades to improve its functioning but throwing the baby with the bathwater is not the solution. The DFI Committee made many recommendations to improve the system, increase the number of APMC mandis (more than 6,500 of them), modernize them and 'upgrade' 22,000 village 'haats', keeping them outside the APMC ambit (as is the case now) to provide competition and expand procurement to cover as many of the 23 crops for which MSP is announced every year (procurement is mainly restricted to wheat and paddy). State government do have private wholesale markets for agriculture produce: 21 states/UT have enabling provisions, and 11 states have notified the rules to implement private wholesale markets (Ministry of Agriculture & Farmers' Welfare, 2017a, 2017c, 2018).

A strong case was made for a central law to bypass APMCs because of the dominance of commission agents or 'arhtiyas' in Punjab and Haryana, but the new law doesn't keep them out. Rather, it makes them integral to the trade and allows them to operate across the country by defining a 'trader' as someone who buys farmers' produce 'either for oneself or on behalf of one or more persons'.

Fear of Dismantling MPS and Limit Procurement

Apart from the Bihar experience, the farmers are worried about MSP and procurement being dismantled, reducing their scope for fair and remunerative price.

Two recent developments sparked a panic among farmers.

One is a letter from the Department of Food and Public Distribution to the FCI, which procures crops at MSP in October 2019. It sought information for a presentation to the PMO examining three options: (a) restricting procurement to PDS requirement, buffer stock and other requirements, (b) introduction of a scheme to pay price differences if farmers don't get MSP prices in open market and (c) procurement of other crops for which MSP is determined in the rice- and wheat-growing states (Sethi, 2020).

Currently, the procurement policy is open-ended, meaning the government has to buy 'whatever wheat and paddy are offered by farmers'. The first option above would seriously curtail official procurement if restricted (Department of Food & Public Distribution, n.d.).

In March 2020, just ahead of the new farm laws, and a report by the Commission for Agricultural Costs and Prices (CACP), which recommends MSPs, reiterated its old stand of reviewing the open-ended procurement of what and paddy and restricting their procurement in Punjab and Haryana (to save ground water), which is why Punjab and Haryana farmers took the lead in the farmers' agitation as they are the major producers and beneficiaries of MSP-based procurement of wheat and paddy (CACP, 2020).

By refusing to guarantee MSP in the parallel, unregulated private market (outside APMC mandis), the government has caused more anxiety, especially since it launched a new CSS to provide production-linked incentive of ₹10,900 crore for promoting food processing units run by private businesses on 31 March 2021. While government is reluctant to assure MSP to farmers outside APMC mandis, it has been steadfastly providing assured return to private entities in all its PPP projects and other business dealings across the spectrum (MoFPI, 2021; Mohanty, 2021).

Why does procurement at MSP matter if only 6 per cent farmers benefit it from directly?

Firstly, declaration of MSP sends a signal to market that farmers have an option of better pricing and, thus, overall market rates remain higher than would be the case otherwise. Second, farmers of states with higher procurement, such as Punjab, Haryana and Madhya Pradesh, have increased their income ,while in Bihar it has decreased. Although market price often crashes after MSP is announced, that is a clear indication of the power of private businesses even when trading is regulated. It would be naïve to expect that unregulated markets will provide better price and double farmers' income by 2022, as the government promises (Mohanty, 2020a, 2021a).

Contract Farming's Benefits Are Debatable

The second farm law seeks to create a parallel contract farming system by bypassing state governments contract laws and provides that farmers will directly negotiate 'mutually agreed remunerative price' or 'guaranteed price' with private corporates and for 'any additional amount over and above the guaranteed price', a reference can be made to 'prevailing prices in specified APMC yard or electronic trading and transaction platform'. This 'prevailing price' is, more often than not, below the MSP prices and hence a double trouble for farmers.

Contract farming is not new to India. It has existed since the 1960s in the seed sector, which has spread across the country. In the 1990s, Punjab and Haryana allowed multinational companies for contract farming of tomato and potato. At least *20 states* have their own contract farming laws (as part of their APMC Acts); 14 of them have notified contract farming rules though only in Maharashtra, Haryana, Punjab, Karnataka, Gujarat, Madhya Pradesh and Chhattisgarh companies/firms have registered for contract farming (Ministry of Agriculture & Farmers' Welfare, 2018). Punjab has a separate Contract Farming Act of 2013 (Ministry of Agriculture & Farmers' Welfare, 2017a).

In spite of all this, contract farming has not really taken off in a big way, and wherever it has been tried, the result hasn't been good either for many reasons. Former Agriculture Secretary Siraj Hussain points out that farmers are apprehensive as they are 'not organized' and 'ill equipped for any legal battle with corporates' of which there have been a few; companies are reluctant to sign agreements fearing that states may hold them responsible if the agreed price is below MSP. More importantly, in the relatively more successful poultry farming business (66% of production through contract farming), contract farmers actually get substantially lower than market price. A 2015 study in Andhra Pradesh, Karnataka and Telangana found that contract farmers' net return was ₹11.06 per bird (broiler) as against ₹17.06 by non-contract farmers. Even in the USA, poultry farming has benefitted producers more than farmers (Hussain, 2020; Sasidhar & Suvedi, 2015).

Professor Sukhpal Singh of IIM Ahmedabad, who has studied contract farming for three decades, lists several more, including law price and stagnation in pricing: default by companies as well as farmers, farmers' grievances such as undue quality cut on produce or no procurement of produce, delayed payments and no compensation for crop failure (Chaba, 2021).

So the chances of farmers getting MSP or fair price in the unregulated and unsupervised contract farming are not bright at all.

One of the DFI reports (Ministry of Agriculture & Farmers' Welfare, 2018) stated that global experience showed that 'contract farming has not been able to easily attract small and marginal farmers' and recommended that while contract law should be made attractive for them (over 85% of Indian farmers are small and marginal farmers with less than 2 ha landholding). The new does include Farmer Producer Organisation, registered firms of small farmers, in the definition of 'farmer', but their growth has been disappointing so far, as they do face too many problems, mainly lack of capital, skilled manpower and business know-how (Ministry of Agriculture & Farmers' Welfare, 2017a; Mohanty, 2021a).

Agriculture is a state subject. The State List mentions agriculture, agriculture marketing, land, revenue, rents, etc.: items 14, 18, 26, 27, 28, 30, 45 and 46. Even for agriculture marketing, the State List mentions three items (items 26, 27 and 28), against item 33 in the Concurrent List, though items 26 and 27 are subject to item 33). The Economic Survey of 2015–2016 admitted it: 'Presently, markets in agricultural products are regulated under the Agricultural Produce Market Committee (APMC) Act enacted by State Governments.' It listed 2,477 regulated principal APMC markets and 4,843 sub-markets under those (Constitution of India, n.d.).

Yet the new law on farm trade disenfranchises states by denying them tax right, removes their role in interstate and intrastate trade (Section 3), empowers the centre to issue any instruction to states and its authorities regarding parallel private markets (Section 12) and overrides all state laws (Section 14).

Similarly, as per the new law on contract farming, the centre reserves rights to issue guidelines on direct agreements between farmers and private traders/corporations (Section 3[4]), makes such contracts 'exempt from the application of any State Act, by whatever name called' (Section 7[1]) and removes restrictions on stock piling by private traders/

corporations, thereby disempowering states to act against hoarding and profiteering (Section 7[2]).

But this attempt to have 'one nation one market' wouldn't be easy. A day after the law came into being, Haryana stopped Uttar Pradesh farmers from selling paddy in its jurisdiction. Six states have passed resolutions against the new laws in the assemblies, three of them (Punjab, Chhattisgarh and Rajasthan) passed their own laws to bypass the central laws. There probably was no need to do so as 27 states had already implemented many of the new provisions such as single license, direct marketing and private wholesale markets. Most states had earlier adopted the model APMC Act circulated from time to time by the centre in the past decade and more (Singh, 2021).

States and Courts Out of Dispute Resolution

This is another area of concern as the new laws on trade and contract farming keep both states and courts of law out of it, leaving farmers at the mercy of private business and the centre's whims.

The dispute resolution provided for is a three-tier-mechanism: Board of Conciliation to be set by a SDM, failing which the SDM will hear it, failing which collector or additional collector nominated by collector would be the final appellate authority. On the face of it, states have a role to play but by inserting provisions such as the centre will issue guidelines about the resolution process and direct both SDM and collector directly, states' role has been eliminated. These officials enjoy the powers of civil courts.

Similarly, both the laws bar jurisdiction of any civil court by stating, 'No civil court shall have jurisdiction to entertain any suit or proceedings in respect of any matter…' This is another contentious issue that farmers want to be removed (Vishwanath, 2020).

Myths of Market Efficiency

The new farms laws are premised on the conviction that free market is more efficient and will provide better price realization to farmers. Nothing could be further from truth.

The USA is a shining example of this, as the outcome of its 40 years of corporatization of farming narrated at the beginning shows. Here is more.

An OECD paper 'Agricultural Policy Monitoring and Evaluation 2020' stated that 54 countries studied (all OECD and EU countries, plus 12 key emerging economies) provided over $700 billion a year in total support to the agricultural sector in 2019. At the top was China with $185.9 billion, European Union with $101.3 billion and the USA with $48.9 billion. The vast majority of this, *$536 billion, was in the form of payments to producers*; the rest consumer support and enabling services such as infrastructure investment or research and development (Calder, 2020).

Had free market been kind to farmers, would these government be spending so much subsidizing producers?

Extract from TradeVistas' 2020 Report

Total Estimated Agricultural Supports in 2019

Ranked by Spend as a % of Gross Farm Revenue		Ranked by Total Spend (% Gross Farm Revenue)	
1. NORWAY - $3.03 billion	57.6%	1. CHINA (12.1%)	$185.9 billion
2. ICELAND - $223.2 million	54.6%	2. EUROPEAN UNION (19.0%)	$101.3 billion
3. SWITZERLAND - $6.16 billion	47.4%	3. UNITED STATES (12.1%)	$48.9 billion
4. KOREA - $20.8 billion	46.1%	4. JAPAN (41.3%)	$37.6 billion
5. JAPAN - $37.6 billion	41.3%	5. INDONESIA (23.3%)	$29.4 billion
6. PHILIPPINES - $7.3 billion	27.1%	6. KOREA (46.1%)	$20.8 billion
7. INDONESIA - $29.4 billion	23.3%	7. RUSSIA (9.2%)	$7.9 billion
8. EUROPEAN UNION - $101.3 billion	19.0%	8. PHILIPPINES (27.1%)	$7.3 billion
9. ISRAEL - $1.5 billion	17.4%	9. TURKEY (13.5%)	$6.7 billion
10. TURKEY - $6.7 billion	13.5%	10. SWITZERLAND (47.4%)	$6.2 billion

Source: OECD Data, Agricultural Policy Monitoring and Evaluation 2020 Reference Tables.

India is missing from this list because Indian farmers end up paying more tax than subsidies they get. The report states that India spends over $11 billion on farm subsidies every year in the form of direct payments and input subsidies (irrigation water, power and fertilizers), but this is offset by 'negative market price support', that is, farmers are implicitly taxed due to complex regulations and trade policy to the tune of $77 billion: a –14.8 per cent hit in terms of farm receipts.

This comes from a 2018 OECD-ICRIER study which found that Indian farmers lost ₹2.65 lakh crore per annum, at 2017–2018 prices, or *₹45 lakh crore cumulatively for 17 years* between 2000 and 2016, because of implicit tax through restrictive marketing and trade policies that have an in-built consumer bias of controlling agri-prices (OECD, 2018).

At the height of farmers' protest in December 2020 French political scientist Christophe Jaffrelot asked about the new farm laws:

> Why should agriculture be liberalised in the first place when in most countries governments subsidise this sector? In the US, the agriculture sector is expected to receive $46 billion in federal subsidies this year. This accounts for about 40 per cent of the total farm income and, if not for those subsidies, the US farm income was poised to decline in 2020, according to a report by the *New York Times*. Similarly, the European Union's Common Agricultural Policy spending has averaged €54 billion annually since 2006.... Without some support from the state, *the smallest of Indian peasants would be even more vulnerable....*
> (Jaffrelot & Thakker, 2020)

He also explained why Indian farmers are scared of private corporations.

> The farmers' suspicion is understandable. Not only because big players have a lot of clout, but also because *past experiences have not been rewarding.* For instance, the management of the crop insurance scheme against natural disasters, introduced in 2017, was handed over to one of Anil Ambani's companies, among others. As P. Sainath has reported, the farmers did not profit from it.

Indian farmers and Indian agriculture have many pressing problems that need urgent attention.

More than 85 per cent of Indian farmers are small and marginal with less than 2 ha land, providing subsistence-level income; per capita operational landholding has fallen from 2.28 ha in 1970–1971 to 1.08 ha in 2015–2016, one of the lowest in the world, primarily because of land acquisition for industrial projects; land reforms has been permanently stalled; 55 per cent of total agricultural workforce is landless and agriculture labour, unlike in China where none is landless; 22.5 per cent farm households live below poverty; private investment in agriculture is falling after private involvement was encouraged; indebtedness at ₹47,000 per farm household is 7.3 times their average income; more than 10,000 farmers commit suicide every year, etc. (Mohanty, 2018, 2020b, 2021b, 2021c, 2021d).

None of these pressing issues are addressed by the new farm laws. The least that the protesting farmers want is corporatization of farming that would cause further harm. The USA is a shining example for them.

Takeaways

- ⇨ New farm laws don't address basic problems of farmers, such as rapidly falling landholding, low income and growth of landless agriculture workers, remain unaddressed.
- ⇨ New laws encourage corporatization of farming.
- ⇨ They promote centralization of power and take away protections that states and state laws provide.
- ⇨ They pit farmers directly with private corporates and keep recourse to courts of law for dispute resolution out, thereby making them more vulnerable to exploitation.
- ⇨ They threaten to hurt farmers' interest as the USA has seen by corporatizing farming 40 years ago.
- ⇨ No farm law can claim to benefit farmers and yet not consult or listen to their worries, forcing them to stage a sit-in for months.

References

Bera, S. (2021, 8 March). What trade freedom did to Bihar's farmers. *Mint.* https://www.livemint.com/news/india/what-trade-freedom-did-to-bihar-s-farmers/amp-11615132324103.html?__twitter_impression=true

CACP. (2020, March). Price policy for Kharif crops. The marketing season 2020–21. https://cacp.dacnet.nic.in/ViewQuestionare.aspx?Input=2&DocId=1&PageId=39&KeyId=702

Calder, A. (2020, 15 October). Agricultural subsidies: Everyone's doing it. Hinrich Foundation. https://www.hinrichfoundation.com/research/article/protectionism/agricultural-subsidies/

Chaba, A. A. (2021, 17 February). Dr Sukhpal Singh: 'Land leasing provisions under present laws worry farmers the most'. https://indianexpress.com/article/india/sukhpal-singh-interview-contract-farming-7191898/

Chatterjee, S., Krishnamurthy, M., Kapur, D. & Bouton, M. M. (2020). A study of the agricultural markets of Bihar, Odisha and Punjab. Center for the Advanced Study of India, University of Pennsylvania. https://casi.sas.upenn.edu/sites/default/files/uploads/A%20Study%20of%20the%20Agricultural%20Markets%20of%20Bihar%2C%20Odisha%20and%20Punjab.pdf

Constitution of India. (n.d.). Seventh Schedule. https://www.mea.gov.in/Images/pdf1/S7.pdf

Dash, D. K., & Gupta, S. (2021, 16 June). Rising prices of pulses, edible oils sear household budgets. *The Times of India.* https://timesofindia.indiatimes.com/business/india-business/rising-prices-of-pulses-edible-oils-sear-household-budgets/articleshow/83556869.cms

Department of Food & Public Distribution. (n.d.). Procurement policy. https://dfpd.gov.in/Procurement-Policy.htm

Hussain, S. (2020, 6 June). Will India's contract farming ordinance be a corporate lifeline for agriculture? *The Wire.* https://thewire.in/agriculture/india-contract-farming-ordinance-corporate-lifeline

IANS. (2018, 18 May). Farmers forced to sell wheat below MSP in Bihar. *Business Standard.* https://www.business-standard.com/article/news-ians/farmers-forced-to-sell-wheat-below-msp-in-bihar-118051801502_1.html

Jaffrelot, C., & Thakker, H. (2020, 3 December). Why should Indian agriculture be liberalised when in most countries governments subsidise it? *The Indian Express.* https://indianexpress.com/article/opinion/columns/farm-bills-protets-indian-agriculture-sector-7078237/

Jebaraj, P. (2021, 11 January). 'No record of consultations on farm laws'. *The Hindu*. https://www.thehindu.com/news/national/no-record-of-consultations-on-farm-laws/article33552859.ece

Kumar, S. (2015, 19 January). Report of the High Level Committee on Reorienting the Role and Restructuring of Food Corporation of India. https://fci.gov.in/app2/webroot/upload/News/Report%20of%20the%20High%20Level%20Committee%20on%20Reorienting%20the%20Role%20and%20Restructuring%20of%20FCI_English_1.pdf

Ministry of Agriculture & Farmers' Welfare. (2013, 22 January). Final report of Committee of State Ministers, In-charge of Agriculture Marketing to Promote Reforms. https://dmi.gov.in/Documents/stminprreform.pdf

Ministry of Agriculture & Farmers' Welfare. (2017a). Report of the Committee on Doubling Farmers' Income (Vol I). https://agricoop.gov.in/sites/default/files/DFI%20Volume%201.pdf

Ministry of Agriculture & Farmers' Welfare. (2017b). Report of the Committee on Doubling Farmers' Income (Vol. II). https://agricoop.gov.in/sites/default/files/DFI%20Volume%202.pdf

Ministry of Agriculture & Farmers' Welfare. (2017c). Report of the Committee on Doubling Farmers' Income (Vol. IV). https://agricoop.gov.in/sites/default/files/DFI%20Volume%204.pdf

Ministry of Agriculture & Farmers' Welfare. (2018). Report of the Committee on Doubling Farmers' Income (Vol. XIII). https://agricoop.gov.in/sites/default/files/DFI%20Volume%2013.pdf

Ministry of Law and Justice. (2020a, 24 September). The Farmers (Empowerment and Protection) Agreement on Price Assurance and Farm Services Act, 2020. https://egazette.nic.in/WriteReadData/2020/222040.pdf

Ministry of Law and Justice. (2020b, 26 September). The Essential Commodities (Amendment) Act, 2020. http://egazette.nic.in/WriteReadData/2020/222038.pdf

Ministry of Law and Justice. (2020c, 27 September). The Farmers' Produce Trade and Commerce (Promotion and Facilitation) Act, 2020. https://egazette.nic.in/WriteReadData/2020/222039.pdf

MoFPI. (2021, 31 March). Cabinet approves Production Linked Incentive Scheme for food processing industry. https://mofpi.nic.in/sites/default/files/cabinet_approves_production_linked_incentive_scheme_for_food_processing_industry_1.pdf

Mohanty, P. (2018, 9 March). Land grab in the name of development. *Business Line*. https://www.thehindubusinessline.com/opinion/land-grab-in-the-name-of-development/article22498363.ece

Mohanty, P. (2020a, 21 September). Rebooting economy XXIX: Exposing farmers to unregulated market is more likely to harm them. *Business Today*. https://www.businesstoday.in/opinion/columns/indian-economy-agriculture-sector-exposing-farmers-to-unregulated-market-is-more-likely-to-harm-them/story/416571.html

Mohanty, P. (2020b, 17 December). Seven reasons why India's agriculture sector needs a fresh churn. *India Today*. https://www.indiatoday.in/diu/story/seven-reasons-why-india-agriculture-sector-needs-a-fresh-churn-1750587-2020-12-17

Mohanty, P. (2020c, 28 December). Rebooting economy 54: Will bypassing APMC-based procurement improve farmers' income, ensure food security? *Business Today*. https://www.businesstoday.in/opinion/columns/indian-economy-will-bypassing-apmc-based-procurement-improve-farmers-income-and-ensure-food-security/story/426298.html

Mohanty, P. (2021a, 3 January). Rebooting economy 55: Farmer producer organisations best bet for small, marginal farmers. *Business Today*. https://www.businesstoday.in/opinion/columns/farmer-producer-organisations-could-be-the-best-bet-for-small-and-marginal-farmers/story/426814.html

Mohanty, P. (2021b, 25 January). Rebooting economy 61: All that's wrong with guaranteed MSP outside APMC. *Business Today*. https://www.businesstoday.in/opinion/columns/indian-economy-all-thats-wrong-with-guaranteed-msp-outside-apmc/story/429060.html

Mohanty, P. (2021c, 30 January). Rebooting economy 63: Budgeting FY22 with critical information gaps. *Business Today*. https://www.businesstoday.in/union-budget-2021/columns/indian-economy-budgeting-fy22-with-critical-information-gaps/story/429601.html

Mohanty, P. (2021d, 14 December). Rebooting economy 52: The unfinished agenda of land reforms nobody talks about. *Business Today*. https://www.businesstoday.in/opinion/columns/indian-economy-the-unifinished-agenda-of-land-reforms-nobody-talks-about-landless-agricultural-labour/story/424811.html

OECD. (2018, 4 July). Review of agricultural policies in India. http://www.oecd.org/officialdocuments/publicdisplaydocumentpdf/?cote=TAD/CA(2018)4/FINAL&docLanguage=En

Pain, B. (2021, 8 March). How 'Big Ag' ate up America's small farms. https://timesofindia.indiatimes.com/world/us/how-big-ag-ate-up-americas-small-farms/articleshow/81384027.cms

Parth, M. N. (2021, 26 February). Farm laws: Fate of farmers in Bihar points to what those across India might soon face. *The Wire*. https://thewire.in/agriculture/farm-laws-farmers-bihar-apmc-msp

Pohit, S., Kannan, E., Singh, R. K. P., Bandyopadhyay, S., Alawadhi, A., & Sayal, L. (2019, November). Study on agricultural diagnostics for the state of Bihar in India. National Council of Applied Economic Research. https://www.ncaer.org/publication_details.php?pID=311&pID=311

Ray, U. K. (2020, 7 December). Nitish cites Bihar example as guarantee of farm laws' success; state farmers disagree. *The Wire*. https://thewire.in/agriculture/nitish-cites-bihar-example-as-guarantee-of-farm-laws-success-state-farmers-disagree

Ray, U. K. (2021a, 27 January). Rice racket: From the paddy fields of Bihar to the mandis of Punjab. Gaon Connection. https://en.gaonconnection.com/rice-racket-from-the-paddy-fields-of-bihar-to-the-mandis-of-punjab/

Ray, U. K. (2021b, 1 March). Why Bihari farmers are looking to sell their sugarcane in Nepal. *The Wire*. https://thewire.in/agriculture/why-bihari-farmers-are-looking-to-sell-their-sugarcane-in-nepal

Sasidhar, P. V. K., & Suvedi, M. (2015, June). Integrated contract broiler farming: An evaluation case study in India. https://meas.illinois.edu/wp-content/uploads/2015/04/MEAS-EVAL-2015-Broiler-India-short-Sasidhar-Suvedi-July-2015.pdf

Sethi, C. K. (2020, 7 December). A 2019 email & a govt report—Why farmers are refusing to trust MSP, procurement promises. *The Print*. https://theprint.in/india/a-2019-email-a-govt-report-why-farmers-are-refusing-to-trust-msp-procurement-promises/558339/

Singh, S. (2020, 6 December). Bihar procurement at snail's pace, farmers forced to sell paddy much below MSP. *The Indian Express*. https://indianexpress.com/article/india/bihar-procurement-at-snails-pace-farmers-forced-to-sell-paddy-much-below-msp-7093413/

Singh, S. (2021, 15 March). Food security and markets: Understanding the protests over India's changing social contract with farmers. The Hindu Centre for Politics and Public Policy. https://www.thehinducentre.com/the-arena/current-issues/article34060554.ece

The Indian Express. (2020, 5 December). On table now, issues which Opp raised in House, govt dismissed. https://indianexpress.com/article/india/farm-laws-protest-msp-apmc-parliament-7092197/

The Wire. (2020, 21 September). A blow-by-blow account of how the Rajya Sabha passed the farm bills. https://thewire.in/politics/rajya-sabha-harivansh-derek-obrien-farm-bills

Vishwanath, A. (2020, 21 December). Explained: In farm laws, the dispute settlement provision govt has offered to roll back. *The Indian Express*. https://indianexpress.com/article/explained/explained-in-farm-laws-the-dispute-settlement-provision-govt-has-offered-to-roll-back-7106606/

VIII NEW LABOUR CODES

Weakening Workers, Empowering Employers

In contrast to the UPA's 10 years of 'job-less' growth, the PLFS of 2017–2018 showed a 'job-loss' growth during the Modi government. This shows the acerbity of the situation (Mohanty, 2021a, 2021b).

The state of Indian workforce hasn't been good, especially after the liberalization when providing flexibility to industries and promoting industrial growth took precedence over workers' rights and protections. India's growth did reach a new high in the first two decades of the new millennium witnessing the highest ever GDP growth, but the growth in employment declined—a trend which has been witnessed world over because of technological advancements.

India's workforce received one shock after another when the new government came in 2014. It unleashed a series of decisions, such as demonetization, GST and an untimely and unplanned overnight lockdown, leading to massive job and business losses. It took no remedial action, but rather brought four new labour codes which increased their precarity even further.

The new codes came when the workforce was under tremendous pressure and yet the industry was cutting both jobs and wages. Business portal CMIE analysed financial reports of more than 4,000 listed companies to find that these companies posted 'their highest ever profit in the midst of a severe lockdown' in Q2 of FY2021, accompanied with cuts in jobs and wages. It stated, '53% profits growth companies slashed wages.' In Q3 of FY2021, these companies surpassed their historic high profits with *net profits* soaring from ₹142,200 crore in Q1 to ₹162,000 crore in Q3 of FY2021. For the entire fiscal of FY2021, their net profits went up by 57.6 per cent to ₹5.31 lakh crore (*Business Today*, 2021; Kant, 2021; Mohanty, 2021c).

How Legit Are the New Labour Codes?

In all, four codes were passed, beginning with the Code on Wages (Ministry of Law and Justice, 2019) of 2019, followed by three more during the pandemic lockdown in September 2020: Industrial Relations Code (IR Code), Code on SS (SS Code) 2020 and the Occupational Safety, Health and Working Conditions Code (OSHW Code). These codes amalgamated 44 central laws relating to workers covering all aspects of labour regulations.

None of the codes had come into force by June 2021 as their rules had not been notified. Unlike the farm laws, the new codes were brought in after prolonged discussions with labour unions and experts but, just like those, the codes weakened workers' rights and protections while boosting that of employers.

The following paragraphs examine these codes for their impact on wages, job and SS, working hours, oversight mechanisms, etc.

Minimum Wages

The Wage Code was the first to be notified in August 2019, promising (a) equity and welfare of workers through a universal minimum wage and (b) improvement in ease of doing business to help enterprises and create more employment (Ministry of Law and Justice, 2019).

By June 2021, there was no sign of a national minimum wage or floor rate. The national minimum wage remained unchanged at ₹176 per day, fixed in 2017, since an upward revision of ₹2 (to ₹178) announced by the Union Cabinet days before this code was passed in 2019 was not notified. A hike of ₹2 came after an internal committee of the Ministry of Labour and Employment recommended a national minimum wage of ₹375. The Economic Survey of 2018–2019 had also highlighted the low minimum wages in the informal sector and sought a higher benchmark, arguing that this would pull up wages by enhancing the bargaining power of vulnerable and informal workers because of the 'lighthouse effect' (Ministry of Finance, 2020; Ministry of Labour and Employment, 2019; Mohanty, 2020a).

The new Wage Code provides for an elaborate mechanism for fixing minimum wages on the basis of multiple considerations but does not provide a linkage between minimum wage and minimum standard of living, and time-bound revisions remain vague. The draft rules of the code do provide for retaining the older norm of ensuring 2,700 calories per day per adult and other requirements such as housing rent, education, health and other expenses for a 3-adult unit (as against 3.6 units the internal committee had recommended), but this is missing from determining the 'floor wage' to be fixed below which no minimum wage can be set.

Both the code and its draft rules provide that minimum wage would be revised 'at an interval not exceeding five years', unlike dearness allowance (DA) which, according to the draft rules, would be computed twice every year (before April and 1 October). This is a clever mechanism to keep wages low, as explained in an ILO paper of 2020. It stated that such differential provisions for minimum wage and DA had cost Indian workers dearly for 72 years as states would revise only DA but leave minimum wage out, thereby short-changing workers on full revision. It stated that this was the method the Delhi and Maharashtra governments adopted to stop revising basic wage rates for 22 years and 9 years, respectively (ILO, 2020b).

Why this clever mechanism is a big concern would be clear from the ILO's 2018 'India Wage Report' which stated that Indian workers were deprived of fair share of rise in profits and productivity. Its estimates showed that 'average labour productivity' (as measured by GDP per worker) increased more rapidly than 'real average wages' in the post-liberalization era, but the labour share declined from 38.5 per cent in 1981 to 35.4 per cent in 2013 (ILO, 2018).

The ILO attributed this to labour flexibility achieved by the *'substitution of permanent employees with contract workers, increasing working hours,* substitution of women for men as permanent workers, substitution of capital for labour and substitution of technology for less skilled labour'. With the global rise in capital mobility and falling cost of capital, it warned that workers were even more vulnerable and amenable to flexibility (low-wage growth).

The Azim Premji University's 2018 paper, titled 'State of Working India', showed that real labour productivity (as measured by real gross value added per worker) grew at *5.5 per cent* a year, while real wages grew at *1.4 per cent* a year, on an average, between 1982 and 2015, in the organized manufacturing. This was attributed to job-less growth (delaying wage growth) and poor enforcement of labour protection laws (Azim Premji University, 2018).

The new Wage Code and its draft rules don't link wages to labour productivity either; thus, workers are likely to be denied their fair share in productivity growth in the future. This is not a progressive approach as another 2020 ILO report showed that Indians were among the lowest paid globally. In the Asia-Pacific region, India's minimum statutory wage was the third lowest (in 2019) after Bangladesh and Solomon Islands (ILO, 2020a; Mohanty, 2020c).

Millions Out of Wage Protections

Contrary to the perception created, the Wage Code is not universal; Section 50 excludes establishments with five or less workers engaged in 'agriculture and domestic purpose' from maintaining a 'register' or a 'wage clip'—the areas where most workers are engaged.

According to the Sixth EC (last one) released in 2014, excluding agricultural establishments with five or less workers alone would exclude *98.6 per cent* of all agricultural establishments. Agricultural establishments account for 22.4 per cent of the total (13.13 million establishments). This exclusion would keep *22 per cent of the total* (12.94 million) establishments out of the minimum wage coverage (Ministry of Statistics & Programme Implementation, 2014).

Add to this domestic workers, gig workers, platform workers and home-based workers (the last three are excluded from the definition of 'worker' in the code, but are included in the SS Code 2020). Their number is not even known. Also, the millions of MGNREGA workers, numbering 84 million (five years' average between FY2012 and FY2021), have specifically been kept out (Section 66; Government of India, 2021).

Added to this are 1.4 million Anganwadis that employ one or more workers and helpers and also 1.05 million Accredited Social Health Activist (ASHA) workers. Both are government employees but are officially considered 'honorary workers' and paid 'honorarium', not wages or salary. Taken together, the numbers of those excluded from the code would reach 100 million (Mohanty, 2020c; PIB, 2019, 2020).

The Economic Survey of 2018–2019 pointed out that how, despite a complex and multiple minimum wage structure, *19.4 per cent of regular workers and 42 per cent of casual workers* received less the national floor-level minimum wage. Since penalties and inspections have been virtually eliminated in the Wage Code, this could further worsen (Ministry of Finance, 2020).

No Equal Pay for Equal Work

The Wage Code does not provide for 'equal pay for equal work' between temporary and permanent workers as mandated by the Supreme Court's 2016 judgement in the case of *State of Punjab v. Jagjit Singh and others* (Supreme Court of India, 2016).

Further, it removes pay discrimination between men and women but is silent on pay discriminations against *ethnic minorities and lower castes*. The ILO's 2018 India Wage Report found such pay discriminations (against women, ethnic minorities and lower caste groups) to be a 'a significant source of wage inequality' in India (ILO, 2018).

The SS Code provides for equal pay between a fixed-term employee—contract or temporary worker—and a permanent employee of a firm, but not among FTEs themselves who can be hired at different wages for the same or similar work. This is a normal practice in the private sector, and it depends on the bargaining power of the individual workers. There is no such protection for a vast majority of contract workers without a written contract. The PLFS of 2018–2019 stated that *69.5 per cent of regular wages/ salaried in the non-farm sector have no written contract* (MoSPI, 2020).

Further, there is a maximum penalty for not paying minimum wage at ₹50,000 and for a repeat offender ₹1 lakh and/or three months of imprisonment. But there is no minimum penalty, which means that a penalty of any amount—₹10 or even ₹1—can be imposed and is, thus, discretionary. Besides, the Parliamentary Standing Committee, which examined the Wage Code (originally introduced in 2017) and submitted its recommendation in 2018, said that this provision 'is not substantial enough to act as a deterrent'. Hence, it proposed to raise the maximum penalty to ₹10 lakh (Parliamentary Standing Committee on Labour, 2018).

This was ignored.

Working Hours up from 8 to 12 Hours

The new codes have extended working hours to 12 hours a day, though the total hours of work in a week remains 48 hours, which is on the higher side globally. The Wage Code is silent on the issue, but its draft rules (Rule 6[2] provides for 'spread over' working time to 12 hours in normal times, even while talking about 8-hour-a-day work). In 'emergency', 'preparatory' and 'complementary', purposes, Rule 9 stated (without explaining) that the 'spread over' time can go up to 16 hours, but 'either physical activity or sustained attendance shall not exceed 9 hours in any day' (Ministry of Labour and Employment, 2020).

This is a license to exploit workers because of weak oversight mechanism. Physical inspection has been ruled out. 'Inspector' becomes 'inspector-cum-facilitator'; physical inspection is replaced with virtual or 'web-based inspection' (Section 51[2]). Besides, higher working hours may lead to reducing three shifts of work (8 hours each) to two shifts, thereby reducing the number of workers (job loss).

What is the mechanism to detect violations? 'Inspector-cum-facilitator' would generate 'web-based inspection' and call for information 'electronically' (Section 51[2] of the code), if needed. Otherwise, he/she will go by self-declarations of employers. His/her responsibilities have been expanded to include the supply of information and give advice to both employers and workers to enable effective compliance, in which case the incentive to side with employer becomes greater.

Then, the draft rules state that the Chief Labour Commissioner (Central) *shall formulate* an 'inspection scheme'. There is no role for workers or their unions. Taken together, oversight becomes a *self-certification* or tilted against workers. The parliamentary panel had objected to the changing of 'inspector' into 'facilitator' for its negative connotations and the 'ILO norms', but that was also ignored.

Health and Safety Protections Curtailed

Similar to the Wage Code, the OSHW Code 2020 leaves out millions of workers from health and safety protections at workplace.

This has been done by changes in the definition of 'factory'. 'Factory' is now defined as a manufacturing unit where 20 or more workers are working with the aid of power and 40 or more are working without the aid of power. Earlier, the thresholds were set at 10 or more and 20 or more, respectively (Ministry of Law & Justice, 2020a).

How many workers would get excluded through this change in definition alone? The Sixth EC, the last of its kind published in 2014, showed that 97.9 per cent of total workers in manufacturing units (Code 06 or factories) were employing 1–9 workers (less than 10), 99 per cent workers were in units employing 1–19 workers and *99.3 per cent in units employing 1–29 workers*. It is unclear from this how many workers work in units employing up to 39 workers (Ministry of Statistics & Programme Implementation, 2014).

Thus, the OSHW Code will, at best, provide health and safety protections to *0.7 per cent of workers* in factories as against 1.1 per cent earlier. Factories are the places where risks to health and life are higher (Mohanty, 2020b).

When it comes to 'establishments' (a place where any industry, trade, business, manufacturing or any other occupation is carried out, including 'factory'), the limit remains 10 or more workers and will protect only 1.7 per cent workers. Although this threshold will not be applicable to establishment where 'hazardous or life-threatening activity is being carried out', what constitutes hazardous and life-threatening activity is left for the central government to notify later.

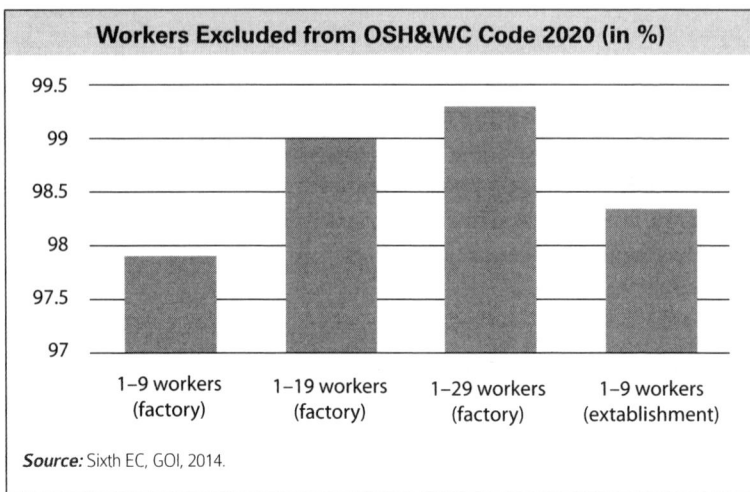

Source: Sixth EC, GOI, 2014.

The OSHW Code 2020 also has Section 127 with two provisions that represent a potential threat to anything good that it may contain. These are as follows:

> (i) Section 127 (1): The appropriate Government may, by notification and subject to such conditions and restrictions, if any, and for such period or periods as may be specified in the notification, direct that **all or any of the provisions of this Code or the rules** or the regulations made thereunder **shall not apply to or in relation to any establishment or class of establishments.**
>
> (ii) Section 127(2): Without prejudice to the generality of sub-section (1), where the State Government is satisfied in the public interest that it is necessary to create more economic activities and employment opportunities, it may, by notification, **exempt,** subject to such conditions as it may think fit, **any new factory or class or description of new factories from all or any of the provisions of this code....**

Taken together, Section 127 states that government can *exclude protections to workers in any establishment or factory*. Several years in the making, this code does not even provide a minimum health and safety standards.

Social Security

The SS Code provides more lip service, less security to workers. Although unorganized sector workers, such as migrants, gig workers, self-employed, home-based and platform workers find a place in the code, the actual security cover remains vague, not universal in nature. It is not spelt out as a right of workers (SS Code 2020).

All the existing thresholds—in terms of workers in an establishment and their monthly incomes—for the applicability of PF, ESI, gratuity and maternity benefits, etc., remain unchanged. Even for migrants, there are same thresholds and protections. The protections under the OSHW Code are also restricted to establishments employing 10 or more workers (Mohanty, 2020b).

Given the fact that three labour codes (except Wage Code) were introduced during the pandemic-induced crisis for millions of workers who lost their jobs and incomes, there is no provision for 'unemployment allowance'. For unorganized workers, Section 109 states that the central and state governments 'shall formulate and notify' welfare schemes for them. There is no concrete plan, no timeline or definitive funding architecture for such schemes yet.

Hire and Fire Gets a Boost

Ironically, the IR Code 2020 expands the scope of hire-and-fire power of employers rather than curtailing it.

This has been facilitated through Section 28 which states that the 'standing orders' shall apply to industrial establishments with *300 or more workers—from 100 or more workers hitherto applicable* (Ministry of Law and Justice, 2020b).

'Standing orders' are mandatory provisions under the Industrial Employment (Standing Orders) Act of 1946, which requires employer to 'define with sufficient precision the conditions of employment' (nature of employment such as permanent, temporary or probationers; wages and hours of work; termination of employment and notice thereof, means of grievance redressal mechanism, etc.) and 'make the said conditions known to workmen' (Government of India, 1946).

The 'standing orders' become critical to stop arbitrariness in hiring and firing workers because written contracts are not a legal requirement (except for fixed-term employment [FTE] incorporated in this code). The last PLFS of 2018–2019 showed that *69.5 per cent of regular wage/salaried employees* in the non-farm sector 'had no written job contract'. Not to talk of other categories of workers (casual and self-employed). Increasing the threshold for 'standing orders' would leave a greater number of workers vulnerable to exploitation. Analysis of the Annual Survey of Industries (ASI) 2017–2018 data showed that around *90 per cent of working factories and 44 per cent of their workers would be left completely outside the purview* of new 'standing orders' (Sundar, 2020).

Further, Section 77 increases threshold for lay-off and retrenchment *from 100 or more workers to 300 or more workers* in industrial establishments for which no prior government approval is needed. This would further expand hire and fire to more industries and may reduce workforce once these laws are enforced after the rules are notified.

The compensation to workers, however, remains the same: 15 days of average pay for every completed year of continuous service (Section 70). Section 83 adds a 'reskilling fund' to which the employer will pay equivalent to 15 days' wages of a retrenched employee, which will then be passed on to the retrenched worker within 45 days (Mohanty, 2020b).

Ironically, the fund is meant for 'training of retrenched workers' without any training scheme or plan in place or even source of money for it since the employer's contribution will be paid to the retrenched worker. The only other source of money for this fund will be 'the contribution from such other sources as *may be prescribed* by the appropriate Government' in Section 83(2b).

Push for Temporary Contract Work

The new labour codes expand the scope of contractual work, which will increase the precarity of workers. Here is how.

First, in the OSHW Code, Section 45 increases threshold for health and safety protections to establishment having 50 or more *contract workers*—up from 20 or more provided in the Contract Labour (Regulation and Abolition) Act of 1970—leaving a larger number of workers vulnerable in the process.

Although contract worker is prohibited in 'core activity' (defined as 'any activity for which the establishment is set up and includes any activity which is essential or necessary to such activity…') in this code, it *excludes works of 'perennial nature'* such as sanitation works, watch and ward services prohibited under the Contract Labour (Regulation and Abolition) Act of 1970 (Section 10).

Second, Section 57 provides enough *flexibility to hire contract workers for 'core activity'* in different circumstances and its Sub-section 2 states that the government retains the power to determine if 'any activity of an establishment is a core activity or otherwise'. Section 47(2) allows 'work specific licence' to contractors to supply contract workers even when a contractor 'does not fulfil the requisite qualifications or criteria'.

Third, the SS Code expanded the number of contract workers by providing for FTE and defined 'the engagement of an employee on the basis of a written contract of employment for a fixed period'. Such workers will get the benefits available to permanent workers, but their work will be *limited to the contract period and non-permanent in nature*, but they can be fired at any time at short notice (usually a month) for which all such contracts provide for. SS and other benefits will, thus, be restricted to their (written) contract period, which, for example, typically runs for 11 months in auto industries. What happens thereafter to workers' job or SS linked to it?

Fourth, the IR Code removes distinction between 'contractor' supplying contract workers and 'employer' by including the former in the definition of the latter. And then, it does not even define 'contractor'. This is a license to 'employer' to act as 'contractor' and hire workers (or fire them **without legal oversight**) on contract.

The other two codes also define 'employer' to include 'contractor' obscuring the responsibility of employer for violations of the codes relating to contract workers, except in the case of welfare facilities under the OSHW Code, which specifically mentions that the 'principal employer' will be liable for violations.

It is no secret that contractual employment increases the precarity of workers because it is not permanent (ends if not renewed). For loss of jobs on contract, workers don't need to be given advance notice, compensation or even be told the reason for the non-renewal of their contracts. Good performance is no guarantee of renewal of contract.

As per the ASI, the share of contract labour in the organized factory sector increased from *13 per cent in 1993–1994 to 36 per cent in 2016–2017*. No economy-wide contract labour data are available, even though it is widely prevalent, including the government sector. Professor Ravi Srivastava of the Institute for Human Development says:

> The pandemic has exposed and highlighted the precarity of Indian workforce and its implications not only for workers but the entire economy in terms of holding up demand. Instead of aligning the labour codes to reduce precarity and increase formalization of workforce, the Indian government has chosen to do the reverse.

He adds that contract work has an adverse impact on long-term productivity and disincentivizes skill development in non-core areas (Mohanty, 2020b; Sundar, 2020).

Myths about Fixed-term Employment/Fixed-term Contract

The introduction of FTE or fixed-term contract (FTC) in the IR Code is not a benign move to help contract workers get equal pay, PF, gratuity and other SS at par with permanent employees as the government claims. It will end up harming workers further, as it already has in Europe from which India borrowed the idea (Mohanty, 2020e).

There are several reasons for this. *First*, FTE is included in the Standing Orders (First Schedule of the IR Code) applicable to all industrial establishments, adding a new category of employees to the existing five: permanent, temporary, apprentices, probationers and *badlis*. It will swell the 'temporary' category of workers.

Second, the Central Rules of 1946 under the Industrial Employment (Standing Orders) Act of 1946 provided that 'temporary' and 'probationers' will become 'permanent' after a 'period of *three months* in the same or another occupation in the industrial establishment'. Such protection or facility is not available in the FTE, which acquires universal character also as a part of the SS Code. The centre has adopted it for its hiring, and it has been around for about two decades in the formal private sector. The author had a first-hand experience of this in 2002. Such employment can be terminated at any time with a month's notice. The FTE, thus, doesn't provide job security even during the contract period.

Third, the gazette notification of March 2018, which introduced the FTE for the first time, had a restriction on its applicability: 'No employer of an industrial establishment shall convert the posts of the permanent workmen existing in his industrial establishment on the date of commencement of the Industrial Employment (Standing Orders) Central (Amendment) Rules, 2018 as fixed term employment thereafter' (Ministry of Labour and Employment, 2018).

This restriction does not find a place in the codes.

This makes a permanent employment vulnerable to conversion into FTE any time and be fired at will. Although there is no restriction on renewal of such contracts, there is no legal provision to convert it into a permanent contract or any compulsion for renewal either. In practice, FTC/FTE is a *permanently temporary job even during the contract period*.

Often FTC/FTE is supported with the argument that it is consensual and not forced on anyone. That is true in theory, but not in practice. When chronic job crisis and massive job loss are the order of the day, workers hardly have any choice. A top-ranking leader of the BJP/RSS-affiliated Bharatiya Mazdoor Sangh told the author on a condition of anonymity that 'consent' for Indian workers meant 'consent under pressure'. He should know because he has been fighting for workers for decades (Mohanty, 2020e).

Flexibility for industry (employer) remains one of the major economic arguments for FTC/FTE. Here is an interesting finding. In 2014, the WB surveyed Indian establishments (manufacturing and services) while preparing its 'Ease of Doing Business' report and found that India's rigid labour laws were hardly an obstacle: 35.7 per cent of firms marked it as a 'minor obstacle', 17.3 per cent marked it as a 'moderate obstacle' and 10.4 per cent marked it as a 'major obstacle' (World Bank, 2015).

Fourth, FTE comes from Europe where it was adopted it in the early 2000s. It was meant to provide flexibility to industry and serve as *a stepping stone for young and raw hands* to establish their suitability for permanent employment. But Europe has witnessed a meltdown, the promised changes were little but the damage to workers was massive: transition rate to permanent employment fell; a duality was created in labour market with a high wage difference; the duration of FTE shortened (in Spain, 25% of new contracts last less than a week and 40% last less than a month); FTE hires are more likely to be low-wage workers, concentrated in the lowest income bracket, increasing wage volatility and lowering job security (Weel, 2018).

Two studies of the European Parliament found that the risk of workers' precariousness increased due to a rise in 'temporary and marginal part-time contracts' and the share of full-time permanent contracts fell from 62 per cent in 2003 to 59 per cent. Studies in OECD countries show that temporary contracts 'negatively affect aggregate labour productivity' and are 'more damaging in skilled sectors'. A study of outsourcing in public sector organizations in the UK found that it weakened trade unions and collective bargaining, causing increased insecurity and worsening of work terms (European Parliament, 2016, 2017; Lisi & Malo, 2017; Sargeant & Sutschet, 2015).

Unlike in Europe, India's new codes *don't provide for transition from contract to permanent employment* (stepping stone for raw hands). The Supreme Court had, in 2001, overturned its earlier judgement of 1996 that made it obligatory to make contract workers permanent where contract system was abolished by the Contract Labour (Regulation and Abolition) Act of 1970 (Supreme Court of India, 2001).

India should have learnt Europe's lessons but chose to follow the same path to provide flexibility to industry where none was needed. FTE was first introduced in India in 2016 in apparel industry and then extended to all other sectors in the budget for FY2019. A 2019 study of organized manufacturing stated that 'immediate cost advantages', rather than flexibility, *influenced* hiring on contract. It ruled out labour market *rigidity* for contract hiring by stating that the effect of protective labour legislation on flexibility in the labour market (rigidity) is 'insignificant' and 'diminishing' (Mohanty, 2020e; Singh et al., 2019).

Another study of organized manufacturing found that the *productivity* of contract workers was significantly lower than that of directly hired workers in both capital- and labour-intensive industries. It pointed at their 'deplorable conditions' of work, little or no job security and fewer benefits in terms of health, safety, welfare and SS compared to directly hired workers. This finding resonates well with the ILO's 2018 report which stated that temporary jobs (marked by low pay and wage inequalities) 'remain a *serious challenge* to India's inclusive growth' (ILO, 2018; Kapoor & Krishnapriya, 2019a, 2019b).

India's promotion of contractual work is self-defeating; it will reduce productivity, increase precarity of workers and undermine future growth.

Ban on Right to Strike

The new codes don't stop here. They do more harm than good.

Strikes and lockouts are prohibited by the IR Code altogether. Section 62 of the code states that no employee can go on strike or lockout (a) without giving notice of strike 'within 60 days before striking', (b) 'within 14 days of the data of strike specified', (c) 'during the pendency of arbitration proceedings' before a tribunal and 60 days after the conclusion of such proceedings, (d) during the pendency of arbitration proceedings before an arbitrator and 60 days after the conclusion of such proceedings and (e) during any period in which a settlement or award is in operation (Ministry of Law and Justice, 2020b).

That leaves no room for strikes at all and curtails workers' right to use strike as the last resort to protest against exploitation. The penalty for violation is stiff: a fine up to ₹10,000 and/or a month's imprisonment.

India's workforce faces a long list of problems, but the new codes don't address any of those. Rather, it adds to their woes. Some of their major concerns are as follows:

1. India has the highest share of informal workers at 88.2 per cent, compared to 70 per cent in emerging economies (peers) and 18 per cent in developed economies, and these workers face 'greater in-work poverty risk than formal economy worker' (OECD & ILO, 2019).
2. Informalization/temporization is growing in the government sector rapidly; a 2014 study (the last of its kind) found that two-thirds of the incremental hiring was temporary, with 43 per cent (12.3 million) of it being 'temporary' (ISF, 2014).
3. Regular jobs are rapidly disappearing in the central government and a large number of vacancies remain unfilled for years even in the face of a massive job crisis (Mohanty, 2020d).
4. The Indian workforce remains one of the lowest paid in the world (ILO, 2020a).

Takeaways

⇨ New codes increase the precarity of workers by weakening protections against arbitrary hiring and firing, work and health safety.

⇨ Minimum wage provisions leave out millions of workers out of their ambit, are not universal, are not linked to productivity, don't promise equal pay for equal work and are merely on paper with no concrete plans and funds.

⇨ The promise of SS is not universal because it leaves out millions of workers.

⇨ Temporary employment, on contract, is expanded with a new category of FTE added to dilute job security and, consequently, SS linked to it.

⇨ Workers' rights are compromised by banning strike and lockouts.

⇨ Oversight mechanisms have been diluted to the point of being irrelevant.

⇨ None of the key concerns of the workforce is addressed.

References

Azim Premji University. (2018). State of working India. https://cse.azimpremji university.edu.in/state-of-working-india/swi-2018/

Business Today. (2021, 17 February). India Inc's profits touch another high in Q3; finserv leads, manufacturing bleeds. https://www.businesstoday.in/current/corporate/india-inc-profits-touch-another-high-in-q3-finserv-leads-manufacturing-bleeds/story/431565.html

European Parliament. (2016). Precarious employment in Europe: Patterns, trends and policy strategies. https://www.europarl.europa.eu/RegData/etudes/STUD/2016/587285/IPOL_STU(2016)587285_EN.pdf

European Parliament. (2017). Temporary contracts, precarious employment, employees' fundamental rights and EU employment law. https://www.europarl.europa.eu/RegData/etudes/STUD/2017/596823/IPOL_STU(2017)596823_EN.pdf

Government of India. (1946, 23 April). The Industrial Employment (Standing Orders) Act, 1946. https://legislative.gov.in/sites/default/files/A1946-20.pdf

Government of India. (2021). At a glance. http://mnregaweb4.nic.in/netnrega/all_lvl_details_dashboard_new.aspx?Fin_Year=2020-2021&Digest=ueg/HtV54GGJ8ZQ6GUB2ew

ILO. (2018). India wage report. https://www.ilo.org/wcmsp5/groups/public/---asia/---ro-bangkok/---sro-new_delhi/documents/publication/wcms_638305.pdf

ILO. (2020a). Global wage report 2020-21: Wages and minimum wages in the time of COVID-19. https://www.ilo.org/wcmsp5/groups/public/---dgreports/---dcomm/---publ/documents/publication/wcms_762534.pdf

ILO. (2020b, August). Discussion paper: Wage code and rules—Will they improve the welfare of low-paid workers in India? https://www.ilo.org/wcmsp5/groups/public/---asia/---ro-bangkok/---sro-new_delhi/documents/publication/wcms_753465.pdf

ISF. (2014). Flexi staffing in government and public sector. http://www.indianstaffingfederation.org/wp-content/uploads/2015/05/Flexi-Staffing-in-Govt.-Public-Sector.pdf

Kant, K. (2021, 31 May). Corporate profit to GDP ratio hits 10-year high of 2.63% in FY21. Business Standard. https://www.business-standard.com/article/companies/corporate-profit-to-gdp-ratio-hits-10-year-high-of-2-63-in-fy21-121053100041_1.html#:~:text=The%20combined%20net%20profit%20of,in%20the%20last%20financial%20year

Kapoor, R., & Krishnapriya, P. P. (2019a, January). *Explaining the contractualisation of India's workforce* (Working Paper No. 369). https://icrier.org/pdf/Working_Paper_369.pdf

Kapoor, R., & Krishnapriya, P. P. (2019b, 18 March). Facts and myths on rise of contract labour. *Business Line*. https://www.thehindubusinessline.com/opinion/facts-and-myths-on-rise-of-contract-labour/article26571045.ece

Lisi, D., & Malo, M. A. (2017). The impact of temporary employment on productivity. *Journal for Labour Market Research, 50*, 91–112. https://labourmarketresearch.springeropen.com/articles/10.1007/s12651-017-0222-8#:~:text=Among%20innovators%2C%20temporary%20employment%20seems,agencies%2C%20decreases%20labour%20productivity%20growth

Ministry of Finance. (2020). Economic survey 2018–2019. https://www.indiabudget.gov.in/budget2019-20/economicsurvey/index.php

Ministry of Labour and Employment. (2018, 16 March). Part II—Section 3—Sub-section (i). GSR no. 235(E). https://labour.gov.in/sites/default/files/FTE%20Final%20Notification.pdf

Ministry of Labour and Employment. (2019). Report of the Expert Committee on determining the methodology for fixing the national minimum wage. https://labour.gov.in/sites/default/files/Commitee_on_Determination_of_Methodology.pdf

Ministry of Labour and Employment. (2020, 7 July). G. S. R. 432(E). https://labour.gov.in/sites/default/files/gazette%20notification.pdf

Ministry of Law and Justice. (2019, 8 August). The Code on Wages, 2019. http://egazette.nic.in/WriteReadData/2019/210356.pdf

Ministry of Law & Justice. (2020a, 29 September). The Occupational Safety, Health and Working Conditions Code, 2020. https://labour.gov.in/sites/default/files/OSH_Gazette.pdf

Ministry of Law and Justice. (2020b, 29 September). The Industrial Relations Code 2020. http://egazette.nic.in/WriteReadData/2020/222118.pdf

Ministry of Statistics & Programme Implementation. (2014, July). Provisional results of Sixth Economic Census, All India Report. http://www.mospi.nic.in/sites/default/files/economic-census/sixth_economic_census/sixth_ec_prov_result_30july14.pdf

Mohanty, P. (2020a, 5 April). Coronavirus lockdown IV: How reverse migration will affect the informal economy as livelihood options dry up. *Business Today*. https://www.businesstoday.in/current/economy-politics/coronavirus-lockdown-reverse-migration-will-affect-informal-economy-labourers-daily-wagers/story/400209.html

Mohanty, P. (2020b, 27 September). Rebooting economy 31: Will new labour codes protect more workers or less? *Business Today*. https://www.businesstoday.in/opinion/columns/indian-economy-will-new-labour-codes-protect--more-workers-or-less-unorganised-workers/story/417146.html

Mohanty, P. (2020c, 29 September). Rebooting economy 32: Wage code leaves millions of workers out in cold. *Business Today*. https://www.businesstoday.in/opinion/columns/indian-economy-wage-code-leaves-millions-of-workers-out-in-cold-labour-productivity-minimum-wages/story/417260.html

Mohanty, P. (2020d, October 5). Rebooting economy 33: Where have the good old full-time decent jobs gone? *Business Today*. https://www.businesstoday.in/opinion/columns/indian-economy-where-have-the-good-old-full-time-decent-jobs-gone-contract-temporary-unemployment-informal-workers/story/417922.html

Mohanty, P. (2020e, 12 October). Rebooting economy 35: Is fixed term employment a boon or bane for India's workforce? *Business Today*. https://www.businesstoday.in/opinion/columns/indian-economy-is-fixed-term-employment-a-boon-or-bane-for-indias-workforce-coronavirus-pandemic-covid19-lockdown/story/418552.html

Mohanty, P. (2021a, 11 January). Rebooting economy 57: When and how will industry take India to next level of growth? *Business Today*. https://www.businesstoday.in/opinion/columns/indian-economy-when-and-how-will-industry-take-india-to-next-level-of-growth/story/427557.html

Mohanty, P. (2021b, 14 December). Rebooting economy 52: The unfinished agenda of land reforms nobody talks about. *Business Today*. https://www.businesstoday.in/opinion/columns/indian-economy-the-unifinished-agenda-of-land-reforms-nobody-talks-about-landless-agricultural-labour/story/424811.html

Mohanty, P. (2021c, 21 February). Rebooting economy 68: How private wealth creators are serving Indian economy and people. *Business Today*. https://www.businesstoday.in/opinion/columns/rebooting-economy-68-how-private-wealth-creators-are-serving-indian-economy-and-people/story/431736.html

MoSPI. (2020, June). PLFS (July 2018–June 2019). http://mospi.nic.in/sites/default/files/publication_reports/Annual_Report_PLFS_2018_19_HL.pdf

OECD & ILO. (2019, 21 May). Tackling vulnerability in the informal economy. OECD Development Centre. https://www.oecd-ilibrary.org/docserver/939b7bcd-en.pdf?expires=1615718853&id=id&accname=guest&checksum=F9D546A0B5116C928186FC17D4FD678A

Parliamentary Standing Committee on Labour. (2018, December). Standing committee report. https://www.prsindia.org/sites/default/files/bill_files/SCR-%20Code%20on%20Wages%20Bill%2C%202017%20%281%29.pdf

PIB. (2019, 21 November). Increase in salary of workers and helpers. https://pib.gov.in/PressReleasePage.aspx?PRID=1592815

PIB. (2020, 13 March). ASHA workers. https://pib.gov.in/PressReleseDetailm.aspx?PRID=1606212

Sargeant, M., & Sutschet, H. (2015). Non-standard working in the public service in Germany and the United Kingdom. ILO. https://www.ilo.org/wcmsp5/groups/public/---ed_dialogue/---sector/documents/publication/wcms_442069.pdf

Singh, J., Das, D. K., Kumar, A., & Kukreja, P. (2019, 10 June). Factors influencing the decision to hire contract labour by Indian manufacturing firms. *Oxford Development Studies*. https://www.tandfonline.com/doi/full/10.1080/13600818.2019.1624705

Sundar, K. R. S. (2020, 22 September). What is wrong with the centre's new labour codes. NewsClick. https://www.newsclick.in/what-wrong-centre-new-labour-codes

Supreme Court of India. (2001, 30 August). *Steel Authority Of India Ltd. & ... vs National Union Water Front...on 30 August, 2001*. https://indiankanoon.org/doc/277653/

Supreme Court of India. (2016). *State of Punjab and Ors vs Jagjit Singh and Ors on 26 October, 2016*. https://indiankanoon.org/doc/106416990/

Weel, B. E. (2018). The rise of temporary work in Europe. *De Economist*. https://link.springer.com/article/10.1007/s10645-018-9329-8

World Bank. (2015, 8 October). Enterprise Survey 2014, India, 2013–2014. https://microdata.worldbank.org/index.php/catalog/2225/variable/F2/V557?name=l30a

IX BANKING 'REFORMS'

Risks to Finance

The current government's penchant to promote private interests at the cost of public interest is amply evident in the banking-related 'reforms' that are in the work. True to the style, it sprang surprises in the budget for FY2022 by announcing two big bang changes: (a) privatize two PSBs, along with a general insurance company and set up a bad bank to address banking stressed assets.

None of it had been discussed inside or outside the Parliament for their merits and needs. Just like other major decisions of demonetization, locking and unlocking of the economy, AatmaNirbhar Bharat Abhiyan, etc., this was a top-down decision without the details being worked out. The third banking 'reform' is the RBI's Internal Working Group (IWG) proposal to let large industrial houses to run banks. All these are interlinked to ensure that private banking gets a bigger role.

The Logic Behind Privatization of PSBs

About the privatization of banks, the government just made an announcement in the budget on 1 February 2021. This hadn't been part of the privatization of public assets in the work until then. The logic was never explained and isn't known yet.

Writing about the need for banking reforms in 2020, former RBI Governor Raghuram Rajan and his deputy Viral Acharya had specifically forbidden privatization and explained why. They wrote:

> *It would be a mistake*...to sell a public sector bank to an untested industrial house. Far better to professionalize public sector bank governance and sell stakes to the broader public—that would help promote a shareholder culture, as well as distribute wealth more widely. This could be coupled with some large stakes sold to financial institutions, who can bring governance, as well as financial and technological expertise to the bank. It would be 'penny wise pound foolish' to replace the poor governance under the present structure of these banks with a highly conflicted structure of ownership by industrial houses. (Acharya & Rajan, 2020b; emphasis added)

They had earlier argued that *'corporate houses must be kept from* acquiring significant stakes, given their natural conflicts of interest' and sought regulatory and market reforms to improve banking (including bank governance and ownership) in line with other experts' committees—Narasimham Committee (1991) and Nayak Committee (2014; Acharya & Rajan, 2020a, emphasis added).

Needless to say, enough is known about the dangers of privatization of banks and the need for improving governance of public banks. These apart, the denationalization of banks would also mean that India hasn't learnt the lessons that led to the nationalization in the first place; subsequent progress and also the lessons of the 2007–2008 financial crisis.

Why Banks Were Nationalized?

Until 1969, Indian banking was entirely in private hands. The historic change from private banks to public banks (though some private banks were allowed) that happened in late 1969 and the 1970s has been recorded by the RBI and needs to be retold (RBI, 1967–1981).

The change happened at a time when India had plunged into political uncertainties after the deaths of first two prime ministers, Nehru and Shastri, within two years. The 1962 war with China and 1965 war with Pakistan, and drought and famines caused immense economic stress. The treasury was empty and a balance of payment crisis hit, delaying the Third Five-Year Plan by three years.

But there were three main banking reasons:

1. The lack of banking facilities for agriculture, small-scale industrial units and self-employed.

2. Bank expansion during 1951–1967 'un-served' rural and semi-urban areas as focus was firmly on urban areas.

3. Private banks were 'seen as being excessively concerned with profit alone' and 'unwilling to diversify their loan portfolios'.

This would be better explained through comparative data for the pre- and post-nationalization changes in (a) the share of credit to agriculture, industry and personal sectors and (b) the distribution of bank branches.

The following two graphs use the RBI data to map the status in 1950–1951, 1966–1967 (pre-nationalization) and 2019–2020 (RBI, 2008).

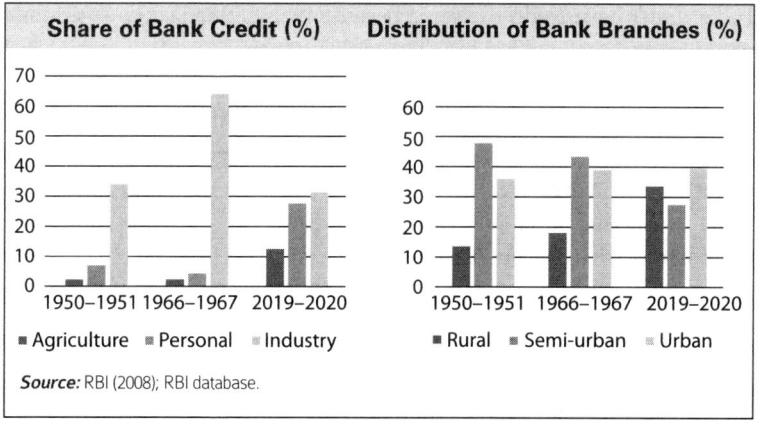

Source: RBI (2008); RBI database.

Banking 'Reforms' 211

What is clear from the two graphs is that the share of credit was far more skewed in 1950–1951 and 1966–1967 and so was the distribution of bank branches (in rural, semi-urban and urban/metro areas). Post-nationalization, in 2019–2020, the shares are more evenly matched—meaning these sectors are far more fairly served. It would be wise to remember that during the pandemic crisis, it is the industry, especially large industry, which is dragging down credit growth—as the RBI said in its 2021 report (RBI, 2021a).

If that doesn't give the lessons of nationalization of banks, noting never will. Privatization threatens to take India back to 1966–1967, if not 1950–1951.

Financial Crisis of 2007–2009

Poorly regulated private banks and shadow banks and other financial institutions have caused a series of economic crises all over the world, right from the Great Depression of 1929 to the Great Recession of 2007–2009. During the 2007–2009 crisis, the USA had to bail out many of those, such as Bank of America, Citigroup, AIG and Bear Stearns, at a huge cost to its taxpayers. It nationalized two big shadow banks (NBFCs) in the housing mortgage markets, Fannie Mae and Freddie Mac. By then, these two had run up a combined debt of *$5.4 trillion* (Davis, 2019; Mohanty, 2020b).

India didn't have to do the same because its banking sector was dominated by nationalized banks which didn't use the complex, opaque and high-risk financial instruments to maximize profits and pose serious threat to economy that those in the USA did. The world learnt a big lesson from the crisis. It started increasing government ownership (asset share) in banking. A WB report ('Rethinking the Role of the State in Finance') mapped this change. Surprisingly, while the developed nations had learnt their lessons and increased their government shares, the developing nations didn't. Its graph is reproduced below (World Bank, 2012).

The report explained that government ownership of banks was critical to 'stabilizing aggregate credit' and helped in limiting the damages during

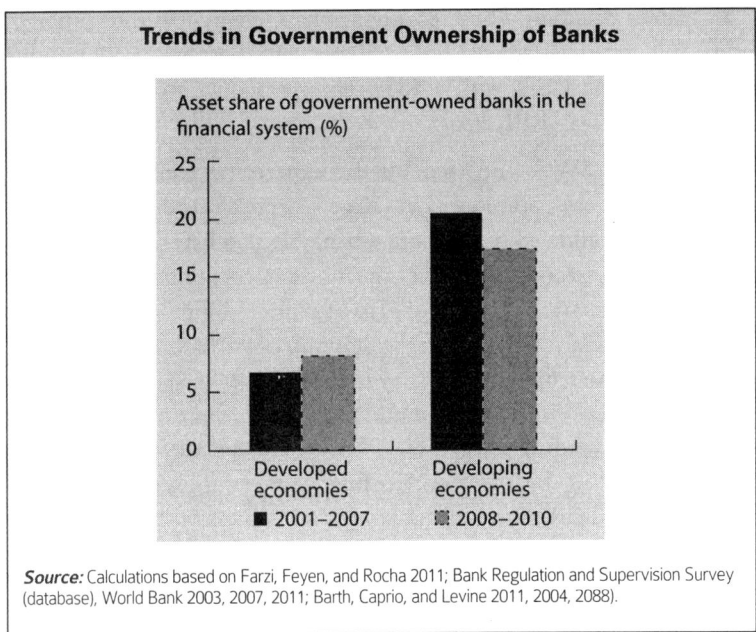

Source: Calculations based on Farzi, Feyen, and Rocha 2011; Bank Regulation and Supervision Survey (database), World Bank 2003, 2007, 2011; Barth, Caprio, and Levine 2011, 2004, 2088).

the financial meltdown of 2007–2009 in several countries. India and China benefitted from this and limited their losses.

India can ignore this lesson at its own peril.

Relinquishing Banks to Corporates

India is on the verge of making another big mistake by letting large industries with a large presence in non-banking to run banks.

The USA, for example, doesn't allow corporations to run banks. Its laws specifically prohibit big industrial houses with ownership and controlling stakes in non-banking businesses (manufacturing and others) from owning or controlling banks (Global Legal Insights, 2020).

The only logic that an IWG of the RBI proposed in October 2020 to allow large industrial houses (corporations) to own and run banks was that India needed to match the credit-to-GDP ratios of developed economies such as the USA, Japan, China and South Korea to make India a $5 trillion economy. Those economies have credit-to-GDP ratios of over 150 per cent, as against India's 50 per cent (both in 2019). It didn't explain why the USA, with a $35 trillion economy, would studiously avoid such a move (RBI, 2020).

Ironically, the IWG said that 'all the experts (it consulted) except one were of the opinion that large corporate/industrial houses should not be allowed to promote a bank.' It also listed their reasons: (a) 'prevailing corporate governance culture in corporate houses is not up to the international standard'; (b) 'it will be difficult to ring fence the non-financial activities of the promoters with that of the bank' and stress in non-financial activity may spill over to bank; (c) corporate houses 'may either provide undue credit to their own businesses or may favour lending to their close business associates'; (d) they 'may influence lending by the bank to finance the supply and distribution chains and customers of the group's non-financial businesses' and (e) 'there are various ways of circumventing the regulations on connected lending and due to complex structures of entities, cross-holding of capital, the disbursal/diversion of funds to group concerns is difficult to check.'

It remains a mystery why did then the IWG proposed what it did and at whose prompting.

Its proposal, however, received strong support from the expected quarters. Arvind Panagariya, former vice chairman of NITI Aayog, now back to teaching at the Columbia University, wrote in February 2021 to claim that India was facing an 'acute problem of credit deprivation' and that its 'credit scarcity' couldn't be addressed 'without recourse to investment resources of corporate houses' (Panagariya, 2021).

Had he done his homework by reading the RBI's reports or checking the relevant RBI data, he wouldn't have said it.

For one, India has been in a credit surplus and, in fact, a liquidity trap since April 2020. This is evident from the following graph, which maps the reverse repo deposits of the RBI. It is in this account that banks park their access liquidity on a daily basis when they are not lending or cannot find any takers. Banks earn 3.35 per cent interest for such deposits (Mohanty, 2021e).

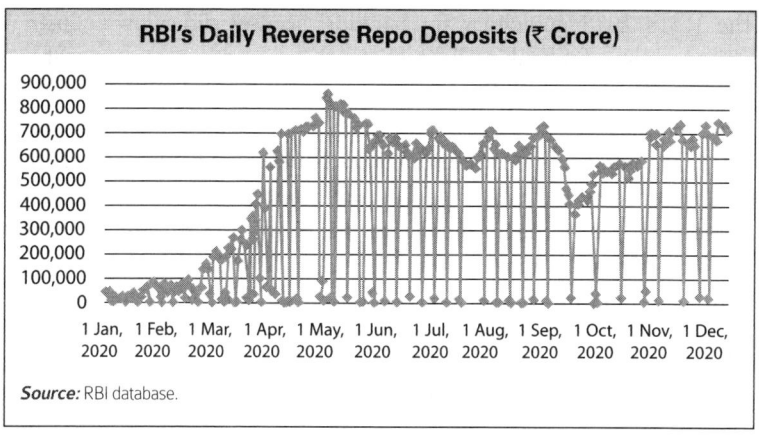

Source: RBI database.

Notice how the reverse repo deposits skyrocketed in March–April 2020, when cheap money was made available by cutting the repo rate (interest RBI charges to banks for lending money) from 4.4 per cent to 4 per cent (on 22 May 2020) and the CRR from 4 per cent to 3 per cent (on 28 March 2020).

The RBI finally admitted this on 5 February 2021, the same day Panagariya's article was published. According to the RBI's Monetary Policy Statement of 2020–2021, India's 'systemic liquidity remained in *large surplus*', thereby 'engendering easy financial conditions' (RBI, 2021a).

In fact, the RBI issued a warning in January 2021 about 'macro-financial risks' to the economy as 'unintended consequences' of fiscal and monetary policies (excess supply of cheap credit) pursued by the government to revive the economy (RBI, 2021b).

The IWG's proposal went against the RBI's stand in 2016 and 2020, as well as two Parliamentary Standing Committee reports of 2013 and 2014. In August 2020, the RBI rejected a similar proposal from the NITI Aayog, stating that this would pose a serious threat to India's financial stability, among other things. The RBI had also rejected a similar suggestion in 2016 while issuing 'Guidelines for "On Tap" Licensing of Universal Banks in Private Sector' (Karthik, 2020; RBI, 2016).

The RBI's 2013 guidelines for banking licenses did allow industrial houses to apply for banking licenses, which provoked a massive pushback from two Parliamentary Standing Committee reports in 2013 and 2014 (pre- and post-2014 change in government). These parliamentary reports listed facts and evidence to recommend that because banking is 'a highly leveraged business involving public money and public welfare', it would be better to 'keep industry and banking separate'. The 2014 report clearly warned: 'The Committee, therefore, reiterate that the Government/RBI should ensure that *no recurrence of the pre-nationalization situation happens*, when the management of private banks deployed their funds to extend undue favour to their own industrial owners without regard to social priorities determined by Government' (Ministry of Finance, 2013, 2014; RBI, 2013, emphasis added).

As expected, several eminent economists opposed the move. Acharya and Rajan wrote that it was a 'bombshell' that was 'best left on the shelf'. Kaushik Basu warned that it was 'almost invariably a step towards crony capitalism'. Arvind Subramanian, Shankar Acharya and Vijay Kelkar wrote that 'mixing industry and finance will set us on a road full of dangers—for growth, public finances and the future of the country itself' (Acharya & Rajan, 2020b; Acharya et al., 2020; Basu, 2020).

Acharya and Rajan questioned the timing too. They asked why now, when India was trying to learn the lessons from the failures such as IL&FS and Yes Bank, and offered two possibilities: (a) the government was trying to expand the set of bidders for privatization of PSBs, and (b) industrial houses holding payment bank wanted to transform into full-fledged banks.

Banking Crisis

Apart from all the above, India's private corporations are problematic for four big other reasons.

First, they are solely responsible for loan defaults and stressed assets in PSBs. The RBI data on 'composition of NPAs of PSB' show that their share of NPAs is, on an average, 98.6 per cent in the past 18 years from FY2003 to FY2020. In six of these 18 years, their share was more than 99 per cent, touching 99.9 per cent in FY2014 (Mohanty, 2021d).

Second, private sector investment in the economy has remained virtually stagnant for several years. Between FY2012 and FY2020, the average private sector investment as a percentage of GDP is 11.9 per cent, ranging from 11.2 per cent (FY2012) to 12.7 per cent (FY2016; Mohanty, 2021e).

The RBI data also show that large industries, which are to be allowed their banks, are particularly responsible for the fall in investment in spite of the surplus liquidity. As the following graph shows, growth in bank credit to industry, particularly large industry, has been falling, dragging down the overall credit growth to the non-food sector.

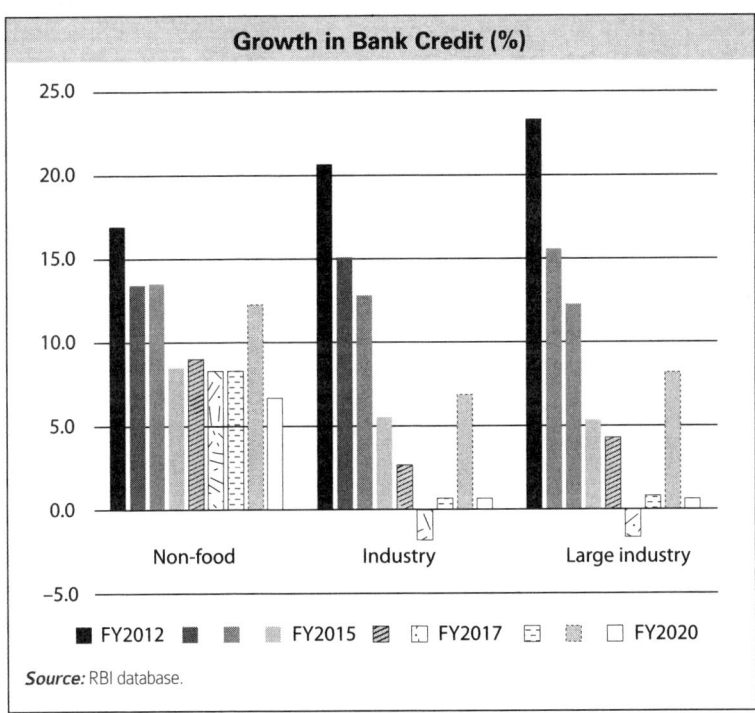

When India needed investment the most, during the pandemic, large industries constituting about 82 per cent of credit off-take to the industrial sector, witnessed the biggest fall. According to the RBI's Fiscal Stability Report (FSR) of 2021, India's number one 'systemic risk' is 'lack of robust private sector investment' (RBI, 2011, 2021b).

Banking 'Reforms'

Third, the private sector is heavily indebted. The Credit Suisse has repeatedly warned about this, particularly about their high *debt stress levels* since FY2017. Its 'India Corporate Health Tracker' of August 2019 showed that *almost all big private businesses houses* were on the list of 'chronically stressed' *corporations* (interest cover ratio of less than 1 for a period of 1 to 12 quarters). The debts of these chronically stressed companies consistently rose from ₹8.9 lakh crore in FY2017 to ₹10.2 lakh crore in FY2019. Further, these stressed debts are spread across infrastructure, manufacturing, telecom, power, metals, textiles, etc. (Gupta et al., 2019; Mohanty, 2020a).

Fourth, their high loan defaults have forced India to write off large sums as NPAs in SCBs, most of which is burdened on the PSBs. Such write-offs skyrocketed after 2014, totalling *₹8.64 lakh crore* during FY2015–FY2020 in SCBSs, with *PSBs accounting for ₹6.83 lakh crore*. The following graph shows how. The recoveries of NPAs have also fallen below 10 per cent since FY2017 (Mohanty, 2021a).

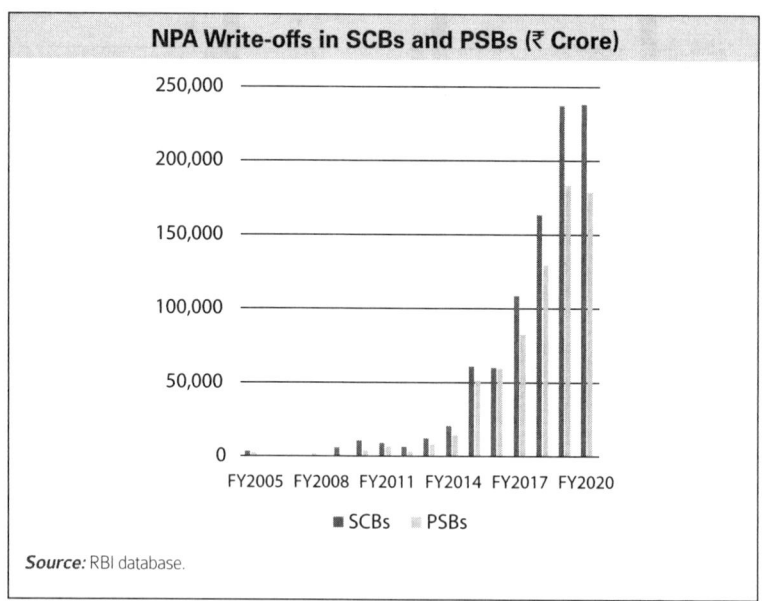

Undoubtedly, the NPAs were not generated only after 2014. In its asset quality review in 2015, the RBI identified three factors for 'the spurt in stressed assets NPAs': (a) aggressive lending practices, (b) wilful default/ loan fraud/corruption in some cases and (c) an economic slowdown. The slowdown accelerated post 2014 due to a series of inappropriate policy decisions such as the demonetization of 2016, a flawed GST of 2017, an untimely and unplanned lockdown and high import tariff imposed since 2014, hurting exports as explained in previous chapters.

Would you expect India's private businesses to channelize their own resources into the Indian economy for India's growth? That would be unwise.

Bad Bank a Solution?

India's another major banking 'reform' is to set up a bad bank for the resolution of stressed assets. The budget for FY2022 proposed this structure under the ARC–AMC model (asset reconstruction company and asset management company). In this, ARC and AMC would consolidate and take over existing stressed debt and then manage and dispose of the assets to alternate investment funds and other potential investors for eventual value realization.

Fundamentally, a bad bank buys stressed assets of other banks and financial institutions and resolves these over a period through turnarounds (resolution) or liquidation. The immediate benefit of it is that it would free up bank balance sheets. The move is clearly timed to separate stressed assets from PSBs before privatization. Indications are that this would be a public–private venture.

ARC as a global phenomenon has proved successful outside of India, but that depends on numbers of factors mentioned later in the chapter. India's experience with bad bank began in 2004, when the IDBI transferred bad loans of over ₹9,000 crore to its wholly owned special purpose vehicle (SPV). This SPV (bad bank) didn't recover substantial amounts, nor did IDBI's lending record improve. The Economic Survey of 2016–2017 pointed that the private sector ARCs in India bought only 5 per cent of the total NPAs and found it 'difficult to recover much from the debtors' in FY2015 and FY2016 (Acharya & Rajan, 2020a; Department of Economic Affairs, 2017).

An RBI study found that 'the growth of the ARC industry has *not been consistent* over time and *not always been synchronous* with the trends in

NPAs of banks and non-banking financial companies (NBFCs)', though it supported the bad bank proposal, stating that it would strengthen the resolution mechanism (RBI, 2021b).

Insolvent and Bankruptcy Code Recovery Rate 21 Per Cent

In 2016, the government launched the Insolvency and Bankruptcy Code (IBC) with fanfare, touting it as the panacea for stress asset resolution, having repeatedly run down the earlier mechanism (the 1980s) Board for Industrial and Financial Reconstruction in which the net yield was 25 per cent recovery.

By now, several other mechanisms had been tried by the RBI: (a) Strategic Debt Restructuring scheme of 2015, which allows creditors to take over firms unable to pay and sell them to new owners, (b) sustainable structuring of stressed assets (S4A) of 2016, which lets creditors to take a 50 per cent haircut to restore a firm's financial viability and (c) ARCs in the private sector, which are registered under the Securitisation and Reconstruction of Financial Assets and Enforcement of Security Interest Act of 2002.

The first two had failed by FY2017 because of governance failures, as detailed in the Economic Survey of 2016–2017. The third one is ineffective as explained earlier. The RBI database shows that 28 private sector AMCs (bad banks) are in operation, but they have made no material difference as their capital base is low.

The IBC failed by 2020. The data provided by the IBC regulator, Insolvency and Bankruptcy Board of India (IBBI), show that the debt recovery ratio is just 20.9 per cent (IBBI, 2020; Mohanty, 2021b).

The following graph maps the 'admitted' claims of financial creditors for resolution, 'realizable' amount (recovery) and haircut (money lost) in IBC proceedings from FY2017 to September 2020 in absolute numbers (the IBC provides two solutions: 'resolution' in which companies continue as going concerns after a haircut and when that fails 'liquidation' follows in which companies' assets are sold off and closed).

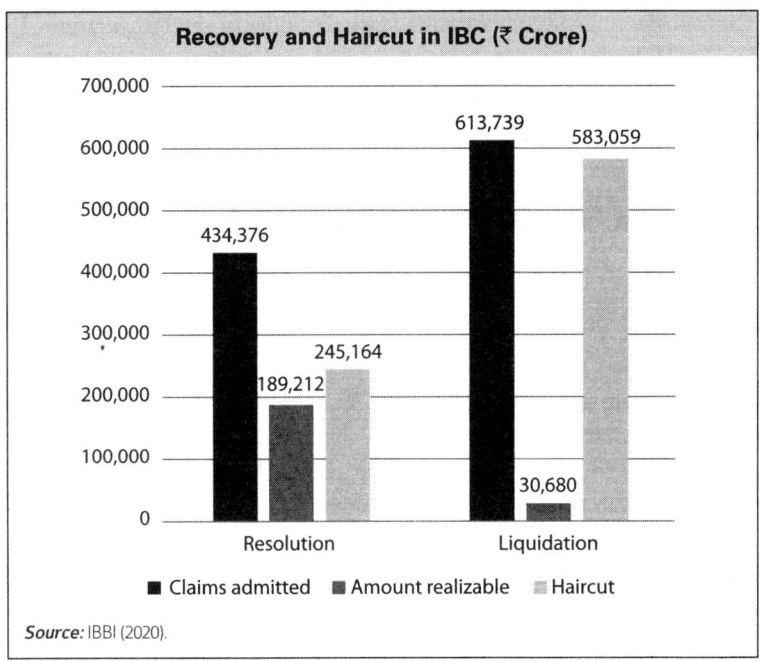

Source: IBBI (2020).

At the end of September 2020, the total claims stood at ₹10.48 lakh crore, the 'realizable' amount was ₹2.2 lakh crore (20.9%) and the haircut was ₹8.3 lakh crore (79%).

The IBC outcomes provide another worrying trend. Most debt claims ended in liquidation—₹6.8 lakh crore or 59 per cent of the total claims. And actual realization (where liquidation had been completed) was only 1.5 per cent.

Such a high liquidation is a triple loss for the economy: loss of bank loans, closure of businesses and loss of jobs arising out of such closures. According to a WB policy note of December 2020, titled 'COVID-19 and Non-Performing Loan Resolution in the Europe and Central Asia region', high liquidation is a sign of 'inefficient insolvency systems'. According to the report, successful insolvency/stressed asset resolution needs 'a legal environment that enables banks to work out bad loans and that *avoids unnecessary losses by steering distressed but potentially viable borrowers towards liquidation*' (World Bank, 2020).

The Videocon insolvency case is a stark reminder of the IBC's failure. In June 2021, its resolution was approved with the creditors taking a haircut of 96 per cent out of admitted claims of ₹64,838.6 crore, creditors will get back only ₹2,962 crore, a mere 4 per cent (PTI, 2021).

Why India Fails to Resolve Stressed Assets?

Poor regulatory mechanism and political interference are the two biggest challenges to PSBs and resolution of their stressed assets (NPAs; Acharya & Rajan, 2020).

India is prone to restructuring (or evergreening) of loans despite its failure. Even after the IBC came in, the RBI allowed a two-year loan restructuring in 26 sectors (following the K. V. Kamath Committee's recommendation) because of the pandemic disruptions, knowing well that *70 per cent of the total moratorium* had been availed by corporates rated A and above—those who have 'comfortable debt–equity ratio' to pay loans easily (Mohanty, 2021c).

Former RBI Governor Urjit Patel had highlighted in his 2018 book, *Overdraft: Saving the Indian Saver*, how the government diluted the IBC and weakened the RBI's regulatory powers to resolve stressed assets after it issued a 'revised framework' on 12 February 2018, instructing banks to start resolution process after a day's default (Mathew, 2020; Mehra, 2020; RBI, 2018).

Problems with PSBs are old and well known. So are the solutions. Yet government control over the appointment of executive heads and boards to loan disbursal decisions continues. PSBs continue to lack independent and professional management, which leads to many governance failures: poor risk management, poor reporting of bad loans, poor evaluation and monitoring of projects and firms bankrolled, etc. Proposals for an independent body for bank appointments and empowering boards have been long ignored.

In such a situation, setting up a bad bank will not make any difference to stressed asset resolution. Rajan and Acharya have stressed on the need to develop a secondary market in stressed assets' sale and transparency to address the tricky issues of pricing stressed assets and write-offs that would entail for providing market benchmarks (Acharya & Rajan, 2020).

What Makes Bad Banks Work?

The WB's policy paper on stress asset resolution highlighted a decade of experiences with ARCs in the Europe and Central Asia (ECA) region, which followed the Great Recession of 2007–2009 (World Bank, 2020).

It listed three sets of policies to be aligned:

1. Robust banking regulation and supervision to ensure proper identification of stressed assets and provisioning for credit losses.
2. Strengthening banks' operational readiness to work out rising volumes of problem assets.
3. A legal environment that enables banks to work out bad loans and that avoids unnecessary losses by steering distressed but potentially viable borrowers towards liquidation.

It then listed seven key lessons for success:

1. Availability of economically meaningful data about banks' exposure to problem assets (key challenge is here to resist industry and political pressures).
2. An orderly transition from current exceptional borrower relief measures and short-term legal measures aimed at flattening the bankruptcy curve needs to be engineered.
3. Banks get operationally ready (with adequate human and financial resources, information system, etc.) for resolving high volumes of bad loans.
4. Banks need to aim for quality in undertaking long-term restructuring (rearranging liabilities and matching future payment obligations with expected cash flows).
5. Unviable and uncooperative borrowers need to be dealt with resolutely.
6. Continued effort to bridge the gap between the modernized insolvency framework and actual practices.
7. Policy coordination is vital to any strategy to resolve stressed asserts, given the many stakeholders involved.

India would do well to take these into consideration before setting up a bad bank.

Takeaways

⇨ Proposed banking 'reforms' pose serious challenges to economic growth and financial stability.

⇨ Privatization of banks is a bad idea because the private sector is responsible for all stressed assets in the banking system.

⇨ Private enterprises are heavily indebted and its investment in the economy is poor. Allowing corporations to run banks would not increase credit flow, which is not even needed given that India is in a credit surplus and is in a liquidity trap because of cheap credit.

⇨ The banking sector needs a robust regulatory mechanism and professional management, the absence of which has led to banking failure, the accumulation of stressed assets and the failure of resolution mechanisms.

⇨ Bad bank is unlikely to make any difference without wholesome reforms in banking.

⇨ Bail-in is an additional incentive for the private sector to indulge in reckless financial behaviour.

References

Acharya, S., Kelkar, V., & Subramanian, A. (2020). Permitting industrial houses to own banks could undermine economic growth and democracy. *The Indian Express*. https://indianexpress.com/article/opinion/columns/rbi-bank-licences-for-corporates-indian-economy-7069713/

Acharya, V., & Rajan, R. (2020a, 21 September). Indian banks: A time to reform? New York University. http://pages.stern.nyu.edu/~sternfin/vacharya/public_html/pdfs/indian-banks-reform.pdf

Acharya, V., & Rajan, R. (2020b, November). Do we really need Indian corporations in banking? https://flossexperiences.files.wordpress.com/2020/11/indian-corporations-in-banking-raghuram-rajan-viral-acharya.pdf

Basu, K. (2020, 27 November). Cronyism in banking feared: Former World Bank chief economist. *The Telegraph*. https://www.telegraphindia.com/

business/cronyism-in-banking-feared-former-world-bank-chief-economist/cid/1798770?utm_source=facebook&utm_medium=social&utm_campaign=tt_daily

Davis, M. (2021, 29 June). US government financial bailouts. Investopedia. https://www.investopedia.com/articles/economics/08/government-financial-bailout.asp

Department of Economic Affairs. (2017). Economic survey 2016–17. https://www.indiabudget.gov.in/budget2017-2018/es2016-17/echapter.pdf

Global Legal Insights. (2020). Banking Laws and Regulations 2021. https://www.globallegalinsights.com/practice-areas/banking-and-finance-laws-and-regulations/usa

Gupta, A., Shah, K., & Kharote, J. (2019, 27 November). India corporate health tracker. Credit Suisse. https://www.dropbox.com/s/83pb0ixle8z0dx0/Health%20tracker%20Nov%2027%2C%202019.pdf?dl=0

Harbert, T. (2019, 21 February). Here's how much the 2008 bailouts really cost. MIT Sloan School of Management. https://mitsloan.mit.edu/ideas-made-to-matter/heres-how-much-2008-bailouts-really-cost

IBBI. (2020). Resolvability: Living will (Vol. 16). https://ibbi.gov.in/uploads/publication/411436dab58c1265aacb015b6b43a215.pdf

Karthik, H. (2020, 6 August). No bank licence to India Inc: RBI sees threat to financial stability. *Business Standard*. https://www.business-standard.com/article/finance/no-bank-licence-to-india-inc-rbi-sees-threat-to-financial-stability-120080600026_1.html

Mathew, G. (2020, 25 July). Govt diluted IBC, its steps hurt RBI's move on bad loans: Urjit Patel. *The Indian Express*. https://indianexpress.com/article/india/urjit-patel-rbi-bad-loans-6522345/

Mehra, P. (2020, 26 July). In Urjit Patel's 'overdraft', a peek at how India's bankruptcy code was slowly diluted. *The Wire*. https://thewire.in/economy/urjit-patel-book-overdraft-bankruptcy-code-rbi-arun-jaitley

Ministry of Finance. (2013, December). Policy on new licenses in the banking sector, 79th report. https://eparlib.nic.in/bitstream/123456789/64184/1/15_Finance_79.pdf

Ministry of Finance. (2014, December). Policy on new licenses in the banking sector, 7th report. http://164.100.47.193/lsscommittee/Finance/16_Finance_6.pdf

Mohanty, P. (2020a, 4 September). Rebooting economy XIII: Why Indian corporates are debt-ridden. *Business Today*. https://www.businesstoday.in/opinion/columns/indian-economy-npas-why-indian-corporates-are-debt-driven-non-performing-assets/story/412124.html

Mohanty, P. (2020b, 2 December). Rebooting economy 49: Who needs corporates to run banks and how will it help Indian economy? *Business Today.* https://www.businesstoday.in/sectors/banks/indian-economy-who-needs-corporates-to-run-banks-and-how-will-it-help-indian-economy/story/423707.html

Mohanty, P. (2021a, 21 January). Rebooting economy 60: India in a financial mess of its own making. *Business Today.* https://www.businesstoday.in/opinion/columns/indian-economy-india-is-a-financial-mess-of-its-own-making-npas-loan-defaults/story/428549.html

Mohanty, P. (2021b, 7 February). Rebooting economy 65: IBC has failed; will a bad bank succeed? *Business Today.* https://www.businesstoday.in/opinion/columns/rebooting-economy-65-ibc-has-failed-will-a-bad-bank-succeed/story/430537.html

Mohanty, P. (2021c, 10 February). Rebooting economy 66: Is India facing credit deprivation to warrant corporation banks? *Business Today.* https://www.businesstoday.in/opinion/columns/rebooting-economy66-is-india-facing-credit-deprivation-to-warrant-corporation-banks/story/430868.html

Mohanty, P. (2021d, 14 February). Rebooting economy 67: Set the record straight before setting up a bad bank. *Business Today.* https://www.businesstoday.in/opinion/columns/rebooting-economy-67-set-the-record-straight-before-setting-up-a-bad-bank/story/431212.html

Mohanty, P. (2021e, 21 February). Rebooting economy 68: How private wealth creators are serving Indian economy and people. *Business Today.* https://www.businesstoday.in/opinion/columns/rebooting-economy-68-how-private-wealth-creators-are-serving-indian-economy-and-people/story/431736.html

Panagariya, A. (2021, 5 February). Corporates for banking: To address India's credit scarcity problem, allow corporate houses to set up banks. *The Times of India.* https://timesofindia.indiatimes.com/blogs/toi-edit-page/corporates-for-banking-to-address-indias-credit-scarcity-problem-allow-corporate-houses-to-set-up-banks/

PTI. (2021, 16 June). Videocon insolvency: Creditors to take 96% haircut on dues; NCLT requests increase in pay-out. *Business Today.* https://www.businesstoday.in/current/corporate/videocon-insolvency-creditors-to-take-96-haircut-on-dues-nclt-requests-increase-in-pay-out/story/441755.html

RBI. (1967–1981). RBI history (Vol. III). https://m.rbi.org.in/scripts/RHvol-3.aspx

RBI. (2008, 4 September). Evolution of banking in India (Chapter III). https://rbi.org.in/scripts/publicationsview.aspx?id=10487#:~:text=The%20major%20banks%20were%20organised,up%20in%201906%20in%20Mumbai

RBI. (2011, 11 January). Fiscal stability report. https://rbidocs.rbi.org.in/rdocs/PressRelease/PDFs/PR92249126040B81448D6B4BFFC88889EDCA8.PDF

RBI. (2013, 22 February). RBI releases guidelines for licensing of new banks in the private sector. https://www.rbi.org.in/Scripts/BS_PressReleaseDisplay.aspx?prid=28191

RBI. (2016, 1 August). RBI releases guidelines for 'on tap' licensing of universal banks in the private sector. https://rbidocs.rbi.org.in/rdocs/PressRelease/PDFs/PR2815FAA5AE631014639A2A11222024E5730.PDF

RBI. (2018, 12 February). Resolution of stressed assets—Revised framework. https://rbidocs.rbi.org.in/rdocs/notification/PDFs/131DBRCEC9D8FEED1C467C9FC15C74D01745A7.PDF

RBI. (2020, November). RBI releases the report of the Internal Working Group to Review Extant Ownership Guidelines and Corporate Structure for Indian Private Sector Banks. https://rbidocs.rbi.org.in/rdocs/PressRelease/PDFs/PR667D315DFDCDF4B4FA98C3AEC2329939B25.PDF

RBI. (2021a, 5 February). Monetary policy statement, 2020–21. Resolution of the Monetary Policy Committee (MPC) February 3–5, 2021. https://www.rbi.org.in/Scripts/BS_PressReleaseDisplay.aspx?prid=51077

RBI. (2021b, 26 April). ARCs in India: A study of their business operations and role in NPA resolution (RBI Bulletin). https://rbidocs.rbi.org.in/rdocs/Bulletin/PDFs/02AR_26042021568788EADB07475AACD1100AD7C06766.PDF

World Bank. (2012). Global financial development report 2013: Rethinking the role of the state in finance. https://openknowledge.worldbank.org/handle/10986/11848

World Bank. (2020, December). COVID-19 and non-performing loan resolution in the Europe and Central Asia region. http://pubdocs.worldbank.org/en/460131608647127680/FinSAC-COVID-19-and-NPL-Policy-Note-Dec2020.pdf

X PRIVATIZATION

Public Assets, Private Profits

India is poised to take up privatization of public assets on a massive scale, the kind it witnessed during the Atal Bihari Vajpayee government in the early years of the millennium. This is a marked shift from the disinvestment and privatization attempt during the first five-year term of Prime Minister Narendra Modi.

The first-term of the current government saw a disinvestment drive. Its privatization plans, for which the NITI Aayog drew up a list of 38 PSUs, including that of national carrier Air India, it didn't take off for various reasons. A new urgency was seen during the pandemic crisis when the AatmaNirbhar Bharat packages proposed a string of 'reforms', including the privatization of public assets. The budget for FY2022 surprised everyone by declaring the privatization of two PSBs and a general insurance company.

The prime minister added to it by declaring his goal of privatizing 100 central PSUs spanning oil, gas, port, airport and power sectors, with the exception of a few in strategic sectors. The new plan envisages the privatization of profit-making PSUs that were previously excluded. The prime minister has justified his privatization drive arguing that 'there are many underutilized and unutilized assets under the control of the government' (Mishra, 2021).

This announcement came after he and his government declared that the government had no business to be in business and advocated for a bigger role for private sector 'wealth creators' so that such wealth could be distributed among people, though there is little evidence to support this claim. In fact, in the pandemic year of FY2020, corporate profits (of listed companies) reached historic highs, accompanied by job and wage cuts (Mohanty, 2021).

Privatization has been promoted in India and all over the world in the past four decades and more in the name of private sector efficiency. Before taking a look at what India plans to do and its ramifications, it would be prudent to first see what economic literature tells about private sector efficiency.

Myths of Private Sector Efficiency

In 2015, the UNDP published an analysis of all existing global studies on comparative efficiencies of public and private sectors with a view to help in achieving its SDGs rolled out the same year, which bring a higher focus to reducing poverty and inequality after realizing that the Millennium Development Goals had not eliminated poverty, 'inequality is a roadblock to progress' (inequality was added as a goal) and, more importantly, 'growth' in the traditional sense was not enough to eliminate poverty and inequalities (Mohanty, 2019).

The title of the UNDP's analysis leaves nothing to imagination: 'Is the Private Sector More Efficient? A Cautionary Tale'. It reached three conclusions: (a) 'no model of ownership'—public, private or mixed—'is *intrinsically more efficient*' than the other and (b) literature broadly comparing efficiency 'lacks rigour', with more 'opinion pieces', and sectoral literature (health and education) 'is more rigorous though often inconclusive' and (c) efficiency under all ownership models 'depends on *competition, regulation, autonomy* and wider issues of *institutional development*'. Therefore, it asserted that a positive outcome of change in ownership was more likely in developed countries because of better regulatory and institutional developments, but a *mixed one in the middle income and developing countries* where these factors were weak (Rao, 2015).

Nobel laureate Joseph Stiglitz and fellow economists carried out a cross-country empirical study comparing how change in ownership from public to private changed their performance. It found no conclusive proof of private sector superiority. According to the study, 'a basic insight is *that institutional quality matters more than ownership*', and profitability (measure of efficiency) post-ownership change was most directly tied to '*protection of private investors* against expropriation and better enforcement of contractual rights'. It also stressed that, more likely, such ownership change happened in the case of public enterprises 'that *perform well, biasing traditional tests* of performance effects of privatization' (Knyazeva et al., 2013).

As the WB's chief economist in the 1990s, Stiglitz has had first-hand experience as part of the Washington Consensus that drove global privatization, and he has written extensively on the subject. He has written that the theoretical case for ownership change (from public to private) 'at best, is *weak or non-existent*' and that 'while there have been some successful cases of privatization, it has often turned out to be *more disappointing than some of its advocates originally expected, and in some places, it has generated great social unrest.*' He mentioned how a few individuals grabbed 'previously state-owned resources *for a pittance* and become millionaires—or billionaires', particularly in Russia, where 'by some estimates, $1.5 trillion in assets were stolen' after the fall of communism towards the end of the 1980s and is now marked by great inequality, as bad as many in Latin America (Stiglitz, 2008; UNGA, 2018).

The Guardian marked 20 years of privatization (ownership change) in the UK rail in 2013 with a report ('"The Private Sector Is Superior." Time to Move on from This Old Dogma') which cited the rail regulator's report stating that 'the single remaining state-run mainline rail service (East Coast rail services) required *less public subsidy than any of the 15 privately run rail* in Britain'. In the UK, the railway ownership changed with the promise of eliminating subsidies, increasing efficiency and reducing fares (through competition). None of it happened. Subsidies rose dramatically from *£2.74 billion* in 1993–1994 to *£20.9 billion* in 2019–2020. The UK now has some of the most expensive rail tickets in Europe. About the privatization of healthcare, *the Guardian* stated, 'some of the UK's largest private care home providers effectively *bankrupted themselves* and had to be *saved by public intervention*' (BBC, 2019; Office of Rail and Road, 2020; *The Guardian*, 2013).

During the pandemic, the predominantly private and insurance-based healthcare system of the USA failed spectacularly. Despite spending about 17 per cent of annual GDP—far higher than the OECD average of 8.7 per cent (during 2010–2019)—the *pandemic defeated*, and it failed to save lives. In 2019, the USA spent $11,100 per person on healthcare, while the average for OECD countries (excluding the USA) was merely $5,500. Yet the USA doesn't have *universal healthcare*, partly because of its 'original sin of slavery', and its performance in health metrics, such as life expectancy, infant mortality and diabetes, is worse than the peers (Krugman, 2020; Peter G. Peterson Foundation, 2020; Yong, 2020).

During the pandemic, economic historian Dirk Philipsen of the Duke University bluntly criticized private sector efficiency. He wrote:

> ...*without massive public assistance*, late-stage extractive capitalism, turbocharged by private interest and greed, would long be dead.... Boeing, Goldman Sachs, Bank of America, Exxon—all would be bust without *public bailouts and tax breaks and subsidies*. Every time the private system works itself into a crisis, public funds bail it out.... When private companies are back up and running, they *don't hold themselves accountable to the public who rescued them*...often go *right back to milking the public*.... As others have noted, for more than a century, it's a *clever machine that privatises gains and socialises costs*. (Philipsen 2020, emphasis added)

An interesting case came to notice in March 2021. The governments of Argentina and Bolivia reversed their privatization of pension schemes that had now failed. Private insurance corporations sued governments for this at the International Centre for Settlement of Investment Disputes of the WB. Their reason: a loss of potential profits. Stiglitz and more than 100 development experts not only condemned the move, pointing out that pension policy wasn't about securing profit for private insurance corporations but rather to provide income security in old age, but they also wrote that a majority of 30 countries that had privatized their pension schemes were reversing their decisions (IPS, 2021).

They listed the many failures of privatized pension schemes: (a) coverage rates decreased or stagnated, (b) pension benefits deteriorated, (c) old-age poverty worsened due to low pensions, (d) gender and income inequality increased, (e) private systems were expensive, (f) financial and demographic risks were transferred to individuals and pensioners had to suffer the loss of benefits when these risks occurred, such as during the Global Financial Crisis.

These are surely not the signs of private sector efficiency.

India's privatization drive during the Vajpayee government was remarkable for how cheaply (Stiglitz's 'pittance') PSUs were handed over to private businesses. The CAG listed many such instances in its 2006 audit report. These were as follows:

1. Core assets of Modern Food such as leasehold *land and plant and machinery, were not valued* before the change of ownership.
2. Leasehold *land housing the plant and fully developed township* of Bharat Aluminium Company Limited (BALCO) *were not valued*.
3. *Non-core assets were not identified* and properly valued for BALCO and Indian Petrochemicals Corporation Limited; real estate, land and building of Videsh Sanchar Nigam Limited and Paradeep Phosphates were 'either discounted or not considered' in the absence of clear title, for which the administrative ministries made no effort.
4. Only one of three operational mines of Hindustan Zinc was valued.
5. 'Far too conservative assumptions' were made in valuation of *7 out of 9 PSUs* under the discounted cash flow methodology *without recording the reasons* for such assumptions, etc. (CAG, 2006).

Besides, India's private sector has been a burden on the public.

Every single year in the past decade, India has been *routinely writing off huge loan defaults* of big corporate entities. The RBI database shows that ₹8.6 lakh crore have been written off by SCBs between FY2015 and FY2020. There are other ways too.

In 2019, for example, when the Modi government decided to privatize Air India, it waived off ₹29,474 crore of debt to 'sweeten the deal' for private players, and more was in the offing, but it didn't take off. The same year, when private airline Jet Airways was grounded because of high debt, the central government asked PSBs led by the SBI, which had lent money to it in the first place, to bail it out by infusing more funds, allowing the *private owner to get away with losses and putting the burden on the public*. Now that it wants to privatize PSBs, it proposes to *hive off debts* (NPAs) to the proposed bad bank and *shift out some bank employees* to sweeten the deal (PTI, 2019, 2021; *The Telegraph*, 2019).

This is why American cognitive scientist Noam Chomsky keeps saying: 'A basic principle of modern state capitalism is that *costs and risks are socialized to the extent possible, while profit is privatized.*'[1]

Are Indian PSUs Less Efficient?

There are studies on the efficiency of the private sector in India as well. Professor Sushil Khanna of IIM Calcutta examined the relative performance of central PSUs and private sector companies in manufacturing over a two-decade period from 2004 to 2014. His study concluded:

> A comparison of the performance of large private and public sector firms in the manufacturing sector shows that the CPSEs have provided *higher returns on capital employed*. And, performance in terms of *technical parameters is in no way inferior to that of their private counterparts*. Yet the Modi government intends to either privatise these CPSEs or sell a significant part of their equity shares, a decision that is *devoid of both strategic and business sense*. (Khanna, 2015, emphasis added)

Professor R. Nagaraj of the Indira Gandhi Institute of Development Research, Mumbai, studied the performance of PSUs in the second half

---

[1] https://twitter.com/noamchomskyT/status/896771696551759874

of the last century and published his findings in a paper titled, 'Public Sector Performance since 1950: A Fresh Look'. Although he didn't compare relative performances, his conclusions were on similar lines: public sector productivity saw an 'impressive rise', and there was 'a steady rise in the profitability of the central PSEs'. He wrote:

> [M]uch of the preoccupation of current policy of changing public ownership and control to get greater efficiency seems misplaced. Such reforms are unlikely to make a difference as ownership has little relation to economic outcomes, either in theory or in contemporary experience. Moreover, as this study has shown, *the real problem is not the lack of efficiency in production, but one of pricing and collection of user charges.*
> (Nagaraj, 2006, emphasis added)

There is yet another route to championing private interests through PPP, in which projects, particularly those in infrastructure that are long-term and cost more, are run jointly in the name of private sector efficiency and also to draw in private resources on the plea that government resources are limited. The murky business of PPPs was known to the IMF, which has played a major role in pushing privatization and PPPs.

In a paper of 2004, the IMF examined the impact of PPP in providing infrastructure assets and services, which was then taking off in many countries across the world, and stated:

> ...it *cannot be taken for granted that PPPs are more efficient than public investment and government supply of services.* One particular concern is that PPPs can be used mainly to bypass spending controls, and to move public investment off budget and debt off the government balance sheet, while the *government still bears most of the risk* involved and *faces potentially large fiscal costs.* (IMF, 2004)

In India, the PPP model, accompanied with VGF—upfront 40 per cent public funding to private partner—had already failed and was virtually abandoned by the UPA government, which promoted it first, but was revived by the Modi government to promote private healthcare during the pandemic and earlier (as detailed in an earlier chapter). The PPPs in the UPA era, particularly in highway projects, with 40 per cent VGF, would later lead to a massive NPA crisis (what Arvind Subramanian referred to as a 'twin balance sheet problem').

An 'internal paper' of the erstwhile PCI and an RTI response revealed horrifying details. PSBs had given *loans nearly twice the total project costs* (TPCs) in 20 projects under scrutiny—a loan of ₹25,940 crore against TPCs of ₹13,646 crore, *without collaterals* to the private partners, plus 40 per cent of VGF (of ₹13,646 crore). Taken together, this would mean that for a project costing ₹100 crore, private partners walked away with ₹240 crore (₹100 crore of additional money without collaterals and ₹40 crore of VGF; Bansal, 2010).

Reviewing India's Policy Framework

Ironically, India doesn't have a privatization policy.

And it is pursuing it despite strong opposition from several of its own ministries and opposition parties. A series of investigative reports have revealed that the Ministry of Health and Family Welfare pointed at the pandemic and the key role central public sector enterprises (CPSEs) played in fighting it; the Ministry of Chemicals and Fertilizers sought to keep all state-owned pharmaceutical firms with it; the Ministry of Defence stated that all defence manufacturing should be under state control 'in the interest of national security', particularly to keep control over inter-country transfer of critical defence technologies; the Ministry of Ports, Shipping and Waterways sought the 'strategic' tag and flagged how multiple private firms went into bankruptcy and how no shipping company was set up using the 100 per cent FDI route in the past 20 years. Even the Ministry of Coal, which has been opened to private sector mining, pointed at how that has affected coal production adversely (Jha, 2021; *The Quint*, 2021).

India has a disinvestment policy reframed by the Modi government. The Vajpayee-era disinvestment ministry, which carried out disinvestment and privatization of PSUs, was dismantled by the UPA government. The new disinvestment policy adopted by the Modi government lists three 'salient features': (a) PSUs are the *wealth of the nation* and public ownership of CPSEs should be promoted to ensure that this wealth remains in the hands of the people, (b) while pursuing disinvestment through minority stake sale in listed CPSEs, the government will retain majority shareholding, that is, at least 51 per cent of the shareholding and management control of the PSUs and (c) strategic disinvestment by way of sale of a substantial portion of the government's shareholding in identified CPSEs, up to 50 per cent or more, along with the transfer of management control. Outright privatization is out of the question.[2]

Has India achieved any of its disinvestment objectives since 2014? According to two CAG reports that looked into it, it hasn't. The reports cited several failures, the most important of which are as follows: (a) a significant part of the disinvestment proceeds came from PSU-to-PSU sales in FY2018 and FY2019, with the comment that 'such disinvestments only resulted in the *transfer of resources already with the public sector* to the government and *did not lead to any change in the stake*', (b) in FY2018, the goal of having 25 per cent public shareholding in CPSEs was not met in 17 cases and (c) in FY2018, disinvestment of strategic holdings in the Specified Undertaking of Unit Trust of India holding shares of blue-chip private companies was used as a 'sweetener' to increase the attractiveness of some central PSUs, against the advice of the Department of Economic Affairs, leading to an 'avoidable discount of ₹170.74 crore' (CAG, 2019, 2020).

Global experience shows that privatization is dangerous for democracies in more ways than one.

A UN report, titled 'Extreme Poverty and Human Rights', tabled in the General Assembly in September 2018 looked at the impact of privatization. It stated that ownership change (privatization) 'often involves the systematic elimination of human rights protections and further marginalization of the interests of low-income earners and those living in

---

[2] https://www.dipam.gov.in/dipam/disinvestment-policy

poverty', and that as some 'aspects of criminal justice systems are privatized, many different charges and penalties are levied with far greater impact on the poor, who then must borrow to pay them or face default' (UNGA, 2018).

It also stated that the neoliberal shift towards private ownership had changed the very definition of personal freedom.

> Freedom is thereby redefined as an emaciated public sector alongside a private sector dedicated to profiting from running key parts of the criminal justice system and prisons, determining educational priorities and approaches, deciding who will receive health interventions and social protection, and choosing what infrastructure will be built, where and for whom.

But Why Privatization?

According to the UNGA report (UNGA, 2018) mentioned above:

> Internationally, privatization was promoted as *an antidote to patronage* through public sector employment and to *reduce the size of government*. It became a central feature of the programmes promoted in the post-communist States of Eastern Europe and, under the auspices of the Washington Consensus, *spread to Africa, Latin America and Asia*. Development finance and structural adjustment support were made conditional upon the transfer of ownership of 'burdensome and inefficient public enterprises'.

to private companies. Public utilities, especially in water and sanitation, were the subject of large-scale privatization.

The UNDP report of 2015 mentioned earlier listed 7 reasons why country after country has promoted private interest at the cost of public interest:

- Political support for undermining the benefits of the public sector.

- Neoliberal push (*public choice theory*) that public service is inherently self-serving and need to be checked.
- Commercial gains (profits) for consultants and businesses.
- Politicians' need for *deflecting criticism* of their own failures.
- Relatively *lower pay* for professional posts in the public sector.
- *Obstructive* public sector labour unions and unhelpful bureaucrats.
- 'Both elected leaders and senior administrators benefit from creating a "*permanent revolution*" of *ceaseless reforms* and reorganisation of the public service…the *temptation to appear to be shaking up* supposedly lazy and incompetent bureaucrats is all too great' (Rao, 2015).

The public choice theory of neoliberal economist James McGill Buchanan (for which he was awarded the Nobel Prize in economics in 1986) attacked state and public institutions, theorizing that government failure was the rule and it happened because of private interests 'capturing' policymakers through nepotism, cronyism, corruption or rent-seeking, misallocation of resources and crowding out private investment, etc. (Buchanan, 1962).

Why Do Governments Hurt Public Interest and Champion Private Interest Thus?

That question was once answered by Stiglitz to investigative journalist Greg Palast. Palast wrote in his 2002 book *The Best Democracy Money Can Buy*:

> Rather than object to the selloffs of state industries, he (Stiglitz) said, national leaders—using the World Bank's demands to silence local critics—happily flogged their electricity and water companies. 'You could see their *eyes widen*' *at the prospect of 10 per cent commissions* paid to Swiss bank accounts for simply shaving a few billion off the sale price of national assets.
> (Palast, 2002)

What the SOP Says?

Chomsky once explained how privatization takes place.

> ...there is a *standard technique* of privatization, namely defund what you want to privatize. Like when Thatcher wanted to *defund* the railroads, first thing to do is defund them, then they don't work and people get angry and they want a change. You say okay, privatize them and then they get worse. In that case the government had to step in and rescue it. *That's the standard technique of privatization: defund, make sure things don't work, people get angry, you hand it over to private capital.* (Chomsky, 2011)

The technique is not alien to it. The last few years have seen exactly the same pattern.

Several PSUs—Life Insurance Corporation, ONGC, PFC, National Buildings Construction Corporation, Water and Power Consultancy Services—and public sector port consortiums, among others, have picked up the tab on India's disinvestment until now. Once cash-rich, oil PSU ONGC is now heavily in debt after buying Hindustan Petroleum Corporation Limited and taking over the bankrupt, scam-tainted Gujarat State Petroleum Corporation. In FY2020, its 'cash and bank balances' fell to ₹968.2 crore in FY2020 from ₹10,798.9 crore in FY2016—a fall of 91 per cent—and is saddled with a huge 'net debt' of ₹11,704 crore. As a result, the ONGC is forced to reduce its oil exploration and development work (ONGC, 2020; Singh, 2021).

Similar is the case with other PSUs, such as NTPC and PFC, which were forced into buying public stakes in other PSUs. They are PSUs that are facing pressure of transferring cash surpluses as dividends. The following graph maps how 'dividends and profits', which comprise dividends and profits from PSUs as well as the RBI surplus, have been transferred to the government. Notice the surge after Modi came to power, even while the economy nosedived post-demonetization of FY2017 (Mohanty, 2020b).

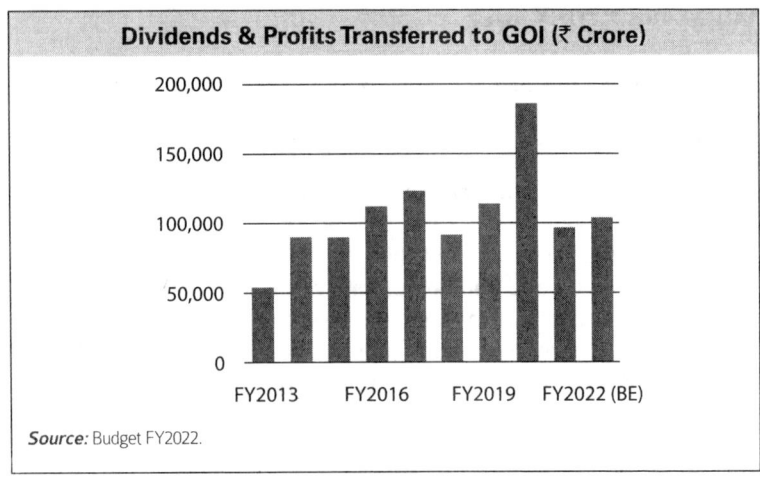

The PM CARES Fund, a so-called public trust that acts like a private one and is out of the RTI purview (not a public authority), though headed by the prime minister, has sucked PSUs further dry. Response to RTI queries showed that 101 PSUs, including the ailing ONGC, which topped the list, and the ailing BSNL, donated ₹*2,422.9 crore* from their corporate social responsibility (CSR) funds, meant for the development of local communities, and ₹*154.9 crore from staff salaries* to this fund. The armed forces also donated ₹203.67 crore from their salaries (Yadav, 2020a, 2020b, 2020c).

Between FY2015 and FY2020, one analysis shows that oil PSUs, ONGC, Bharat Petroleum Corporation Limited, Indian Oil Corporation Limited and Gas Authority of India Limited gave ₹1,355 crore from their CSR funds to the temple towns, the PM CARES Fund and the Statue of Unity instead of spending on the development of communities around their operation areas (Nair, 2021).

Meanwhile, another disturbing development has taken place.

Creeping Cronyism

Under Modi's governance, cronyism is soaring. Japan's business portal *Nikkei Asia*'s article stated: 'Modi risks turning India into a *nation of gangster capitalists*'. It stated that a clutch of billionaire cronies was growing richer at everyone else's expense because of their proximity to power. It admitted that the trend wasn't new, but that it 'has accelerated during the tenure of Prime Minister Narendra Modi'. It warned: 'In the absence of a dynamic economic environment in India, today's cronies can become tomorrow's gangsters, exactly as has happened in Russia' (Subramanya, 2021).

As per *the Economist*, due to 'political influence and privileged access to capital', the fortunes of some have skyrocketed at the cost of others during the pandemic year of 2020. It stated that while India's economy tanked and millions lost jobs and sunk into poverty during the pandemic crisis, the fortunes of India's two richest people have swollen—one's personal wealth (running a conglomerate from ports to mines to food) doubled to $32 billion and another's (oil refining, telecoms and retail, among others) grew (by just 25%) to 'an intimidating $75 bn or so' (*The Economist*, 2020).

It stated that inequality in wealth and income has increased around the world, with the top 1 per cent cornering the maximum, but India has surpassed all.

> Last year they (share of top 1%) hoovered up 21.4% of earnings, just ahead of their counterparts in Russia, said the World Inequality Database. Credit Suisse, a bank, puts share of top 1% Indian's wealth at 39%, well ahead of the richest 1% of Americans or Chinese. Most alarmingly, in India some of the rich have become super-rich by using their *heft to crush smaller competitors and thus corner multiple chunks of the economy.* The tilt in fortunes has rewarded *not so much technical innovation or productivity growth* or the opening of new markets as the *wielding of political influence and privileged access to capital* to capture and protect existing markets.

The way one private corporation with no prior experience or expertise in running airports had a clean sweep of all airports privatized in recent years is evidence of the wrong turn India is taking. This happened despite strong objections from the Ministry of Finance and NITI Aayog as an investigative report revealed. This report also pointed out how multiple investigative agencies filed criminal complaints and FIR under a stringent law—the Prevention of Money Laundering Act—against a leading player in building and maintaining major airports in India a month before it withdrew from the biddings process (Mukul & Sasi, 2021a).

The same group reaped a bonanza of ₹500 crore in refunds on customs duty it claimed to have paid on raw materials and consumables (coal imported for the generation of electricity) but had not, in fact, paid the duty amounting to approximately ₹1,000 crore that was due by March 2015 (Thakurta et al., 2017).

Another report stated how this favoured group saw 'the biggest wealth surge' in the world because of his proximity to power: 'After spending two decades building a business empire centred around coal, Indian billionaire Gautam Ambani is now looking beyond the fossil fuel to cement his group's future. His ambitious plans are getting a boost from Prime Minister Narendra Modi' (Bloomberg, 2021).

The government's gift of corporate tax cut to the tune of ₹1.45 lakh crore in September 2019, amid economic slowdown and shrinking revenues, can't really be disconnected from the government–corporation nexus increasing its hold over the economy. The opaque electoral bond is another manifestation of it. History provides enough evidence of how this deadly cocktail of crony capitalism and a regime with poor democratic instincts can overrun any society or country.

Rise in inequality is a gift of 1991 liberalization, as French economists Lucas Chancel and Thomas Piketty showed in their 2017 book *Indian Income Inequality, 1922–2014: From British Raj to Billionaire Raj?* (Details are provided in the AatmaNirbhar Bharat chapter). In his subsequent visit to India, Chancel cautioned against the government's disinvestment in PSUs. He reasoned that disinvestment stripes government of its assets, thereby reducing its capacity to address income inequality. This is more relevant now that the pandemic would have sent millions of Indians into poverty (Mohanty, 2020a).

As economist Pronab Sen often argues, privatization during a recessionary phase is even more reprehensible as it would mean the 'transfer' of private investment for acquiring existing capacity rather than the creation of fresh capacities, which drive growth.

A mindless drive without economic logic and evidence is surely not what India can afford when its economy has already collapsed.

Takeaways

⇨ India's proposed privatization is top-down and arbitrary. It is not enough to say that governments have a business to be in business, especially in a poor and underdeveloped country like India, which is going through a recessionary phase.

⇨ It doesn't even have a privatization policy. It has a disinvestment policy, and the objectives of it are completely different.

⇨ There is no evidence either in India or the world to claim that the private sector is more efficient.

⇨ Mindless promotion of private interest at the cost of public interest and blatant crony capitalism threatens to weaken the economy and harm people's interest.

References

Bansal, R. (2010, 8 September). Wrong road, Kamal! *Governance Now*. https://www.governancenow.com/news/regular-story/wrong-road-kamal

BBC. (2019, 14 August). Are UK train fares the highest in Europe? https://www.bbc.com/news/uk-49346642

Bloomberg. (2021, 25 March). World's biggest wealth surge heralds rise of India's next Ambani. *The Times of India*. https://timesofindia.indiatimes.com/business/india-business/worlds-biggest-wealth-surge-heralds-rise-of-indias-next-ambani/articleshow/81683315.cms#:~:text=The%20net%20worth%20of%20Adani,the%20title%20of%20world's%20richest

Buchanan, J. M. (1962). The calculus of consent: Logical foundations of constitutional democracy. In *The collected works of James M. Buchanan* (Vol. 3). Liberty Fund. http://files.libertyfund.org/files/1063/Buchanan_0102-03_EBk_v6.0.pdf

CAG. (2006). Report no. 17 of 2006 for the period ended March 2005 performance audit of disinvestment of government shareholding in selected PSUs during 1999–2003. https://cag.gov.in/en/old-audit-reports/view/13768

CAG. (2019). Disinvestment in CPSEs (CAG Report No. 18; Chapter VII). https://cag.gov.in/uploads/download_audit_report/2019/Chapter_8_Disinvestment_in_CPSEs_of_Report_No_18_of_2019_General_Purpose_Financial_Reports_of_Central_Public_Sector_Enterprises.pdf

CAG. (2020, 23 September). Report of the Comptroller and Auditor General of India for the year 2018–19 (No. 4 of 2020). https://cag.gov.in/webroot/uploads/download_audit_report/2020/Report%20No.%204%20of%202020_Eng-05f808ecd3a8165.55898472.pdf

Chomsky, N. (2011, 7 April). The state–corporate complex: A threat to freedom and survival (text of lecture given at the University of Toronto). https://chomsky.info/20110407-2/

IMF. (2004, 12 March). Public–private partnerships. https://www.imf.org/external/np/fad/2004/pifp/eng/031204.pdf

IPS. (2021, 29 March). Nobel economist and 100 experts condemn corporate action against Argentina and Bolivia after rollback of failed pension privatization. https://www.ipsnews.net/2021/03/nobel-economist-100-experts-condemn-corporate-action-argentina-bolivia-rollback-failed-pension-privatization/

Jha, S. (2021, 24 March). Privatisation files: Modi's flagship policy faces pushback from key ministries—BQ exclusive. *Bloomberg | Quint*. https://www.bloombergquint.com/business/privatisation-files-modis-flagship-policy-faces-pushback-from-key-ministries-bq-exclusive

Khanna, S. (2015, 31 January). The transformation of India's public sector: Political economy of growth and change. *Economic & Political Weekly, 50*(5). https://www.epw.in/journal/2015/5/public-sector/transformation-indias-public-sector.html

Knyazeva, A., Knyazeva, D., & Stiglitz, J. E. (2013). Ownership change, institutional development and performance. *Journal of Banking & Finance*. https://www8.gsb.columbia.edu/faculty/jstiglitz/sites/jstiglitz/files/2013_Ownership_Change.pdf

Krugman, P. (2020, 2 June). Opinion. *The New York Times*. https://messaging-custom-newsletters.nytimes.com/template/oakv2?campaign_id=116&emc=edit_pk_20200602&instance_id=19018&nl=paul-krugman&productCode=PK&regi_id=116687270&segment_id=29881&te=1&uri=nyt%3A%2F%2Fnewsletter%2F49d108af-1245-4020-bae1-d171091d33d1&user_id=01c171186a86a3bb5bcbec529dceab76https://scholar.harvard.edu/files/glaeser/files/why_doesnt_the_u.s._have_a_european-style_welfare_state.pdf

Mishra, A. R. (2021, 25 February). PM signals PSU assets sale. *Mint*. https://www.livemint.com/news/india/pm-signals-psu-assets-sale-11614212183277.html

Mohanty, P. (2019, 10 April). Part II. NYAY complements PM-KISAN in fighting poverty and inequality. *DailyO*. https://www.dailyo.in/politics/lok-sabha-elections-2019-nyay-pm-kisan-rahul-gandhi-congress-narendra-modi-bjp-welfare-poverty-inequality-in-india-doles-subsidies-ayushman-bharat/story/1/30252.html

Mohanty, P. (2020a, 30 January). Budget 2020: CAG questions Modi govt's disinvestment process for failing to meet its objectives. *Business Today*. https://www.businesstoday.in/union-budget-2020/news/budget-2020-cag-modi-govt-disinvestment-process-psus-public-sector-undertakings-minimum-public-shareholding/story/395000.html

Mohanty, P. (2020b, 31 January). Budget 2020: Strategic disinvestment, a questionable source of off-budget financing. *Business Today*. https://www.businesstoday.in/union-budget-2020/news/budget-2020-strategic-disinvestment-as-source-of-off-budget-financing/story/394626.html

Mohanty, P. (2021, 21 February). Rebooting economy 69: What do workers gain from growth and profits? *Business Today*. https://www.businesstoday.in/opinion/columns/rebooting-economy-69-what-do-workers-gain-from-growth-and-profits/story/431857.html

Mukul, P., & Sasi, A. (2021, 15 January). Finance Ministry and NITI Aayog had raised red flags before Adani's clean sweep of six airports. *The Indian Express*. https://indianexpress.com/article/business/adani-airports-finance-ministry-niti-aayog-7146853/

Nagaraj, R. (2006, 24 June). Public sector performance since 1950: A fresh look. *Economic 8 Political Weekly*, *41*(25). http://www.igidr.ac.in/newspdf/19_Chap_Nagaraj_Public%20Sector%20Performance%20since%201950,%20with%20an%20Update.pdf

Nair, R. (2021, 18 June). ₹1,355 cr—How much oil PSUs have given temple towns, PM Cares, statue of unity as CSR. *The Print*. https://theprint.in/economy/rs-1355-cr-how-much-oil-psus-have-given-temple-towns-pm-cares-statue-of-unity-as-csr/677548/

Office of Rail and Road. (2020, 26 November). Rail industry finance (UK), 2019–20. https://dataportal.orr.gov.uk/media/1889/rail-industry-finance-uk-statistical-release-2019-20.pdf

ONGC. (2020). Annual report 2019–20; Making a strategic move. https://www.ongcindia.com/wps/wcm/connect/31cce834-fb8f-49c1-a2c4-38df2f712f7c/ONGC_AR_2019-20.pdf?MOD=AJPERES8CONVERT_TO=url8CACHEID=ROOTWORKSPACE-31cce834-fb8f-49c1-a2c4-38df2f712f7c-noD1QT5

Palast, G. (2002). *The best democracy money can buy*. Pluto Press.

Peter G. Peterson Foundation. (2020, 14 July). How does the U.S. healthcare system compare to other countries? https://www.pgpf.org/blog/2020/07/how-does-the-us-healthcare-system-compare-to-other-countries

Philipsen, D. (2020, 24 April). Private gain must no longer be allowed to elbow out the public good. *Aeon*. https://aeon.co/ideas/private-gain-must-no-longer-be-allowed-to-elbow-out-the-public-good?utm_source=Aeon+Newsletter&utm_campaign=9b9179ef1d-EMAIL_CAMPAIGN_2020_04_20_05_07&utm_medium=email&utm_term=0_411a82e59d-9b9179ef1d-69098213

PTI. (2019, 17 December). Government looking to shift more debt out of Air India balance sheet before disinvestment. *The Economic Times*. https://economictimes.indiatimes.com/industry/transportation/airlines-/-aviation/government-looking-to-shift-more-debt-out-of-air-india-balance-sheet-before-disinvestment/articleshow/72850384.cms?utm_source=contentofinterest&utm_medium=text&utm_campaign=cppst

PTI. (2021, 23 February). Bank privatisation: NPA hive-off, employee transfers being considered. *The Economic Times*. https://m.economictimes.com/news/economy/policy/psb-privatisation-npa-hive-off-staff-transfers-being-considered/amp_articleshow/81140877.cms

Rao, S. (2015). *Is the private sector more efficient? A cautionary tale* (Discussion Paper No. 10). UNDP Global Centre for Public Service Excellence. https://gsdrc.org/document-library/is-the-private-sector-more-efficient-a-cautionary-tale/

Singh, K. (2021, 15 February). Cash reserves sliding, ONGC trims exploration and development works. *The Indian Express*. https://indianexpress.com/article/business/cash-reserves-sliding-ongc-trims-exploration-and-development-works-7188884/

Stiglitz, J. (2008). Foreword. In G. Roland, *Privatization: Successes and failures* (p. ix). Columbia University Press. https://host.kelley.iu.edu/nagupta/gupta_surveychapter.pdf

Subramanya, R. (2021, 5 February). Modi risks turning India into a nation of gangster capitalists. *Nikkei Asia*. https://asia.nikkei.com/Opinion/Modi-risks-turning-India-into-a-nation-of-gangster-capitalists

Thakurta, P. G., Palepu, A. R., Jain, S., & Dasgupta, A. (2017, 19 June). Modi government's ₹500-crore bonanza to the Adani Group. *The Wire*. https://thewire.in/business/modi-government-adani-group

The Economist. (2020, 3 December). India's super-rich are getting much richer; Even as the economy shrinks by a tenth. https://www.economist.com/asia/2020/12/03/indias-super-rich-are-getting-much-richer

The Guardian. (2013, 18 April). 'The private sector is superior'. Time to move on from this old dogma. https://www.theguardian.com/commentisfree/2013/apr/25/private-sector-superiority-mythbuster

The Quint. (2021, 26 March). Key ministries opposed Modi govt's privatisation policy: Report. https://www.thequint.com/news/india/modi-government-ministries-oppose-privatisation-push#read-more

The Telegraph. (2019, 19 March). Govt asks banks to bail out Jet Airways. https://www.telegraphindia.com/business/govt-asks-banks-to-bail-out-jet-airways/cid/1687169

UNGA. (2018, 26 September). Extreme poverty and human rights. https://undocs.org/A/73/396

Yadav, S. (2020a, 19 August). Maharatnas to navratnas: 38 PSUs give ₹2,105 crore from CSR to PM CARES. *The Indian Express.* https://indianexpress.com/article/india/maharatnas-to-navratnas-38-psus-give-rs-2105-crore-from-csr-to-pm-cares-6560452/

Yadav, S. (2020b, 7 December). 101 PSUs give ₹155 crore from their staff salaries to PM fund. https://indianexpress.com/article/india/101-psus-give-rs-155-crore-from-their-staff-salaries-to-pm-cares-fund-7094510/

Yadav, S. (2020c, 18 December). Armed forces gave ₹203.67 cr from day's salary to PM-CARES Fund. *The Indian Express.* https://indianexpress.com/article/india/armed-forces-gave-rs-203-67-cr-from-days-salary-to-pm-cares-fund-7109235/

Yong, E. (2020, 20 September). How the pandemic defeated America. *The Atlantic.* https://www.theatlantic.com/magazine/archive/2020/09/coronavirus-american-failure/614191/

XI NEOLIBERAL ECONOMICS MASQUERADE

India took the neoliberal turn in 1991 under pressure from the WB and IMF to which it had turned for a bailout from its balance of payment (forex) crisis. In that sense, the new government under Prime Minister Narendra Modi has not done something entirely new, but it went to an extreme in adopting many of its concepts and principles without application of mind.

Neoliberalism is a set of economic concepts and principles pushed in the 1970s, first by the Chicago school of economics, to essentially promote private sector interest and limit the role of state (small state) in running economies. In the 1980s, this was imposed on non-Anglo-Saxon countries by the WB and the IMF when these countries sought loans to tide over economic crises known as the Washington Consensus or structural adjustment programme (SAP). The focus was laid on deregulation and opening domestic markets to foreign capital, corporate tax cuts, privatization and fiscal austerity. It gained immense political clout first when British Prime Minister Margaret Thatcher and later US President Ronald Reagan adopted it in the late 1970s and 1980s, respectively, earning it two new names—Thatcherism and Reaganism (Kapur & Subramanian, 2018; Mohanty, 2020a; Ostry et al., 2016).

During the Great Recession of 2007–2009, many capitalism economists (liberal) exposed the many fallacies of neoliberalism and wished for its immediate end. Nobel laureate Joseph Stiglitz repeatedly dismissed it as economics, branding it as 'political doctrine' with no evidence of effectiveness. In 2008, he wrote:

> Neoliberal market fundamentalism was always a *political doctrine* serving certain interests. It was *never supported by economic theory*. Nor, it should now be clear, is it supported *by historical experience*. Learning this lesson may be the silver lining in the cloud now hanging over the global economy.
> (Stiglitz, 2008)

In 2019, he wrote that 40 years of neoliberalism in advanced economies 'has been a *spectacular failure*', with growth lower than what was in the quarter-century after the Second World War (economic literature describes it as the golden age of capitalism) and most of it accruing to the very top. He added: '…neoliberalism must be pronounced *dead and buried*.' Later that year, he wrote:

> Well, after 40 years, the numbers are in: growth has slowed and the fruits of that growth went overwhelmingly to a very few at the top. As wages stagnated and the stock market soared, income and wealth flowed up, rather than trickling down. How can wage restraint—to attain or maintain competitiveness— and reduced government programmes possibly add up to higher standards of living? Ordinary citizens felt like they had been sold a bill of goods. They were right to feel conned.
> (Stiglitz, 2019a, 2019b)

Stiglitz was an insider. He quit the WB as chief economist in 1999 in protest of the adverse impacts on poor countries. He described the neoliberal agenda as a four-step programme: step 1: privatization; step 2: capital market liberalization; step 3: market-based pricing and step 4: free trade (Palast, 2002).

Nobel laureate Paul Krugman blamed neoliberal economics squarely for the Great Recession in his famous 2009 essay, 'How Did Economists Get It So Wrong?' In 2020, he wrote a book describing it as 'zombie ideas', the 'ideas that should have been *killed by contrary evidence, but instead keep shambling along, eating people's brains*', but '*monetary support from right-wing billionaires* is a powerful force propping up zombie ideas' (Krugman, 2009, 2020).

French economist Thomas Piketty used historical data to show that inequality had surged globally due to neoliberal economics 'due largely to the political shifts of the past several decades, especially in regard to taxation and finance' (Piketty, 2017).

The previous chapter dealt with privatization—a key neoliberal tool to limit state (small state) and enlarge private business. This chapter looks at other major neoliberal concepts and how they measure up to economic logic and evidence.

Neoliberalism Oversold?

The IMF woke up to the reality later. Its three leading economists published their study in 2016, provocatively titled 'Neoliberalism: Oversold?', which examined the impact of two neoliberal policies: (a) capital market liberalization (removing restrictions on movement of capital across borders) and (b) fiscal consolidation or 'austerity'. This was a long-term study of 53 emerging market economies between 1980 and 2014 for the impact of capital inflows and 149 countries between 1970 and 2010 for fiscal austerity (Ostry et al., 2016).

They arrived at 'three disquieting conclusions':

- The *benefits in terms of increased growth seem fairly difficult to establish* when looking at a broad group of countries.
- The *costs in terms of increased inequality are prominent*. Such costs epitomize the trade-off between the growth and equity effects of some aspects of the neoliberal agenda.

- *'Increased inequality in turn hurts the level and sustainability of growth*. Even if growth is the sole or main purpose of the neoliberal agenda, advocates of that agenda still need to pay attention to the distributional effects.'

Further, they wrote, '*austerity policies not only generate substantial welfare costs* due to supply-side channels (bottlenecks), *they also hurt demand—and thus worsen employment and unemployment*.' Refuting that fiscal consolidation could be expansionary (increase in output and employment), they wrote 'in practice, episodes of *fiscal consolidation have been followed, on average, by drops rather than by expansion in output*'—on average, a consolidation of 1 per cent of GDP increased long-term unemployment rate by 0.6 percentage points and raised income inequality by 1.5 per cent within five years.

There is much more to capital market liberalization.

Growth of Financial Sector

In 2015, the IMF had produced a study of over 100 countries, spanning from 1980 to 2013, to conclude that the financial market needs tighter regulations and 'speed limits'. It admitted the role of large, unregulated and complex financial growth in the Global Financial Crisis of 2007–2009. Later in 2020, another IMF study found that financial deepening helps up to a point before leading to a financial crisis. Its keys findings were as follows:

- Initially, financial depth is associated with lower inequality (as financial inclusion is achieved), *but only up to a point*, after which inequality rises.
- Greater financial *inclusion* tends to be associated with reductions in inequality.
- *Higher inequality is associated with greater financial risks*. When inequality increases, credit tends to rise. For example, in the USA, too much credit, including to lower income households, contributed to the 2007–2008 crisis. The crisis led to higher default rates, which made the lower income households worse off after the crisis.

- *Inequality increases before a financial crisis;* inequality falls during the crisis and begins to rise afterwards as *lower income households* disproportionately experience *income loss,* and *higher growth in debt* is associated with a greater probability of a *banking crisis* (IMF, 2015a, 2020).

By now, the world knows how unbridled growth and greed of financial sector have caused multiple economic crises in the world, from the Great Depression of 1929 to the Great Recession of 2007–2009. In between, there have been several others, such as the dot-com bubble (2000–2001), the Asian financial crisis (late 1990s), the Latin American crisis (1990s–2000s) and the Japan crisis (1990s–2000s; Mohanty, 2020b).

Among many others, Nouriel Roubini of the New York University, who first forewarned an impending a 'US housing burst' in 2006, wrote a book explaining how the deregulated private banks, shadow banks (NBFCs) and others in the USA used complex, opaque and high-risk financial instruments to *maximize profits* that first derailed the USA and then the rest of the world, causing the Great Recession of 2007–2009 (Roubini & Mihm, 2010).

Here is what the unregulated expansion of the financial sector did to the UK.

British tax expert and author Nicholas Shaxson wrote that it proved to be counterproductive. In his 2018 book, he wrote that the UK's banking assets, which stood at 50 per cent of the GDP for 100 years until 1970, grew to 500 per cent by 2006 (1,000% if insurance and others are added) and remained there. A century ago, *80 per cent of bank lending* went to finance businesses, which reduced to *10 per cent,* the rest being lent among themselves, housing and real estate. The UK's per capita GDP was lower than that of its northern European peers; it was much more unequal and had poorer overall scores in health and well-being (Shaxson 2018, emphasis added).

Mariana Mazzucato of the University College London says that the financial sector was brought into GDP estimates in the 1970s, until which it was treated as an 'intermediate input'—a service contributing to the functioning of other industries that were the 'real' value creators—and perceived as 'a *distributor, not a creator of wealth*'. This coincided with the financial sector's deregulation (tightened after the Great Depression of 1929), *increasing its hold on the 'real' economy* (producing goods and services, such as agriculture, industry, services, rather than banks and stock markets; Mazzucato, 2018; emphasis added).

Today, she wrote, the issue is not just the size of the economy, but its effect on the *behaviour of the rest of the economy*, large parts of which have been 'financialized'. Rather than creating value by investing in the long-term future of businesses, the financial sector is *capturing value* from other sectors through interest differentials and expensive transaction costs, and when PE and venture capitals control non-financial companies, the main objective is not to produce new things but to *maximize shareholders' value* through stock buybacks (to boost stock prices and executive pay).

In India, the growth of the financial sector has led to a massive rise in bank frauds (doubling every year during 2017–2020), the growth and collapse of shadow banking (NBFCs), rising stressed assets in banks and NPA write-offs, the domination of tax haven in FDI inflows and outflows (more than 80% transactions) and a bigger role of shell companies, particularly during the Modi government. Amid the pandemic crisis, India is in a liquidity trap because of cheap loans (Mohanty, 2020c, 2020e, 2021a, 2021b, 2021c; Sen, 2021).

Fiscal Austerity Problematic?

The pandemic crisis saw India reluctant to spend. Its AatmaNirbhar Bharat relief and stimulus packages were big on paper, but the actual fiscal spending was just 1.2 per cent of the GDP—while developed economies spent more than 5 per cent of their GDP—and FY2021 ended with India among the worst hit nations. India was more concerned about fiscal austerity and ignored repeated advice of eminent economists such as Amartya Sen, Abhijit Banerjee and Raghuram Rajan.

The IMF has been imposing fiscal authority on the world. Since 1985, the IMF has been imposing it on about 100 countries, including India. Its 2017 rulebook prescribes it for *96 countries*. *It comprises two elements*: (a) limiting fiscal deficit to *3 per cent* of GDP and (b) limiting government (pubic) debt-to-GDP to *60 per cent* of GDP. Mazzucato explored the history of these 'magical numbers', as well as how they work on the ground and concluded that 'these numbers are taken out of thin air, supported by neither theory nor practice' (IMF, 2017; Mazzucato, 2018).

At the height of the pandemic, Stiglitz warned the USA that 'the true danger is austerity' and explained that lower government spending would constrain GDP growth and cause a higher debt-to-GDP ratio, contrary to what fiscal austerity seeks to achieve. In 2014, he declared that 'austerity has failed' in the context of the Eurozone crisis (Stiglitz 2014, 2020).

Now, it is clear that capital market liberalization and fiscal austerity are not the magic formula that neoliberal economics claims. They create economic crisis, impoverish ordinary people and benefit private business interest. The previous chapter described how privatization does the same.

There are plenty of absurd theories India has fallen victim to. The three key ones are as follows: (a) trickle-down theory, which posits that wealth created at the top trickles down; a variation to this is the argument that corporate tax cut leads to higher investment and creation of jobs; (b) a high wage for workers is detrimental to workers as it leads to lower employment generation and (c) the market is free, neutral and efficient in terms of price discovery.

Trickle-down Theory and Corporate Tax Cut

The trickle-down theory is the most popular one in India. One variation popular with neoliberal economists is that 'a rising tide lifts all boats.'

After former US President Donald Trump announced a corporate tax cut using this logic, the Wharton University of Pennsylvania published a paper in 2017 tracing its history and validity to conclude: 'The term "trickle-down economics" doesn't really represent a cohesive economic theory. It's a term used, often negatively, to characterize the view that reducing taxes on the rich will benefit the non-rich.' It traced the origin of the phrase to humourist Will Rogers' 1932 column in which he made fun of an engineer's understanding of water trickling down from the top to money trickling down (it trickles up, he wrote) and described the theory as 'the great hobgoblin of our time' to push tax cuts for the rich and industries on the plea that lower taxes *lift all boats together* (Wharton University of Pennsylvania, 2017).

In his article, Warren Buffet dismissed it, stating that between 1982 and 2018, '…the tsunami of wealth didn't trickle down. It surged upward.' Long ago, in 1984, economist John Galbraith described it using the 'horse-and-sparrow' metaphor, implying that if the horse is fed enough oats, some will pass through to the road for the sparrows (Buffet, 2018; Galbraith, 1984).

The IMF knows this too. Its 2015 study of more than 150 countries concluded that 'the benefits do not trickle down.' On the contrary, an increase in the income of the rich (top 20%) drags down GDP growth, whereas an increase in the income of the poor (bottom 20%) drives up GDP growth (IMF, 2015b).

What did the US and Indian corporates do with tax cuts?

After the then President Trump cut corporate tax drastically, from 35 per cent to 21 per cent, the US Congress found that corporations used it for *stock buyback, which reached an all-time high of $1 trillion in 2018*. Stock buybacks are problematic for draining out cash surplus and manipulating stock prices to benefit a selected few. The Congress found no evidence of growth in investment and jobs but led to revenue loss of $40 billion. But cut in personal taxes that accompanied it raised revenue collection by $45 billion by boosting consumptions (Gravelle & Marples, 2019).

The RBI found that India's corporate tax cut (from 25%–30% to 15%–22% without exemptions) amounting to annual loss of ₹1.45 lakh crore amid a prolonged slowdown and fall in revenue was used for 'debt servicing, build-up of cash balances and other current assets rather than restarting the capex cycle' (PIB, 2019; RBI, 2020).

The IMF tracked the sharp fall in corporate tax in the past 30 years in different economies to ask a question: how low can you go? It stated that this sharp fall was problematic because it undermined both tax revenue and faith in the fairness of the overall tax system; it was especially harmful to low-income countries as it deprived them of revenue needed to achieve higher growth and reduce poverty (IMF, 2019).

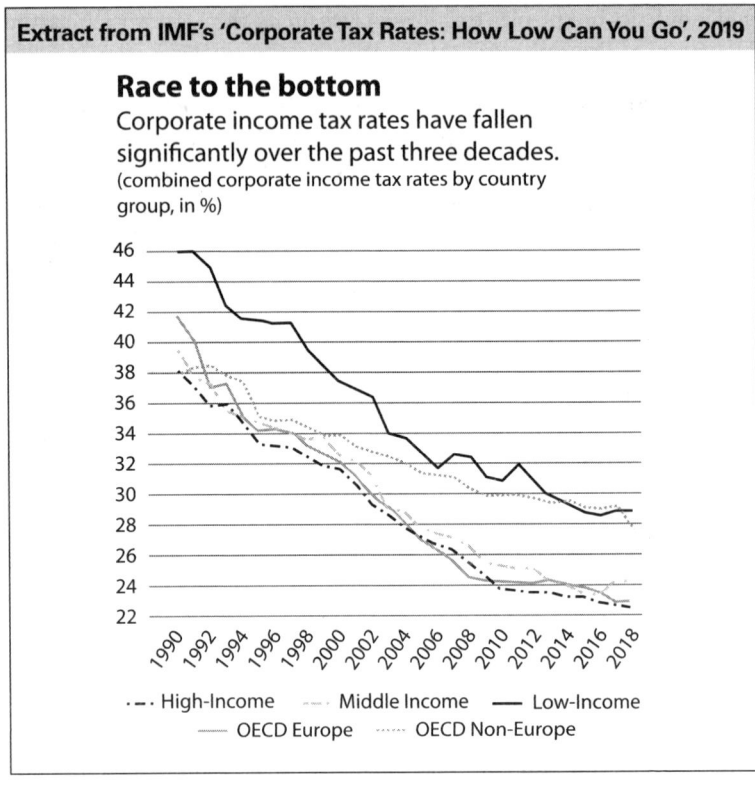

A UN report warned developing countries about such tax cuts, stating that this might '*entail significant costs, such as revenue loss, low economic efficiency, increased administrative and compliance costs, and excessive tax planning and tax evasion*, which may exceed their benefits and considerably erode the general tax base' (UN, 2018).

Here is a good lesson from history.

During the golden age of capitalism between the 1950s and the 1970s—when both developed and developing countries registered the highest ever GDP growth (3.8% and 3%, respectively) and inequality was lower—the average top corporate tax rate was 70–80 per cent in the USA and 80–99.25 per cent in the UK (Mohanty, 2020a; Shaxson, 2018).

It was in June 2021 that the G7 agreed on imposing a global minimum corporate tax of at least *15 per cent* to deter multinational companies from avoiding taxes by stashing profits in low-rate countries. US President Biden has proposed the same (down from 28% he proposed earlier) for American corporations (Chan & McHugh, 2021; Renshaw & Shepardson, 2021).

High Wage Bad for Employment

Neoliberalism posits that higher wage is bad for employment growth as it leads to higher cost of production and services, which in turn lowers demand for goods and services, and hence leads to lower economic activities and job cuts.

This may sound logical for an isolated and individual business entity, but it doesn't apply to the entire economy. Rise in wages raises consumption expenditure of a large population base (lower income groups), significantly boosting economic growth (in a country like India, for example) and creating more jobs as demand goes up and investment in production of goods and services goes up. Low wage, on the other hand, keeps consumption and demand low, pulling down growth and job creation—just the opposite.

India seems to believe the neoliberal theory and has kept national minimum wage rates low at ₹176 for three years after its internal committee recommended ₹375 (in 2019) and passing of the Code on Wages (2019). The ILO's 2018 India Wage Report stated that Indian workers were getting increasingly short-changed in their share of productivity growth and profits (ILO, 2018; Mohanty, 2020f).

Neoliberalism has another bizarre neoliberal concept called 'voluntary unemployment'.

This concept posits that high unemployment is because workers choose not to work and that they have financial incentives not to work. Casey Mulligan of the Chicago school is credited with this concept. His colleague John Cochrane went a step ahead to add that *unemployment is good, recession is good*, adding for good measure that 'People who spend their lives pounding nails in Nevada need something else to do' (Krugman, 2009).

The obvious flaw in the argument is that voluntary abstention or withdrawal from work is not counted as unemployment. Unemployment is a status of labour looking for work, not holidaying in a hill station. But that never crossed the minds of neoliberal economists. Bibek Debroy, who heads the EAC-PM, stated that voluntary unemployment was growing in India to explain the job crisis in 2017. The PLFS 2017–2018 report showed that India's unemployment rate had reached a 45-year high (Dhoot, 2017).

No wonder neoliberalism is described as 'snake-oil economics'—deceptive or misleading—by a Harvard publication (Mankiw, 2019).

Free and Efficient Market

The terms 'neoliberalism' and 'free market' are inseparable and interchangeable, and neoliberals are, indeed, referred to as free-market economists. The term 'free market' refers to a market where all exchanges are voluntary, supply and demand determine prices and there is no government interference.

Stiglitz bursts this by myth saying that there is no such impersonal or natural law that makes market free or neutral; markets are *shaped by public policy*, pre-setting which has how much market power, and most markets are *far from competitive* (Stiglitz, 2019c).

Krugman burst the myth of rational individuals interacting in perfect markets which get the right price, else there wouldn't be stock market bubbles that burst, sinking economies into crisis. Referring to studies by behavioural economists in the context of the 2007–2009 market crash, Krugman wrote:

> Practitioners of this approach (behavioural finance) emphasise two things. First, many real-world investors bear little resemblance to the cool calculators of efficient-market theory: they're all too subject to *herd behavior*, to *bouts of irrational exuberance and unwarranted panic*. Second, even those who try to base their decisions on cool calculation often find that they can't, that problems of trust, credibility, and limited collateral force them to run with the herd. (Krugman, 2009)

Who Are Neoliberals and Who They Work For?

Neoliberalism is a new way of interpreting the classic 'free-market' or *laissez-faire* concept.

Its origin is traced to a group of radical right thinkers from the USA and Europe which set up the Mont Pelerin Society (MPS) in 1947. Nancy MacLean, a history professor at the Duke University, wrote that they called themselves 'neoliberals' to signal that they were 'retooling' the classical pro-market ideas of Adam Smith and John Stuart Mill. The society got its name from the Swiss mountain where they met. About their goal, she wrote: 'Their concern was how they might, together, *shift the tide of history away from what they called* "statism" or what we might call a *strong role for government*' (MacLean, 2017).

She wrote that the society was led by Austrian polymath Friedrich Hayek (Nobel in 1974) and included fellow Austrian Ludwig von Mises and US economists Milton Friedman (Nobel in 1976) and Frank Knight (both from the Chicago school of economics). Nobel laureate Buchanan, an alumnus of the Chicago school, joined later. His public choice theory helped strengthening the fight against 'statism' by focusing on government failure to pave a greater role of the private sector. It is his strategy, described as 'crab-walk' for its deviousness, that was used in the decades-long fight to privatize the highly successful government-run SS programme of the USA and, far more than Friedman, he played a vital role in Chile's economic rearrangements under Augusto Pinochet's dictatorship in the 1970s, which brought mass-scale privatization.

US billionaire and one of the richest people in the world, Charles Koch, the elder of the famous Koch brothers, joined the society in 1970. He has been championing 'drastically lower personal and corporate taxes, minimal social services for the needy, and much less oversight of industry—especially environmental regulation' (Mayer, 2010).

Neoliberals gained the upper hand during the 1970s due to multiple economic crises; growth slowed down, inflation picked up (multiple oil crises), unemployment rose and resource-strapped governments needed new ways to boost growth. Friedman's belief that the Fed policy, rather than changes in government spending, should be used to stabilize the economy triumphed over the Keynesian thinking. Stiglitz explained that 'the fact that most of the post-war recessions were associated with the Fed tightening credit excessively confirmed conservatives' prejudices that it was government failures, not market failures, that were responsible for any aberration from perfection' (Stiglitz, 2019c).

They all worked for private corporates.

MacLean detailed Buchanan's active collaborations with big corporations for the most part of his working life, especially with Charles Koch, for which he received generous funding. His public choice theory sought to weaken the state (or reduce its excessive regulation) to promote private interest. Stiglitz revealed that Friedman provided intellectual defence to corporates in weakening anti-trust laws in the USA, which had broken up big corporate monopolies and constrained mergers that would lead to new monopolies. Shaxson revealed that Hayek, after leaving the London School of Economics in 1950, never held a permanent appointment that was not paid for by corporate sponsors. He also revealed that the very first meeting of 1947 at MPS where the 'neoliberal revolution' began 'was financed by Switzerland's three largest banks, its two largest insurance companies, the Swiss Central Bank, the Bank of England and City of London interests' (Shaxson, 2018; Stiglitz, 2019c).

As for the WB and the IMF, Kapur and Subramanian wrote that through structural adjustment lending, they '…effectively became a *debt collector for creditors*. The result was a lost decade for Latin America, but not for the bankers' (Kapur & Subramanian, 2018).

An opening line in Mazzucato's chapters reads: 'Economics emerged as a discipline in large part to assert the productive primacy of the private sector.'

Relationship between Neoliberalism and Democracy

The fact that neoliberalism has strived to weaken democracy is integral to its attempt to limit the state (small state, fiscal austerity) and promote private business interest.

MacLean titled her study of Buchanan and neoliberalism 'Democracy in Chains' to which Stiglitz agreed and said very categorically that 'neoliberalism has undermined democracy for 40 years.' He explained:

> The form of globalisation prescribed by neoliberalism left individuals and entire societies unable to control an important part of their own destiny...if a leading presidential candidate in an emerging market lost favour with Wall Street, the banks would pull their money out of the country. Voters then faced a stark choice: give in to Wall Street or face a severe financial crisis.... (Stiglitz, 2019c)

Just as Shaxson described tax havens, neoliberalism is a *project of the world's rich and powerful*—big corporations and governments—who seek to run the economy their way using the power of money and the language of political theorists masquerading as economists undermine democracy.

Harvard Professor Dani Rodrik provided a good perspective about policy choices recently. He wrote:

> All of our previous policy paradigms—whether mercantilist, classical liberal, Keynesian, social–democratic, ordoliberal, or neoliberal—had *important blind spots* because they were *conceived as universal programs* that could be applied everywhere and at all times. Inevitably, each paradigm's blind spots overshadowed the innovations it brought to how we think about economic governance. The result was overreach and *pendular swings between excessive optimism and pessimism....* The right answer to any policy question in economics is, 'It depends.' We need *economic analysis and evidence* to fill out the details of what the desired outcome depends upon. The keywords of a truly useful economics are *contingency, contextuality, and non-universality.*
>
> Economics teaches us that there is a time for fiscal expansion and a time for fiscal retrenchment. There is a time when government should intervene in supply chains, and a time when it should leave markets to their own devices. Sometimes, taxes should be high; sometimes, they should be low. Trade should be freer in some areas, and regulated in others.

> Mapping the links between real-world circumstances and the desirability of different types of interventions is what good economics is about.... *Our goal should be not to create the next ossified orthodoxy, but to learn how to adapt our policies and institutions to changing exigencies.*
> (Rodrik, 2021, emphasis added)

The point of this chapter is the same: no economic policy should be adopted without being sure of its economic logic and evidence: neoliberal or something else. The purpose of all policies should be to do greater good to greater number of people, not the top 1 per cent or top 0.1 per cent, as neoliberalism has done in the last four decades.

Manmohan Singh's Neoliberal Lessons

As finance minister, Manmohan Singh brought in neoliberalism under pressure from the IMF. As prime minister for 10 years (2004–2014), he talked about 'inclusive growth' and brought in a series of progressive laws, particularly rights-based ones, to address the distortions his policies had unleashed.

Some of the key ones were as follows:

1. Rural job guarantee scheme, Mahatma Gandhi National Rural Employment Guarantee Scheme (MGNREGS) of 2005, to address years of rural distress.
2. The National Rural Health Mission of 2005 to provide accessible, affordable and quality healthcare to the rural population, with ASHA workers serving as the 'interface' between people and the health system.
3. The Forest Rights Act of 2005 to 'undo the historical injustice' to tribals and others living in forest areas who were displaced by forcible land acquisition for development projects.
4. The Right to Fair Compensation and Transparency in Land Acquisition, Rehabilitation and Resettlement Act of 2013 to adequately compensate those who lost everything due to development projects.

5. The NFSA of 2013 to provide subsidized food grains to 75 per cent of the rural population and 50 per cent of the urban population.
6. The National Urban Health Mission of 2013 to provide primary healthcare to the urban poor.

Two of these, MGNREGS and NFSA, saved millions of Indians from starvation during the untimely, unplanned and overnight pandemic lockdown. Manmohan Singh didn't privatize public assets. Very few know that he didn't approve the neoliberal economic policies of the WB and the IMF, but he was forced to accept them. In 1990, just before he liberalized the economy in 1991, he wrote the South Commission report drawing attention to many flaws in the SAP.

Among other things, he wrote:

> ...they were generally shaped by a doctrinaire belief in the efficacy of market forces and monetarist policies. This combination of priorities and policies *aggravated the developing countries' economic woes and social distress* in a number of ways. 'In particular, the complete disregard of equity in prescriptions for structural adjustment consisting of cuts in public spending and changes in relative prices had *devastating effects* on vital public services like health and education, with especially harmful consequences for the most vulnerable social groups...after several years of "adjustment" many countries found themselves in the position of having *unwillingly or unwittingly caused large and irrecoverable losses to their economy and undermined their growth prospects*; their levels of public savings remained inadequate for financing vital investments that would allow the economy to make a sustainable recovery....'
> (South Commission, 1990, emphasis added)

The above narration raises one final question that needs to be answered.

Why Does Neoliberal Economics with All Its Flaws Doesn't Go Away?

Stiglitz answered it in his 2019 book, *People, Power and Profits*, explaining how neoliberal economics work in money-driven political systems such as the USA and India. He wrote that money power (of private business) translates into political power, ultimately evolving into an economy and democracy of, for and by the 1 per cent. The collusion between political power and money power leads to government failures as the powers that enable the state to improve societal well-being can be used by some groups or individuals to advance their self-interests at the cost of others. Thus, he wrote, the real problem is 'not economics but politics'.

The politics need to change before neoliberal economics change. In the case of India, a beginning for this can be made by dismantling the opaque electoral bond, which facilitates the politics–business nexus by allowing unhindered flow of unaccounted corporate money into the political system (Stiglitz, 2019c).

Takeaways

- Neoliberal economics is a political construct with no economic logic or evidence for support. There is no place for such economics in a democratic polity.
- If India's recent economic decisions and 'reforms' are tilted towards private interest at the cost of public interest, some of which have demonstrably hurt the economy and people, it is because those are entirely guided by neoliberal thinking.
- It aims to weaken the state, expand private interests and profits, and undermine democracy.
- It is a project of the rich and powerful corporations and politicians.

References

Buffet, W. (2018, 4 January). Warren Buffett shares the secrets to wealth in America. *Time.* https://time.com/5087360/warren-buffett-shares-the-secrets-to-wealth-in-america/

Chan, K., & McHugh, D. (2021, 6 June). G-7 back steps to deter tax dodging by multinational firms. *Pittsburgh Post-Gazette.* https://www.post-gazette.com/news/2021/06/05/G-7-back-steps-to-deter-tax-dodging-by-multinational-firms/stories/202106050061

Dhoot, V. (2017, 11 May). Aayog member Bibek Debroy sees dramatic rise in voluntary unemployment. *The Hindu.* https://www.thehindu.com/news/national/voluntary-unemployment-rising-says-bibek-debroy/article18427026.ece

Galbraith, J. K. (1984, 2 September). The heartless society. *The New York Times Magazine.* https://www.nytimes.com/1984/09/02/magazine/the-heartless-society.html

Gravelle, J. G., & Marples, D. J. (2019, 22 May). The economic effects of the 2017 tax revision: Preliminary observations. Congressional Research Service. https://www.everycrsreport.com/files/20190522_R45736_8a1214e903ee2b719e00731791d60f26d75d35f4.pdf

ILO. (2018). India wage report. https://www.ilo.org/wcmsp5/groups/public/---asia/---ro-bangkok/---sro-new_delhi/documents/publication/wcms_638305.pdf

IMF. (2015a, May). *Rethinking financial deepening: Stability and growth in emerging markets* (IMF Staff Discussion Note). https://www.imf.org/external/pubs/ft/sdn/2015/sdn1508.pdf

IMF. (2015b, June). *Causes and consequences of income inequality: A global perspective* (IMF Staff Discussion Note). https://www.imf.org/external/pubs/ft/sdn/2015/sdn1513.pdf

IMF. (2017, March). Fiscal rules at a glance. https://www.imf.org/external/datamapper/fiscalrules/Fiscal%20Rules%20at%20a%20Glance%20-%20Background%20Paper.pdf

IMF. (2019, 15 July). Corporate tax rates: How low can you go. https://blogs.imf.org/2019/07/15/corporate-tax-rates-how-low-can-you-go/

IMF. (2020, January). *Finance and inequality* (IMF Staff Discussion Note). https://www.financialcapability.gov.au/files/finance-and-inequality.pdf

Kapur, D., & Subramanian, A. (2018, 4 December). Can the World Bank redeem itself? *Business Standard.* https://www.business-standard.com/article/opinion/can-the-world-bank-redeem-itself-118120400030_1.html

Krugman, P. (2009, 2 September). How did economists get it so wrong? *The New York Times Magazine*. https://www.nytimes.com/2009/09/06/magazine/06Economic-t.html

Krugman, P. (2020). *Arguing with zombies*. W. W. Norton & Company.

MacLean, N. (2017). *Democracy in chains: The deep history of the radical right's stealth plan for America*. Viking Press.

Mankiw, N. G. (2019, 3 January). Snake-oil economics: The bad math behind Trump's policies. *Foreign Affairs*, *98*(1), 176–180. https://scholar.harvard.edu/mankiw/publications/snake-oil-economics-bad-math-behind-trumps-policies

Mayer, J. (2010, 23 August). Covert operations: The billionaire brothers who are waging a war against Obama. *The New Yorker*. https://www.newyorker.com/magazine/2010/08/30/covert-operations

Mazzucato, M. (2018). *The value of everything: Making and taking in the global economy*. Penguin.

Mohanty, P. (2020a, 24 June). Deconstructing neoliberalism III: Why neoliberalism calls for a rethink. *Business Today*. https://www.businesstoday.in/current/economy-politics/deconstructing-neoliberalism-neoliberal-ideas-call-for-a-rethink-indian-economy-free-market/story/407915.html

Mohanty, P. (2020b, 25 June). Deconstructing neoliberalism IV: How neoliberals won the world but India can ill afford their economics. *Business Today*. https://www.businesstoday.in/current/economy-politics/deconstructing-neoliberalism-how-neoliberals-won-the-world-indian-economy-jobs-unemployment/story/408055.html

Mohanty, P. (2020c, 29 July). Rebooting economy XI: Why are private companies so prone to financial frauds? *Business Today*. https://www.businesstoday.in/opinion/columns/indian-economy-why-are-private-companies-prone-to-financial-frauds-corporates-tax-havens/story/411453.html

Mohanty, P. (2020d, 1 August). Rebooting economy XII: Is private sector inherently more efficient than public sector? *Business Today*. https://www.businesstoday.in/opinion/columns/indian-economy-is-private-sector-inherently-efficient-than-public-sector-ownership/story/411696.html

Mohanty, P. (2020e, 12 August). Rebooting economy XVII: Why governments promote shadow banking. *Business Today*. https://www.businesstoday.in/opinion/columns/indian-economy-why-governments-promote-shadow-banking-nbfcs-non-banking-financial-companies/story/412786.html

Mohanty, P. (2020f, 6 October). Rebooting Economy 34: Temporary Jobs Hurt Both Workers And Economy. *Business Today*. https://www.businesstoday.in/opinion/columns/story/indian-economy-temporary-jobs-hurt-both-workers-and-economy-contractual-workers-informal-sector-274841-2020-10-06

Mohanty, P. (2021a, 10 February). Rebooting economy 66: Is India facing credit deprivation to warrant corporation banks? *Business Today*. https://www.businesstoday.in/opinion/columns/rebooting-economy66-is-india-facing-credit-deprivation-to-warrant-corporation-banks/story/430868.html

Mohanty, P. (2021b, 14 February). Rebooting economy 67: Set the record straight before setting up a bad bank. *Business Today*. https://www.businesstoday.in/opinion/columns/rebooting-economy-67-set-the-record-straight-before-setting-up-a-bad-bank/story/431212.html

Mohanty, P. (2021c, 19 February). Rebooting economy 68: How private wealth creators are serving Indian economy and people. *Business Today*. https://www.businesstoday.in/opinion/columns/rebooting-economy-68-how-private-wealth-creators-are-serving-indian-economy-and-people/story/431736.html

Ostry, J. D., Loungani, P., & Furceri, D. (2016). Neoliberalism: Oversold? *Finance & Development*, *53*(2). https://www.imf.org/external/pubs/ft/fandd/2016/06/ostry.htm

Palast, G. (2002). *The best democracy money can buy*. Pluto Press.

PIB. (2019, 20 September). Corporate tax rates slashed to 22% for domestic companies and 15% for new domestic manufacturing companies and other fiscal reliefs. https://pib.gov.in/PressReleaseIframePage.aspx?PRID=1585641

Piketty, T. (2017). *Capital in the twenty-first century* (translated by Arthur Goldhammer). Harvard University Press.

RBI. (2020, 25 August). Annual report, 2019–20. https://www.rbi.org.in/Scripts/AnnualReportPublications.aspx?year=2020

Renshaw, J., & Shepardson, D. (2021, 4 June). Biden proposes 15% corporate minimum tax to win Republican backing of infrastructure plan. Reuters. https://www.reuters.com/business/biden-offers-drop-corporate-tax-hike-proposal-source-2021-06-03/

Rodrik, D. (2021, 11 May). Beware economists bearing policy paradigms. Project Syndicate. https://www.project-syndicate.org/commentary/economic-policy-must-abandon-universal-paradigms-by-dani-rodrik-2021-05

Roubini, N., & Mihm, S. (2010). *Crisis economics: A crash course in the future of finance*. Penguin.

Sen, S. (2021, 29 January). The curious case of rising bank frauds. *Deccan Herald*. https://www.deccanherald.com/opinion/in-perspective/the-curious-case-of-rising-bank-frauds-944528.html

Shaxson, N. (2018). *The finance curse: How global finance is making us all poorer*. Penguin.

South Commission. (1990). *The challenges to the south*. Oxford University Press. https://www.southcentre.int/wp-content/uploads/2013/02/The-Challenge-to- the-South_HRes_EN.pdf

Stiglitz, J. (2008). Foreword. In G. Roland, *Privatization: Successes and failures* (p. ix). Columbia University Press. https://host.kelley.iu.edu/nagupta/gupta_surveychapter.pdf

Stiglitz, J. (2014, 1 October). Austerity has been an utter disaster for the eurozone. *The Guardian*. https://www.theguardian.com/business/2014/oct/01/austerity-eurozone-disaster-joseph-stiglitz

Stiglitz, J. (2019a, 30 May). Neoliberalism must be pronounced dead and buried. Where next? *The Guardian*. https://www.theguardian.com/business/2019/may/30/neoliberalism-must-be-pronouced-dead-and-buried-where-next

Stiglitz, J. (2019b, 26 November). The end of neoliberalism and the rebirth of history. *Social Europe*. https://www.socialeurope.eu/the-end-of-neoliberalism-and-the-rebirth-of-history

Stiglitz, J. (2019c). *People, power and profits: Progressive capitalism for an age of discontent*. W. W. Norton & Company.

Stiglitz, J. (2020, April). Four priorities for pandemic relief efforts. Roosevelt Institute. https://rooseveltinstitute.org/wp-content/uploads/2020/07/RI_Four-Priorities-for-Pandemic-Relief-Effort-WP-202004-1.pdf

UN. (2018). Design and assessment of tax incentives in developing countries. https://www.un.org/esa/ffd/wp-content/uploads/2018/02/tax-incentives_eng.pdf

Wharton University of Pennsylvania. (2017, 12 December). Does trickle-down economics add up—Or is it a drop in the bucket? *Knowledge@Wharton*. https://knowledge.wharton.upenn.edu/article/trickle-economics-flood-drip/

XII REIMAGINING INDIAN ECONOMY

India's immediate and biggest challenge undoubtedly is to pull out millions of people who would have slipped into extreme poverty because of a series of disastrous economic decisions taken since 2014 which have caused massive loss of jobs and businesses, starting from the illogical demonetization of 2016 and the slapdash GST of 2017 to the untimely and unplanned locking and unlocking and gross mismanagement of the pandemic crisis in 2020 and 2021 and an inward-looking regressive import substitution policy that began in 2014 and embodies the AatmaNirbhar Bharat Abhiyan of 2020.

The Pew Research Center's study of March 2021 estimated that 75 million Indians are likely to have been impoverished—accounting for 60 per cent of all globally—out of which 35 million (also 60% of the global total) would have slipped into extreme poverty (living below $2 daily) and the middle class shrunk by 32 million during the 2020 lockdown. According to the Brookings Institution's October 2020 estimates, the number is even higher at 85 million Indians slipping into extreme poverty in 2020 (Kharas, 2020; Kochhar, 2021).

The devastating second wave would have added many more millions to the list. This is a dramatic reversal of India's fortune. The global multidimensional poverty estimate of

2018 showed that India pulled *273 million Indians* out of poverty from 2004–2005 to 2015–2016. Even then, India was home to most of the poor at *377.5 million* (Oxford Poverty & Human Development Initiative & UNDP, 2020).

According to the WB's 2020 report, India was home to *284.6 million extreme poor* at per capita per day living expense of $1.9. At $3.2, which is the WB's poverty line for a low–middle-income country like India, *half of Indians or 659 million were poor* (World Bank, 2019, 2020).

Besides, India is far more unequal than other major economies. The World Inequality Report of 2018 showed that India rose to the *very top* in income inequality during 1980–2016. Its 2019 report stated that this rise in income inequality in India 'has no precedent in recent history', and that, since 1980, the top *0.1 per cent* of earners have captured a higher share of total growth than the *entire bottom half* of the Indian population (Alvaredo et al., 2018; Bharti & Chancel, 2019).

The first priority, therefore, is to provide direct income support to millions of Indians to pull them out of poverty, reduce income inequality and restore the demand and growth momentum in the economy.

Direct Income Support

One of the best solutions to fight poverty has been direct income support. Call it universal basic income (UBI), as is commonly known, or minimum income guarantee (MIG), or by any other name, the essence is to give direct cash support to as many people as possible to ensure a life of dignity and minimum living standard, which is also good economics.

In India, the Economic Survey of 2016–2017 first proposed this and sought MIG of ₹*7,620 per annum* (Tendulkar's poverty line of 2011–2012 inflation-indexed to 2016–2017) to *75 per cent of population*. It was estimated that this would cost *4.9 per cent of the GDP* and could be funded from 5.2 per cent of the GDP allocated for 950 central sector and centrally sponsored sub-schemes (Ministry of Finance, 2017).

The difference between UBI and MIG is that the former is linked to poverty line, whereas the latter is discretionary and could be equal to, more than or less than poverty line. During the 2019 general elections, the Congress proposed giving ₹6,000 per month (₹72,000 per annum) to 20 per cent of the poor (50 million families). It called this 'Nyuntam Aay Yojana' or 'NYAY' (Mohanty, 2019a).

There have been many global studies which show that such a policy works. Pilots have been conducted in more than 100 countries, including developed economies such as Canada, Finland, the Netherlands, Italy, the UK and the USA. Their main concerns have been a sharp rise in inequality and the threat of automation creating joblessness (Khosla, 2018).

March 2021 brought good news on this front. A study found that California's UBI programme, in which $500 dollar was given every month (for two years) to 125 randomly selected median-income households with no strings attached, had paid off. The study was conducted during February 2019–February 2020 (Kornfield, 2021; Stockton Economic Empowerment Demonstration, 2021).

The study listed four key findings of the guaranteed income: (a) income volatility was reduced; (b) recipients were able to find full-time employment; (c) recipients were healthier, showing less depression and anxiety, and enhanced well-being and (d) financial scarcity was alleviated, creating new opportunities for self-determination, choice, goal-setting and risk-taking. One more finding was in the report: 36.9 per cent of the money was spent on food, 22.7 per cent on sales/merchandise, 11 per cent on utilities and 'less than 1 per cent' was spent on tobacco and alcohol. Apart from turning people lazy, wasteful expenditure on tobacco and alcohol is often cited to rule out income support plan all over the world.

These findings are on expected lines. A similar study was carried out in Odisha by behavioural economists of MIT, University of California and University of Chicago. For the study, workers engaged in odd jobs (in this case, making leaf plates) were given ₹1,400 in advance (one month's wage). The study found that labour productivity went up by 6.2 per cent, with the effect being 'concentrated' among relatively poorer workers, and mistakes declined. It explained that having more cash-on-hand improved cognition by removing worry, stress and sadness, and enabled them to work faster with fewer errors (Kaur et al., 2021).

Several such studies have been carried out in India, including those in Madhya Pradesh in 2011–2012; and Delhi and Alwar in 2011, which led to introduction of direct cash transfer (DBT) during the UPA years (Khosla, 2018).

India has several such schemes running. The Ujjwala Yojana for LPG connections (₹1,600); PM-Kisan (₹6,000 a year to farmers); Telangana's Rythu Bandhu (₹10,000); Odisha's Kalia and other such schemes in West Bengal and Jharkhand. The genesis of DBT goes back to 1991's National Social Assistance Programme when India provided pensions to the elderly, widows and disabled (Mohanty, 2019c).

For years, economists have advocated for UBI to fight poverty in India. They include Nobel laureates Amartya Sen and Abhijit Banerjee, as well as Pranab Bardhan and Jean Dreze (Banerjee, 2016; Dreze, 2017a, 2017b; Gupta, 2019; Khosla, 2018).

Now India needs it all the more. Money is not a constraint. Here is why.

The Economic Survey of 2016–2017 had suggested that its MIG to be funded from central schemes (*4.9% of the GDP, out of 5.2% of central schemes*). This apart, fiscal space can always be found if political will is present. For example, amid a fiscal crisis, India cut corporate tax in September 2019 by ₹1.45 lakh crore. During the pandemic-hit financial crisis and a prolonged stand-off with farmers over new farm laws, a new central scheme of ₹10,900 crore was launched to provide production-linked incentive to food processing units (PIB, 2021).

India routinely writes off huge amounts of loans defaults (NPAs) of private corporations. During FY2015 and FY2020, India wrote off *₹8.64 lakh crore as NPAs* (details in the banking 'reforms' chapter). Estimates show that *revenue foregone* in corporate and personal income tax together cost *1.4–2.2 per cent of the GDP* in FY2020 (details in GST and other taxes chapter). Taken together, these write-offs amount to *2.6–3.4 per cent of the GDP* a year. Since these are given to the financially better off, this could be diverted to UBI/MIG for the poor.

In June 2021, the G7 countries decided to impose a 15 per cent global minimum corporate tax, and the USA proposes to do the same for American companies. India could think of this and many other ways to increase revenue. In 2019, a group of economists had proposed, in response to Gandhi's NYAY, a 2 per cent wealth tax on households owning more than ₹2.5 crore of wealth; a 2 per cent tax on land and building above ₹2 crore; new tax bracket for top 0.1 per cent by 20 percentage points and new tax bracket of 70 per cent tax rate, etc. (Bharti & Chancel, 2019; Renshaw & Shepardson, 2021; Stein & Farzan 2021).

These are eminently doable measures.

Identifying the beneficiaries is the least of the problem. The bottom 40 per cent of the population is already identified and linked to the Ayushman Bharat scheme (Pradhan Mantri Jan Arogya Yojana) since 2018. It uses the database of the 2011 Socio-Economic Caste Census, which mapped household monthly incomes, and remains the only-of-its-kind census (mapped 100% households; Mohanty, 2019b).

Cash Support to Revive MSMEs

The MSMEs are key to the well-being of Indian workers. They contribute 45 per cent to manufacturing output, more than 40 per cent of export, over 28 per cent of the GDP and 24 per cent of total employment. About 99.5 per cent of MSMEs are micro-units providing self-employment and have suffered the most due to demonetization and lockdown (RBI, 2019).

This sector is in a dire straight. The GST closed a large number of MSME units, leading massive job losses. The lockdowns of 2020 and 2021 did more of the same. This sector was allocated a mere ₹15,700 crore in FY2022 budget. Until December 2020, the government had disbursed ₹1.58 lakh crore of collateral-free credit to MSMEs (out of ₹3 lakh crore earmarked) under the AatmaNirbhar Bharat packages. This was expected to revive *45 lakh units*. The budget allocation of ₹15,700 crore for FY2022 would mean that an additional 5 lakh units would resume business, taking the total to 50 lakh units. This is just 7.8 per cent of the total 6.44 crore MSME units in India. The rest 92.2 per cent of MSMEs need cash support for revival as well (Mohanty, 2021d; PIB, 2020).

A survey in May 2021 showed that 59 per cent MSMEs and start-ups might be sold off or shut down by the end of 2021 due to pandemic disruptions. The industry association Federation of Indian Chambers of Commerce and Industry (FICCI) wrote to government for financial assistance for MSMEs, stating that they faced an existential crisis due to the second wave of lockdowns and sought several measures, including the clearance of all dues and payments, interest rate subvention, etc. According to its statement: 'It is extremely important to ensure the flow of money into the working capital of such enterprises otherwise there will be a risk to the survival of these enterprises' (Dave, 2021; FICCI, 2021).

NEP to Protect and Create Jobs

India entered into a job-loss growth during FY2012–FY2018 as the PLFS of 2017–2018 showed. Its unit-level data analysis showed that 9 million jobs had been lost during this period, a phenomenon that, according to the Azim Premji University report, 'happened for the *first time in India's history*' (Mehrotra & Parida, 2019).

India is yet to formulate the National Employment Policy (NEP). Following the 2007–2009 financial crisis, many countries, including Pakistan (2010), Nepal (2017) and Sri Lanka (2012), framed their NEPs. So did a number of African countries; China did it much earlier in 2002. So far, 36 countries have adopted NEPs, 20 are in the process and 13 are revising theirs (GOI, 2020).

During the job-less era of the UPA, the government initiated an NEP. A decade later, there is no sign of it yet. India doesn't even have a reliable database on the total number and composition of workers. A national policy is a dire need; else, ministers will keep repeating inanities like 'job seekers (are) becoming job creators' in India (Haq, 2019).

One of the first things that NEP should do is to frame 'JR' schemes similar to those used by the OECD countries to protect 50 million jobs during their lockdowns in 2020. The USA—apart from its universal unemployment allowances of weekly $600 or more—launched several new measures, such as the short-term compensation programme, the Coronavirus Aid, Relief, and Economic Security Act Act of 2020, the Paycheck Protection Program and the employee retention tax credit. These programmes provide loans to pay salary that are forgiven if employment and compensation (salary/pay) levels are maintained and give refundable tax credit to firms (OECD, 2020).

Germany's 'Kurzarbeit' allows employers to reduce working hours, instead of laying off workers. Workers get paid for their actual hours of work plus 60 per cent (67% for workers with children) for their non-work hours. The government fully reimburses the cost and also provides SS assistance to workers. France's 'Activité Partielle' allowed all workers to *receive 70 per cent of their gross wage* from their employer, which the government reimburses.

Such a JR scheme is important given that the pandemic year of FY2021 saw the Indian corporate sector first registering 'their highest ever profits in the midst of a severe lockdown' in Q2 of FY2021 by cutting jobs and wages, and then surpassed it in Q3 of FY2021, again with job and wage cuts, with net profits rising from ₹142,200 crore in Q2 and ₹162,000 crore in Q3. For the entire fiscal of FY2021, their profits hit a decade high, with combined net profits increasing by 57.6 per cent (Kant, 2021; Mohanty, 2021e).

The same practice was seen in the government-run steel plants of Durgapur and Asansol, which cut jobs and wages even while their revenues and profitability soared after the lockdown due to higher prices of steel. Hundreds of contract workers lost jobs, and many more suffered wage losses in the largest steel producers (about 30% of Steel Authority of India Limited's production) and most profitable state-run companies (Bhattacharya, 2021).

The other key concern for NEP would be to address structural distortions in the workforce.

A 2021 study by Ashoka University and CMIE on the sectoral share of employment showed three disturbing trends between 2016–2017 and 2020–2021.

1. The share of *agriculture went up* by 4 per cent, taking its share in the economy from 36 per cent to 40 per cent.
2. The share of services went up by 13 per cent.
3. The share of manufacturing halved (declined by 46%) in five years. A critical aspect of this is that the job loss was mostly in labour-intensive sectors such as textiles, construction material and the food processing industry (Bhardwaj, 2021; Misra, 2021).

According to the Azim Premji University's State of Working 2021 paper, during the pandemic year of 2020, India lost 100 million jobs due to the lockdown, of which 15 million were lost permanently. It also showed a *50 per cent rise in informal workers*, as the maximum impact was on salaried/regular wage workers, who moved to the informal sector (APU, 2021).

India's informal workers constituted 88.2 per cent of total workforce, while it is 18 per cent in developed economies and 70 per cent in other developing and emerging economies. The large presence of informal workers is a big concern as informal workers face 'high risks of poverty' and 'often face a greater range of general and occupational risks than formal economy workers' (OECD & ILO, 2019).

All of this means that NEP must aim at structural transformation. Agriculture is not only low-paying and labour-surplus, but it has also attracted more workers, which is neither sustainable nor good for growth. India already has a higher share of informal workers, and their number is also going up. There is a need for formulating a policy to address precarity of these workers and low productivity (skilling).

Redrafting Labour Codes

The new labour codes need to be revisited to universalize minimum wages and set a higher bar; universalize and improve SS, health and safety covers; tighten protections against arbitrary hire-and-fire and reverse expanding short-term contracts (FTE/FTC), all of which harm rather than help workers (detailed in labour codes chapter). The Wage Code was passed in August 2019, but two years down the line there is no sign of a new national minimum wage, which remains ₹176. Setting it at ₹375, as an internal committee of the Ministry of Labour and Employment suggested in 2019, could be a good beginning. There is no provision for unemployment allowance either, which needs to be added since India's existing unemployment allowance is flimsy and helps next to none (Mohanty, 2020b).

There will be no economic growth without a secure and healthy workforce. The new codes would end up harming productivity and economic growth in both short and long run, apart from increasing the precarity of workers, as has been explained in an earlier chapter.

Filling Government Vacancies

To address job crisis, the first obvious step is to immediately fill up large vacancies in the government sector and to stop cutting down sanctioned posts. The number of central government vacancies (regular civilian) is steadily increasing from 5.51 lakh in 2006 to 6.61 lakh in 2010, growing further to 7.47 lakh in 2014 and declining slightly to 6.84 lakh in 2018. At the same time, the number of sanctioned posts of the central government is declining since 1994 (post-liberalization era): from 41.76 lakh in 1994 and 40.49 lakh in 2014 to 38 lakh in 2018. In education, 42 central universities had 6,210 vacancies in teaching and 12,437 in non-teaching posts as on 1 September 2020; vacancies of teachers in government schools stood at 10.6 lakh, or 17 per cent of the total sanctioned strength (61.8 lakh), during the 2020–2021 academic sessions, as per the government's answers to the Parliament (Mohanty, 2020d).

In FY2021, amid the prolonged job crisis, central government hiring dropped by 27 per cent and state hiring fell by 21 per cent compared to the previous year. There is no reason why this be so and why vacancies in government sector continue. There is also no reason why sanctioned posts be cut down when there is a job crisis (Nanda, 2021).

The number of vacancies in the state is not known. There must be a centralized database to provide such information and fill vacancies at the earliest.

It is not just about vacancies. A large number of appointments in the government sector are ad hoc and honorary in which employees don't get promotion, increments and SS cover; scope for permanent employment is non-existent. Health and education are significant for growth and development but, in the public sector, health and education have a large presence of 'honorary' workers who are paid 'honorarium', such as Anganwadi and ASHA workers. Government-run schools, colleges and universities across states have ad hoc teachers. In Delhi University, for example, 43 per cent teachers are ad hoc, on a four-month contract, who get no increment, no promotion and no SS. So is the case with *niyojit shikshak* (employed teacher) and 'para-teachers' in several states (Mohanty, 2020a, 2020c).

The pandemic health crisis revealed a massive shortage in health infrastructure, including health workers. A study by the Public Health Foundation of India states that India's health workers are not only grossly inadequate by WHO standards, but their distribution is also highly skewed across states, rural–urban and public–private lines. It also points out that a large number of health workers are not adequately qualified, while 'more than 20% of qualified health professionals are not active in labour markets' (Karan et al., 2021).

Bias against Agriculture and Services

For more than 70 years, India has relied on industry to bring high growth, prosperity and employment. That hasn't happened. Since 1950–1951, it is the agriculture and services which are providing maximum employment and income; yet they are not given the same importance that industry gets.

The following graph maps the income shares (GDP) of the three sectors using the 2011–2012 GDP series (from 2004–2005), which corresponds to the trend since 1950–1951 (Mohanty, 2021b).

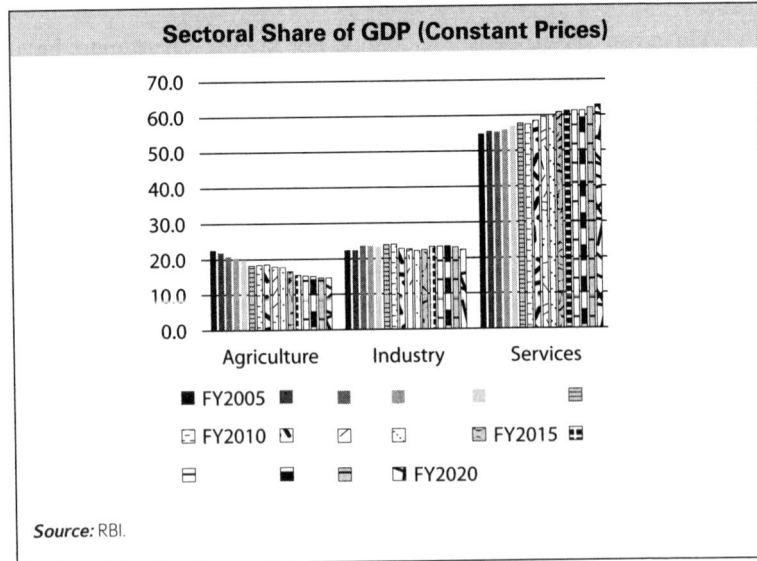

Source: RBI.

As the graph clearly shows, maximum income (GDP) is generated by the services sector—more than 60 per cent and rising. Agriculture's share is falling, and so is the case with industry. As Bhardwaj's study (2021) showed earlier, the fall in agriculture's share is a bigger worry as more workers are fleeing to it.

When the employment share is mapped, it is seen that, while income is falling, agriculture still provides maximum employment (more than 40%), followed by services (more than 40%). Industry's share of jobs has remained stuck at just over 10 per cent. These are long-term trends, not restricted to post-2004–2005 years that the GDP of 2011–2012 base provides.

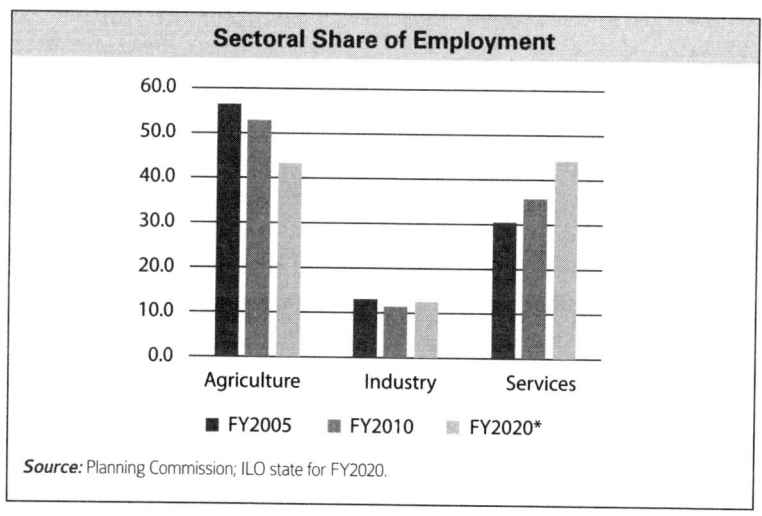

Source: Planning Commission; ILO state for FY2020.

The systemic bias against labour-intensive industries is a legacy issue. Economists have pointed out how historically India failed to transform its labour-intensive ecosystem and integrate with global economies (such as Bangladesh and Vietnam, for example, in textile) because of a protectionist approach and the dominance of the informal sector even in manufacturing. The Make in India and AatmaNirbhar Bharat programmes are no different (Misra, 2021).

The excessive emphasis on industry, particularly large industries, should be shifted to agriculture and services to create better and more employment, as both sectors are largely informal. That would require structural reforms and, hence, it is important that India frames its NEP.

True, industry led the growth and development in most developed economies, but that didn't happen for India. It shouldn't lose sight of the fact that there have been many exceptions, particularly closer to home. The most successful, industrialized and fast-growing Asian economies, such as Japan, South Korea, China and Vietnam, followed 'agricultural development-led industrialization pathway' to success, as a study of Asian Development Bank concluded. It argued that 'growth in agriculture supports the subsequent growth of industry', not the other way round that India pursues. In the reform era, India ignored agriculture and promoted industry (manufacturing included), which has neither provided jobs nor added much to the GDP (Mohanty, 2021a).

There is no reason why India can't try it. A beginning should be made by reviving the incomplete land reforms of the early decades of Independence. China did, and 'landlessness is virtually absent' there. In contrast, 55 per cent of India's total agriculture workforce is landless agriculture labour. Throwing open farming to the corporate sector is the wrong answer, as the US experience shows that their countries ate up small farmers. With less than 2 ha of landholding, 85 per cent of farmers in India are small and marginal (Fan & Gulati, 2008; *The Times of India*, 2021).

Similarly, the services sector should get far greater attention.

This sector has traditionally been neglected in India and the world because, as a WB report stated, 'it has been argued for *more than 200 years that economic growth is associated with the manufacturing sector*. Services have been considered non-tradable, menial, low productivity and low-innovation' (Ghani & O'Connell, 2014).

But that is no longer valid. This report showed that the conventional path of manufacturing-led growth hit a roadblock in many parts of the world, especially in low-income countries in Africa and South Asia. Unlike the East Asian Tigers or the Western developed economies earlier, some of these economies, like the Lions of Africa (Tanzania and Ethiopia) and India, witnessed growth driven by services.

Given the consistent contributions of service to India's growth, it must be treated as an independent sector, not divided into components which are then treated as adjunct to agriculture, industry, energy, transport, communication, rural development, urban development, etc., as is the practice now. There is no policy, ministry or department to deal with services. A large number of people don't have basic services such as safe drinking water, sanitation, quality health and education. While its income share (GDP) has grown, employment share has not kept its pace (Mohanty, 2021c).

Reviving Democratic Institutions and Practices

A lot needs to change for India to go back to high growth and improvement in the living standards of its vast population of poor. The single most important is the restoration of democratic processes of decision-making with robust institutional checks and balances to ensure accountability and transparency in governance, all of which have significantly declined since 2014.

Democracies survive and thrive on the strength of their institutions. More than 70 years of constitutional democracy later, India is witnessing a series of rash, top-down and self-serving policies since 2014, which have been explained in detail in earlier chapters, which strengthens the politics–business nexus to the detriment of ordinary people. Several economic decisions have been taken without economic logic and evidence to back, such as demonetization, new farm laws, new labour codes, blanket privatization of public assets, including PSBs, as previous chapters have detailed.

That India's GDP numbers (2011–2012 series) lack credibility, that its statistical system has lost the faith of economists and experts, and that Indian policymakers are working in a complete data vacuum on all critical areas such as job and business loss, growing poverty and inequality, and health and education deprivations (detailed in GDP and data vacuum chapter) are the consequences of weakening of India's democracy and governance. So long as that continues, there is no hope for change in India's fortune.

The other phenomenon that has noticeably seen in India since 2014 is rise in discrimination and violence on caste and religion lines. Dalits and Muslims have been consistently attacked. Weakening social fabric through caste and religion-related violence not only harms Indian citizens but also hurts the economy.

Once these issues are taken care of, the many ills that afflict the people and the economy at present would begin to recede, and India would be back to growing and developing in the right direction.

It should always be kept in mind that India is home to most of the poor in the world. A 2015 study of the IMF stated that 'the poor and the middle class' are 'the main engines of growth'. It looked at data from 156 to 159 economies across the most advanced, emerging markets and developing countries (EMDCs) from 1990 to 2012 to conclude that rise in the income of the bottom 20 per cent (the poor) drives GDP growth, while rise in the income of the top 20 per cent (the rich) reduces GDP growth (Dabla-Norris et al., 2015; emphasis added).

The way forward may appear to be easy, but history tells us that it is never so.

Takeaways

- ⇨ Direct cash support to poor and MSMEs must be given to overcome the humanitarian and business crises and also to revive demand in the economy.
- ⇨ Growing poverty, hunger and job crisis call for new thinking and policy responses.
- ⇨ All such policies that potentially harm people, such as the new farm, new labour laws, indiscriminate privatization of pubic assets, should be revised after due deliberations.
- ⇨ Systemic bias against agriculture and services must end as they are providing maximum jobs and incomes since 1950–1951, not industry.
- ⇨ Revival of democratic and constitutional institutions is the key to reversing the negative trends in economic growth, people's well-being and democracy.

References

Alvaredo, F., Chancel, L., Piketty, T., Saez, E., & Zucman, G. (2018). World inequality report 2018. World Inequality Lab. https://wir2018.wid.world/files/download/wir2018-summary-english.pdf

APU. (2021, 5 May). State of working India 2021. Azim Premji University. https://cse.azimpremjiuniversity.edu.in/state-of-working-india/swi-2021/

Banerjee, A. (2016, 16 September). Universal basic income: The best way to welfare. Ideas for India. https://www.ideasforindia.in/topics/poverty-inequality/universal-basic-income-the-best-way-to-welfare.html

Bhardwaj, A. (2021, 4 May). CEDA-CMIE bulletin: Manufacturing employment halves in 5 years. CEDA, Ashoka University. https://ceda.ashoka.edu.in/ceda-cmie-bulletin-manufacturing-employment-halves-in-5-years/

Bharti, N., & Chancel, L. (2019). *Tackling inequality in India: Is the 2019 election campaign up to the challenge?* (Issue Brief No. 2019/2). World Inequality Lab. https://wid.world/document/india2019/

Bhattacharya, A. (2021, 15 April). SAIL plants show how workers, wages are being sacrificed during economic recovery. *The Wire*. https://thewire.in/labour/sail-lockdown-workers-wages-low-recovery

Dabla-Norris, E., Kochhar, K., Suphaphiphat, N., Ricka, F., & Tsounta, E. (2015). Causes and consequences of income inequality: A global perspective. IMF. https://www.imf.org/external/pubs/ft/sdn/2015/sdn1513.pdf

Dave, S. (2021, 27 May). 59% of startups and MSMEs may shut shop, sell off or scale down: Survey. *The Economic Times*. https://economictimes.indiatimes.com/small-biz/sme-sector/covid-second-wave-59-of-startups-and-msmes-may-shut-shops-sell-off-or-scale-down-localcircles-survey/articleshow/82974477.cms?utm_source=contentofinterest&utm_medium=text&utm_campaign=cppst

Dreze, J. (2017a, 16 January). Universal basic income for India suddenly trendy. Look out. NDTV. https://www.ndtv.com/opinion/decoding-universal-basic-income-for-india-1649293?pfrom=home-lateststories

Dreze, J. (2017b, 2 February). The tale and maths of universal basic income. NDTV. https://www.ndtv.com/opinion/the-tale-and-maths-of-universal-basic-income-1655225

Fan, S., & Gulati, A. (2008, 28 June). The dragon and the elephant: Learning from agricultural and rural reforms in China and India. *Economic & Political Weekly*. http://www.indiaenvironmentportal.org.in/files/7_6.pdf

FICCI. (2021, 23 March). MSMEs may not survive if cash flow problem occurs amid lockdown, FICCI tells govt; suggests steps. https://ficci.in/ficci-in-news-page.asp?nid=20856

Ghani, E., & O'Connell, S. D. (2014, July). *Can service be a growth escalator in low income countries?* (World Bank Policy Research Working Paper No. 6971). World Bank. https://openknowledge.worldbank.org/bitstream/handle/10986/19352/WPS6971.pdf?sequence=1&isAllowed=y

GOI. (2020). Concept note on national employment policy (NEP). https://www.dropbox.com/s/tryx7yzyynmqpe3/NEP%20concept%20note%202020.pdf?dl=0

Gupta, A. (2019, 14 January). Amartya Sen: Granting basic income to all may lead to more privatisation. *The Indian Express.* https://indianexpress.com/article/cities/kolkata/amartya-sen-universal-basic-income-ashok-rudra-memorial-lecture-5536609/

Haq, Z. (2019, 2 February). Budget: Job seekers are now becoming job creators, says Piyush Goyal. *Hindustan Times.* https://www.hindustantimes.com/budget/budget-job-seekers-are-now-becoming-job-creators-says-piyush-goyal/story-MtuyshvOlxPQfkegVgeIIM.html

Kant, K. (2021, 31 May). Corporate profit to GDP ratio hits 10-year high of 2.63% in FY21. *Business Standard.* https://www.business-standard.com/article/companies/corporate-profit-to-gdp-ratio-hits-10-year-high-of-2-63-in-fy21-121053100041_1.html#:~:text=The%20combined%20net%20profit%20of,in%20the%20last%20financial%20year

Karan, A., Negandhi, H., Hussain, S., Zapata, T., Mairembam, D., De Graeve, H., Buchan, J., & Zodpey, S. (2021). Size, composition and distribution of health workforce in India: Why, and where to invest? Public Health Foundation of India. https://human-resources-health.biomedcentral.com/track/pdf/10.1186/s12960-021-00575-2.pdf

Kaur, S., Sendhil, M., Oh, S., & Frank, S. (2021). *Do financial concerns make workers less productive?* (Working Paper No. 28338). National Bureau of Economic Research. https://www.nber.org/system/files/working_papers/w28338/w28338.pdf?utm_source=PANTHEON_STRIPPED&amp%3Butm_medium=PANTHEON_STRIPPED&amp%3Butm_content=PANTHEON_STRIPPED&amp%3Butm_term=PANTHEON_STRIPPED&amp%3Butm_campaign=PANTHEON_STRIPPED&amp%3Butm_id=PANTHEON_STRIPPED&amp%3Borgid=151

Kharas, H. (2020, 21 October). The impact of COVID-19 on global extreme poverty. Brookings Institution. https://www.brookings.edu/blog/future-development/2020/10/21/the-impact-of-covid-19-on-global-extreme-poverty/#:~:text=Compared%20to%20the%20baseline%20path,in%20poverty%20could%20be%20permanent

Khosla, S. (2018). India's universal basic income. Carnegie India. https://carnegieendowment.org/files/CEIP_Khosla_Report_FNL_w_covers.pdf

Kochhar, R. (2021, 18 March). In the pandemic, India's middle class shrinks and poverty spreads while China sees smaller changes. Pew Research Center. https://www.pewresearch.org/fact-tank/2021/03/18/in-the-pandemic-indias-middle-class-shrinks-and-poverty-spreads-while-china-sees-smaller-changes/

Kornfield, M. (2021, 4 March). A city gave people $500 a month, no strings attached, to fight poverty. It paid off, study says. *The Washington Post.* https://www.washingtonpost.com/nation/2021/03/03/stockton-universal-basic-income/

Mehrotra, S., & Parida, J. K. (2019, October). *India's employment crisis: Rising education levels and falling non-agricultural job growth* (CSE Working Paper No. 23). Azim Premji University. https://cse.azimpremjiuniversity.edu.in/wp-content/uploads/2020/10/Mehrotra_Parida_India_s_Employment_Crisis_October_2019.pdf

Ministry of Finance. (2017, January). Economic survey 2016–17. https://www.indiabudget.gov.in/budget2017-2018/es2016-17/echapter.pdf

Misra, U. (2021, 18 May). ExplainSpeaking: Why has Indian manufacturing been losing jobs since 2016? *The Indian Express.* https://indianexpress.com/article/explained/explainspeaking-why-has-indian-manufacturing-been-losing-jobs-since-2016-7318114/

Mohanty, P. (2019a, 29 January). How does Rahul Gandhi plan to finance his 'minimum income guarantee to every poor' scheme? Can this be done? *DailyO.* https://www.dailyo.in/politics/rahul-gandhi-minimum-income-guarantee-scheme-non-performing-assets/story/1/29177.html

Mohanty, P. (2019b, 28 March). NYAY: The scheme brings focus back to poverty and income inequality in India. *DailyO.* https://www.dailyo.in/voices/nyay-minimum-income-guarantee-income-disparity-rahul-gandhi-minimum-income-guarantee-gdp/story/1/30089.html

Mohanty, P. (2019c, 10 April). Part II. NYAY complements PM-KISAN in fighting poverty and inequality. *DailyO.* https://www.dailyo.in/politics/lok-sabha-elections-2019-nyay-pm-kisan-rahul-gandhi-congress-narendra-modi-bjp-welfare-poverty-inequality-in-india-doles-subsidies-ayushman-bharat/story/1/30252.html

Mohanty, P. (2020a, 20 August). Rebooting economy XIX: How India relies on low-paid ad hoc teachers for schooling children. *Business Today.* https://www.businesstoday.in/opinion/columns/education-sector-how-india-relies-on-low-paid-ad-hoc-teachers-for-school-children/story/413481.html

Mohanty, P. (2020b, 29 August). Rebooting economy XXII: Why is India reluctant to provide unemployment allowance? *Business Today.* https://

www.businesstoday.in/opinion/columns/why-is-india-reluctant-to-provide-unemployment-allowance-to-its-organised-unorganised-workforce/story/414510.html

Mohanty, P. (2020c, 29 September). Rebooting economy 32: Wage code leaves millions of workers out in cold. *Business Today*. https://www.businesstoday.in/opinion/columns/indian-economy-wage-code-leaves-millions-of-workers-out-in-cold-labour-productivity-minimum-wages/story/417260.html

Mohanty, P. (2020d, 5 October). Rebooting economy 33: Where have the good old full-time decent jobs gone? *Business Today*. https://www.businesstoday.in/opinion/columns/indian-economy-where-have-the-good-old-full-time-decent-jobs-gone-contract-temporary-unemployment-informal-workers/story/417922.html

Mohanty, P. (2021a, 6 January). Rebooting economy 56: Why India should follow agricultural development-led industrialisation growth model. *Business Today*. https://www.businesstoday.in/opinion/columns/why-agricultural-development-led-industrialisation-could-be-a-better-growth-model-for-india/story/427213.html

Mohanty, P. (2021b, 11 January). Rebooting economy 57: When and how will industry take India to next level of growth? *Business Today*. https://www.businesstoday.in/opinion/columns/indian-economy-when-and-how-will-industry-take-india-to-next-level-of-growth/story/427557.html

Mohanty, P. (2021c, 13 January). Rebooting economy 58: The untold story of India's services sector. *Business Today*. https://www.businesstoday.in/opinion/columns/indian-economy-the-untold-story-of-indias-services-sector-despite-being-main-driver-of-countrys-growth-story/story/427788.html

Mohanty, P. (2021d, 6 February). Rebooting economy 64: Budget numbers don't add up to 10% or more growth in FY22. *Business Today*. https://www.businesstoday.in/union-budget-2021/columns/indian-economy-budget-numbers-dont-add-up-to-10-or-more-growth-in-fy22/story/430462.html

Mohanty, P. (2021e, 21 February). Rebooting economy 69: What do workers gain from growth and profits? *Business Today*. https://www.businesstoday.in/opinion/columns/rebooting-economy-69-what-do-workers-gain-from-growth-and-profits/story/431857.html

Nanda, P. K. (2021, 26 May). Govt job hiring in FY21 drops to lowest in three years. *Mint*. https://www.livemint.com/news/india/govt-job-hiring-in-fy21-drops-to-lowest-level-in-three-years-11621966062774.html

OECD. (2020, 12 October). OECD Policy Responses to Coronavirus (COVID-19). Job retention schemes during the COVID-19 lockdown and beyond. http://www.oecd.org/coronavirus/policy-responses/job-retention-schemes-during-the-covid-19-lockdown-and-beyond-0853ba1d/

OECD & ILO. (2019, 21 May). Tackling vulnerability in the informal economy. OECD Development Centre. https://www.oecd-ilibrary.org/docserver/939b7bcd-en.pdf?expires=1615718853&id=id&accname=guest&checksum=F9D546A0B5116C928186FC17D4FD678A

Oxford Poverty & Human Development Initiative & UNDP. (2020). Charting pathways out of multidimensional poverty: Achieving the SDGs. Global multidimensional poverty index 2020. http://hdr.undp.org/sites/default/files/2020_mpi_report_en.pdf

PIB. (2020, 13 December). Finance Minister Smt. Nirmala Sitharaman reviews implementation of Aatma Nirbhar Bharat package with secretaries of all ministries/departments concerned. https://pib.gov.in/Pressreleaseshare.aspx?PRID=1680343

PIB. (2021, 31 March). Cabinet approves Production Linked Incentive Scheme for food processing industry. https://pib.gov.in/PressReleasePage.aspx?PRID=1708691

RBI. (2019, June). Report of the Expert Committee on micro, small and medium enterprises. https://rbidocs.rbi.org.in/rdocs/PublicationReport/Pdfs/MSMES24062019465CF8CB30594AC29A7A010E8A2A034C.PDF

Renshaw, J., & Shepardson, D. (2021, 4 June). Biden proposes 15% corporate minimum tax to win Republican backing of infrastructure plan. Reuters. https://www.reuters.com/business/biden-offers-drop-corporate-tax-hike-proposal-source-2021-06-03/

Stein, J., & Farzan, A. N. (2021, 6 June). G-7 countries reach agreement on 15 percent minimum global tax rate. *The Washington Post.* https://www.washingtonpost.com/us-policy/2021/06/05/g7-tax-us-yellen/

Stockton Economic Empowerment Demonstration. (2021). Preliminary analysis: SEED's first year. https://static1.squarespace.com/static/6039d612b17d055cac14070f/t/6050294a1212aa40fdaf773a/1615866187890/SEED_Preliminary+Analysis-SEEDs+First+Year_Final+Report_Individual+Pages+.pdf

The Times of India. (2021, 8 March). How 'Big Ag' ate up America's small farms. https://timesofindia.indiatimes.com/world/us/how-big-ag-ate-up-americas-small-farms/articleshow/81384027.cms

World Bank. (2019). Poverty & equity brief. https://databank.worldbank.org/data/download/poverty/33EF03BB-9722-4AE2-ABC7-AA2972D68AFE/FM2019/Global_POVEQ_IND.pdf

World Bank. (2020). Reversal of fortune. https://openknowledge.worldbank.org/bitstream/handle/10986/34496/9781464816024.pdf?sequence=27&isAllowed=y

XIII STATE OF ECONOMY AND FUTURE GROWTH

The pandemic hit India hard, harder than most other countries with the growth plunging to −7.3 per cent in FY21 (PE). This reduced India to Rank 142 among 194 countries in IMF's World Economic Outlook report of April 2021, making it one of the slowest growing economy in the world—from the fastest-growing major economy in 2015—lower than the global average of −3.5 per cent. China reclaimed its tag as the fastest-growing major economy at +2.3 per cent growth rate. India was beaten by Bangladesh with +3.8 per cent growth to Rank 5; it surpassed India in per capita income at $2,277 in FY21, against India's $1,947 (from about half of India's per capita income in 2007). Pakistan (Rank 33), Nepal (Rank 56) and Sri Lanka (Rank 86) also finished ahead of India with higher growth (*Indian Express*, 2021a; IMF, 2021a, 2021b).

The GDP numbers for FY21 (PE) show continuation of the sad state of the economy noticed in FY20 (before the pandemic hit). In FY20, three engines (private consumption, investment and net exports) had stalled and only one, government expenditure, was working. In FY21, private consumption (private final consumption expenditure [PFCE]) shrunk by −9.1 per cent, investment (gross fixed capital formation) to −10.8 per cent and net export to −65 per cent with both exports and imports taking a beating. Government expenditure (government final consumption expenditure [GFCE]), which contributes 11–12 per cent to the GDP, grew at +2.9 per cent—too small to prevent the growth from falling to –7.3 per cent (MoSPI, 2021b).

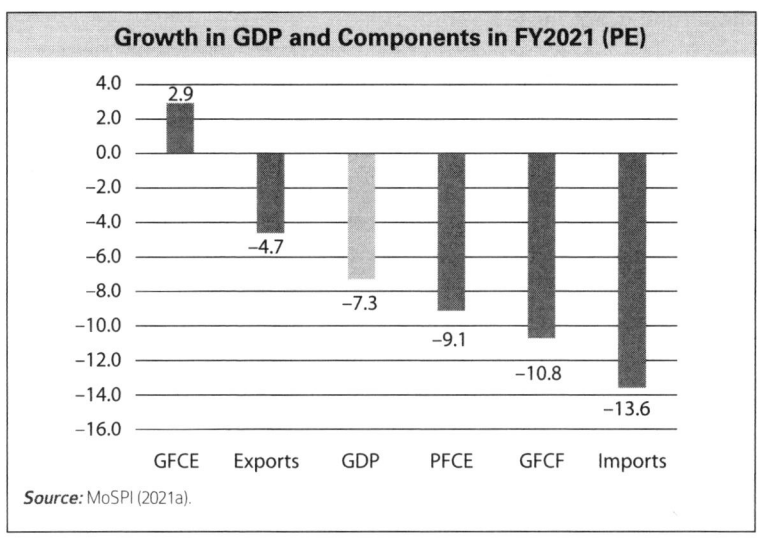

Source: MoSPI (2021a).

India, however, can take comfort from the fact that its foreign exchange reserves have remained high and healthy all these years because of robust foreign investment—FDI and FII; the latter shows up in the stock market boom described later. At the end of FY21, the forex reserve was $576.98 billion. The current account balance turned negative in Q3 of FY21 (0.2% of the GDP), after a surplus in Q2 (of 2.4%) and Q1 (3.7%) due to trade deficit and increase in net investment income payments. Trade deficit is an age-old problem. Growth in exports and imports both turned negative in FY20 and FY21 (PE)—with imports falling much more than exports (RBI, 2021b, 2021d).

Sectoral growth numbers showed agriculture and allied was the only sector that grew by +3.6 per cent. All others shrunk. Growth of policymakers' favourite growth driver, manufacturing GVA (part of industry), fell to –7.2 per cent—more than the overall fall in the GVA (–6.2%). Given India's flagship programme of 'Make in India', which was supposed to boost growth and raise its share to 25 per cent of the GDP, this is ironic. Instead, its share in the GVA for FY21 was 16.9 per cent (MoSPI, 2021b).

The worst hit were the services subsectors of trade, hotels, transport (–18.2%) and construction (–8.6%), followed by the industry subsector, mining and quarrying (–8.5%).

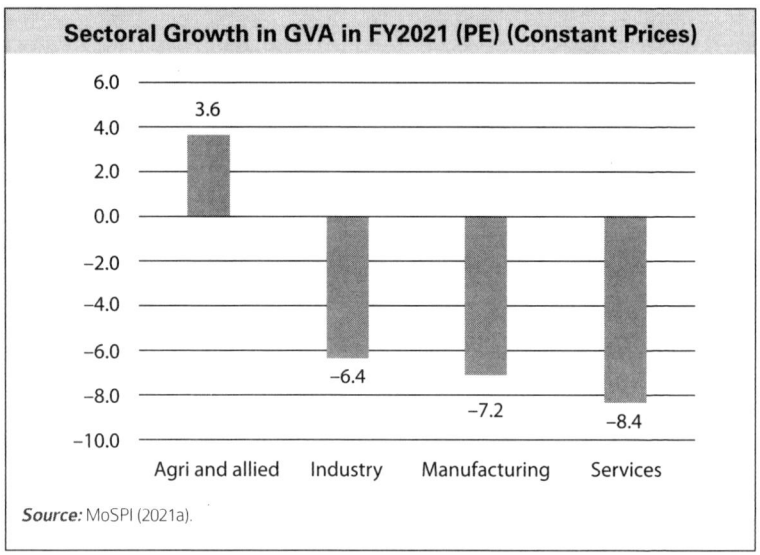

Source: MoSPI (2021a).

The stress was reflected in the growth of IIP as it fell from –0.8 per cent in FY20 to –8.6 per cent in FY21. CU in manufacturing fell to 66.6 per cent in Q3 of FY21—from 70 per cent in Q4 of FY20. Gross bank credit growth in SCBs fell to 5 per cent in March 2021, compared to 6.8 per cent in March 2020. Credit growth to industry was the lowest among sectors (0.4%), large industries registering –0.8 per cent in FY21, in spite of cheap credit, tax cuts (of ₹1.45 lakh crore in September 2020) and fiscal stimulus. Services also saw low growth of 1.4 per cent. If the overall credit growth was positive, it was because of agriculture (12.3% growth) and personal loans (10.2% growth; RBI, 2021c).

All this indicated large-scale disruptions to industry and services and an abject failure of the AatmaNirbhar Bharat packages to address the pandemic crisis.

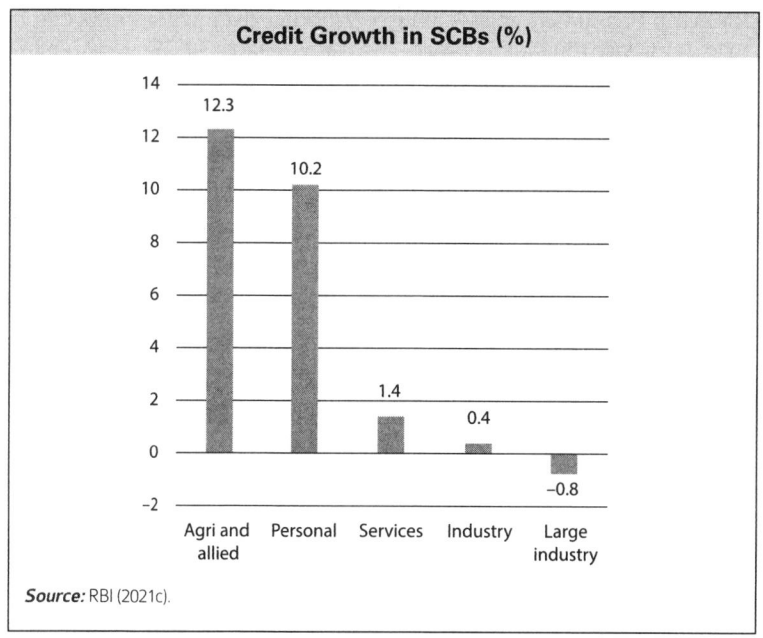

Source: RBI (2021c).

The Need to Address Livelihood Crisis and Demand Shock

There is a livelihood crisis which is yet to register with the government. One reason is high health expenditure. By 31 March 2021, India had *12.2 million cases* and *162,927 deaths*. A SBI paper said households would have spent additional ₹66,000 crore in FY21 over FY20 (11% higher) due to the pandemic[1] (SBI, 2021).

In normal times, official documents show that 60–63 million people slip below poverty line (BPL) every year due to 'exorbitant' health expenditure (also high out-of-pocket expenditure). Imagine the cost the pandemic would have imposed on the millions of households, far more than the official numbers reveal because of gross under-reporting (GOI, 2015; National Health Authority, 2018).

---

[1] https://ourworldindata.org/coronavirus-data?country=~IND

The Azim Premji University's State of Working 2021 paper shows that in 2020, India lost 100 million jobs due to the lockdown, of which 15 million jobs were lost permanently. It also showed a *50 per cent rise in informal workers* as the maximum impact was on salaried/regular wage workers and they moved to informal self-employment (30%), casual (10%) or informal salaried (9%) work. It also found a fall of 17 per cent in average monthly income of workers and impoverishment of 230 million who fell below a minimum wage threshold of ₹375 per day recommended (but not accepted or implemented) by the Anoop Satpathy Committee (APU, 2021).

The US-based Pew Research Institute showed that 35 million low-income people would have slipped below $2 dollar of living expenses (extreme poverty) and 32 million middle-income people below $10 (low income) due to the pandemic in 2020. This estimate does not include those who would have slipped into extreme poverty earlier because of the slowing economy and the impact of demonetization, GST (as explained in earlier chapters) or the second wave in 2021. This is a reversal of India making historic record of lifting 271 million out of poverty during 2005–2006 and 2015–2016. A large number of them would now be back to BPL status (Oxford-UNDP, 2018; Pew Research Center, 2021).

The massive job loss and rise in low-paying informal work were reflected in the rising demand for job guarantee scheme MGNREGS, which provides manual work, in FY21. Households who worked under the scheme went up from 54.8 million in FY20 to 75.5 million in FY21. During the same period, individuals who worked went up from 79 million to 111.9 million. The budget for FY22 reduced allocation for the scheme, which needs to be brought back.

The aforementioned Azim Premji University study said that food intake fell as 90 per cent households suffered a reduction in food intake during the 2020 lockdown. Net physical assets have been falling fast—from 16.3 per cent of the GDP in FY12 to 11.7 per cent in FY20—indicating liquidation of physical assets (including gold and silver) to meet demands for essentials before the pandemic hit. Past few months have seen a big step up in auctioning of gold kept as collateral for loans by gold financiers like Manappuram Finance due to factors like income stress (BloombergQuint, 2021a, 2021c; MoSPI 2021a).

The National Accounts Statistics reveal that per capita income (GDP) shrunk by −8.2 per cent and per capita disposable income (gross national disposable income) by −3.8 per cent in FY21 (PE). The GDP numbers, however, don't tell the full story of the impact of the pandemic, particularly on household pain because of the loss of lives and livelihoods and additional expenditure on healthcare. Per capita income (GDP) takes into account all incomes—households, government and corporations—thus, masking the sufferings of households. India doesn't have data on household expenditure (proxy for income) after 2011–2012. The 2017–2018 NSSO survey of household consumption expenditure was junked for showing that the real expenditure had fallen for the first time in 40 years—from ₹1,501 in 2011–2012 to ₹1,446 in 2017–2018 (*Business Standard*, 2019).

RBI's latest report shows that household financial savings fell to 8.2 per cent of the GDP in Q3 of FY21, reflecting a sequential moderation from an unusually high of 21 per cent in Q1 when the lockdown led to high financial savings. The moderation, it said, 'was driven by a significant weakening in the flow of household financial assets', with the ratio of household (bank) deposits declining to 3 per cent of the GDP in Q3, from 7.7 per cent in the previous quarter. More worryingly, household debt, which has been increasing steadily since March 2019, rose sharply to 37.9 per cent of the GDP at the end of December 2020 (Q3) from 37.1 per cent in the previous quarter. No data is available about physical assets of household for FY21 yet (RBI, 2021h).

That the economy didn't recover fully is clear. The IIP fell in January and February before picking up in March and gain in employment reversed as Q3, the last quarter, saw 3 million job loss. As Indian states went into another round of lockdowns because of the second wave, job loss and unemployment rate mounted. According to the CMIE, India lost 22.3 million jobs during April–May 2021, 17.2 million of them daily wagers (25.3 million jobs during January–May 2021). The unemployment rate rose to 11.9 per cent in May 2021—double the unemployment rate of 6.1 per cent in 2017–2018, which was at a 45-year high. As a consequence, labour force participation rate never recovered from the 2020 lockdown. Industrial hum came down and labour shortages hit due to the second wave of workers' migration and when they returned, they found work hard to come by in places such as Delhi, Mumbai and Goa. Services sector contracted in May, reversing the gains made in previous eight months, forcing job cuts at the fastest pace since October (CMIE, 2021a, 2021b; *Indian Express*, 2021b; Mint, 2021b; Reuters, 2021).

All these were before the far more *devastating second wave* of the pandemic hit in late February and peaked in April–May 2021. Our World in Data shows, as against *12.2 million cases* and *162,927 deaths* until 31 March 2021, the numbers climbed up to *30.1 million cases* and *393,338 deaths* as on 25 June 2021—a quantum leap. More cases and more deaths mean higher cost to the economy and more pain on households in terms of loss of income and higher expenditures too—apart from the loss of lives.[2]

Demand Shock, the Biggest Worry!

The biggest worry for the economy remains a prolonged weakening of the main driver—private consumption demand (PFCE), which constitutes 56–57 per cent of the GDP. It went down as the economy slowed down from FY18. The *pent-up demand*, which shot up in the second half of FY21, started falling right from the beginning of FY22 (April 2021). The RBI said the second wave of the pandemic delivered *a demand shock* to the economy due to loss of mobility, discretionary spending and employment, besides inventory accumulation (*India Today*, 2021; RBI, 2021c).

The latest GDP numbers show that consumption in FY21 fell below FY19—₹124.5 lakh crore against ₹127 lakh crore in FY19 (MoSPI, 2021b).

The household health expenditure is likely to be far higher than in FY20, squeezing out other consumptions to aggravate demand for other goods and services. The second wave has caused havoc in rural areas too. Unless demand is revived, there would be no improvement in production of goods and services, fresh investment or employment generation and the recovery would be delayed.

---

[2] https://ourworldindata.org/coronavirus-data?country=~IND

Unlike in the first wave, rural areas were hit harder by the pandemic spread. At the peak in May, 53 per cent of new cases and 52 per cent of deaths were reported in rural areas. Rural economy was impacted due to breakdown in supply chain and mandi arrivals sharply fell, despite localized shutdowns (BloombergQuint, 2021b; *Times of India*, 2021).

Amidst ruin all around, stock markets boomed, reaching historic heights and giving a false sense of hope and misleading state of the economy.

Yes, Stock Markets Boomed!

The only markets which boomed during the pandemic crisis were the stock markets. Both BSE Sensex and NSE Nifty50 kept creating new historic highs even as the economy was collapsing and millions of people were ruined through the pandemic.

This is not surprising because contrary to popular notions, stock markets have repeatedly demonstrated since the Great Depression of 1929 that their performance is not linked to macroeconomic and business fundamentals. The RBI has repeatedly warned against the stock market *bubble*, highlighting the *disconnect* between stock markets and the real economy and pinning the blame on the government's fiscal stimulus and liquidity infusion to speed up recovery but instead having the 'unintended

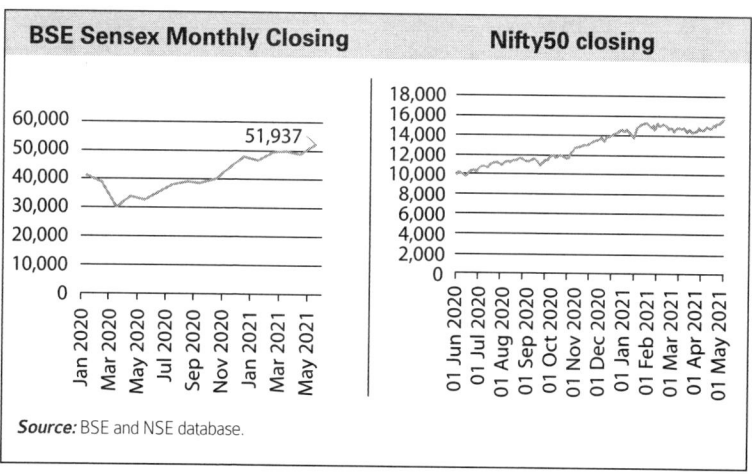

Source: BSE and NSE database.

consequences', posing 'macrofinancial risks' to the economy. Ironically, the RBI has played a big role in facilitating this liquidity by keeping key interest rates low (Mohanty, 2020a, 2021d; RBI, 2021e).

Stock market behaviour has shown that the concepts of rational and well-informed investors participating in an efficient and self-correcting market that always gets stock prices right are deeply flawed. Globally, stock markets and billionaires remained immune to the pandemic crisis and boomed. A study by two multinational giants, UBS and PwC, said, 'huge fiscal and quantitative easing packages' given by governments around the world drove a V-shaped recovery of stock markets, and billionaires' wealth surged to $10.2 trillion by the end of July 2020 (Mohanty, 2020c).

What the Future Holds?

At the end of FY21, India seems very precariously poised. Long-term trends paint a very scary picture and indicate India is more likely to go back to 'Hindu' rate of growth, rather than regain the pre-pandemic growth which was bad enough.

As the devastating second wave hit, the RBI lowered India's growth projections for FY22 to 9.5 per cent from 10.5 per cent. The World

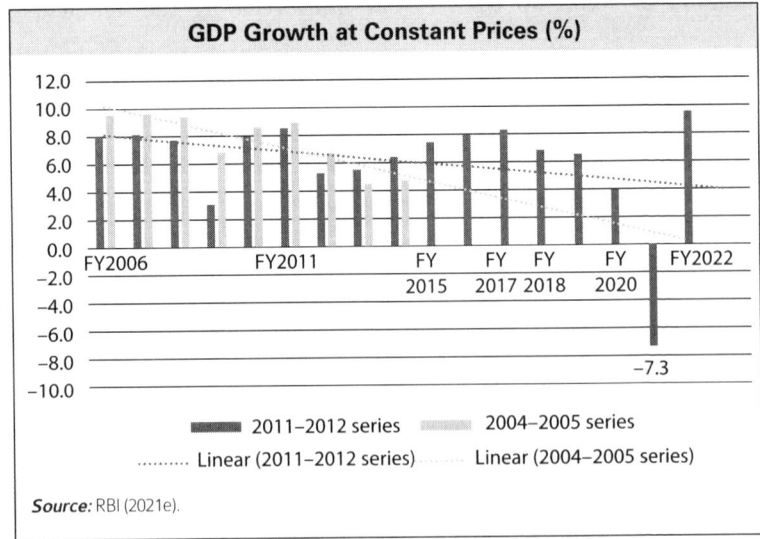

Bank's Global Economic Prospects, released at the same time, pegged it at 8.3 per cent (up from 5.4% projected in January 2021; RBI, 2021f; World Bank, 2021).

The previous graph uses RBI's projection for FY22 at 9.5 per cent. On the face of it, a 9.5 per cent growth looks as if India would be back to high growth trajectory again. This is very misleading as the high number is due to an extremely low base (−7.3% in FY21). In absolute numbers, a 9.5 per cent growth in FY22 actually translates to a GDP growth of 1.6 per cent over FY20—far from being inspiring. Even then, with 9.5 per cent growth for FY22 means an average growth of 5.4 per cent during the eight years of the Narendra Modi government (FY15–FY22). This is a significant fall from the average annual growth of 7.6 per cent in the 2004–2005 series and 6.7 per cent in the 2011–2012 series during Manmohan Singh government's nine years (FY06–FY14)—which deliberately lowered the UPA era growth numbers as explained in a previous chapter.

The growth trendlines in the previous graph show that under the 2004–2005 and 2011–2012 GDP series, growth is dipping towards 0 and below 4 per cent, respectively—the *Hindu* rate of growth. Not to forget that the 2011–2012 GDP series is overestimated by at least 2.5 per cent (2.5–3.7 percentage points during 2011–2012 and 2016–2017), as the then CEA, Arvind Subramanian, had pointed out. If this is taken into account, then the average annual growth during Narendra Modi's eight years in office will be 2.9 per cent.

Apart from a high growth number for FY22 (9.5% or 8.3%), the other misleading picture comes from the stock market booms, which were explained earlier. Stock market investments are speculative activities divorced from the real economy and, hence, should be discounted. Besides, stock market bursts have led to financial crisis all over the world multiple times beginning with the 1929 Great Depression. The last one caused the Great Recession of 2007–2009. Now the RBI is warning of stock market bubble being built up because of the government and RBI's policy of cheap credit (excess liquidity). A stock market burst in future means another massive shock to the economy as it would lead to massive job and business loss again.[3]

---

[3] https://ourworldindata.org/coronavirus-data?country=~IND

Shankar Acharya, former CEA, thinks the FY22 growth would more likely be 6–8 per cent, taking the national output (GDP) to below the FY20 level. More worrisome, he writes, is that India would have lost 10–12 per cent of GDP increment forever. Since the pandemic and lockdowns would leave deep scars on the society and the economy, India is unlikely to go back to the pre-pandemic growth level and 'the likely medium-term potential growth will almost certainly be markedly lower than that experienced in pre-pandemic years' (Acharya, 2021).

There are several disturbing trends that have emerged following the second wave.

RBI's consumer confidence surveys reflecting citizens' expectations regarding the current state of economy, employment, prices, income and spending, which were declining since March 2019, hit all time low in May 2021 with negative sentiments expressed for all, except spending. Future expectations (one year ahead) turned negative, except for income and spending but less than the previous round of survey in March 2021. Since the overall trends in sentiment about the current and future expectations were negative in the last round of survey in March 2021, it is not just the second wave that has fuelled such pessimism (RBI, 2021g).

A business confidence survey by the industry association FICCI in May revealed sharp deterioration in the optimism level of corporate India. The overall index fell to 51.5 after reporting a decadal high of 74.2 in 2020. It was the second wave that pulled down the overall index, citing weak demand, lower household savings and fear of a third round, besides permanent loss of household incomes. It sought direct income support to rural as well as urban poor, income tax reductions for the middle class and temporary reductions in indirect taxes. More disturbingly, a survey showed that 59 per cent MSMEs and start-ups might be sold off or shut down by the end of 2021 due to the pandemic disruptions (*Economic Times*, 2021; FICCI, 2021).

A long-term study of employment for the period of FY17–FY21 by the Ashoka University and CMIE said (a) agriculture is now employing more people than five years ago and (b) manufacturing employment fell by nearly half in these five years, the job loss being in labour-intensive manufacturing such as textiles, construction and food processing units but not in capital-intensive ones. It shows instead of moving out of low-productive and low-paying agriculture, more workers are going back to agriculture due to loss of jobs in industry and services and economic slowdown. It also shows that relying on manufacturing to create more jobs is a myth (CEDA-CMIE, 2021).

Growth will not revive automatically on its own. The only growth engine capable of firing in a recession is the government expenditure (GFCE), which grew at +2.9 per cent in FY21. The budgetary allocation in FY22 is just 1 per cent higher than FY21 (RE). This is unlikely to bring back high growth, especially when the growth rate of all other engines fell drastically in FY21 (PE): private consumption (PFCE) by −9.1 per cent, investment (price to free cash flow) by −10.8 per cent, exports by −4.7 per cent and imports by −13.6 per cent. Nobel laureate Abhijit Banerjee recently called for an additional 2 per cent of the GDP, while the Azim Premji University study proposed 3–5.5 per cent of additional spending to handle the pandemic (APU, 2021; Banerjee, 2021).

The key to revival is fiscal spending that can raise consumption demand (fallen below the FY19 level) and raise investment. A 1 per cent rise in fiscal spending is not enough to do this. A dramatic rise in fiscal spending is unlikely because of high deficit (FY22 budget proposes to bring it down from 9.5% of the GDP in FY21 to 6.8% in FY22) and the revenue collapse forcing the central government to violate the GST law by refusing to pay the GST compensation to states. Instead, it has started borrowing the compensation from the RBI and lending it to states, not transferring it, as should be the case. Private investment remains the weakest link in reviving growth as RBI's Fiscal Stability Report of 2021 said (RBI, 2021a).

India has been blundering along with one man-made disaster after the other since 2014. The list is long: gross mismanagement of the pandemic, no planning and preparations for the second wave and botched vaccination; fiscal mismanagement and misdirected fiscal stimulus; reliance on liquidity when demand is depressed, leading to macrofinancial risks; incentivizing loan default by routinely writing off huge amounts of NPAs and then restructuring loans; off-budget spending that hides fiscal deficit and bypasses the FRBM Act; the budgeting for FY22 which assumes the pandemic crisis is over, pays little attention to direct income support and revival of employment generation, doesn't address health and education deprivations and proposes to spend 1 per cent more, etc. (Mohanty, 2021a, 2021b, 2021c).

The gross under-reporting of COVID-19 cases and deaths only mean the magnitude of the pandemic and cost to the economy and society will never be known and hence, not remedied. The SBI estimates that there would be a 11 per cent rise in health expenditure of households (additional expense of ₹66,000) in FY22 but the actual may be far more given the quantum jump in numbers of cases and deaths and rising healthcare cost (SBI, 2021).

Vaccination of population is the best bet against future waves of the pandemic, particularly the fear of variants like 'Delta Plus', and long-term safety. Newer and more deadlier variants can emerge as the daily cases still remain very high, close to 50,000. India's biggest challenge in the short-term is the threat of a prolonged pandemic. India's vaccination drive has been seriously jeopardized because of multiple flip-flops, definite move to turn it into trade and for-profit venture for the private manufacturers, as against other major economies where it is free and fast. As on 25 June 2021, India had fully vaccinated only 3.7 per cent of its population and partly 14 per cent of its population, while the UK had fully vaccinated 47 per cent of its population; Israel, 51 per cent; the USA, 45 per cent; France, 26 per cent; Turkey, 17 per cent; and Brazil, 12 per cent in comparison.[4]

The other emerging threat is the rising inflation. In May 2021, wholesale inflation shot up to 12.9 per cent, largely driven by spike in fuel and power inflation and supply side constraints due to the local lockdowns. International crude price is also going up, with the Brent price crossing $63 in June 2021, from $41.96 in 2020. Then international commodity prices are on the rise as economic activities pick up in the USA and Europe (*The Hindu*, 2021; Mint, 2021a; Statista, 2021).

Given its tight fiscal position and reluctance to fire the only engine working, government expenditure (GFCE), the only miracle that can

---

[4] https://ourworldindata.org/coronavirus-data?country=~IND

save it is large-scale disinvestment of public assets and privatization of banks. But as economist Pronab Sen keeps saying, disinvestment would mean investment in existing production capacity, rather than creating capacity and, hence, is not a good idea as a private investment going into acquiring public assets could be better utilized in greenfield projects. Moreover, India's corporate sector is making profits but runs on debt, accumulates high level of NPAs every year, is cutting down jobs and wages and not investing despite cheap credit and excess liquidity (India is long in liquidity trap). There is no reason to believe investment will grow by handing public sector banks to them.

Consumption expenditure, which contributes 56–57 per cent to the GDP, is unlikely to rise without the income level of households rising. There seems no attempt to give direct income support other than the pre-poll sop of ₹6,000 being given to farm households annually (₹500 a month). Import substitution policy has impacted both imports and exports adversely (as explained earlier). Similarly, unless the damage to informal economy, which contributes 50 per cent to the GDP and where about 90 per cent of workers are engaged, caused by successive policies such as the demonetization, GST and the misdirected fiscal response to the pandemic (as explained earlier), the economic health is unlikely to improve (Mohanty, 2020b).

Overall analysis of the economy shows two areas of improvement since 2014. Infrastructure has got a boost. The government has been laying 36 km of highways a day, on average, far higher than 8–11 km build during the previous UPA regime. Renewable energy (solar and wind) has doubled in five years—a significant achievement towards climate change mitigation. Given the overall failures of the economy, this isn't enough to take India back to pre-pandemic growth (BBC, 2021).

The other is what economist Arvind Subramanian calls 'new welfarism'— access to bank accounts, electricity, sanitation and clean cooking fuel has improved. At the same time, child malnutrition has worsened, as the latest National Health Survey (NHS-5 of 2019–2020) showed; poverty, hunger and income inequality have risen. The negatives far outstrip the damages to the people and economy (*Indian Express*, 2020; *The Wire*, 2020).

The preceding chapters have also explained how India's economic problems are not just because of economic missteps but are also political and ideological in nature.

Takeaways

- India is passing through a massive livelihood crisis that needs to be addressed before expecting economic recovery.
- India's challenges are aplenty—from the pandemic mismanagement to fiscal management and misdirected policies.
- India needs to raise fiscal spending several notches higher to generate demand and kickstart investment that can revive growth.
- Medium-term growth prospects seem low unless dramatic changes happen.

References

Acharya, S. (2021, 28 May). India may have LOST 10–12% of GDP growth FOREVER. Rediff.com. https://www.rediff.com/money/column/shankar-acharya-india-may-have-lost-10-12-of-gdp-growth-forever/20210528.htm

APU. (2021, 5 May). State of working India 2021. Azim Premji University. https://cse.azimpremjiuniversity.edu.in/state-of-working-india/swi-2021/

Banerjee, A. (2021, 26 May). Spend more: Nobel Laureate Abhijit Banerjee's advice to Indian govt. *The Week*. https://www.theweek.in/news/biz-tech/2021/05/26/spend-more-nobel-laureate-abhijit-banerjees-advice-to-indian-govt.html

BBC. (2021, 22 June). India economy: Seven years of Modi in seven charts. BBC. https://www.bbc.com/news/world-asia-india-57437944

BloombergQuint. (2021a, 5 May). Why lenders have stepped up auctions of gold jewellery. https://www.bloombergquint.com/business/why-lenders-have-stepped-up-auctions-of-gold-jewellery

BloombergQuint. (2021b, 11 May). Covid-19 second wave: Farm arrivals drop despite localised lockdowns. https://www.bloombergquint.com/economy-finance/covid-19-second-wave-farm-arrivals-drop-despite-localised-lockdowns

BloombergQuint. (2021c, 26 May). Manappuram Finance stepped up gold auctions in Q4. https://www.bloombergquint.com/business/manappuram-finance-stepped-up-gold-auctions-in-q4

Business Standard. (2019, 15 November). Consumer spend sees first fall in 4 decades on weak rural demand: NSO data. https://www.business-standard.com/article/economy-policy/consumer-spend-sees-first-fall-in-4-decades-on-weak-rural-demand-nso-data-119111401975_1.html#:~:text=The%20survey%20%E2%80%94%20Key%20Indicators%3A%20Household,Rs%201%2C501%20in%202011%2D12.&text=In%20cities%2C%20it%20rose%20by,report%20reviewed%20by%20Business%20Standard

CEDA-CMIE. (2021, 6 May). CEDA-CMIE Bulletin No 4: May 2021. Bulletin: Manufacturing Employment Halves in 5 Years, CEDA, Ashoka University and CMIE. https://ceda.ashoka.edu.in/ceda-cmie-bulletin-manufacturing-employment-halves-in-5-years/

CMIE. (2021a, 10 May). LPR never recovered fully from lockdown, slides again. https://www.cmie.com/kommon/bin/sr.php?kall=warticle&dt=2021-05-10%2014:14:07&msec=723

CMIE. (2021b, 1 June). 15 million jobs lost in May 2021. https://cmie.com/kommon/bin/sr.php?kall=warticle&dt=2021-06-01%2018:06:45&msec=766

Economic Times. (2021, 27 May). 59% of startups and MSMEs may shut shop, sell off or scale down: Survey. https://economictimes.indiatimes.com/small-biz/sme-sector/covid-second-wave-59-of-startups-and-msmes-may-shut-shops-sell-off-or-scale-down-localcircles-survey/articleshow/82977477.cms?utm_source=contentofinterest&utm_medium=text&utm_campaign=cppst

FICCI. (2021, May). Business confidence survey. https://ficci.in/Sedocument/20566/business_confidence_survey.pdf

GOI. (2015). *Draft national health policy 2015.* Author. https://www.nhp.gov.in/sites/default/files/pdf/draft_national_health_policy_2015.pdf

IMF. (2021a, April). World economic outlook update. https://www.imf.org/en/Publications/WEO/Issues/2021/03/23/world-economic-outlook-april-2021

IMF. (2021b). Ranking. https://statisticstimes.com/economy/countries-by-projected-gdp-growth.php

India Today. (2021, 18 May). Explained: How lower demand impacts India's Covid-hit economy. https://www.indiatoday.in/business/story/explained-how-lower-demand-impacts-india-s-covid-hit-economy-1804054-2021-05-18

Indian Express. (2020, 22 December). New Welfarism of Modi govt represents distinctive approach to redistribution and inclusion. https://indianexpress.com/article/opinion/columns/national-family-health-survey-new-welfarism-of-indias-right-7114104/

Indian Express. (2021a, 21 May). Bangladesh outpaces India on per capita income. https://indianexpress.com/article/business/economy/bangladesh-outpaces-india-on-per-capita-income/

Indian Express. (2021b, 7 June). As states begin unlocking, returning migrants struggle to find work. https://www.hindustantimes.com/india-news/lockdown-curbs-eased-returning-migrants-continue-to-struggle-for-work-101623058233660-amp.html

Mint. (2021a, 1 May). Why prices of commodities, from metals to food, are soaring. https://www.livemint.com/market/commodities/why-prices-of-commodities-from-metals-to-food-are-soaring-11619857342043.html

Mint. (2021b, 11 May). Factories hum becomes faint as Covid wave rages. https://www.livemint.com/industry/manufacturing/factories-hum-becomes-faint-as-covid-wave-rages-11620669637880.html

Mohanty, P. (2020a, 2 July). Rebooting Economy I: Why stock market is booming when COVID-19-hit economy sinks. *Business Today.* https://www.businesstoday.in/current/economy-politics/indian-economy-economic-growth-stock-market-investors-equities-covid19-pandemic-coronavirus/story/408626.html

Mohanty, P. (2020b, 5 April). Coronavirus lockdown IV: How reverse migration will affect the informal economy as livelihood options dry up. *Business Today.* https://www.businesstoday.in/current/economy-politics/coronavirus-lockdown-reverse-migration-will-affect-informal-economy-labourers-daily-wagers/story/400209.html

Mohanty, P. (2020c, 20 October). Rebooting Economy 38: What makes stock markets and billionaires immune to coronavirus pandemic? *Business Today.* https://www.businesstoday.in/opinion/columns/indian-economy-what-makes-stock-market-and-billionaires-immune-to-coronavirus-pandemic-v-shaped-recovery/story/419524.html

Mohanty, P. (2021a). Rebooting Economy 60: India in a financial mess of its own making. https://www.businesstoday.in/opinion/columns/indian-economy-india-is-a-financial-mess-of-its-own-making-npas-loan-defaults/story/428549.html

Mohanty, P. (2021b). Rebooting Economy 62: Economic growth for whom and for what? https://www.businesstoday.in/union-budget-2021/columns/indian-economy-economic-growth-for-whom-and-for-what-gross-domestic-product-gdp/story/429579.html

Mohanty, P. (2021c). Rebooting Economy 64: Budget numbers don't add up to 10% or more growth in FY22. https://www.businesstoday.in/union-budget-2021/columns/indian-economy-budget-numbers-dont-add-up-to-10-or-more-growth-in-fy22/story/430462.html

Mohanty, P. (2021d, 10 February). Rebooting Economy 66: Is India facing credit deprivation to warrant corporation banks? *Business Today.* https://

www.businesstoday.in/opinion/columns/rebooting-economy66-is-india-facing-credit-deprivation-to-warrant-corporation-banks/story/430868.html

MoSPI. (2021a, 29 January). First revised estimates of national income. http://mospi.nic.in/sites/default/files/press_release/PressNote_FRE%202019-20%20-%20Website.pdf

MoSPI. (2021b, 31 May). Provisional estimates of national income 2020–21. http://mospi.nic.in/sites/default/files/press_release/Press%20Note_31-05-2021.pdf

National Health Authority. (2018). About Pradhan Mantri Jan Arogya Yojana (PM-JAY). https://pmjay.gov.in/about/pmjay

Oxford-UNDP. 2018. Global multidimensional poverty index 2018. https://ophi.org.uk/wp-content/uploads/G-MPI_2018_2ed_web.pdf

Pew Research Center. (2021, 18 March). In the pandemic, India's middle class shrinks and poverty spreads while China sees smaller changes. https://www.pewresearch.org/fact-tank/2021/03/18/in-the-pandemic-indias-middle-class-shrinks-and-poverty-spreads-while-china-sees-smaller-changes/

RBI. (2021a, 21 January). *Financial stability report*. Issue No. 22. https://rbidocs.rbi.org.in/rdocs//PublicationReport/Pdfs/FSR_F06B552BF8B144B80B4AEFEDEB3D62218.PDF

RBI. (2021b, 31 March). Developments in India's balance of payments during the third quarter (October–December) of 2020–21. https://www.rbi.org.in/Scripts/BS_PressReleaseDisplay.aspx?prid=51356

RBI. (2021c, 30 April). Sectoral deployment of bank credit—March 2021. https://rbidocs.rbi.org.in/rdocs/PressRelease/PDFs/PR423D3373D1FDD640E5915DE3DFE539E42C.PDF

RBI. (2021d, 12 May). Report on management of foreign exchange reserves. https://rbi.org.in/Scripts/PublicationsView.aspx?id=20359

RBI. (2021e, May). *Annual report 2020–21*. https://rbidocs.rbi.org.in/rdocs/AnnualReport/PDFs/0RBIAR202021_F49F9833694E84C16AAD01BE48F53F6A2.PDF

RBI. (2021f, 4 June). Monetary policy statement, 2021–22. https://rbidocs.rbi.org.in/rdocs/PressRelease/PDFs/PR318MPC439D2DC49B89429A90F832CAD7447B1C.PDF

RBI. (2021g, 4 June). Consumer confidence survey. https://www.rbi.org.in/Scripts/PublicationsView.aspx?id=20373

RBI. (2021h, 23 June). Preliminary estimates of household financial savings for Q3: 2020–21 and household debt-GDP ratio at end-December 2020. https://www.rbi.org.in/Scripts/BS_PressReleaseDisplay.aspx?prid=51776

Reuters. (2021, 3 June). India's services activity shrank in May on lockdowns, job cuts quicken. https://www.reuters.com/world/india/indias-services-activity-shrank-may-lockdowns-job-cuts-quicken-2021-06-03/

SBI. (2021, 17 May). Pandemic, discretionary spends and headline inflation, Ecowrap, SBI, Issue No 11, FY21. https://sbi.co.in/documents/13958/10990811/17052021_Ecowrap_20210517.pdf/c81deb06-409c-cde1-abdc-f1b9696d165c?t=1621232824140

Statista. (2021, 7 May). Brent crude oil price annually 1976–2021. https://www.statista.com/statistics/262860/uk-brent-crude-oil-price-changes-since-1976/

The Hindu. (2021, 14 June). Surging fuel prices push wholesale inflation up to nearly 13%. https://www.thehindu.com/business/Economy/surging-fuel-prices-push-wholesale-inflation-up-to-nearly-13/article34810370.ece

The Wire. (2020, 14 December). Child nutrition levels in India worsened over last five years, finds NHFS survey. https://science.thewire.in/health/child-nutrition-levels-in-india-worsened-over-last-five-years-finds-nhfs-survey/#:~:text=According%20to%20a%20World%20Bank,14%25%2C%20the%20report%20said

Times of India. (2021, 5 June). Covid-19: Rural India worst hit in 2nd wave, says report. http://timesofindia.indiatimes.com/articleshow/83248710.cms?utm_source=contentofinterest&utm_medium=text&utm_campaign=cppst

World Bank. (2021, June). Global economic prospects. https://openknowledge.worldbank.org/bitstream/handle/10986/35647/9781464816659.pdf

ABOUT THE AUTHOR

Prasanna Mohanty is a journalist and researcher with three decades of professional experience. Most recently, he was working as Editor, Policy, with India Today Group until June 2021. He writes on public policy, politics and governance. His area of work includes economics, social, socio-economic development, law and justice, and environmental governance. His articles have appeared in the group's various platforms, including *India Today*, *Business Today*, *DailyO* and *Aaj Tak*.

Prior to this, he worked with Delhi-based think tank Thought Arbitrage Research Institute (2014–2018) as a principal consultant, where his work involved macroeconomics, corporate governance and sustainability.

Earlier, he was deputy editor with *Governance Now* (2009–2013), a specialized fortnightly magazine on public policies and governance, in which he wrote on public policies covering a wide range of area, including national security, tribal rights, rural development and environmental governance. Prior to that, he worked for several national dailies and digital platforms, including *the Statesman* (1991–2000), *Deccan Herald* (2000–2001), *the Newspaper Today* of India Today Group (2002–2003), *Mid-Day* (2003–2005), IBN7 (2005–2009) and News9 (2009). In 1999, he received an award for excellence in human development reporting.

He is a contributing author of *Handbook for Independent Directors* (2015, 2016), research contributor to *CSR in India: Steering Business towards Social Change* (2017) and co-authored a chapter in *Corporate Governance in India: Change and Continuity* (2016).

His articles have been published in several international publications such as *India Climate Dialogue*, *Village Square* and *Asia Times*. His opinion pieces have been published in national media platforms such as *the Hindu Business Line*, *Firstpost*, *the Financial Express*, *Mint*, *the Wire* and others.

He did his BSc (Hons) in chemistry and has a master's degree in journalism.

He is an avid photographer and a wildlife enthusiast. Lately, he has taken into birding and bird photography. He enjoys travelling, meeting new people and learning about their lifestyles.

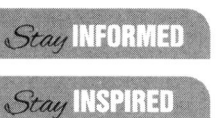

Read up on the most contentious and compelling topics in history and the contemporary world.

For special offers on these books and more, visit **stealadeal.sagepub.in** **Steal A Deal**
YOUR ONE-STOP-SHOP FOR LOWEST PRICE

www.sagepub.in

ScS000321 OL/APM/NS/22/0022/ 14.4.22/2

(7J559552-1)

B-22